YOUR OWN WORDS

Judith Wainwright
&
Jackie Hutton

Nelson

Thomas Nelson and Sons Ltd
Nelson House   Mayfield Road
Walton-on-Thames   Surrey
KT12 5PL   UK

51 York Place
Edinburgh
EH1 3JD   UK

Thomas Nelson (Hong Kong) Ltd
Toppan Building 10/F
22A Westlands Road
Quarry Bay   Hong Kong

Thomas Nelson Australia
102 Dodds Street
South Melbourne
Victoria 3205   Australia

Nelson Canada
1120 Birchmount Road
Scarborough   Ontario
M1K 5G4   Canada

Cover illustration: Pippa Sterne

First published by Thomas Nelson & Sons Ltd 1992

ISBN 0-17-432336-0
NPN 9 8 7 6 5 4 3

Printed in Hong Kong

Contents

Section One: Language in Theory

Chapter 1: In the beginning was the word
– the basic units of language – major word classes
What factors affect our word choice? ... 7
Nouns: making sense of the universe ... 8
Adjectives: modification – direction or information? ... 12
Verbs: the muscles of sentences ... 16
Adverbs: where, when, how and why? ... 21

Chapter 2: Stringing words together
– the importance of function words ... 23
Determiners ... 23
Pronouns ... 26
Prepositions ... 30
Conjunctions – introducing co-ordination and subordination! ... 31
Phrases and clauses ... 33

Chapter 3: The sentence
– three ways of looking at a sentence ... 34
What is a sentence anyway? ... 34
Word order in sentences ... 35
Basic elements ... 36
Sentences are made of clauses ... 36
What purpose do sentences serve? ... 37
Summary ... 38

Chapter 4: Writing about talking
– discourse analysis ... 39
General features of spoken language ... 39
Idiolect ... 39
Transcriptions: the way to write down speech ... 40
Speech strategies, or The verbal games people play ... 41
Noises and paralinguistic features ... 43
Individual speech features ... 43
Clues to personal identity ... 43
Summary ... 45

Chapter 5: Linking the theory to the practice
– a suggested approach to any text ... 46
A system for text analysis ... 46

Section Two: Language in Action

Chapter 6: Private persuasion
– words used to express feelings ... 51
Love songs ... 52
Literary expressions of love ... 55
Breaking up ... 59
Expressing sympathy ... 59

Chapter 7: Public persuasion
– words used to sell ... 61
Catchphrases and slogans ... 62
Market research ... 63
Target audience ... 64
Public speaking ... 68

Chapter 8: Letting off steam, or Swearing is good for you
  – words used for venting spleen   74
Letters   74
An example from literature   79
Authentic disputes   81

Chapter 9: Contracts and promises
  – words to close the loopholes   84
Legal language   87
Contracts and Promises: P.S.   89

Chapter 10: Jargon
  – words used to baffle the uninitiated   91
Features of jargon   92
A receiver's guide to the language of estate agents   95
Academic jargon   96
Summary

Chapter 11: Just gimme the facts
  – words used by journalists   99
If it's in the paper it must be true ...   104
Never mind the quality, read all about the bonking   104
Bias   110
Audiences within audiences   112

Chapter 12: House style to sell life style
  – words used to foster group identity   116
Style   116
A style to suit the audience   117
Different audiences   121
More pieces of rock   125

Chapter 13: Literature   127
What is literature?   127
What is the purpose of a literary text?   130

Chapter 14: Establishing voice and point of view   131
A different person   133
Viewpoint in poetry   134

Chapter 15: Creating a sense of place   139
Places in poetry   143

Chapter 16: Sending a message   150
Poetry for the people   155
Didactic prose   159
Our analysis of Blake's *London*   164

Chapter 17: Make 'em cry   166
Prose   170

Chapter 18: Humour – make 'em laugh   178
Humorous verse   188
Parody   192

Section Three: Language Investigation

Chapter 19: What can I look at?
  – the collection and recording of data   196
What can I look at?   197
Scientist or detective?   199
Suggestions   201

Working with spoken data 201
How much should you transcribe? 205
Projects on spoken language which do not involve taping 206
Working with written data 207
Grey areas: written or spoken? (or even sung!) 210
Comparisons between written and spoken language 211
General points 211

Chapter 20: What can I look for?
   – how to ask questions of your data 213
Questions to ask 213
Focus 217
Narrowing down – looking at the language 218

Chapter 21: How should I present my findings?
   – *hints on how to submit your investigation* 220
Consider your reader 220
Start in good time 220
Title 221
Style 221
How to begin? 222
Explain your methods 222
Where do I present the data? 222
How should I present data? 223
Terminology 225
Framework for analysis 226
The conclusion 226
Sources 226
Presentation 226

Chapter 22: Inside a marker's head
   – *examples of good and bad practice* 228
First impressions 228
Every cover sheet tells a story 228
What do you get marks for? 229
Phonetic transcription 231
If you has to ask you ain't got it: rhythm 233
Can you manage your grammar? 234
Is the knowledge displayed relevant? 235
Structure 235
Summary 243

Chapter 23: Your own words
   – *the link with creative writing* 245
Pastiche and parody 245
Fiction 250
Newspapers 250
Adverts 252
More persuasive language 253
Poetry 253
Literary prose 256
Informative and instructive writing 265

Glossary of terms 267

Acknowledgements 272

• S E C T I O N O N E •

LANGUAGE IN THEORY

This section provides a vocabulary for describing language.

Chapter 1: In the beginning was the word
The basic units of language – major word classes, noun, pronoun,
adjective, verb and adverb

Chapter 2: Stringing words together
The importance of function words: determiners, conjunctions,
prepositions and pronouns.

Chapter 3: The sentence
Three ways of looking at a sentence.

Chapter 4: Writing about talking
Discourse analysis

Chapter 5: Linking the theory to the practice
A suggested approach to any text

Chapter 1

In the beginning was the word ...

In every piece of speech or writing we find words, words, words, and any consideration of language ought, reasonably, to start with them. Their selection is by no means random: every user of words, consciously or otherwise, weighs several possibilities before plumping for the chosen word. Slips of the tongue such as 'blix the ingredients' betray the fact that we are selecting from options – here 'blend' and 'mix'.

The fact that our language, English, has the largest wordstock of any language means that English users have a particularly large range of possibilities to choose from:

Are you drinking from a mug, beaker or cup?
Do you say the dress is scarlet, crimson or just plain red?
Is the man hurrying, dashing or rushing?
Is he hurrying impatiently, desperately or determinedly?

Notice that in each case the three alternatives are interchangeable because they all do the same job. Depending on the job they are doing, words in their context are ascribed to WORD CLASSES* such as NOUN, ADJECTIVE, VERB and ADVERB. As a native speaker you do not need to be familiar with these terms to know that you would never say 'Are you drinking from a scarlet?' or 'Is the dress mug?' If, however, you want to analyse or describe language as well as use it, you need explicit terms in addition to implicit knowledge.

Implicit knowledge tells us that not only do we need a certain sort of word, we also need to combine words in certain ways. In English, we place adjectives before nouns, for example, although this is not usually the case in French. The importance of word order (SYNTAX) will be discussed in a later chapter when we consider phrases, clauses and sentences. To begin with, we will look at the four major word classes and what makes us choose one word from the numerous options available within each class.

What factors affect our word choice?

Sometimes the need to be precise, to label correctly and describe accurately is what motivates us. Sometimes a desire to praise or blame will push us toward emotive adjectives (inspiring emotion) like willowy or skinny (the first laudatory, the second pejorative) rather than the more neutral 'thin'. Sometimes a desire to impress makes us select the longest possible LATINATE word where an ANGLO-SAXON one would serve just as well – consider perambulate and walk. Of course, down-to-earth Anglo-Saxon can be speciously sincere.

Our word choice is affected by context, audience, intellect ... a whole host of factors. It is a useful exercise to try to 'read between the lines' of a text in order to

*Terms whose first occurrence in the text is in capitals are defined in the Glossary.

discover what linguists call the SUBTEXT. Some things you might consider include:

What is the SENDER up to?
What is he trying to tell the RECEIVER about himself?
What is he actually telling the receiver about himself?
Why are words so important to us all anyway?

Nouns: *making sense of the universe*

Most of us remember very little about learning our own language – it just occurred as if by magic. This is not the time or place for a lengthy digression about child language acquisition, but the first words children use tell us a lot about what words mean to, and do for, us all.

The first words children use are nearly always not only nouns but CONCRETE NOUNS. Children do not want to discourse upon love, loyalty or other abstractions. They have quite enough to cope with learning labels for the really important things in life like 'juice' and 'biccies'. When you comfort a child who is afraid of a big alsatian you cut it down to size by saying 'It's only a dog'. Give it a label and it isn't so frightening any more, because it's placed in the universe. The names for things allow us to talk about them when they aren't there. This gives us the ability to talk about other times and places, indeed unreal ones. Names have enormous potency: some stand for something so disturbing that we come to avoid the word itself. This explains the numerous euphemisms for cancer, 'the big C', and death. As one child remarked, 'Death wouldn't be so bad if it was called hig.'

It isn't only children who have an obsession with labelling (giving something a name and thus getting control over it.) Many adults take great pride in knowing a pippit from a peewit, a spitfire from a hurricane, an elm from an oak. Clearly, this is partly a practical matter – it takes far longer to describe the differences between two birds/planes/trees than to attach to them a generally agreed label. Knowing lots of labels is useful in terms of precision as well as ego-boosting! More and more precise labels become necessary among specialist groups, be they drug traffickers saying what's available or ornithologists discussing the mating habits of guillemots and puffins.

Concrete nouns seem to be eminently practical things, giving useful or interesting information. All English speakers above a certain age and intellectual level share a set of mental pictures ready to be conjured up by words like snow, boy and bucket.

As an experiment, draw now on a piece of paper a sun, a house and a flower. Turn to the end of the chapter and see if your pictures and ours coincide.

Concrete nouns, however, are not so straightforward as they appear. Consider the following options:

1 Bird
2 Troglodytes Troglodytes
3 Wren
4 Teeny Brown Birdie

All are labels for the same thing – they have the same DENOTATION or dictionary meaning – but they do not have the same CONNOTATIONS (associations). 1 is very general; 2 likely to seem unnecessarily technical except among true specialists; 3 is precise and workaday and 4 could be patronising or appropriate, depending on the age of the receiver.

To judge their efficiency as labels you'd need to consider context. Quite often people deliberately go up or down the scale of specialism for their own purposes. Some men oversimplify technical terms in order to convey to women that they don't expect *them* to understand such things; doctors, lawyers and even teachers use specialist terms to exclude and intimidate non-specialists. In such a situation you have to be either very confident or very close to the speaker to say 'Don't talk to me as though I'm an idiot' or 'What the hell are you talking about?' Your worry stems from the fact that (if the speaker plays it convincingly enough) you feel the fault lies with you. You feel that everyone else in the room understands and it's just you who is dense, or that the speaker is not meaning to talk down to you and means kindly, so you mustn't be rude. Choice of labels, then, can be significant in the power politics of conversation.

In the wider political arena, choice of label indicates a point of view. Sometimes this point of view is deliberately expressed and received: we would expect to hear of 'the rationalisation of the Health Service to improve its efficiency' from one side of the House, but of 'an attack on the Welfare State to drain its lifeblood' from the other. It is interesting to note whose version of the truth a particular reporter chooses, since we would not expect a deliberate expression of viewpoint from a reporter.

Many noun choices reflect the word user's stance, consciously or not. In what contexts or from what speakers might you expect to hear the following sets of labels, which could all denote the same two things?

house	girl
home	woman
property	lady
place	tart
abode	female

Labels seem to matter to us. You only need to think of the frustration of not being able to remember a name or the awful feeling of powerlessness engendered when trying to get what you want in a foreign country to realise that words for things are vital to us all.

What of labels for the intangible – abstracts such as joy, justice and truth? Could these concepts exist if we did not symbolise them in words? What exactly do they represent? Such words certainly carry a massive emotional weight, perhaps the greater because each individual will have their own interpretation of each of them. 'Love' and 'freedom' will probably not carry precisely the same mental pictures for any two people: the words are nevertheless hugely suggestive. ABSTRACT NOUNS are of little use in imparting information, but for discussing possibilities and ideals they are invaluable.

So what is the implication of all this for analysis of language? To summarise, we might say that a communicator who wants to be precise, specific and convey facts will lean heavily on concrete nouns. This will enable the receiver to have a clear mental image and it will lend an air of realism to the TEXT (either written or spoken). A communicator who wants to discuss ideas, to philosophise and suggest without stating will employ more abstract nouns.

It is always worth looking at the selection of nouns that a writer uses. If they are predominantly concrete, are they related to a similar field of life or activity? You often find that a tone is established by clustering related words, or words within the same SEMANTIC FIELD. For example, in the first paragraph of *A House For Mr Biswas* by

V. S. Naipaul, 'dollars', 'interest', 'money' and 'rent' concentrate the reader's mind on Mr Biswas's financial problems:

> Ten weeks before he died, Mr Mohun Biswas, a journalist of Sikkim Street, St James, Port of Spain, was sacked. He had been ill for some time. In less than a year he had spent more than nine weeks at the Colonial Hospital and convalesced at home for even longer. When the doctor advised him to take a complete rest the Trinidad Sentinel had no choice. It gave Mr Biswas three months' notice and continued, up to the time of his death, to supply him every morning with a free copy of the paper.
>
> Mr Biswas was forty-six, and had four children. He had no money. His wife Shama had no money. On the house in Sikkim Street Mr Biswas owed, and had been owing for four years, three thousand dollars. The interest on this, at eight per cent, came to twenty dollars a month; the ground rent was ten dollars. Two children were at school. The two older children, on whom Mr Biswas might have depended, were both abroad on scholarships.

V. S. Naipaul: A House for Mr Biswas

A cynic might feel that the use of abstract nouns makes it more difficult to pin down meaning. Advertisers can promise that you'll be 'at peace with your pipe' and it's well-nigh impossible to disprove them. When the next political conference takes place, count the abstract nouns in the party leader's big speech.

Let's look at a literary writer using abstract nouns:

> ... thanks to the occult tyrannies of those blandly saluting clocks, I had been mysteriously handcuffed to history, my destinies indissolubly linked to those of my country. I had become heavily embroiled in fate.

Salman Rushdie: Midnight's Children

Notice here the predominance of abstract, somewhat mysterious nouns. Also notice the cluster of words in the semantic field of fate. Neither of these things are accidental: they create an aura of mystery about the central character. They also make us suspect that he is rather pleased with himself!

What's in a name?
We all have a large number of labels stuck onto us in the course of our existence. They can signal our relationship with the speaker, be it familial (Auntie), emotional (luv) or formal (madam). What we are called helps to establish the right tone, on a scale from the totally formal to the intimate. Deliberately using an inappropriate name signals that something is wrong: thus the angry parent lengthens Sam to Samantha; the boss on his dignity reintroduces the surname which had been dropped as you'd become more friendly. A secretary would not expect the boss's spouse to ring up and ask for chubby-poos, and if you're unfortunate enough to be taught by your mother, you'd certainly avoid calling her Mum at school. Very young children, naturally, break the rules, embarrassing the milkman by calling him Dad or mortifying their older sister by calling the next-door neighbour Snoopy Sam to his face.

Nicknames are an interesting phenomenon: used overtly they're a matter of peer group identity; used covertly they are often a harmless rebellion against authority.

Look at the following greetings. How would you scale them in terms of intimacy?

1 Wotcher, Cock.
2 Hi, Fred.
3 Morning, Linda.
4 Good-day, Madam.
5 How's things?
6 Good morning, Mrs Brown.

Could you make any guesses about the age of speaker five, the regional background of speaker one or the sort of context within which speaker four is operating? Of course you could: we all recognise such differences fairly easily. What you need to do is raise this intuitive knowledge to the surface when doing analysis.

We all know that a first name is friendlier than a surname – otherwise 'Call me John' would be a pointless utterance – it is seen as a marker of favour. Similarly, we all know that surnames mark formality or respect (but they can also mark hostility, which is, I think, important to remember.) If two people speak, one using the first name and one the surname, the surname-user is almost certain to be younger or inferior in status.

Sometimes our liking for someone, which predisposes us to use their first name, clashes with a social duty to show them respect by using their surname. Many people solve this problem by referring to the person by both their names, thus signalling respect and affection. Older students often do this when talking about teachers. Do you? It's usually younger pupils who have relatively less power who use nicknames (often beginning with 'old'!) Meeting people in a different context can be difficult, too. You can't really say 'Would you like a drink, Miss?' but would you sound over-familiar using her first name?

Names, then, are clear indicators of role, status and intimacy in conversation. They are equally significant in writing. Journalists' terms for politicians make their allegiances quite clear. When in power, was she Maggie, the Prime Minister, Mrs Thatcher, the Iron Lady or Margaret Thatcher? Could you make an intelligent guess as to which newspaper would have used which appellation?

If someone you've never met writes to you using their first name, aren't they certain to be selling you something, be it a cause or a course?

Writers of fiction, Charles Dickens for example, sometimes use names to indicate the character of a person (Gradgrind in *Hard Times* and Bumble in *Oliver Twist*) or the nature of an institution (Dotheboys Hall in *Nicholas Nickleby*). Funny, memorable names are a stock-in-trade of comic writers (in both meanings of the word comic: consider Billy Bunter and Olive Oyl as well as Podsnap and Toby Belch in Shakespeare's *Twelfth Night*.) Alliteration in names is often used by writers to catch the reader's attention.

You will have noticed the large incidence of capital letters at the beginning of words in the last few paragraphs. These are the typographical markers of PROPER NOUNS. These are those nouns which are most truly 'naming words'. They stress particularity and individuality, and as such they are numerous in news reporting, realistic fiction and guide books, to name but a few! However, not all writers want to be precise and informative – some prefer to make their creations mysterious.

The man with no name

Storytellers sometimes avoid giving their characters names, as these would endow them with identity. Names can give clues to racial and social background. You don't find many Alexandras or Henrys in inner city Manchester, for example, and there are no prizes for guessing the origins of Jacob Epstein or Michael O'Flaherty. When anonymity is necessary a pronoun is used. But more of this in the next chapter.

Normally, pronouns are used to replace a previously named thing or person and thus to avoid useless repetition. This is their straightforward grammatical function. However, when they are favoured above a name, you can be sure that writers have their reasons. One character in a novel may refer to another only as him or her because of their disgust: they cannot even humanise the person with a name. John Fowles uses this technique when Miranda talks about her captor in *The Collector*. This is not such a surprising effect when you remember that pronoun use is generally regarded as rude: we have all been told that 'she is the cat's mother'. Feminists, entirely reasonably, object to the use of he/him as generic pronoun, and calling anyone older than a small baby 'it' is a terrible insult. Personal pronouns can be just that.

Possessive pronouns are often interesting, too. Do couples refer to our or my house, car or children? How often do they feel the need to mark ownership anyway? (Again, if children are anything to go by, this impulse is very basic – 'That's mine' and 'That's not yours' are early favourites!) Why do adults sometimes replace the possessive pronoun with the definite article? Is referring to 'the wife' more or less offensive than talking about 'my wife'? Is it true to say that 'the' distances and makes you less responsible than 'my'? It is easier, certainly, to give 'my' an intonation suggesting pride, affection etc. whereas 'the' sounds very matter-of-fact.

I hope that by now you are beginning to see that all word choices can give us clues about a communicator's intentions and emotions. Try to train yourself to notice whether a writer uses a lot of proper nouns, or many concrete ones, or numerous abstracts. When you have noticed what is there, don't leave it at that: ask yourself why. Who is the writing or speaking aimed at? Does the writer seem confident/patronising/ironic? The answer will be there in the words and structures chosen. It is not a mystery, available only to a privileged few; it's there for all to see if only they look carefully and thoughtfully enough.

Adjectives: modification – direction or information?

When we first start writing, we are soon encouraged by our teachers to make our writing more colourful or precise by adding adjectives. In response to the request 'Tell us more about it: what sort of man? What kind of house?' we might transform the sentence 'The man walked up to the house' into 'The tall, thin man walked up to the old, ruined house'. It's still not exactly inspired but the picture is already coming into sharper focus. Extra qualities are being added to the nouns. More information makes the reference more specific. The nouns 'man' and 'house' have been MODIFIED. Since, in English, adjectives precede the nouns they modify unless separated by a verb, they can condition our response to them, and most of us capitalise fully upon the opportunity adjectives give us to direct the response of the reader or listener. A few adjectives do add strictly factual information to the noun, but more reflect some personal judgement of the speaker or writer.

One of the most neutral, factual ways of adding information to a noun is to use another noun as an adjective: 'plastic spoons', 'brick wall' and 'safety catch' are all examples of phrases in which the modifier, in other contexts, is a noun. Do any other examples spring to your mind?

Other purely physical visual properties can be similarly added – take 'woollen rug' and 'luminous signs'. There is much PRE-MODIFICATION in technical writing since it allows you to pack in lots of information.

Pick out nouns being used as modifiers and the visual adjectives from this extract:

> The parallel current flow through the metallic coils allows the
> relay logic operation to be followed precisely.

Other words which add physical properties to nouns might seem at first sight to be similarly factual, but a moment's thought will make us realise that 'large' and 'tall' are purely relative. Such adjectives as fat, thin and pretty are value judgements: your viewpoint depends on your own starting-point. From a height of five feet, five feet nine *is* tall, and many people consider themselves fat because they are comparing themselves to an ideal. Children think you are old at thirty – in fact the older you become, the farther away 'old' seems! To people in developing countries, we in the West would all seem rich, and even the question of whether or not human beings are mortal depends on religious viewpoint.

It is actually very difficult to choose adjectives which are not highly personal, even when we are trying not to be emotive. How we describe other things and people is intimately linked to our attitudes, tastes and personal attributes. Not only might one girl describe a lad as hanging (Lancastrian dialect for ugly) and another girl describe him as handsome, but the same two girls could describe the same shade of dark red as maroon or plum. It is well-nigh impossible to ensure that your listener will DECODE (interpret) your message in the desired way.

In short, adjectives are frequently subjective and imprecise: this is at the same time their charm and their fault. Adjectives clearly express personal, cultural and political bias, but they are unclear guides to action: how much should I spend on a 'reasonable' present? Do I really give her a 'teeny drop' of sherry? When he refers to his son-in-law as 'dark' is he referring to his hair or his skin? All these confusions can be, and are, exploited by writers, who often use deliberately ambiguous words. The rest of us rarely realise how biased and misleading our words can be.

We may not intend to mislead, but there is little doubt that a chocolate manufacturer who sells 'fun-sized bars' is being 'economical with the truth': a more dispassionate observer could call them plain 'small'. Advertisers generally exploit the unspecific nature but powerful impact of adjectives: thus Ford tell us that the Fiesta is 'strong and sophisticated, potent and practical'. Emotive adjectives (wonderful, happy, sad, tragic and many more) and evaluative ones (good, bad, stupid, brilliant, wrong) are heavily used by advertisers and journalists to attribute praise or blame. In argument, we have all been guilty of piling one emotive or extreme adjective upon another to vent our spleen.

Sorting the fact from the opinion

Find and list the adjectives in the article overleaf.

First, select those which are factual. Then divide the others into favourable, neutral and unfavourable. It might help if you scale them from one (very favourable) to five (very unfavourable). For example

1   mature   experienced   elderly   old   decrepit   5

The bombing of the Pan Am flight 103 with the loss of 259 passengers and 11 local people in Lockerbie was a sickening atrocity. It could not conceivably serve the interest of workers or oppressed nations. If it proves to be true that a Palestinian group was responsible for the appalling bombing then it will have done nothing whatsoever for the cause of the Palestinian people. It could undermine the gains made by the magnificent intifada the biggest Palestinian mass movement for 50 years.

In 13 months there have been countless demonstrations, strikes and general strikes as the mass of the population become involved in this vital struggle. Even the atrocious brutality of the Israeli army which has resulted in over 400 deaths has failed to dampen the courageous struggle for democratic and national rights.

The great sweep and scale of the mass uprising has had a profound effect upon the working class in Israel.

The Militant

Now find your own examples to analyse in the same way.

Politicians are not averse to using the same technique, even if the Speaker tells them it is unseemly (a pretty emotive word in itself). An easy way to get some practice in spotting loaded adjectives is to listen to Radio 4's parliamentary summary programme, which includes recordings of politicians in action.

Sow's ear or silk purse?

Adjectives also allow us to be euphemistic. Asked what we think of a dress we might say 'It's very nice.' 'Nice' has become little more than a polite noise. We say someone is poorly when we cannot face their being really ill; and it is more socially acceptable to be affluent than rich; more desirable to be curvaceous than well-padded.

Any stretch of reading or listening can provide countless examples of the ways in which adjectives are used and abused. In the second part of this section we shall look at some more.

Post-modification – justice for all?

As we have seen, the usual place for an adjective is in front of a noun, unless of course it is the COMPLEMENT in a sentence, as in 'The tea was too hot' or 'She seems very clever'. It is extremely unusual to find an adjective directly after a noun – 'the body beautiful' is the only example that springs to mind. When it does occur it's usually for literary or stylistic effect, and thus well worth noticing.

However, adjectives are not the only way to modify nouns. A word-user can, instead, POST-MODIFY using a group of words.

Consider the following pair of sentences:

The starving children crowded into the refugee camp.

The children, who were starving, crowded into the refugee camp.

❖ What is the difference between them?
❖ Is there a difference in emphasis in that 'starving' is stressed in one and 'children' in the other? To what effect?
❖ When might you choose to use each sentence?

Some would argue that if the adjective comes before the noun it colours your impression before you hear or see the noun itself, whereas if the modification comes afterwards it is separable from the noun – almost an afterthought. It is impossible to make blanket rules about what form of modification is most effective or noticeable, but in looking at language it's worth noticing which method has been used and suggesting why.

Look at another example. Is there a difference in emphasis between these two sentences?

> The dying man wrote his will.

> The man, who was dying, wrote his will.

Of course, it isn't always a straightforward either/or choice. If you want to pack in lots of information, you are likely to use both pre- and post-modification: 'The new and innovative theatre complex, which is almost complete, will open in May.'

You have probably noticed that post-modification sounds more formal, and it is more typical of the written mode. In conversation, you would never say 'My dentist, portly, middle-aged stock-car racing enthusiast, is moving to a new surgery', but you surely recognise where you might read it.

Post-modification is often more precise than a single adjective can hope to be. 'The pink flower' paints a far less precise picture than 'The flower, which was tinged with the palest possible shade of pink'. Using an adjectival or RELATIVE CLAUSE to follow a noun rather than butting in also has the advantage of seeming fairer.

Certain varieties of language are either more or less likely to make use of post-modifiers. They are seldom used by advertisers and frequently used by legal writers. Method of modification sometimes divides the quality press (*The Times*, *The Guardian*, *The Daily Telegraph* and *The Independent*) from the popular press (*The Sun*, the *Daily Star*, the *Daily Mirror* and the rest). Writers seeking to make a direct emotional impact are likely to lean heavily on adjectives, talking of 'terrorised pensioners', 'macho men' and 'sexy starlets'. If, conversely, they want to give detail, they might prefer adjectival and relative clauses. We are being somewhat simplistic here for the sake of clarity. This topic is covered in more detail in Chapter 11.

A final word on adjectives

The range of choice of adjectives is enormous. The right shade of meaning can be differentiated by selecting just the right adjective, and the hallmark of a good writer is unerringly succeeding to do this. If inspiration fails the rest of us, there's always Roget's Thesaurus!

As readers, we likewise make precise judgements: 'wealthy', 'affluent', 'rich' and 'comfortable' do not mean exactly the same thing, though they are in the same range of meaning (or, to put it more technically, the same semantic field.) Expressions like 'well-heeled' and 'well off' are separated from the others by being more informal (COLLOQUIAL), which is another factor writers need to consider. How sophisticated and formal a writer chooses to be will depend largely upon AUDIENCE.

'Audience' is the term linguists use to describe language receivers, whether they are listening or reading. If an audience is relatively uneducated, there is little point in using a word like 'quintessential'. Children's writers have to edit out sophisticated LEXIS (vocabulary) in order to be understood. A word which is simply too difficult cannot fulfil another of the two functions of an adjective – to inform or to move. All the same, constant use of the simplest, most common and therefore somewhat meaningless words such as 'nice' and 'lovely' is equally ineffective and has the added disadvantage of insulting the receiver's intelligence.

Verbs: the muscles of sentences

Language can't get very far without verbs. They are the muscles of sentences, and give them direction and point, telling us what all these sundry things and people are doing – or having done to them. Try to imagine a diary entry without verbs:

> Out of bed. Breakfast. Letters. Car. At The Bistro. Home.

At first glance this might appear to make sense, in the way that telegrams or notes make sense. Supply the verbs that the other words suggest, to make a complete narrative.

Have you used 'got', 'ate', 'read', 'washed', 'dined' and 'went'? Some are easier to predict than others – for instance 'car' would most regularly be COLLOCATED with 'drove', 'mended' or 'started'. The point is that there are very many possibilities and that verb choice greatly affects meaning. Consider this alternative diary entry:

> Leapt out of bed. Skipped breakfast. Wrote letters. Crashed car!
> Drank at The Bistro. Staggered home.

This depicts a rather more dramatic day! It also gives an impression of a more dynamic character.

Since the context of this writing is a diary, the assumption we have made is that the subject of the verbs is first person – most probably the singular 'I' but possibly the plural 'we'. If we gave ourselves the freedom to change the subjects governing the above verbs, we could produce a different story:

> John leapt out of bed. The rest of his family had skipped
> breakfast. His sister was writing some letters when their neighbour
> crashed his car. He had been drinking at The Bistro. His friends had
> staggered home.

In this version, there are many more characters. Each subject has its own verb, and this has to be FINITE one. In its infinitive form (e.g. to leap, to skip) the verb is NON-FINITE and has not been activated or made sense of by a subject. Once subject and verb have been brought into relation, you have a meaningful grammatical unit: the CLAUSE or SIMPLE SENTENCE. We will discuss these larger units in subsequent chapters.

Let us now return our attention to the verb itself. There are two broad types of verb, STATIVE and DYNAMIC. Stative verbs such as to be, seem, appear and know tell us what *is*. They can sound extremely matter-of-fact. However, if they are clustered, their subject is seen as passive, ineffective and even victimised.

The effect is very different where the subject is followed by numerous dynamic verbs. Dynamic verbs tell us what the subject does. This person, it seems, is active, effective and in charge of their own destiny, making things happen as opposed to allowing things to happen to them. Consider this brother and sister:

> He knew he would never be a success. He was too unambitious. He
> appeared apathetic. He seemed made for failure.

> She told him to pull his socks up. She insisted that he needed
> confidence, suggested therapy and nagged him to visit a psychiatrist.

The verbs associated with the brother – 'was', 'appeared' and 'seemed' – are stative ones, but those associated with the sister – 'told', 'insisted', 'suggested' and 'nagged' – are all dynamic. We might not like the sound of the sister – doers are often a nuisance – but we recognise her dynamism. We may pity the brother, but we suspect that he is a lost cause.

In our writing we can explore verbs in different ways. Chosen carefully, they can carry a lot of the meaning within a text by adding to the descriptive effect. How many verbs can you think of as an alternative to the relatively neutral 'walk'? To replace it with 'stroll' or 'amble' enables the reader to see the scene (and character) more clearly. We need not explicitly state that a character is violent if many of the verbs associated with him/her suggest violence. Verbs don't necessarily draw attention to themselves in the way that unusual adjectives might because they are such an integral part of the sentence structure. In analysis, it is easy to overlook verbs. *Don't* – they are frequently very significant.

Take a close look at the verbs in the following passage.

❈ What meaning do they seem to carry?
❈ What effect do they have on you?

> The first thing the midwife noticed about Michael K. when she helped him out of his mother into the world, was that he had a hare lip. The lip curled like a snail's foot, the nostril gaped. Obscuring the child for a moment from its mother, she prodded open the tiny bud of the mouth and was thankful to find the palate whole.
>
> To his mother she said, 'You should be happy, they bring good luck to the household.' But from the first Anna K. did not like the mouth that would not close and the living, pink flesh it bade to her. She shivered to think of what had been growing inside her all these months. The child could not suck from the breast and cried with hunger. She tried a bottle; when it could not suck from the bottle, she fed it with a tea-spoon, fretting with impatience when it coughed and spluttered and cried.
>
> 'It will close up as he gets older,' the midwife promised. However, the lip did not close, or did not close enough, nor did the nose come straight.

J. M. Coetzee: The Life and Times of Michael K

When and how did it happen?

Apart from choosing particular verbs carefully, the TENSE of those verbs may also be varied for different purposes. A little earlier when you were asked to add the verbs to the diary entry, you almost certainly used the past tense. This is because you were describing events which had already occurred. People automatically use the past tense for storytelling, for reporting and, of course, for diary-writing. If a writer deliberately selects another tense, for example the present, this will be for a particular effect.

Here is an extract from *David Copperfield* by Charles Dickens, in which David is describing the house in which he was brought up. Why, do you think, does he use the present tense?

> Looking back, as I was saying, into the blank of my infancy, the first objects I can remember as standing out by themselves from a confusion of things, are my mother and Peggotty. What else do I remember? Let me see.
>
> There comes out of the cloud, our house – not new to me, but quite familiar, in its earliest remembrance. On the ground-floor is Peggotty's kitchen, opening into a back yard; with a pigeon-house on a pole, in the centre, without any pigeons in it; a great dog-kennel in a corner, without any dog; and a quantity of fowls that look terribly tall to me, walking about in a menacing and ferocious manner. There is one cock who gets upon a post to crow, and seems to take particular notice of me as I look at him through the kitchen window, who makes me shiver, he is so fierce. Of the geese outside the side-gate who come waddling after me with their long necks stretched out when I go that way, I dream at night; as a man environed by wild beasts might dream of lions.

Charles Dickens: David Copperfield

This is a literary example, but the usage is also familiar from speech: consider 'I'm walking down the street and he comes up to me and says ... ' More expected uses for the present tense include the stating of opinion, commenting, describing a habitual action or state, or summing up a situation. Examples of these usages would be

I think she's very talented.

He is a fool to himself.

I go dancing every Monday.

He belongs to the Scout Movement.

The Muslim world is in ferment.

If any of these verbs were changed to the past tense, for example 'He was a fool to himself' or 'The Muslim world was in ferment' we would immediately have the action placed in time. The SIMPLE past describes completed action whereas the present is timeless. You can talk about someone who is dead and nevertheless use the present tense, for example 'Mozart is the greatest composer of all time'.

If you want to describe the past but sequence events within it, you would have recourse to the PLUPERFECT. This is the verb form which includes the word 'had' and it precedes the simple past. An example will make this much clearer:

When I had told him off (pluperfect) he began to cry (past or perfect).

By using those particular verb tenses, I have made it clear that the telling off occurred before the crying. In narrative, this sort of information is vital and is usually referred to as SEQUENCING.

Non-native speakers often confuse tense, unaware of subtle differences. They may use the pluperfect 'had' too often, thus going too far into the past. Or they may use 'used to' instead of the simple past, not appreciating that 'used to' implies past HABITUAL action and not one self-contained act: consider the difference between 'I used to smoke when I was younger' (subtext 'But now I don't') and 'I smoked when I was younger', which is a statement of fact and has no clear subtext.

There is yet another complication in verb forms and that is the difference between the simple and the CONTINUOUS. The simple present and past we have already mentioned: they deal with what is always true or what happened once: 'I write' and 'I washed the glasses' will serve as examples. Consider the change in meaning if we use the continuous forms 'I am writing' and 'I was washing the glasses'. What words might you add to either clause? Jot them down.

To 'I am writing' most people would add 'at the moment' or 'a book' because the continuous suggests a very precise moment in time, not an activity which is habitual but may not be happening at this very moment. A speaker whose first language is English would not say 'I am writing every day' or 'I write now', but a second or foreign language speaker could be forgiven for not recognising the difference. As analysts, you need to be aware of these subtle differences.

Taking our second example, most English speakers would follow 'I was washing the glasses' with 'when ... ' We use the past continuous to suggest interrupted action. This use helps to sequence: you were doing one thing when something else happened. Notice the interruption occurs only once, so the simple past is used. Perhaps the telephone rang; perhaps the light went out. Either way you were interrupted. You find a good many past continuous plus simple past formations in mystery and horror stories. They are useful for narration and atmosphere creation: 'I was sleeping peacefully when I heard a strange sound' is far more effective and clear than 'I was asleep. I heard a strange sound.' The terseness of the two simple forms would be very appropriate in other contexts, for example action-packed narratives: 'He dashed in. Furiously, he searched the drawers. He could not find it.' By now, you will see that one tense is not as good as any other. Nor is it just a matter of past, present or future.

Before we leave tense let us look quickly at the future. It would seem self-explanatory: it describes that which is yet to occur. Either 'going to' or 'will'/'shall' can be used, but it is worth noticing that the future can also be marked by use of an adverb, as in 'Tomorrow I meet my fate'. Some languages and dialects prefer to use a function word rather than a tense change: for example, in Black English you find 'mi go yisede' not 'I went'. Language gives us enormous creative flexibility: something you should remember as a sender and receiver of it.

It is not the case that once you pick your tense you have to stay with it. Very often it is more interesting or subtle to alter tense. A change from the predominant tense of a narrative – past to present or continuous to simple past – can indicate a change of perspective or mode. The CONDITIONAL tense, for example, might indicate an interior monologue, daydreaming or a speculative passage. We could continue on this subject forever: let's leave tense for now and look at the voice of verbs.

Passivity means lack of responsibility
An interesting phenomenon is the way writers use the ACTIVE and PASSIVE forms of the verb. Before we go any further let's clarify what these are.

In an active sentence the subject is followed by the verb, then the sentence is completed by an object or complement, for example 'The dog bit the man'.

In a passive sentence the recipient of the action becomes the subject of the verb. The verb is followed by 'by' plus the AGENT, which is the person or thing which performed the action. For the example above the passive form would be 'The man was bitten by the dog'.

Here is another example:

> Lee Harvey Oswald shot President Kennedy. (active)

> President Kennedy was shot by Lee Harvey Oswald. (passive)

Turn these active sentences into the passive:

> Michelangelo painted the Sistine Chapel.

> Blackburn Rovers won the FA cup.

> Prime Minister sacks Home Secretary.

What difference does it make?

As in the last example above, journalists and literary writers use the active form of dynamic verbs to make responsibility for actions abundantly clear. 'Doctor slams her critics' and 'Chief Constable blasts Archbishop' are both headlines from a quality newspaper. In both cases it's very clear who is doing the slamming and blasting. These are active verbs. The subject or agent is clear, and we can praise or blame the agent accordingly.

Suppose, however, that the journalist had wanted to suggest that the Archbishop or his opinions were unpopular with the police force but couldn't quote the Chief Constable directly on it. He might then have written 'Archbishop criticised in police circles'. In this headline the Archbishop is made the subject of a passive verb rather than as previously the object of an active one. The source of the criticism therefore remains mysterious.

Look at these two further examples:

> The Captain fought the blaze all night. He sent women and children to safety then set about tackling the problem.

> Dutton attacked Emma viciously. He broke six of her ribs, burnt her body and knocked out her front teeth.

In either of the above cases a switch to the passive would make a significant difference. The second example above will probably have shocked you, whereas its passive version makes the horrible truth a little more palatable:

> All night the fire was fought. After women and children were sent away, the problem was tackled.

> Terrible injuries were sustained. The child was viciously attacked. Six of her ribs were broken, her body burnt and six of her teeth knocked out.

In the passive versions emphasis is placed on *what* occurred, not who was responsible for what occurred. A reader may well wonder who did this terrible or wonderful thing, but the writer chooses not to give this information. The sentences include no agents, so we can only guess at their identity; the hero and the culprit have both disappeared. How did you respond to the two versions?

Use of the passive is also typical of reports and technical and scientific writing. In all of these, what is done is more important than who is doing it:

The test tube was heated to a temperature of 100 degrees.

When the material is exposed to light ...

Use of the passive is more frequent in formal, written English than in speech. A straightforward spoken narrative or account of events will usually be delivered in the active voice, because we are interested in the personalities involved: 'Then do you know what he did?' We may, of course use the passive to describe a state of affairs:

When I got home (active – personal interest) **the door had been broken and the window smashed** (passive).

We do not know who did the breaking and smashing, so we are forced to use the passive.

When we are looking at verbs within a text or transcript, or are thinking of ways to exploit them in our own writing, there are three main things to look for:

1 The choice of the verb itself – dynamic or stative, vague or precise
2 The tense(s) used – especially any shifts in tense
3 The voice that has been used – active or passive.

Adverbs: where, when, how and why?

Just as the adjective functions as additional information to a noun, an adverb goes with a verb to tell us more about it. It clarifies where, when, how or why something was being done.

Some critics would argue that adverbs are really a sign of careless choice of verb. If the writer had troubled to use 'amble' and not 'walk' he would not need the how-adverb 'slowly'. Most how-adverbs would, in fact, join the ranks of the unemployed if writers were more willing to vary their verbs. Writing dialogue is a case in point. You cannot shout quietly or stammer fluently, and good writers of dialogue eschew adverbs as 'unnecessary letters'.

The adverb comes into its own when it is answering the more factual questions 'when?' and 'where?' You cannot include the notion of 'yesterday' or 'nearby' in a verb, and these clarifications are sometimes vital. Try to give someone instructions without using adverbs and you will discover how valuable they can be. 'How often?' must be answered by adverbs like 'repeatedly' or 'seldom' – where would the writers of questionnaires be without them? There are clearly times when the use of ADVERBIALS gives necessary precision.

This is true whether the adverb is a single word or a group of words. As we found with adjectivals, there is more room to clarify in clauses than in single words. In answer to the question 'Where did he go?' the reply 'Out' is positively unhelpful; an adverbial phrase is much better. You might say 'To the park' or 'Up the pub' (if you're a Cockney).

Helpful, informative adverbials are very common in factual writing, be they 'when' ones in history writing or 'where' ones in directions. When we tell a story, sequencing – getting things in clear order – is vital, and adverbs enable us to do this:

First he noticed the silence. Next the unpleasant odour assailed his nostrils. Then he saw it. Finally, he knew.

Notice in this extract how the writer has placed the adverbs in initial position in the sentences for greater emphasis and drama. As children we are taught that

21

adverbials come after the verb they modify. However, there is actually far more flexibility in the placing of adverbs than of adjectives. Novelists and journalists like initial adverbials; novelists for the sake of drama, journalists for re-establishing the important facts in the readers minds:

> Yesterday, the Prime Minister ...
> In Regent's Park last night, police arrested ...

All writers can see the virtues of where- and when-adverbials, but there is less unanimity of enthusiasm for 'how' and 'why' ones. The reason for this is that how- and why-adverbials are far more subjective. All the how-adverbs of manner, most of which end in *ly*, are matters of personal opinion, just like evaluative adjectives. One listener may feel that the miners' leader 'unreasonably refused to talk to the Coal Board chief'; another commentator would replace 'unreasonably' with bravely or resolutely.

Bias, then, can very often be signalled by adverbs: 'He washes his hair daily' is a statement of fact but 'He washes his hair obsessively' is a very different matter.

Clearly (like 'obviously' a rather assertive, dogmatic adverb with which to start a sentence) one can see that, for a speaker or writer trying to establish mood or character, how- and why-adverbials are extremely valuable:

> Tenderly, she picked up her child and cradling it lovingly in her arms softly hummed a lullaby

> Gradually, the light faded. The water lapped repeatedly but gently against the boat, making it sway rhythmically, in tune with its surroundings.

The next time you are looking at a text, look especially carefully at the adverbials. Are they there to move us or to clarify for us? Keep asking yourself what the writer's purpose was, using the adverbials as a clue. They can reverse the impact of a verb – 'She held him to her, frigidly' – or create a paradoxical effect – 'The child smiled sadly.' Sometimes their use is blatantly persuasive – 'insincerely', 'cruelly' and 'generously' make the writer's intentions quite apparent – at other times a little more thought is required to decide what the subtext is really saying. The only way into the subtext is through careful and systematic consideration of the text.

Chapter 2
Stringing words together

In the previous chapter we looked at the four major word categories (sometimes called as a group LEXICAL WORDS), words which seem directly to carry meaning. In this chapter we go on to look at other words which are vital when we begin to string words together. As soon as we do this, FUNCTION WORDS become very important.

Within this 'umbrella' term there are several different kinds of function word, but what they have in common is that usually they only come into play when we want to combine words into sentences or utterances. They are very important, although almost impossible to discuss in terms of what they mean in isolation. For example, we could all begin to try to describe what 'car' or 'happy' or 'walk' or 'sleepily' mean, either by using other words of similar meaning, or by mime or drawing. Could we do the same of 'the', or 'of' or 'but'? It would be wrong to imply that such words do not contribute significantly to meaning, as 'Do you want it cut and washed?' is clearly very different from 'Do you want it cut or washed?' but the significance of such words arises from their position in the string.

There are relatively few of these sorts of words. We have a limited stock of them, and they change very little. We are constantly adding to our stock of lexical words by coinings and borrowings for many different reasons. For example, when television was invented we needed a name for it, and one was created. The four major word classes are therefore called 'open'. It would be unlikely, however, for us suddenly to need a new function word, and these are therefore closed word classes. We use them all the time and they provide the 'cement' between the bricks of language. Any kind of language structure would be impossible without them.

The importance of function words in our language is made clear when we consider small children's language use. At the two-word stage they frequently use one lexical word and one function word. Thus 'Mummy up' means 'Pick me up, please, mummy' and 'Sock off' would be a request to go bare-footed.

We are going to look at four types of function words. There are more, but these are possibly the most important: determiners, pronouns, prepositions and conjunctions.

Determiners

DETERMINERS introduce nouns, or noun phrases. They 'modify' them in the sense that they give us information about the noun or noun phrase, before we hear or read the noun itself. The most common ones are the indefinite and definite ARTICLES 'a' and 'the'.

Indefinite and definite articles

The indefinite article is 'a', or 'an' before a word which begins with a vowel. It comes before a noun – 'a house', 'a holiday', 'an orange' – or before a noun phrase – 'a new house', 'a long hot holiday', 'a rotten orange'. In English, adjectives almost always come between the article and the noun.

You may not think that such an apparently insignificant word is giving us much information, but when its use is compared with that of the definite article, 'the', then we can see that the choice can be crucial. If we say 'the house' it means something very different from 'a house'. 'The long hot holiday' seems to carry references to or comparisons with other holidays – brief wet ones perhaps – built into it, as 'the rotten orange' implies the existence of other, ripe ones. Normally we are only able to use 'the' in writing if there has been a previous reference to the noun, or in speech if it is obvious from the context or from shared experience which particular thing we are referring to.

If, for example, we say 'Pass me a book' we can deduce that either all the possible books are the same, so that it doesn't matter which is given, or that the purpose for which the book is required (to prop up a broken chair leg, for example) means that it doesn't matter whether the book is a novel or a chemistry text book, the important thing is that it's a book.

If, on the other hand, we say 'Pass me the book' we know that it's either the only book available, or it's a book we've been discussing: the important thing is that it's *that* book – using 'the' relies on shared knowledge. Often the use of 'the' functions as a linking device carrying an automatic reference back to an earlier sentence or utterance.

Or the definite article can be used to exclude, to insist: 'the method we could adopt is ... ' rather than 'a method we could adopt is ... ' In 1988, a politician's fate seemed to depend on whether she had declared in a speech 'I do not want to belong to a racist Labour party' or 'I do not want to belong to the racist Labour party.' What is the difference between these two statements?

There is no need to list exhaustively the implications or uses which choice of the definite or indefinite article might have – your intuitive understanding of language will tell you once you start to think about it. Sometimes the definite article indicates uniqueness – 'the sun', 'the moon', 'the queen'. It would be unusual, but perfectly possible, to use the indefinite article with these nouns, and this would alert us to a particular effect. When a character in Shakespeare's *Timon of Athens* says 'Men shut their doors against a setting sun' it is not only context which tells us that this has a metaphorical as well as a general, literal meaning; it is also the use of the indefinite article 'a'.

It is surprising, given that we have said that use of the definite article implies a shared reference between addresser and addressee either from context or previous reference, how often writers begin with the definite article. Look at this opening from an article in a magazine about medicine in the Third World:

> The health workers were eager. They demonstrated their 'baby-weighing' scheme, complete with animated health talks. Then, sitting down under a giant fig tree with the mothers and children of the village, they boasted of the dramatic fall in child deaths and reduction in malnutrition over the past two years.
>
> *New Internationalist*

If you chose to begin a story with 'The sunlight streamed through the broken window' rather than 'Sunlight streamed through the broken window', why would you have made that choice? (You may not even have been aware that you were making a choice!)

Omissions

As you can see from the preceding example, nouns or noun phrases do not have to be preceded by an article or determiner: 'Cars drive too fast through busy streets' means something different from 'The cars drive too fast through the busy streets.'

To leave out these function words before nouns gives a statement a more general meaning. If we say 'School is boring' or 'Swimming is good for you' we are making general pronouncements. Circumstances in which these words are consciously omitted are newspaper headlines – 'MP in Scandal' – and notices in personal columns where space costs money (literally) and such words can be omitted without seriously affecting meaning:

> Petite, Pretty Brunette – Slim, warm, intelligent, 36, 5'2". seeks professional man, 30s-mid 40s, with good sense of humour and a kind heart. Photo/note/phone, please.

Consider some of the following examples, and discuss the effect of the choice of definite or indefinite article:

> Let's seek the opinion of the man in the street.

> The long sandy beaches and the exciting night life are part of San Pedro's main attractions.

> He was always a good father to his children.

> The curfew tolls the knell of parting day,
> The lowing herd winds slowly o'er the lea.

> A cat may look at a king.

In coming before nouns or noun phrases and modifying them in some way, determiners function in a similar way to adjectives. While you may be fairly sure that you wouldn't confuse 'a' or 'the' with an adjective, it may be easier to confuse some of the other determiners which seem closer to adjectives. But the main difference is that where we can choose to modify a noun with an adjective (or not), many single nouns must be preceded by a determiner. Here is a list of words which can function as determiners:

the	a/an	this	that
these	those	all	some
any	no	every	each
either	neither	one	several
enough	such	many	much
more	most	few	fewer
fewest	little	less	least
what	which	whatever	whichever

These words are functioning as determiners if they are replacing 'a' or 'the'. You will notice that many of them denote quantity or number. All add information to the noun and can be more precise than the article – they sharpen the focus:

> This man is my father. (i.e. the one next to me – or not that one)

> Those tomatoes are mouldy. (not the ones in the window)

> All dogs like bones. (every single one)

Several astronauts have reached the moon. (more than one but not too many)

The words in the list are not however always determiners. In the sentence 'Look at those lovely bluebells', 'those' is clearly functioning as a determiner, coming before the noun and giving us more information about it. But if we merely say 'Look at those!' the noun itself disappears, and 'those' stands in place of it. (In this case it also stands in place of the adjective, replacing a whole noun phrase.) It is being used as a PRONOUN.

Pronouns

Pronouns are words which stand in for, or replace, a noun or noun phrase. For example, in the sentence 'The girl kicked the cat', 'she' could replace 'the girl', and 'it' could replace 'the cat': 'She kicked it.'

We speak of pronouns as being in the first, second or third person, starting with self 'I' (first person) and moving through the direct addressee 'you' (second person) to the other 'she', 'he' or 'it' (third person). Pronouns may take different forms if they are plural, if they are the object rather than subject of the verb, and if they are possessive.

	First Person	Second Person	Third Person
Subject			
Singular	I	you	he/she/it
Plural	we	you	they
Object			
Singular	me	you	him/her/it
Plural	us	you	them
Possessive			
Singular	my/mine	your/yours	his/her(s)/its
Plural	our/ours	your/yours	their/theirs

As with the definite article, we can see that use of pronouns depends on shared knowledge between speaker/writer and listener/reader. For pronouns to work for us, we need to have some idea of which nouns they are replacing. In this way they make obvious links to previous sentences or utterances and shared context. For instance, in the example 'John had kumquats for breakfast. He had never eaten them before', 'He' can replace 'John' and 'them' can replace 'kumquats' in the second sentence because we already know what these pronouns refer to. In writing, the pronoun usually replaces a previous noun; in speech it is usually obvious from the context what is meant, for example 'Give it to me!' or 'Look at her!'

According to the sociologist Basil Bernstein, dense pronoun use is one of the markers of the RESTRICTED VARIANT – as used in institutions where everyone knows everyone else (and their business).

Pronouns are very useful words, helping us to avoid repetition of nouns and noun phrases, and, because of their referential function (referring back), they provide a cohesion, a cementing together or linkage between sentences or utterances. However, although they function as nouns, or noun phrases, there are limitations as to what we can do with them. We can't add adjectives to modify or qualify pronouns. We can say 'the old man' but not 'the old he'.

In public life we often hear the first person plural pronoun being used to suggest a feeling of identity or inclusiveness. If we are being included (and we want to be) we share in this feeling; if the 'we' being used does not include us, we end up feeling excluded. We are all familiar with the expressions 'he is not one of us' or 'it ended up in a them and us situation', where the distance between first and third person pronouns is used to imply a division. Most of us at some time have probably said something like 'Well, *we* don't agree with you' when in fact it was only our own individual opinion we were really sure of, but we wanted the extra weight added by the inclusive 'we'.

Public speakers exploit this cosy feeling all the time. At the point in their speech where they hope to have won you over you suddenly realise that the 'we' being used so expansively includes you. Advertisers use 'we' a lot to give more concerned authority to their claims: 'We know you will love our chocolates' sounds more human somehow than 'The manufacturing division of Arnold's confectioners are sure that you will enjoy their chocolates.' In fact large business concerns and government departments all call themselves 'we' in publicity and information material, even though it was probably written by another public relations firm altogether. Pronouns do sometimes allow us to get away with being rather vague and woolly. Who exactly is this 'we' or 'they'? Sometimes it's important that we know!

The second person pronoun can also be used in a general, non-specific way. I've been addressing 'you' throughout this chapter, for instance, although I have no exact personal knowledge of who you are. In expressions like 'you never know really, do you?' the 'you' takes on a wider reference than just the person(s) you might be addressing. It's rare these days to hear 'one never knows, does one?' which sounds formal and strained. Although accepted in speech, the generalised 'you' is still not accepted in formal written English of the type required by academic essays, but eliminating it can cause problems.

There is currently something problematic about the third person singular pronoun – he or she or it; him, her, his etc. – which leads to particular problems in the age of equal opportunities. Other pronouns which stand in for people's names – I, you, we, they, me, them, their – are not gender-specific – that is, we don't have to specify the sex of the person. For a long time in English it has been conventional, and acceptable, to use the male pronoun 'he' or 'him' to include reference to both sexes in certain situations, for example, in sentences such as 'The person appointed to this post will need many qualities. He will have a wide experience of marketing and promotion' or 'In this College each student will be given the opportunity to develop to his full potential.' The 'he' or 'his' would have been understood to include female applicants or students too, or so the grammarians tell us. Many women, however, have pointed out that such use assumes that the normal state of affairs is that the applicant or student will be male, and can create expectations that he will be. Two solutions have been proposed. One is that both male and female pronouns are included, in writing separated by a stroke: 's/he will have a wide experience', 'his/her full potential'. This is fair, if clumsy, particularly in speech. The other solution is that the third person plural pronoun – which is neutral – replaces the singular: 'The person appointed to this post will need many qualities. They will have a wide experience ... '; 'In this College each student will be given the opportunity to develop their full potential.' This is easier to say – in fact is familiar and common usage in speech – although technically incorrect, as plural pronouns should not replace singular nouns if you take a prescriptive view of grammar. Controversy rages! This shows that even function words are not immune to change – this problem reflects a change in society.

'It', on the other hand, is utterly neutral and a very versatile pronoun. It is even something of an exception to the general rule that pronouns carry a reference back, because we can use it to anticipate subjects, to introduce utterances when it isn't yet quite clear what we are referring to: 'It was a nice day yesterday' or 'It seems to me that ... ' We don't need to know beforehand what 'it' refers to as we know we are going to be told when the full noun is used later in the sentence.

Of course it is possible to use personal pronouns this way, so that 'He had never been seen in the neighbourhood before, the man with the brown check cap' could be the opening of a story but would be a deliberate withholding of information to create suspense. Normally we would not use you, he, she, we, they etc. without some sense of who was being referred to, although some dialects use this form more than others, as in 'He's a great darts player, that Frank Robinson.' In fact one of the most striking features of many dialects is that pronoun use differs from that of Standard English. Thus in Devon one can hear 'I like he' and 'Her's been looking for thee.' In Black English 'mi' stands for 'I', 'me' and 'my'.

How do the following differ from Standard English in terms of pronoun use, and where might you hear them?

> Give us it.
>
> Her's no better than she should be.
>
> I like them big cars.
>
> He gave hisself a nasty shock.
>
> Me like you.

We have already remarked that pronouns take different forms depending on the job they are doing in a sentence. Take for instance these simple sentences involving the third person singular pronoun (male):

> Sid tickles Nancy → He tickles Nancy
>
> Nancy tickles Sid → Nancy tickles him
>
> Sid's tickle annoys Nancy → His tickle annoys Nancy.
>
> Sid tickles himself.

'He', 'him' and 'himself' all stand in place of 'Sid'. 'His' stands in for 'Sid' plus apostrophe s. 'His' is a possessive pronoun and 'himself' is what is called a reflexive pronoun: it refers back to the subject of a verb.

A different sort of pronoun can be used to ask questions:

> **Who** was that?
>
> **Which** is your bicycle?
>
> **What**'s the matter?

and these *wh* pronouns which ask questions can also be used to link clauses in a neat way which avoids repetition of the noun. For example 'The girls picked up the books' and 'The books were on the table' can be linked by replacing the second 'the books' by 'which': 'The girls picked up the books which were on the table.' Similarly, 'I know a man. The man trains weasels' becomes 'I know a man who trains weasels.' 'Who' replaces the second 'the man'. This use of pronouns relates one piece of information to another, and so when 'which', 'who', 'whose' and 'whom' are used in this way they are called relative pronouns. 'That' can be used in the same way: 'These are the shoes. I like the shoes' becomes 'These are the shoes that I like.'

So there are different sorts of pronouns, but all are replacing – standing in for – nouns and noun phrases. We don't stop to think about them much. We acquire them at a very young age, and know when to use them. When and where might we use them – or avoid using them – for special effect?

The use of personal pronouns suggests familiarity. Sometimes this is inappropriate, and we use pronouns instead of proper names deliberately to discuss or belittle – 'she's the cat's mother' – on occasions when familiarity implies disrespect. However in story-writing the central character in a particular episode might well be referred to more frequently by pronouns when other characters are given full names or titles. Here the familiarity suggests intimacy and helps to establish point of view. After all, we rarely think of ourselves by name, but that is often the way we think of and refer to others. Here is a passage from an American novel by Anne Tyler called *Dinner at the Homesick Restaurant*. Different sections of the novel are seen from the point of view of different members of a family, although none are written in the first person. Whose point of view is this?

> Oh, she'd been an angry sort of mother. She'd been continually on edge; she'd felt too burdened, too much alone. And after Beck left, she'd been so preoccupied with paying the rent and juggling the budget and keeping those great, clod-footed children in new shoes. It was she who called the doctor at two a.m. when Jenny got appendicitis; it was she who marched downstairs with a baseball bat the night they heard that scary noise. She'd kept the furnace stoked with coal, confronted the neighbourhood bully when Ezra got beaten up, hosed the roof during Mrs Simmons's chimney fire. And when Cody came home drunk from some girl's birthday party, who had to deal with that?

Anne Tyler: Dinner at the Homesick Restaurant

If we want to sound rather formal or grand in our writing we are more likely to use long sentences in which ideas and information are linked by the use of relative pronouns. A sentence such as this one is clearly characteristic of written, not spoken English:

> Yesterday I was honoured to meet a woman who has discovered a cure for a common disease which has blighted our lives for centuries, and who turned out to be one of the most unassuming people that I have ever met.

This is much more likely in writing than speech as it requires quite a lot of forethought and planning to produce such a complex structure. Legal language, on the other hand, uses fewer pronouns so that there can be no ambiguity about who a particular 'he' is, or what 'it' refers to. Pronouns can be consciously used to achieve various purposes, but as with so many language choices we need to keep an open mind about the effect which use of a particular word – or pattern of words – may be creating.

Prepositions

The easiest way to introduce PREPOSITIONS is to look at some in action:

> Flora walked into the lab. She put the batch of specimens on the bench and called across the room to her assistant, 'In a moment I'll show you something to make your hair curl.'

Prepositions relate words to one another in terms of time:

> **In** a moment
>
> The explosion occurred **during** the race.

or place:

> She put the specimens **on** the bench.
>
> The queue waited **outside** the cinema.
>
> I leaned my bike **against** the wall.

or possession:

> A batch **of** specimens
>
> She was having the time **of** her life.

or direction:

> She called **across** the room.

These examples are relating one thing or action to another. The predominance of any one type in a text might well add to a particular effect. Descriptions of places normally contain many prepositions indicating place, or of direction across, among, between, etc. to achieve a sense of movement. Narratives, where sequence and time is important, will probably contain that type of preposition.

This is a passage from a novel by Graham Swift, describing the fenland landscape. List the pronouns of place and direction.

> We lived in a lock-keeper's cottage by the River Leem, which flows out of Norfolk into the Great Ouse. And no one needs telling that the land in that part of the world is flat. Flat, with an unrelieved and monotonous flatness, enough of itself, some might say, to drive a man to unquiet and sleep-defeating thoughts. From the raised banks of the Leem, it stretched away to the horizon, its uniform colour, peat-black, varied only by the crops that grew upon it - grey-green potato leaves, blue-green beet leaves, yellow-green wheat; its uniform levelness broken only by the furrowed and dead-straight lines of ditches and drains, which, depending on the state of the sky and the angle of the sun, ran like silver, copper or golden wires across the fields and which, when you stood and looked at them, made you shut one eye and fall prey to fruitless meditations on the laws of perspective.

> *Graham Swift: Waterland*

Prepositions are very frequently so closely linked with verbs – as in 'look at', 'care for', 'come in', 'think about' – that they seem to become part of the verb phrase and not a neutral linking device. Coming after verbs they often introduce adverbial phrases or clauses of time or place.

It is striking how many idiomatic and colloquial phrases seem to involve prepositions; we seem to be able to use them to create such phrases. Consider the verb 'break' and how many different prepositions can be added to it. We can

> break out
> break off
> break up
> break in
> break through
> break down

The last three have come to function as nouns in their own right. 'Lock-out' and 'sit-in' are other verb plus preposition phrases which have now become nouns. Combined with existing nouns we have another sort of colloquial phrase: 'by car', 'in hand', 'in action', 'for good'. It is noticeable how many current 'in' phrases coming into common use involve prepositions: 'come out' in its new meaning, 'live-in lover', 'I'm not really into computers.' Many such phrases are currently more acceptable in spoken rather than formal written English and it will be interesting to see how many enter the official lexicon and are still used in fifty years' time. The new use of the preposition 'into' as meaning 'interested in' does seem to be a relatively rare example of a function word broadening its use and meaning.

Conjunctions: introducing co-ordination and subordination!

Rather like prepositions, CONJUNCTIONS are linking words, but they often do more than link single words or groups of words: they can signify a particular relationship between them too. The easiest conjunction to start with is the most common and neutral, the word 'and'.

We can use 'and' to link single words – 'fish and chips', 'dance and sing', 'tall and thin', 'quickly and quietly' – or to link groups of words – 'I am coming to Manchester next week and I hope to see you then.' The word 'or' is a similar sort of conjunction: 'Do you want fish or chips?' 'I can't dance or sing.'

'And' and 'or' are CO-ORDINATING CONJUNCTIONS, linking words or phrases without discriminating between them in terms of importance. There are very few co-ordinating conjunctions, only 'and', 'but', 'either', 'or', 'neither' and 'nor'. If we say, for example, 'I like her but she annoys me', the two statements 'I like her' and 'she annoys me' both have equal importance and weight. Any extra significance we feel 'I like her' has, comes from its position in the sentence. We could change the two statements round and the meaning would not be substantially affected. Co-ordinating conjunctions therefore give equal weight to the two items they are linking.

We would use 'and' if we wanted to link the following three statements in a way which gave them the same emphasis :

> Mary walked along the road
>
> Mary was chewing gum
>
> Mary was wearing a red dress

We would probably replace the second two 'Mary's with the pronoun 'she' to achieve the acceptable (though not very elegant) sentence 'Mary walked along the road and she was chewing gum and she was wearing a red dress.'

This probably reminds you of the writing of young children, and red pencil marks in the margin of your work saying 'too many ands!' There is a stage in language acquisition (usually around three years of age) when children discover 'and', which enables them to generate seemingly endless utterances.

There are other ways of linking the three statements which would sound (or more likely, read) much better, but would probably involve us in the decision that one of the facts about Mary was more important than the others. Let's try linking just two of them in a more comfortable way: 'Mary was chewing gum as she walked along the road.' This reads better, but it has involved us in deciding that 'Mary was chewing gum' is the main fact we wish to convey, and 'as she walked ... ' is providing us with extra information. This main statement has become the main clause of the sentence. Unlike the previous example with 'but' this is not just because the gum comes first, because it would remain true if the sentence were ordered 'As she walked along the road, Mary was chewing gum.'

Conjunctions such as 'as', then, imply a subordination of one piece of information to another. There are many SUBORDINATING CONJUNCTIONS. One broad group of them is related to time, and they link information by sequencing it in some way. Such conjunctions include 'after', 'before', 'until', 'as':

> I will mow the lawn **before** I take the dog for a walk.

> **Until** I see you again, I won't discuss this with anyone.

The clause which begins with the conjunction is the subordinate clause, wherever it comes in the order.

Another group of conjunctions is used in contexts where we wish to suggest cause and effect, and therefore they are common in discursive, persuasive writing and talk. 'Because', 'although', 'unless', 'in order that' are examples of such conjunctions and they suggest causal relationships between pieces of information:

> I can't play basketball tonight **because** I've sprained my ankle.

> **Because** the French army were unprepared, they lost the war.

> You will not be able to take part **unless** you have prepared.

> **Unless** you have £1,000, you cannot join the Enterprise Scheme.

We see from the above examples that it is perfectly possible to begin a sentence with a subordinating conjunction and we often choose to do so if it conveys information we want to stress, although it is not the main clause in the sentence. We may have been told in primary school not to begin sentences with 'because', but it is in fact perfectly acceptable to do so if it is followed by the main clause. It would still probably be only for deliberate stylistic effect – to suggest an afterthought, or a sense of 'piling on the agony' – that we would begin a sentence with the co-ordinating conjunction 'and': 'And another thing is that you said ... ' This in fact sounds more like speech than writing. Written forms that aim to sound like speech often do start sentences with 'and'. Look out for this in advertisements and some popular journalistic styles:

They're both fed on Pedigree Chum Puppy Food. And that's all they're fed, because that's all they need. A growing pup demands two to three times the nutrition of an adult dog. And when it's building new bone and muscle quite literally overnight, it's important that the food it eats is the food it needs to do the job properly.

Co-ordination is much more a feature of speech than subordination. In order to 'subordinate' one piece of information in a sentence or utterance to another we have to plan ahead, to manipulate long stretches of language. In speech we would be more likely to add one fact to another, or pause and start again. Writing is more formal and can be planned and redrafted. We 'craft' our sentences into an appropriate form and divide writing into sentences. However, we do not divide speech into sentences in the same way, and 'Are you coming tonight?' 'Unless I've too much work to do' would be a perfectly understandable spoken exchange. We wouldn't feel the need to answer the question with the full sentence 'I am coming tonight unless I've too much work to do': the 'main' clause is understood from the previous utterance. We consider sentences and spoken English separately in the next two chapters.

Phrases and clauses

In this chapter we have considered words which come into their own when we begin to join words together into larger units. We have referred to units, groups, clauses and phrases without attempting definitions. Before we go on to look at the sentence as a unit of written language we need to clarify 'phrase' and 'clause' and to see what is the difference between them.

A PHRASE is any group of words which does not contain a verb with a subject. It can be as short as two words, or as long as you can make it: the concepts of phrases, clauses and sentences have nothing to do with length. 'Run!' is a sentence, whereas 'the purple grapes on the drooping vines' is not. Phrases are groups of words such as 'my best friend', 'down the high street', 'on a windy day', 'came running'. Put them together in an acceptable order, so that we know who came running, and we have a sentence: 'My best friend came running down the high street on a windy day.'

The clause, not the sentence, is in fact the basic unit of English. The clause is a group of words which contains a verb with a subject, and if it makes sense on its own we would probably re-christen it a sentence. If we return to our earlier example, 'Mary was chewing gum' is a clause, and a sentence; 'who was wearing a red dress' and 'as she walked along the road' are clauses: they both have verbs – 'was wearing' and 'walked' – and subjects – 'who' (a pronoun) and 'she' – but they do not make sense on their own. Put them all together and we have a sentence of three clauses: 'Mary, who was wearing a red dress, was chewing gum as she walked along the road.'

If you want to analyse this sentence you have to begin with it as it stands and break it into smaller parts. We began with the word as our smallest unit of language (there is a smaller one, the MORPHEME) but as we began to discuss combining words we have had to look at them in different groups. There is a limit to what you can say about an individual word. If we are concentrating on meaning or association we usually start to bring in other, similar words to define the word more exactly. If we want to comment on its function in a group of words, we need to know where it comes in the string and what it's doing. There is no simple progression up the hierarchy word-phrase-clause-sentence, and in the next chapter we discuss the larger units in terms of the constituent parts of their overall function.

Chapter 3
The sentence

What is a sentence anyway?

There are really two answers to this question – a 'common sense' one and a grammatical one. As language students you need to be in possession of both.

The common sense view holds that any group of words which make sense on their own equals a sentence, and that the visual markers of a sentence are a capital letter at the beginning and a full stop at the end.

In spoken language we easily recognise a meaningful utterance. Thus an exclamation like 'Out!' or the reply 'Dad' to the question 'Who told you?' makes sense to English speakers. It is context which enables us to supply the missing elements. In this case, these are the understood subject of the verb – 'you' – and the verb which relates to 'Dad' – 'told'. Nevertheless, these utterances do not conform to the grammatical definition of a sentence. This is because the rules for speech and standard written language are simply not the same. Even in written language the rules are not totally inflexible. Poets, novelists headline writers and advertisers use what are known as MINOR SENTENCES all the time.

Minor sentences are useful in creating an atmosphere or image quickly. Inessentials are omitted and we are left with a minor sentence which lacks either the verb or the subject.

In grammatical terms, a complete sentence must have two things:

1 A SUBJECT – the person or thing that the sentence is about, be it Jemima, a tragedy or a triumph

2 A PREDICATE – what the subject is or is doing. In some sentences the predicate will consist of a verb only, for example 'Jemima thinks'. In others, there will be an additional element, the ADJUNCT. This might be an adverb – 'Jemima thinks profoundly' – or a noun phrase – 'Jemima thinks profound thoughts.'

All subjects will include a noun or pronoun. They can be as little as one word – the aforementioned 'Dad' or 'he' – or they can be lengthened with determiners ('a', 'the', 'that' etc.), adjectives and so on; for example 'her somewhat insecure though charming Dad'. We could add information ad infinitum but the group of words would still be the subject.

The important thing is to see the bare bones or structure of a sentence and not to fall into the error that long means hard or complex. No-one would argue that a long list of the animals you saw at the zoo makes a difficult sentence. A feat of memory it may be; a feat of grammar it is not. Grammatical complexity is a matter of how many clauses there are rather than how many words. Remember that as a general guide.

Look at these two sentences:

I talked and he listened.

All the cinemas in town and even the local fleapit are showing the latest film from Walt Disney.

The second is much longer because it has a COMPOUND subject, that is two nouns and a lot of additional information. The predicate is also long since its verb has an adjunct. However, it is still a simple sentence because it has only one verb and therefore only one clause.

The first sentence, though much shorter, has two verbs joined by a co-ordinating conjunction and is thus a compound sentence. More of this later!

Don't be misled by the form of the word in front of you. In some sentences the subject appears at first sight to be a verb – the present continuous to be precise – as in 'Swimming is good for the health'. But here 'swimming' is an activity and thus a noun. The verb proper (or main verb) comes into the sentence with the predicate. We might have the predicate 'took his daughter out for supper' to follow the subject 'Her somewhat insecure though charming Dad', or perhaps 'was a generous man'.

It may seem downright awkward to have two standards of behaviour, one for speaking and another for formal, written language, but such is the situation. The way sentences are formed is not random and if you want people to understand you and to judge you a competent language user it's as well to follow the rules. Most of these rules don't need to be learnt by native speakers. It becomes entirely natural to us to place the subject of a sentence before the verb, for example (unless we're giving a command). No five year-old would write 'Chips I like' or 'Thirty is my Mum.'

Word order in sentences

Subject-Verb sentences

As we have said, all sentences need a subject and a verb (predicate). The most straightforward sentence type in English may thus be called in short S-V. 'Birds fly', 'Teachers teach' and 'People grumble' are all examples of this type.

Subject-Verb-Object sentences

Slightly more complicated is the sentence where the subject is doing something to someone else. This someone or something else is then the OBJECT of the sentence. S-V-O is a very common word order in sentences: 'The lion ate the gnu', 'The sadist whipped the masochist' and 'The teacher bored me' are all examples of this type.

Notice that all the verbs in the above examples are active verbs and can therefore take a DIRECT OBJECT. Verbs which can take a direct object are called TRANSITIVE.

Subject-Verb-Complement sentences

Some other verbs cannot take a direct object and are called INTRANSITIVE. These verbs are stative, i.e. they describe how something is or seems, and instead of a direct object they are followed by what is called a complement. This can be either an adjective or a noun. For example, 'My friend is a hairdresser' (here the complement is a noun) or 'My friend is muscular' (here the complement is an adjective.) Do remember that it is not only the verb 'to be' which is intransitive: so are verbs like 'to seem' and 'to appear'.

Subject-Verb-Indirect Object-Direct Object sentences

Another sentence type involves two kinds of object, the direct, which actually receives the action of the verb and the INDIRECT which has an understood 'to' or 'for' before it. An example will clarify. In the sentence 'I gave him an expensive present' it is the present which is actually given, so this is the direct object. The present is given *to* him, so he is the indirect object. In English it sounds ridiculous to say 'I gave to him a present' (though many other languages do it that way.) Instead we omit the 'to' (or 'for') but leave the indirect object before the direct object. Hence the pattern S-V-I/O-D/O.

Basic elements

Before we go any further it might be an idea to check that you're with it so far. Try to write the patterns of the following sentences down using the symbols S for subject, V for verb, D/O for direct object, I/O for indirect object and C for complement.

> The cannibal ate his cousin.
>
> He is disgusting.
>
> I offered him a pork chop.
>
> He refused it.
>
> I feel sick.
>
> I'm fainting.

It's very easy, isn't it? Of course, these examples are easy because there are no distracting bits tacked on, so all the elements of the sentences show through clearly. Consider if the first sentence said 'The ravenously hungry cannibal ate his cousin, a fat and therefore tempting youth.' The pattern is the same but the sentence appears far more complicated.

We repeat that you must look for the bare bones of a sentence – its basic elements – however long and full of adjectival phrases and adverbials it is.

All this may seem rather pointless, but if you can see the patterns within sentences and you're presented with an enormously long, difficult-looking sentence, it's reassuring to be able to see that it's only really S-V, heavily disguised. Start by finding the main verb. This, in turn, will help you to find the subject and object.

If we consider the sentence above which seemed complicated, 'The cannibal' has had an adjectival phrase tacked onto it: 'ravenously hungry'. We call it adjectival because it is telling us more about the noun 'cannibal'; it is a phrase, not a clause, because it has no verb. 'The cannibal' remains the subject of the sentence; 'ate' is the main verb; 'his cousin' has had the noun phrase 'a fat and therefore tempting youth' added to it. Though there is more information about the cousin, he remains the direct object of the cannibal's appetite!

Sentences are made of clauses

Another way of analysing sentences is by dividing them into clauses. By this system there are three kinds of sentences:

> 1 SIMPLE sentences have one main clause, or, if you prefer, one subject whether simple or compound and one verb; for example 'Grammar isn't difficult.'

> 2 COMPOUND sentences have two or more main clauses – two subjects and verbs. These two clauses are linked by a co-ordinating conjunction. As you know, there are only six co-ordinating conjunctions so simply spot them if you find that easier: they are 'and', 'but', 'or', 'nor', 'either' and 'neither'.

3 COMPLEX sentences are the most complicated, and thus usually signal a relatively sophisticated style. Like compound sentences they have two or more clauses. The difference is that whereas compound sentences have two main, independent clauses, complex ones have an independent clause linked to a dependent one. The two are linked by a subordinating conjunction.

There are a lot more conjunctions of this type than there are co-ordinating ones. They include such words as the relative pronouns 'who', 'which', 'whom' and 'what'; conjunctions relating to time like 'after' and 'while', and purpose such as 'because' and 'since'. The thing to remember is that these conjunctions introduce clauses which do not make sense on their own. That is why they are called dependent: they depend on another, independent clause to complete their sense.

Here are a few examples in case your mind is boggling:

After I ate the soup, I ate the chicken.
(dependent clause + independent clause = complex sentence)

I ate the soup and I ate the chicken.
(independent clause + independent clause = compound sentence)

I ate the soup and the chicken.
(one independent clause – because only one verb, 'ate' – therefore simple sentence)

Have a go at these yourself:

You're reading this book because you're studying English.

My students, who have been the guinea pigs, are helping me.

Writing books isn't easy!

Explaining things verbally is easier but people prefer to read books.

I hope that you understand the book.

Have you managed that?

Notice that in the above examples you could differentiate between the sentences in several ways. First, you could say what pattern they followed as far as S, V, D/O etc. goes. Secondly you could say whether they are simple, compound or complex. Thirdly and finally, you could say what job they're doing, i.e. their function.

What purpose do sentences serve?

By this I simply mean whether they are making a statement, asking a question, giving a command or uttering an exclamation.

If they are statements, they will have a full stop at the end and their technical name is DECLARATIVES. By all means call them statements if you prefer.

If they are questions, then they must end with a question mark and you can call them questions or INTERROGATIVES.

Commands can – depending on how polite they are – end with a full stop or an exclamation mark. They can be called commands or IMPERATIVES.

Exclamations are often minor, i.e. incomplete, sentences. Remember that if they are telling someone what to do they are actually imperatives. Exclamations are emphatic statements like 'What enormous feet you've got!' or 'The nerve of him!'

EXCLAMATORY sentences always end with an exclamation mark.

When you first glance at a piece of prose, you can often judge its general tone by noticing the punctuation marks. If it is awash with question and exclamation marks it is likely to be dramatic and, possibly, persuasive. If it is all statement – that is, all full stops – the tone is likely to be more matter-of-fact: you probably have a piece of informative writing in front of you.

Summary

In this chapter, we have outlined three ways in which you can look at sentences:

1 You can see the basic **structure** of a sentence in terms of its subject, verb and object;

2 You can look at the **type** of sentence in terms of clauses – is it simple, compound or complex?

3 You can see what the sentence's **function** is – statement, question, command or exclamation.

When you analyse prose, it is vital to say something about sentences and it really isn't adequate to talk about 'long' sentences or 'hard' ones. You need instead to recognise why someone's prose style is less accessible – perhaps because there are a lot of subordinate clauses – or why the tone seems matter-of-fact – perhaps because all the sentences are declaratives. Or why the style seems dramatic – perhaps because the sentences are nearly all very short subject-verb structures.

Naturally, you won't always want to talk about all these possible aspects, but at least one of them will be relevant to the particular piece of writing that you're considering. Writers select their structures just as they do their words, so it makes little sense to dwell only on vocabulary in analysis.

Chapter 4

Writing about talking – discourse analysis

The first thing to accept when you are writing about talking is that it is not governed by the same rules as writing. People do not ignore word order and syntax when talking but it is pointless and inappropriate to say that an UTTERANCE is 'not a complete sentence'. We do not always speak in sentences, so when people attempt to do so the effect is very stilted indeed.

Nevertheless, speech is not entirely, or even remotely, anarchic: it does have its own rules and features. These have been recognised by DISCOURSE ANALYSTS.

General features of spoken language

The most striking thing about the average person's speech is the presence of NON-FLUENCY FEATURES. Only a rare few can talk with never a 'sort of' or 'you know' to provide thinking time. These silence-fillers are called just that – FILLERS – and English has plenty of them. Some speakers fill the silence with a meaningless noise, 'erm' being a popular choice. Such a noise is called a voiced pause and by extending its length a signal can be given that talk is about to begin. At other times the silence is left undisturbed and what you get is an UNVOICED PAUSE.

Even when speakers have started on a sentence they sometimes decide to re-phrase what they're saying: 'wouldn't you say ... ' or 'I mean, wouldn't you agree that ... ' This phenomenon is called a FALSE START.

Confusion is also signalled by a speaker's trying to resequence his material. This can be recognised by a remark like 'I should have mentioned this before.' This too has a technical name: it is referred to as back-channelling.

One other feature of many people's speech is perhaps worth mentioning. This is REPETITION. Repeating the same word or phrase gives the speaker time to think. A phrase such as 'I don't know about that' is often said more than once.

We all use non-fluency features, though some of us have more recourse to them than others. They are an inevitable consequence of making up the script as we go along. When we write, we use complete sentences, make a conscious effort to vary our vocabulary, think about the sequence of events. If we don't get it right the first time we can always re-draft. This is not possible in speech which is spontaneous. Speech which is not spontaneous but planned in detail ahead, such as public speeches, sermons, lectures and commentaries, shares many more of the features of written language. It would be naïve to assume that everything spoken is spontaneous.

Idiolect

When we talk, favourite words and phrases will tend to be oft-used. This can be irritating and distracting but it is perfectly normal. It is just one of the ways in which speech is a less crafted and thus more spontaneous mode than writing. An individual's IDIOLECT – their own unique cluster of language features including the volume and pitch of their voice, accent, lexical choice and so on – comes through far more strongly in speech than in writing. Though literary critics may well be able to tell Jane Austen from Charles Dickens, the vast majority of us would find it far easier to differentiate people by the way they talk than by the way they write. So, one approach to analysing and thus writing about speech is to look for the usual features of spoken language. They will be there.

Transcriptions: the way to write down speech

The next thing to do is to look more closely at the individual use of language. If you are going to study spoken language, listening to it is not enough: you will need to make a transcription. This effectively freezes the language so that you can have a good look at it.

Transcriptions are fairly time-consuming, though a little practice speeds you up. Never use speech marks and be careful about the use of question marks and full stops. Many transcribers prefer to use no punctuation marks at all. Rather then theorising, let me give you an example:

T now today we're going to look at business letters
P (quietly) oh no (.) not again
T did someone speak
P1 no sir ...
P2 no-one did, sir
T erm, well, let's get on with it

In the above, teacher and pupil are shown as T and P. A pause is shown by a full stop between brackets, and running full stops ... indicate an unfinished utterance. If two people speak at once this can be shown by bracketing their utterances together. If a pause is particularly long, you can write the number of seconds in the brackets. If a word is strongly stressed this can be conveyed by capitalisation, for example, 'Jenny DID NOT say that'. Sophisticated transcription also shows INTONATION (whether the voice goes up or down in pitch) by a line above the words going up or down. This is particularly useful to clarify whether something is a question or a statement, since questions rise intonationally and statements do not. In the example above the teacher's comment 'did someone speak' is not a genuine question: it is a way of pointing out and objecting to the grumbling. Thus the form may look like a question but the function isn't. Getting quite clear in your mind the difference between these two is vital for good discourse analysis.

The importance of intonation can be fully grasped if you consider an utterance like 'I didn't tell him because you were there.' Does the speaker here mean she did tell him but not because you were there, or that she didn't tell him on account of your presence? The only way to be sure is by marking STRESS and intonation. For the first meaning you would have

I didn't / TELL him because / YOU were there.\

and for the second meaning

I DIDN'T tell him because you were / THERE.\

The simplest way to mark intonation is with the marks used above. You put / on the line before the word that starts a rising intonation. This is often also a word which is stressed, as in 'tell' in the first meaning above. You put \ above the line after the word which starts a falling intonation. A falling intonation often betrays embarrassment or hesitation.

If you want to show the contour of a whole utterance, you can put a horizontal line above it which has an arrow to the right, either level to show flat intonation (statement); pointing up to show rising intonation (question or surprise) or pointing down to show falling intonation (running out of steam or interest, feeling unsure):

I didn't tell him. I er don't know why.

We all use stress and intonation all the time so the problem is not hearing them but putting them on paper correctly. It's a bit of a chore at first but it does make your transcription far more interpretable and it's a very useful skill to develop for project work.

Try to mark the following conversation for stress and intonation:

Are you coming tonight?

Not sure really.

Look, are you or aren't you? I need a decision.

Er well, I don't think so.

Terrific. Thank you very much!

Honestly. You are so unreasonable.

No, I'm not. I'm just utterly fed up with your indecisiveness.

I'm not being indecisive – just polite. Okay. I have absolutely no intention of coming: it'll be a bloody bore. Happy now?

When you've marked the conversation, act it out with a friend. Are their stresses the same as yours? Check if they'd have transcribed it in the same way.

Speech strategies, or the verbal games people play

Most speech is conversational – that is, people speak to one another. All the jokes about talking to oneself are based on the fact that it is deviant behaviour because talking is a social activity. Most conversations start with friendly, reassuring noises of the 'How's things? Nice day, isn't it?' variety. This is called PHATIC COMMUNION and is very socially significant. It is against the unwritten law to answer the polite noise 'How are you?' with a detailed explanation of all the problems in your life. This is mistaking the form or usage (a question) with the function or use (a greeting, expecting a reciprocal 'Fine, how are you?')

The skill of INTERACTION – talking to people – is not hearing what they say but knowing what they mean. If someone says 'Do you think I'm a fool?' they are not asking for your assessment of their IQ, they are pointing out that you are treating them as if you do think that they're a fool. The answer 'Actually, I do' would therefore be both rude and inappropriate.

Question forms can, in fact, function as greetings or statements, or as what are called rhetorical questions, expecting no reply.

Single moves

Every time we make a conversational MOVE (the term discourse analysts use) we are sending a message, and not only with words. The able analyst of the spoken word will be able to sort out what.

The most common opening move is a greeting. Sometimes, however, we are not in the mood for niceties. Few ADDRESSERS would lead into 'Where the bloody hell have you put my cheque book?' with 'How are things going?' Likewise, few ADDRESSEES (people spoken to) would reply with a straightforward answer like 'It's in the top drawer'; they will tend to reply in kind – 'You're in a charming mood, aren't you?' – before answering.

Another possible starting point is the businesslike, organising approach in which chairs of meetings and teachers specialise. 'Now today we are going to ... ' and 'I've convened this meeting in order to ... ' function in two ways: they initiate a certain kind of discourse – the work one – and they make clear that the speaker is in charge.

Let us now take a more detailed look at some of the moves people can make.

INITIATING In this move the speaker starts things off. By their choice of type of lexis (formal or informal) and type of opener (statement, demand, greeting) they effectively set the tone for the conversation. Thus the initiating remark is very important.

SOLICITING This move may follow or replace the opening one. It occurs when a speaker makes a specific demand of their listeners. 'Would you just ... ', 'I would like you to ... ' and 'Who knows what ... ' are all solicitations.

RESPONSES These are the direct, relevant answers to soliciting questions or demands. The range of possible responses is wide but the running sense (COHESION) of conversation depends on responses being appropriate to solicitations. Thus the question 'Did you have a good time?' does not expect the response 'I'm wearing a new dress.' Totally inappropriate responses indicate something seriously wrong with the addressee, such as mental illness or senility. We have all heard conversations where the people involved are following their own train of thought rather than responding to one another. This is more normal, but a sorry comment on their relationship and sensitivity. This kind of 'non-communication situation' is often re-created by dramatists like Harold Pinter for humorous and telling effect.

For the majority of the time normal people follow the rule of TURN-TAKING. That is, they follow what the other person has said and make an appropriate response in terms of content – what they say – and style – how they say it. If people refuse to play this civilised game it can be quite frightening or annoying.

Question and answer sequences are not of course the only kind of conversation people have (though they are firm favourites in the classroom.) Statements can be supported or opposed by other speakers. An EVALUATION or ELUCIDATION may be offered. If an evaluation is given, a clear indication of power has been made, since we only feel able to judge at least our equals and more often our inferiors. Elucidations are really a kind of support since they are helping the previous speaker to get their point of information across. Thus they are often the act of a friend or well-wisher, who understands what the speaker wants to say. 'I think what Fred means is ... ' may sound a bit patronising but it is friendly in intent, whereas 'Look, just what are you trying to say?' is clearly hostile.

Noises and paralinguistic features

If it is at all possible it is far more instructive to watch people talking rather than simply to listen to them. This is because so many of the messages sent by the addresser and addressee are non-verbal or PARALINGUISTIC. This large umbrella term covers gesture, facial expressions, body language in all its manifestations and noises as opposed to words. These latter can certainly signal a good deal: writers refer to people 'tut-tutting' and we all know what that means; 'erm's and 'yeah's with a nodding head will always be read as support, and movements of the shoulders can completely change the meaning of an 'mm' from straightforward 'yes' to 'I'm not too sure about that.' Wagging the head from side to side changes its meaning again to 'perhaps, perhaps not'. All this is rather difficult on paper but I'm sure you take my point.

Individual speech features

Once you've considered general speech features and interactive ones, there only remain the markers of INDIVIDUALITY. The first of these of course is voice – high or low pitched; generally quiet or loud; monotonous or varied in tone. All these features are very difficult to include in transcription but they clearly have an effect on listeners.

Easier to see in a transcript are ACCENT and DIALECT features. It is not usually necessary or practicable to use phonetic symbols to convey precise accentual features. Spelling is often able to do the job. For example 'I'm goin' up the 'igh street wiv me bruvver' is clearly differentiated from 'I'm going to the city centre with my brother.' Not only does the Cockney speaker drop *h*s and say *th* as *v*, which are accent features, he also uses dialect forms such as 'up' for 'to'. Dialectal features include lexical items – do you make, mash or brew tea? Do you eat tea or dinner in the evening? Do you eat sandwiches or butties? – and grammatical ones – do you use Standard English 'I was' or Northern 'I were'? Standard 'I am not' or Cockney 'I ain't'? Clearly one could give numerous examples. The point is that speakers tell us far more about themselves than writers (except of dialect poetry) habitually do.

Clues to personal identity

Regional

Look for letters omitted, like initial *h* and final *s*. Black and East Anglian English have 'she like him'. Northerners use 'sat' for 'sitting' and 'stood' for 'standing'. They also often use adjectives adverbially, though this, like many non-standard dialect features, is common to many areas – we have all heard Emlyn Hughes insist that 'the lads played great.'

Again it is important to remember that non-standard does not equal wrong or inferior; it means different. As I said at the beginning of this chapter, the rules for written and spoken language are not the same. Written language is written in Standard English so that it is comprehensible to all readers; spoken language can be differentiated for different audiences and purposes and regional dialect is often perceived as more 'sincere' and 'friendly' by its users than Standard English. Many of us operate along a language continuum from Standard English in formal contexts to speech marked by regional dialect features in more informal situations. However, formal Standard English is perceived as more prestigious and is associated in many people's minds with educational levels. It's perfectly possible, in fact usual, to speak

Standard English with a regional accent; some speakers do tend towards the more prestigious RECEIVED PRONUNCIATION.

Gender

Research tends to suggest that our sex affects the way we speak. Research as well as instinct tells us that men swear more than women. Women seem more anxious to speak 'correctly' by the standards of written language and use non-standard dialect less than men. Their accents are also less pronounced. Men are less polite when it comes to turn-taking than women and butt in far more often. Women more frequently use tags at the end of sentences like 'don't you agree?' to seek approval and they are more likely to say 'It seems to me that ... ' where men will go for the more assertive 'I think'. These are, of course, huge generalisations but they are supported by evidence and are food for thought. We have not space here to quote much research, but here are two examples. They are quoted from Jennifer Coates' book *Men, Women and Language* which we recommend to those interested in this topic.

The variable [ŋ] in Norwich

100 = RP pronunciation [ŋ] as opposed to non-standard [n]

In casual speech	Middle middle class	men	69
		women	100
	Upper working class	men	3
		women	12
In formal speech	Lower middle class	men	73
		women	97
	Middle working class	men	9
		women	19

Turntaking (Zimmerman and West 1975)

Overlaps	men	9	women	0
Interruptions	men	46	women	2

Incidence of swearing (Gomm 1981)

	single sex	mixed	total
men	21	4	25
women	7	2	9

Jennifer Coates: Men, Women and Language

Age

One can often tell the age of a speaker by the sort of informal lexis they use, since many people adopt colloquialisms in their youth and never update them. (Someone older trying to use the current trendy words can sound very silly anyway, so I suppose you can't win!)

Some examples of informal lexis include

war-time words: prang (crash car), sippers and gulpers (naval slang for small and large rum rations)

words of the fifties: fridge, telly, DA (teddy boy's hairstyle)

words of the sixties: pad (your place, flat etc.), chick, bird (young girl – not popular with feminists), swinging (trendy), pot (marijuana)

words of the seventies: heavy, no way, iffy

words of the eighties: fit, toy-boy, yuppies.

I'm assuming that you don't need the more recent ones translating!

Class

This category is one beset with problems, not least that of defining what is meant by working and middle class. That said, there is a correlation between class and usage, as mentioned in the section on dialect. The difficulty lies in deciding whether a speaker uses a certain phrase or word because of their class or because of their birthplace. 'Mam', for example, could be regarded as a 'working-class' variant of Mum or as a Northern one.

The sociologist Basil Bernstein's theory that the working class used a RESTRICTED CODE which was topic-fixed, based on shared assumptions and highly predictable whereas the middle class used an ELABORATED CODE which was more flexible, generalised and context-free has caused, and continues to cause, great controversy. It is perfectly possible to find examples of 'middle class' speech which exemplify elaborated code; likewise 'working-class' speech that is highly anecdotal, but the problem with Bernstein's theory is that it subdivides people and speech variants on very broad bases. Even his reformed view that the middle class use both restricted and elaborated code while some working-class speakers have no option does seem to take into too little account the fact that any individual speaker is influenced by who they are with, what they are talking about and where they are quite as much as by their 'roots'.

Summary

It seems, then, that we need to consider any speaker from at least four viewpoints:

1 as a speaker, not a writer. Remark the speech features like fillers.

2 as a conversationalist interacting with other people and reacting to feedback. Recognise their motives for saying what they do.

3 as an individual with a basic voice, regional accent, dialect and preferred code. See if you can assess region, sex, class and age.

4 as a member of society who is affected by external factors such as where he is, who he's with and what he's discussing. Decide what register(s) the speaker has adopted and why.

If you look at talking from all these points of view, you should have plenty to say about it!

Chapter 5
Linking the theory to the practice

The foregoing chapters should have given you some food for thought and quite a bit of terminology. Presumably, you'll agree that writing, be it of newspapers, reports or novels, is a craft (amongst other things) and that what is there is there because the writer chose it. It wasn't a happy accident, it was a deliberate policy.

Your job as analyst is, simply put, to do two things. First, you need to recognise *what* is there, then, using your knowledge of language, you need to decide *why* it is there. It is not enough to list how many complex sentences there are, calculate the ratio of passive to active structures and mention a preference for pre- over post-modification. Nor is it enough to say that a text 'moves' you, 'clarifies matters well' or 'sounds sarcastic'. Personal response and recognition of features are legitimate activities, but the only way to do a fair and thorough analysis of any text is to use a system.

A system for text analysis

The exact details of your own system should be evolved by you, and you ought to keep it as flexible and un-mechanical as possible. It will have to allow for the major differences between spoken and written language. We shall deal primarily here with written and prepared spoken (as in a speech or rehearsed interview); we suggested systems of approaching interactional spoken language in Chapter 4.

Somewhere in your system we would suggest the following activities:

Read the text with your full attention. Try not to make pre-judgements on the basis of who wrote it or what it looks like. Keep an open mind.

Jot down first impressions. These will probably be helpful in giving you lines of enquiry. Close analysis may prove them to be false impressions; there again it may prove to you that your instincts are sound.

Take three pieces of paper. Head them Audience, Purpose and Tone respectively and write notes on the appropriate sheet, having asked yourself some broad questions about each of these areas:

Audience (Who was this written for?)
Is the target audience sophisticated?
            well-educated?
            young or old?
            specialist or not?

Purpose (What was the writer's intention?)
Was she attempting to entertain?
            persuade?
            inform?
            instruct?
            do several things at once?

Tone (How did the writer sound?)
Did she seem to you to have a personality?
If not, why not?
If so, of what type?
Did she seem to be factual or emotional?
> consistent?
> direct or subtle?

Try to link your understanding of how particular words and structures work to these broad areas. You might consider these possibilities but please do not use them as a prescriptive checklist; think it through for yourself.

Audience
Educational level/degree of sophistication
Words	Latinate or Anglo-Saxon?
	any foreign words?
	any idioms and clichés?
Structures	simple or complex? (look at clauses)
	very long or short sentences?
	word order usual? (e.g. subject-verb)

Age
Words	very simple vocabulary for children?
	slang associated with a certain period and thus age group?
	archaisms?
	formal or colloquial?
Structures	simple co-ordinators like 'and'
	exclamations for teenagers
	elegant variation (i.e. numerous subordinate clauses)

Specialism
Words	specialist/technical terms
	insider language
Structures	layout including charts, flow-charts, diagrams, tables etc.
	unusual syntax

Purpose
Entertaining
Words	humour through puns
	phonological effects
	'bad' language
	nonsense words
Structures	alliteration and assonance
	form not the same as function (effect is ironic)
	variety of structure to maintain interest

(Entertaining is by far the hardest category to talk about. Look out for unusual words and structures which amuse or interest you. Sequencing – the order in which things are written – is also important.)

Persuading

Words   emotive and extreme language (look at adjectives and adverbs
                carefully)
          'loaded' words (look at verbs)

Structures   repetition for effect
          rhetorical questions
          question and answer
          exclamatory sentences
          two-part, balanced sentences

Informing

Words   precise labels (nouns)
          prepositions (specifying inter-relations.)
          factual adjectives
          adverbials of time and place

Structures   sequencing
          declarative sentences
          lists
          tables

Instructive

Words   prepositions
          'a'/'the' distinction important
          adverbs of manner, time and place

Structures   imperative mood verbs
          sequencing
          format: sub-sections

Tone

Personality

(Remember that the writer may be speaking as a persona and not as herself – try not to confuse the two.)

Words   hyperbolic (exaggerated) or understated
          assertive e.g. 'I think' as opposed to 'it seems to me'
          anxious – question tags
          muddled or clear (look at nouns)
          attitude to others (look at nouns)
          attitude to others (look at adjectives)
          colloquial and chatty or formal?
          original – unusual collocations
          unconventional – taboo words

Structures   active (involved) or passive (objective)?
          first person or third person?
          personal? (lots of 'I's and 'me's)

Is the tone sophisticated or simple?

Words   long and Latinate?
          jokes, puns and plays on words?

	jargon?
	specialist language or simple?
Structures	short statements or long, complex sentences?
	simple co-ordination or lots of subordination?

'stream of consciousness' – where the writer shares their thought process with the reader?

any asides? – jokey or informational?

Is the tone factual or emotional?

Words	nouns mainly concrete or abstract?
	adjectives and adverbs informing or directing?
	articles or possessive pronouns? ('the country' or 'my country'?)
Structures	declaratives or exclamations/questions and answers?
	lists for precision?
	detailed post-modification?
	long, reflective passages or snappy sentences?
	layout – numbered and ordered or anarchic?

Is the tone consistent?

Does the style remain the same throughout or are there shifts?

If there are, can you suggest why?

Does a simple, emotional opening attract your sympathy before the complexities are introduced?

Or does an attempt to be factual disappear as the writer's bias comes through?

Are changes deliberate or a failure?

When you have collected your evidence by looking closely at words and structures, you will be in a position to write an informed, fair appraisal of the text. Plan what you are going to say: decide what your overall opinion of the text is, as well as dealing with how effectively it addresses its chosen audience, whether it achieves its purpose and whether you feel it adopts a suitable and appropriate tone. When you have completed your analysis, look at what you have written:

Is it well-ordered and thus clear?

Is it an expression of your personality – if you want it to be?

Is it thorough or vague?

Is it linguistic – i.e. have you used the appropriate specialist terms?

In short, analyse your own work too!

· S E C T I O N   T W O ·

LANGUAGE IN ACTION

In this section we look at language varieties, using the vocabulary and framework provided in Section One.

Chapters 6 to 12 deal with non-literary varieties; chapters 13 to 18 deal with literature.

Chapter 6

Private persuasion
– words used to express feeling

> They're only words
> and words are all I have
> to steal your heart away.

This pop song of the sixties may not be as laughable as it at first appears. In the matter of winning hearts, words have always been considered a very powerful weapon. Centuries ago, judging by Shakespeare's jokes at their expense, the love-lorn were penning excruciatingly bad sonnets (think of Benedick in *Much Ado About Nothing*, for example.) In the early nineteenth century John Keats was pouring all his longings into his letters to Fanny Brawne. And at the end of that century a very different figure, Queen Victoria, was writing passionate missives to her Albert.

Nowadays, few, if any of us write sonnets and even love letters are largely a thing of the past. The ubiquitous telephone kiosk has made them unnecessary (I say telephone kiosks despite the fact that most homes have a 'phone: nothing is more embarrassing than assuring someone of your unending love with an audience of father complaining about the bill and big brother taking the mickey.)

All of us get involved in love at some time or another. The most dispassionate amongst us could probably not deny singing along with a love song in a pointed way. If we didn't, why would they be so popular? We will look at a love song in detail later: for the moment let us just say that the person reading this book who has never bought or received a record of a sloppy love song or fantasised about doing so is a rare breed indeed!

Likewise, we've all sent hundreds of cards and we'll have chosen a lot of them for 'the nice words'. If we're less open, because more embarrassed, we might have bought humorous ones. The message is still the same, as is the impulse behind it.

Fashions do alter about 'the done thing'. Sonnets are no longer part of everyone's life, the tributes to female beauty no longer stress, as they did in mediaeval lyrics, 'her skinne as whyte as whalle-bone' (whatever would Greenpeace say?) Even the Shakespearean comparison to a rose would strike most twentieth-century women as unoriginal, but then that is just what most compliments are. When universal emotions are being expressed it isn't easy to be original, nor is it necessarily desirable. Sincerity and simplicity are allied in many people's minds, otherwise the success of a love song with the refrain

> I just called to say I love you
> I just called to say how much I care
> I just called to say I love you
> And I mean it from the bottom of my heart

would be hard to understand.

Love songs

Many love songs contain a string of clichés, rhymes which poets would certainly turn their noses up at and well-worn metaphors. Consider the chorus from a Don Williams song:

> You're my bread when I'm hungry
> You're my shelter from troubled winds,
> You're my anchor in life's ocean,
> But most of all, you're my best friend.

Just as the language forms of love songs are predictable, so is the content: 'Nothing you could do could make me untrue to my guy' and 'Stand by your man, give him two arms to cling to' are the Tamla and Country and Western versions of the same sentiment.

Loneliness is another firm favourite: 'It hurts to be alone, so help me make it through the night', 'I'd rather dream than have that lonesome feeling stealing through the night' and

> I can make you mine, taste your lips of wine
> Any time night or day
> Only trouble is – gee whizz!
> I'm dreaming my life away

are different expressions of the same sentiment.

The songs from which the last two quotes are taken make an interesting comparison. Their statement is markedly similar, but their tone and style – because of their intended audience – are very different. Have a close look at the whole of the two songs and see what you can deduce about their intended audiences and their effectiveness as expressions of feeling.

It's Easy To Remember

> Your sweet expression,
> the smile you gave me
> The way we looked when we met
> It's easy to remember
> And so hard to forget.
>
> I hear you whisper,
> 'I'll always love you'
> And though it brings me regret,
> It's easy to remember
> And so hard to forget.
>
> So I must dream
> To have your hand caress me,
> Fingers press me tight;
> I'd rather dream
> Than have that lonely feeling
> Stealing through the night.

Each little moment
Is there before me;
I know it's over and yet
It's easy to remember
And so hard to forget.

Rodgers and Hart

All I Have To Do Is Dream

Dream
When I want you in my arms
When I want you and all your charms
Whenever I want you
All I have to do is dream
Dream, dream, dream;

When I feel blue in the night,
And I need you to hold me tight,
Whenever I want you,
All I have to do is dream.

I can make you mine,
Taste your lips of wine,
Any time – night or day;
Only trouble is – gee whizz!
I'm dreaming my life away.

I need you so that I could die,
I love you so and that is why
Whenever I want you,
All I have to do is dream.
Dream, dream, dream,
Dream.

Boudleaux Bryant

Of course, not all love songs are the same. They are in fact most various because they express the many facets of love: initial fears and doubts, fulfilment, marriage, separation, devotion, passion, affection – the list is endless!

When confronted with a love song or poem, it is useful to decide which category of love experience it deals with and what audience it is seeking to move. For example, the tendency of teenagers to insult people who they are attracted to is clearly reflected in songs written for them. In such songs, as I suspect in real life, the receiver of the message recognises its falseness: that the flippant, insulting tone is masking genuine affection which it would be smarmy and embarrassing to voice openly. A 'see if I care' posture is struck, but observers think 'Methinks he doth protest too much,' or, more colloquially 'Who do you think you're kidding?' Nobody, is, of course, meant to be fooled.

Next let's look at the 10 C.C. song *I'm Not In Love*, which seems a good example of the unwilling love tribute.

I'm Not In Love

I'm not in love, so don't forget it
It's just a silly phase I'm going through
And just because I call you up
Don't get me wrong; don't think you've got it made
I'm not in love ... no, no,
It's because ...

I'd like to see you, but then again
That doesn't mean you mean that much to me
So if I call you, don't make a fuss
Don't tell your friends about the two of us
I'm not in love; no, no
It's because ...

Be quiet, big boys don't cry
Be quiet, big boys don't cry

I keep your picture upon the wall
It hides a messy stain that was lying there
So don't you ask me to give it back
I know you know it doesn't mean that much to me
I'm not in love; no, no
It's because ...

Ooh, you'll wait a long time for me
Ooh, you'll wait a long time

Graham Gouldman and Eric Stewart

Throughout this song the speaker reiterates that he is not in love; presumably because he is frightened to give his emotion that name. The word, in English, is a tremendously potent one: there is no confusion between 'like' and 'love' in our tongue as there might be in French. To like is one thing; to love another. And as for being *in* love ... !

Those in love tell their love almost obsessively – which is what this chapter is all about. Lovers demand of one another verbal reassurance. 'Tell me you love me!' may seem a ridiculous directive: of what value is a sought profession? Yet I am sure such demands are very common.

But to get back to the song. The speaker is at pains to assure the receiver that this is not love but merely 'a silly phase [he's] going through.' His choice of words is interesting: 'silly' suggests foolishness, 'phase' inconstancy. He is really apologising for his condition and making unconvincing excuses. Excuses recur in the third verse where her picture is 'hiding a messy stain.' He knows she knows 'it doesn't mean that much' to him. Really?

The writer's problem – or rather that of the persona of an awkward teenager – is that he cannot bear to seem over-enthusiastic. To do so would court mockery and chance rejection. So eager is he not to be misunderstood that he uses lots of imperatives to insist that she doesn't 'get him wrong' or think she's 'got it made'. Perhaps the most telling of his commands is 'Don't tell your friends about the two of us' which combines the intimacy of a shared secret and the fear of discovery.

The lexis of the song is extraordinarily simple, stressing that the persona is a simple soul. You could not readily imagine him writing sonnets! Indeed many of the lines do not boast a single bisyllabic word. Many of the phrases sound deliberately childlike, for example 'don't you ask me to give it back'. This at once inspires our pity and a certain amount of contempt. Pity predominates when we hear the sour grapes in 'You'll wait a long time for me.'

Most of the statements and imperatives in the song are negative. Even those that are positive are meagre in their praise: 'I'd like to see you', he is prepared to admit, but this is followed by the escape clause 'but then again ... ' He would hate her to think she could 'mean that much' to him.

What, one wonders, would the recipient of such a tribute feel? Would she be moved by the vulnerability and gaucheness of the writer or infuriated by his lukewarm tone and qualifiers? I suspect the former, and that any willing victim would soon unravel the subtext of the song.

A weakness in the song in my view is the large nudge in the ribs of the listener in the form of the line 'Be quiet, big boys don't cry.' Nobody was convinced by his cool stance, so why hit us over the head with the truth?

Literary expressions of love

Unwilling tributes are not, of course, a late twentieth-century phenomenon or necessarily the preserve of the young and inarticulate. Look at this famous passage from the novel *Pride and Prejudice* by Jane Austen.

> In an hurried manner he immediately began an inquiry after her health, imputing his visit to a wish of hearing that she were better. She answered him with cold civility. He sat down for a few moments, and then getting up walked about the room. Elizabeth was surprised, but said not a word. After a silence of several minutes, he came towards her in an agitated manner, and thus began:
>
> 'In vain have I struggled. It will not do. My feelings will not be repressed. You must allow me to tell you how ardently I admire and love you.'
>
> Elizabeth's astonishment was beyond expression. She stared, coloured, doubted, and was silent. This he considered sufficient encouragement, and the avowal of all that he felt and had long felt for her, immediately followed. He spoke well, but there were feelings besides those of the heart to be detailed, and he was not more eloquent on the subject of tenderness than of pride. His sense of her inferiority – of its being a degradation – of the family obstacles which judgment had always opposed to inclination, were dwelt on with a warmth which seemed due to the consequence he was wounding, but was very unlikely to recommend his suit.
>
> In spite of her deeply rooted dislike, she could not be insensible to the compliment of such a man's affection, and though her intentions did not vary for an instant, she was at first sorry for the pain he was to receive; till, roused to resentment by his subsequent language, she lost all compassion in anger. She tried, however, to compose herself to answer him with patience, when he should have done. He concluded

with representing to her the strength of that attachment which, in spite of all his endeavours, he had found impossible to conquer; and with expressing his hope that it would now be rewarded by her acceptance of his hand. As he said this, she could easily see that he had no doubt of a favourable answer. He spoke of apprehension and anxiety, but his countenance expressed real security. Such a circumstance could only exasperate farther, and, when he ceased, the colour rose into her cheeks, and she said,

'In such cases as this, it is, I believe, the established mode to express a sense of obligation for the sentiments avowed, however unequally they may be returned. It is natural that obligation should be felt, and if I could feel gratitude, I would now thank you. But I cannot – I have never desired your good opinion, and you have certainly bestowed it most unwillingly. I am sorry to have occasioned pain to any one. It has been most unconsciously done, however, and I hope will be of short duration. The feelings which, you tell me, have long prevented the acknowledgment of your regard, can have little difficulty in overcoming it after this explanation.'

Mr. Darcy, who was leaning against the mantle-piece with his eyes fixed on her face, seemed to catch her words with no less resentment than surprize. His complexion became pale with anger, and the disturbance of his mind was visible in every feature. He was struggling for the appearance of composure, and would not open his lips, till he believed himself to have attained it. The pause was to Elizabeth's feelings dreadful. At length, in a voice of forced calmness, he said,

'And this is all the reply which I am to have the honour of expecting! I might, perhaps, wish to be informed why, with so little endeavour at civility, I am thus rejected. But it is of small importance.'

'I might as well inquire,' replied she, 'why with so evident a design of offending and insulting me, you chose to tell me that you liked me against your will, against your reason, and even against your character? Was not this some excuse for incivility, if I was uncivil? But I have other provocations. You know I have. Had not my own feelings decided against you, had they been indifferent, or had they even been favourable, do you think that any consideration would tempt me to accept the man who has been the means of ruining, perhaps for ever, the happiness of a most beloved sister?'

As she pronounced these words, Mr. Darcy changed colour; but the emotion was short, and he listened without attempting to interrupt her while she continued.

'I have every reason in the world to think ill of you. No motive can excuse the unjust and ungenerous part you acted there. You dare not, you cannot deny that you have been the principal, if not the only means of dividing them from each other, of exposing one to the censure of the world for caprice and instability, the other to its derision for disappointed hopes, and involving them both in misery of the acutest kind.'

She paused, and saw with no slight indignation that he was

listening with an air which proved him wholly unmoved by any feeling of remorse. He even looked at her with a smile of affected incredulity.

'Can you deny that you have done it?' she repeated.

With assumed tranquillity he then replied, 'I have no wish of denying that I did everything in my power to separate my friend from your sister, or that I rejoice in my success. Towards him I have been kinder than towards myself.'

Elizabeth disdained the appearance of noticing this civil reflection, but its meaning did not escape, nor was it likely to conciliate her.

'But it is not merely this affair,' she continued, 'on which my dislike is founded. – Long before it had taken place, my opinion of you was decided. Your character was unfolded in the recital which I received many months ago from Mr. Wickham. On this subject, what can you have to say? In what imaginary act of friendship can you here defend yourself? or under what misrepresentation can you here impose upon others?'

'You take an eager interest in that gentleman's concerns,' said Darcy, in a less tranquil tone, and with a heightened colour.

'Who that knows what his misfortunes have been, can help feeling an interest in him?'

Jane Austen: Pride and Prejudice

❖ How can we tell that Darcy is unwilling?
❖ Why is Elizabeth so furious?
❖ What tone does each of them adopt?

This is an example of someone being in love despite himself. Austen conveys this by the language which Darcy uses – would you expect a lover to say 'You must allow me to tell you'? He does! A sensitive reading of the passage enables the reader to see warning emotions within both the characters' breasts. Love and pride are designated by different word choices, different structures. So are regret and anger.

Look in detail at their exchanges. Select the key words and try to decide which words relate to which of their emotions. Is Austen's version a passable or excellent representation of how people express their emotions?

It is reasonable to make a judgement of a piece of writing once you have analysed it. You have every right to a personal response: indeed it would be a pity if you did not have one. Remember though, that your remarks should be justified by solid, linguistic evidence. For example, a candidate might write of Darcy's opening remark

The tone Darcy adopts is neither gentle nor affectionate. The fact that he uses an imperative 'You must allow' is significant. So is the fact that he addresses Elizabeth as 'you' and not 'my dear Elizabeth' as a more overtly affectionate man might.'

Another candidate might say: 'Right from the start Darcy is stroppy and rude. No wonder Elizabeth gets mad.'

You will notice that there is a difference in the style of these candidates' analyses as well as in their content. The second is far too colloquial: it is in the wrong register.

Register is an interesting feature of the next passage we would like you to consider. It is a love letter, but it was written by a poet – John Keats to be precise. On first reading, decide whether it works as a love letter. Would you enjoy receiving or be proud of sending such a letter? Does it seem to you sincere or is it too literary in register, too self-conscious?

My dearest girl,

This moment I have set myself to copy some verses out fair. I cannot proceed with any degree of content. I must write you a line or two and see if that will assist in dismissing you from my mind for ever so short a time. Upon my soul I can think of nothing else. The time is passed when I had power to advise and warn you against the unpromising morning of my life. My love has made me selfish. I cannot exist without you. I am forgetful of everything but seeing you again – my life seems to stop there – I see no further. You have absorbed me. I have a sensation at the present moment as though I was dissolving – I should be exquisitely miserable without the hope of soon seeing you. I should be afraid to separate myself far from you. My sweet Fanny, will your heart never change? My love, will it? I have no limit now to my love. Your note came in just here – I cannot be happier away from you. 'Tis richer than an argosy of pearls. Do not threat me even in jest. I have been astonished that men could die martyrs for religion – I have shuddered at it. I shudder no more – I could be martyred for my religion – Love is my religion – I could die for that. I could die for you. My creed is Love and you are its only tenet. You have ravished me away by a power I cannot resist; and yet I could resist till I saw you; and even since I have seen you I have endeavoured often "to reason against the reasons of my love". I can do that no more – the pain would be too great. My love is selfish. I cannot breathe without you.

Yours for ever,
John Keats

It seems only fair to tell you that Keats' love letters are considered (note how I use the passive when I am distancing myself from an opinion!) some of the finest in the English language. Can you see why?

Look at the structures and words he employs. Pick some which seem to you to denote sincerity or strength of feeling.

Consider the purpose of the letter. It seems to us to be persuasive in intent as well as complimentary. Can you see any persuasive elements in this letter? (If you want to revise persuasive language you could have a look at Chapters 6 and 7.)

We have mentioned that terms of address are significant. Note how Keats addresses Fanny (not a Darcy 'you'!) Look also at how he signs off. The starts and ends of letters are always worth considering. They make a sensible starting point to an analysis.

Some might argue (again I refuse to be held personally responsible) that Keats is somewhat literary and egotistical. What evidence is there, if any, in the text to support such a view?

Having considered these general issues, attempt a full analysis of the letter and judge its effectiveness.

Breaking up

Of course, love letters are not always positive and encouraging. At the end of most affairs one or other of the partners has the difficult task of saying 'It's over.' Such letters (and many people find it easier to end a relationship on paper than in person) are popularly known as 'Dear John' letters. Here is an example. See if you can tell anything about the writer and the recipient.

> Dear ...
>
> I don't know how to put this. I feel dead mean but I don't think I want to see you again. I want us to stay friends, but I just reckon we're too young to get so serious. I bet you agree if you really think about it. I don't want you to think it's because I've gone off you or anything. It's just time we had a bit of a break from each other to see how we really feel. I'll probably finish up writing you another letter, asking you to go back!
>
> Please don't get all upset. That's the last thing I want to happen. And please, please don't send one of your mates round to try and talk me round. I bet you'll enjoy having a bit more time to see them, anyway.
>
> Take care of yourself. No hard feelings, all right?
> Stay in touch.

❖ What age and gender do you think the writer was? How could you tell? What attempts does s/he make to soften the blow?
❖ If you received this letter, would you despair, or are there some promising signs for a reconciliation?
❖ Write a reply picking up on the more friendly and hopeful comments in the letter.

Expressing sympathy

Some letters are terribly difficult to write. Imagine that the grandmother of one of your friends has just died. She had been ill for a long time and was eighty-eight years old. All the same, you know your friend will be very upset and you want to write to express your sympathy. Sketch out what you would say.

Everyone will probably have said similar things. Was your opening remark 'I was really sorry to hear about your Gran' or something very similar? Did you then go on to say that at least she wasn't in pain now and that for her it was probably a welcome release? Perhaps you praised her or said that time would lessen the pain. Have I guessed right? If I have, it's not because I'm a genius but because there are limited things you can say at such a time: you can hardly say 'I gather she's finally popped her clogs – best thing all round.' Humour may be an acceptable way of handling love but it's an utterly unacceptable way of expressing grief.

Because grief is problematic to express, many people buy cards to convey how they feel. They are also likely to take a funeral director's advice about what kind of announcement to put in the newspaper. Many phrases recur in In Memoriam columns, and not because their writers are insincere: it is genuinely difficult to find something new to say about mourning. Certain features are noticeable and understandable:

Euphemism A loved one's death is not easily accepted, so the word 'death' is very often avoided. Thus you find 'went to sleep', 'passed away' or 'found his rest' rather than 'died'.

Simple lexis Sincerity is connected with simplicity in many people's minds. Raw emotion is thus seen as best expressed in simple words.

Semantic fields Words relating to God and religion have an obvious place in this context. When sent by children love, hugs and kisses feature largely and family names are often present.

Format Very often In Memoriam announcements are not written in prose but as poetry. Rhyme is employed, presumably for memorability.

The same sort of rhyme – which is easy to laugh at but clearly fulfils a function – can be found in greeting cards:

> I love you, Mummy, very much,
> Just bucketfuls I do,
> So here's a great big birthday wish,
> And a hug and a kiss for you

is fairly representative.

Private persuasion runs the gamut from terrific subtlety and very literary language to the simplest, most obvious language forms: that is why it is so interesting.

Chapter 7

Public persuasion – words used to sell

We may not, as individual members of society, consider ourselves to be of great significance in the whole scheme of things, but very many people spend a great deal of time, effort, and above all money trying to influence our thoughts and our behaviour. Industry and commerce want us to buy various products and services, politicians and pressure groups want us to support them with our votes, money and time.

It might seem shocking to talk in the same breath of attempts to persuade us to change our breakfast cereal and attempts to alter our opinions on an issue such as abortion, but the same techniques will probably be used in the service of both these 'causes'. Increasingly, specialist firms offer to run campaigns, to exploit the media, and to use their expertise to make sure that a message is put across to the public in the most effective ways. Governments speak of 'selling' their policies, politicians bemoan their failure to 'get the message across'. Industry runs million-pound advertising campaigns, not only to sell its products, but to project a 'positive corporate image'.

These activities are entirely legitimate. After all, if there is some issue we believe to be important – cleaning up our environment for example – we would be sure that it was vital to make other people concerned and prepared to act as well. We would try to convey our views and our plan of action as clearly as possible, and in a way which would capture our audience's attention, arouse interest, persuade them of the urgency of the situation and convince them of the need for action. Time devoted to designing the best way to do this would be time well spent, and we would welcome advice from anyone who had experience in such campaigning. We would not consider that in doing this we were tricking or manipulating people, because we would be convinced of the rightness of our aims.

Nevertheless there is something about this whole process which does make us uneasy. For example, an extremely successful public relations executive was heard on television admiring Hitler's 'completely legitimate' propaganda methods, which sent a chill down the spine. Where do we draw the line between 'legitimate' attempts to put a case forcefully in the hope of influencing others, and what we call 'naked propaganda'? Does it depend on how skilfully it's done, or does it depend on whether or not we agree with the point of view which is being put forward? We only have to think of an emotive issue such as abortion or capital punishment to realise how difficult it is to be 'objective' about the techniques employed by one side or another.

We do not intend to spend the rest of the chapter debating this question. Hopefully you can do that for yourselves, and find examples to fuel the discussion. However, it is useful to consider various ways in which language is used to affect our opinions and our feelings, both so that we ourselves may become effective 'persuaders' when we want to be (on behalf of entirely worthy causes, naturally) and so that we can be aware when some of these methods are being used to affect us. Then we will be in a better position to be persuaded, or not, as we see fit.

Catchphrases and slogans

Many of the methods used to persuade us in the 1990s are obviously heavily dependent on extra-linguistic features. 'A picture's worth a thousand words', we are told in newspapers, magazines, on television, film, or advertising hoardings. Is this the case? The picture may be what catches our attention, but the catchphrase or slogan may be what stays in our heads. A short, memorable phrase which seems to capture the 'essence' of the product, campaign or politician, is often the most important part of an otherwise heavily visual approach. A classic example is the Milk Marketing Board's 'Gotta Lotta Bottle' which they obviously considered an effective part of their campaign. Of course it was spoken with lots of glottal stops, as in 'Go' a lo' a bo'l' (swallowing all the *t*s). 'Beanz Meanz Heinz' is another famous example. Will history prove 'Pure Genius' to have been a good slogan for Guinness? There will be many current examples you could think of, some more successful than others.

This technique does not only work in advertising. Headline writers and political opponents love to find a short nickname for a public figure which labels them in the public mind. The leader of the Labour Party struggled throughout the eighties to escape the 'Welsh Windbag' tag. 'The Iron Lady' served Mrs Thatcher for much of her term in office, although whether it was a compliment or an insult tended to depend on the context. John Major, initially at least, is proving rather resistant to attempts to label him, 'Grey Suit' having, not surprisingly perhaps, failed to stick.

Americans seem particularly good at inventing insulting and cutting expressions to expose the supposed shortcomings of presidential candidates. 'Would you buy a used car from this man?' put paid to Richard Nixon's chances – the first time. 'Where's the beef?' (implying lack of practical policies) defeated another candidate, and 'Can he walk and chew gum at the same time?' impugned the intellectual capacities of Gerald Ford.

This is not just a skill practised by American politicians: Labour politician Dennis Healey once paid tribute to the incisive wit of a parliamentary opponent by describing being attacked by him as 'like being savaged by a dead sheep.'

These might just seem the happy inspirations of political or journalistic wits which happened to stick. More probably, they are the calculated inventions of opposing campaign managers and their advertising teams. Whichever is true, they very effectively demonstrate the power of the word. They stick in the memory longer than flattering photographs, and carry a more telling message than campaign theme tunes.

We mention the latter because another important extra-linguistic element in some forms of persuasion is music. On television, radio, or at live meetings well-chosen music can instantly create a mood, set the scene or indicate target audience. Some of this music may be accompanied by words, and the combination of words and music also helps to add to memorability: 'Just one Cornetto' to the tune of *O sole mio* was a stroke of genius.

We do not mean to ignore or to underestimate the role of music and visual images in attempts to influence us, but the main concern of this book is language and from now on we will concentrate on that, and in particular on the main forms such as advertisements, leaflets, letters and speeches, which allow most scope for words to be used persuasively.

Market research

Most advertising and political campaigns are based on a lot of market research. This groundwork of research will have been to discover 'gaps in the market' or how a current product or policy is received. Sophisticated sampling techniques and questionnaires will have been used to these ends.

THATCHER   **VS**   **KINNOCK**

Q1. On this scale, 10 represents a perfect Prime Minister and 1 represents a Prime Minister who does everything wrong. Where on this scale would you put Mrs Thatcher as Prime Minister? ...Mr Kinnock if he were Prime Minister?

10 points   0   10

4.8 (Tory 7.1, Labour 3.0)   4.6 (Tory 3.2, Labour 6.3)

Q2. For each of the following pairs of words can you tell me which applies best to Mrs Thatcher? ...to Mr Kinnock? The bars indicate the net score of the party leaders in each category. For example 93% of respondents said they thought Mrs Thatcher was strong, while 8% thought she was weak. She therefore scored 88% (93%–5%)

100 %   0   100

STRONG   **STRONG**
88% (93-5)   13% (50-37)   *The alternative word was 'weak'*

UNCARING   **CARING**
27% (58-31)   74% (83-9)

DEVIOUS   **TRUSTWORTHY**
15% (52-37)   20% (52-32)

EXTREME   **MODERATE**
45% (69-24)   55% (74-19)

FIT TO GOVERN   **FIT TO GOVERN**
24% (59-35)   4% (47-43)   *The alternative was 'not fit to govern'*

CLEAR HEADED   **CLEAR HEADED**
60% (78-18)   16% (54-38)   *The alternative was 'muddled'*

This is an example of the sort of research on the basis of which a politician plans the next stage of her/his campaign, although this was done for a newspaper. Note the importance attached to the positive adjectives. The expectation will be that Mrs Thatcher will adjust her campaign to win over those members of the public who find her 'uncaring' or 'extreme'. You may be in a better position than us to judge whether she did so.

You are just as likely to be stopped in the street to be asked if the ice cream you've just been given to sample is 'too sweet' or 'too salty'. The product will be adjusted accordingly.

Target audience

One of the first things for you to consider when analysing a persuasive text is whether or not it is addressed to a specific target audience. This advertisement appears to be very specific:

MAY WE SUGGEST YOU TELL THE BOARD YOU'RE CHOOSING A FIVE-SEATER FAMILY SALOON.

So you've spent the last few months diplomatically 'losing' at golf. You've laughed at the MD's jokes (some were even funny) and you kept schtum when the Chairman's wife deliberately forgot you name.

Yesterday it paid off. Your back was patted (not stabbed) and you've just been told to invest some company money in some brand new metal.

Allow us to make a suggestion. Test drive the stunning new CD Carlsson from Saab. Of course, you'll be hooked from the moment you sit in the driving seat, but then there's a problem. People may think you're getting ideas above your already lofty station. And you didn't get where you are today by people thinking you're getting ideas above your already lofty station.

So here's what you tell the Financial Director:

Firstly, the new Saab is a four door, five-seater, family saloon. Don't mention the integrated aerodynamic skirts, alloy wheels, or exclusive badging.

Secondly, inform him there is 23.8 cu. feet of luggage space in the boot, but omit there's 195 b.h.p. 16-valves, and an all new turbo-charged power unit under the bonnet.

Say that it's quite nippy, and jolly safe when overtaking. But please leave out the 0-60 in 7.5 seconds, forget that it's faster than a Ferrari Mondial from 50 to 70 m.p.h.

Oh, and mention the 38.1 m.p.g. Not the 140 m.p.h.

And finally, whatever you do, don't say the new CD was partly developed by Erik Carlsson, the legendary rally driver. Just explain that it's wholly favoured by Harry Dobson, the frugal company car manager.

If all goes well, you'll soon be driving the new Saab Carlsson CD into the company car park. Obviously, you'll be hiding it in a corner until it's time to make your move. That day, in the not-too-distant future when you 'accidentally' park it in the Chairman's space.

Or have we been addressing the Chairman all along?

- Who does this appear (literally) to be addressing?
- How much do we get to know about the supposed addressee's life?
- Is this actually only appealing to high-flying company directors who are about to be bought a new company car? (This would appear to limit the potential market somewhat.)
- If in fact it is really aimed at a wider audience, how is it making its appeal, and what feelings is it appealing to in that audience? Did it appeal to you?
- What qualities are associated with this car?
- Who are the 'we' referred to in the headline? What sort of relationship does the 'we' voice imply it has with the addressee/audience? How is this built up?

Usually we analyse the first text in a chapter, but this one seemed to exemplify so many of the characteristics of persuasive writing that we thought we'd ask you to find them. It is not always quite so clear exactly which audience an advertisement is aimed at. Which group do you think is the target for the following one?

> Set in a most convenient location, Parkfield Court is an attractive development of 1 and 2 bedroomed apartments, all contained within one main building.
> Our aim has been to create the ambience and comfort of a luxury hotel, yet with all the privacy and independence of your own home.
> Wimpey Homes' reputation for quality of construction doesn't mean just building the best homes; we also make sure that we consistently offer the best value for money.

This is a much smaller amount of text, but is it enough for you to work out who it might be addressing? It might help to pick out which qualities of these properties are being stressed.

It is in fact an advertisement for apartments (why not flats?) for retired people. Possibly this is not emphasised because being old is not as desirable as being an upwardly mobile young executive. This may change of course, as the elderly become an increasing proportion of the population.

Does the language used in this advertisement have anything in common with the SAAB advertisement?

The most obvious feature they share is that both use the first person plural – 'Our aim has been ... ' – and address the audience directly – 'of your own home ... ' This is characteristic of much persuasive language, although often the 'we' includes the addressee as well; here it personalises the corporate image. Direct address seems to create a personal connection between writer and reader. Sometimes this is informal and familiar – 'and you kept schtum ... ' – sometimes more formal and respectful – 'of your own home ... '

The other feature the two advertisements have in common is the use of positive lexis to refer to the product. The Parkfield Court advertisement is much less subtle here. It uses adjectives in the first paragraph, 'convenient', 'attractive'; nouns in the second, 'ambience', 'comfort', 'privacy' and 'independence' (isn't it by this last word we most clearly spot the audience?); and in the last paragraph that old superlative standby 'best' twice.

By contrast, the SΛΛB advertisement seems to be giving us facts. But hidden away in this fluent, casual style are such words as 'stunning', 'exclusive', 'new', 'power', 'faster', 'legendary'. True, they are not all applied directly to the car, but they are there, and their associations 'rub off'.

Where the two differ is in tone. The Parkfield Court advertisement is formal, bordering on frozen in the recognisable register of estate agents: 'convenient location', 'attractive development'. The tone of the car advertisement is a mixture of the occasionally formal – 'May we suggest', 'Allow us to make a suggestion' – with the clearly colloquial – 'kept schtum', 'brand new metal'. The effect of this mixture is to create a familiar, 'jokey' tone appropriate to the apparent task in hand, that of conspiring to deceive the Financial Director.

The next text has a clear target audience, and also uses direct address, but it is not a commercial advertisement and it has a much more serious persuasive purpose. It was published by the Health Education Authority as part of the campaign to raise awareness of the danger of AIDS among young people, and to persuade them to change their behaviour.

IS THIS ... UM, HOW YOU'D ... WELL, FEEL ABOUT ... ER, ... ASKING YOUR BOYFRIEND ... TO ... UM ... WELL ... ER ... USE A CONDOM?

- Like the SAAB advertisement, this is designed to sound like direct address. Who is the apparent recipient of this advice?
- If you wanted to reach this audience, where would you place this advertisement?

In fact in this particular Health Education campaign, different advertisements were written to address different 'at risk' groups. This one is aimed at teenage girls, and appeared in a magazine many of them read, *Smash Hits*.

- What impression is the text on the left hand side of the spread intending to make, and how is this conveyed?
- What has been identified (probably on the basis of some market research) as one of the problems girls might have in taking responsibility for 'safer sex'?

Condom.

It's not that difficult to say is it?

Well if it's not, what's stopping you?

He might laugh at you for mentioning it. He might think you're easy.

Well here's something else to think about.

In Britain the number of people with AIDS is still on the increase.

And for every person with AIDS, we estimate there are thirty with HIV.

Human Immunodeficiency Virus is the virus which leads to AIDS.

Someone can have it for several years and still look and feel perfectly healthy.

But through unprotected sex, they can pass the virus on to you.

A condom can help protect you.

So think about using one, and talk about it with your boyfriend.

You never know, he might just be pleased you suggested it.

Think about not having sex at all if you're not certain, or you don't really know him well enough.

And more important, never feel shy about asking him to use a condom.

AIDS. YOU'RE AS SAFE AS YOU WANT TO BE.

The other difficulty this piece is concerned with is one of language. It is that of making the term 'condom' more acceptable and generally used. There are many colloquial expressions in general use for this particular item, but they don't have respectable connotations, vary in different parts of the country and in different age groups, and are more often heard from men. The AIDS campaign had to find a more 'neutral' term which a wider range of people would feel comfortable with. 'Condom' was the solution, but it had to be launched into general use. Only time will tell if this campaign has succeeded. So the embarrassment to be overcome is not only a behavioural one, but a linguistic one, the possibility that the boyfriend might find the *word* funny, as much as the suggestion.

Think about the different types of sentence used in this text:

❖ **Why do you think it begins with questions and continues mainly with statements?**

❖ **What is achieved by asking the readers questions? After all, they can't answer – or can they?**

❖ **Why are three of the last sentences commands? Is this the most important part of the text?**

❖ **Why is the text broken up into so many short major and minor sentences?**

❖ **Why do three of them begin with co-ordinating conjunctions, usually to be found in the middle of sentences and not at the beginning?**

❖ **Can you find any attempts to make this writing sound like speech?**

❖ **What do you think about the vocabulary of this piece? Is it mainly formal or colloquial?**

❖ **Now ask the same question of the style of the advertisement as a whole: formal or informal? Are the answers the same to both questions?**

If you have tried to write this sort of persuasive piece yourself, aiming like this one to reach a lot of people, have you found that the main problem is to get the tone right? If you try to be too chatty and colloquial you run the risk of sounding patronising, and detract from the serious subject. On the other hand, if the tone is too formal or impersonal, it will not engage your target audience. Do you think this advertisement – and it could just as well be a leaflet – is successful in striking a tone which will appeal to its audience, and thus have some hope of being effective in changing people's behaviour?

Public speaking

Having progressed from commercial to public service advertisements, let's look now at a different form of public persuasion altogether, the public speech. Throughout history we know that there have been great orators, people who have been able to sway multitudes by the power of their words. Of course, we know of most of them by report only, and can judge others merely by reading their words on the page, a pale shadow of the real thing. Contemporary examples are harder to find, as modern politicians know that they can reach far more people through the more intimate medium of television. We can, however, still catch a whiff of the excitement of stirring public speech-making at election times, at religious or political rallies, at party conferences, and even (occasionally) now that parliament is televised. But most commentators agree that it is a dying art. It's an art, however, that as language students we should consider, as it is an example of language at full tilt. These orators were the first of the public persuaders.

The example we are going to look at is a famous one. It is President Kennedy's inaugural address, delivered in Washington on January 20th, 1961.

> So let us begin anew – remembering on both sides that civility is not a sign of weakness, and sincerity is always subject to proof. Let us never negotiate out of fear. But let us never fear to negotiate.
>
> Let both sides explore what problems unite us instead of belabouring the problems that divide us.
>
> Let both sides join to invoke the wonders of science instead of its terrors. Together let us explore the stars, conquer the deserts, eradicate disease, tape the ocean depths, and encourage the arts and commerce.
>
> Let both sides unite to heed in all corners of the earth the command of Isaiah – to 'undo the heavy burdens ... and let the oppressed go free'.
>
> Now the trumpet summons us again – not as a call to bear arms, though arms we need – not as a call to battle, though embattled we are – but a call to bear the burden of a long twilight struggle, year in and year out, 'rejoicing in hope, patient in tribulation' – a struggle against the common enemies of man: tyranny, poverty, disease, and war itself.
>
> Can we forge against these enemies a grand and global alliance, north and south, east and west, that can assure a more fruitful life for all mankind? Will you join in that historic effort?
>
> In the long history of the world only a few generations have been granted the role of defending freedom in its hour of maximum danger. I do not shrink from this responsibility – I welcome it. I do not believe that any of us would exchange places with any other people or any other generation. The energy, the faith, and the devotion which we bring to this endeavour will light our country and all who serve it – and the glow from that fire can truly light the world.
>
> And so, my fellow-Americans: ask not what your country will do for you – ask what you can do for your country.
>
> My fellow-citizens of the world: ask not what America will do for you but what together we can do for the freedom of man.

Theodore C. Sorensen: Kennedy

President Kennedy was concerned in this speech not to target one section of the community, but rather to include as many members of it as possible. He had just won the election by the narrowest of margins, and his purpose was to unite these previous opponents by creating a sense of national purpose. He was also keen to make the transition from national politician to international statesman. This is the climax of the speech, which he concludes by addressing 'My fellow citizens of the world' (and you can't get much more inclusive than that!)

This oration has few features in common with spontaneous speech, and many more in common with literature. Yet it was written to be spoken and clearly exploits sound and rhythm.

As you read it through we expect that one of the features which struck you immediately was the balanced structure of many of the sentences. Write down as many as you can find.

If a balanced, parallel structure is used to highlight contrasting or opposite notions, then the technical term for it is antithesis. An example of antithesis is the sentence 'Let both sides explore what problems unite us instead of belabouring the problems that divide us.' In this sentence 'unite us' is balanced by its opposite 'divide us', and although the rhythmic balance is not exact (as it would have been if he had used 'not' rather than 'instead of'), the effect of this is to draw attention to the contrast. The sentence is balanced on the pivot phrase 'instead of'.

Other pivot words or phrases are 'and', 'but' or 'not'; in other cases the pivot is a punctuation feature such as a comma or a dash.

In two noticeable examples, the antithetical contrast is further emphasised by word inversion: 'Let us never negotiate out of fear. But let us never fear to negotiate.' Here 'fear' is used first as a noun, then as a verb. The other example is the famous 'ask not what your country can do for you – ask what you can do for your country.' In this case the two parts of the sentence contain almost identical vocabulary, but by reversing the words in subject and indirect object positions the meaning is dramatically altered.

These are instances of the most carefully structured word-play. The parallel structures, vocabulary and sounds ('not'/'what') combine to make the phrases easily memorable. Some of the earliest language we learn and retain, nursery rhymes and riddles, uses repetitive rhyme and rhythm. It may not be a very technical remark to make, but rhyme, rhythm and word-play give us pleasure and stay in our heads: this is something advertising copywriters are as much aware of as are American presidents. We admire verbal ingenuity.

There are other repetitive features in this speech. Certain key words are repeated frequently, 'both sides' for example. Lists are used to build to a crescendo. They have a sense of predictability with which we can join in. Sometimes the lists are positive ones, suggesting boundless opportunity (the lexis is catching): this is the case in the 'wonders of science' paragraph. Other lists are negative, to suggest the size of the challenge, as in the 'common enemies of man' section.

The invocation 'Let' is used many times as a form of direct address. This is a deliberate echo of the Bible and the pulpit. In fact there is a lot of biblical lexis used, as well as direct quotation. Make a list of all the biblical words you can find here. Why do you think there are so many of them?

You might like to compare the vocabulary with other famous examples of American rhetoric; Lincoln's Gettysburg Address and Martin Luther King's 'I have a dream ... ' speech.

Besides the biblical references, the speech is full of formal, elevated lexis, as of course you'd expect. Kennedy is declaring what he would like to see happen during his presidency, but it is not a practical plan of action. Look at the heavy preponderance of abstract nouns such as 'freedom', 'energy', 'faith' and 'devotion': these are all heavily-charged words which uplift us. However, it isn't going to be easy: we must also 'struggle' and 'fight' against 'tyranny', 'poverty' and 'disease'. An opponent might say that the president hasn't actually said very much, but inaugural speeches are meant to inspire, not to get bogged down in 'concrete' details.

'We' seemed the most natural pronoun to use in the previous paragraph because it is used continually throughout the speech to achieve a sense of inclusive purpose, of common identity. Towards the end of the speech the first person singular 'I' begins to feature, and it is 'my', not 'our', which opens the final sentence. What is the effect of this?

This is a cleverly balanced speech overall. The picture of the future which is painted is not too rosy: it is going to be difficult, but it is a worthy enterprise, and the president makes us feel that we are worthy to join it. He appeals to our better selves, as do most persuaders: berating your audience is not a good selling tactic.

We have spent a long time on that one example because it contains so many language features which are 'foregrounded'. You probably found just as many that we failed to mention. But most persuasive language uses words in this obviously crafted way. After all, if someone is writing to try to change what you buy, what you think, what you feel or what you believe in, the odds are that they are going to put a lot of thought, and a fair bit of craft, into it. Like the president, they have to pay you the compliment of appearing to think that you're worth it.

The next few passages are for you to analyse on your own. The first is an extract from President Bush's inaugural address, for you to compare to the one we've just looked at. This is followed by an example of Winston Churchill's wartime speeches, and then we give an example each of 'good cause' persuasive writing and straightforward commercial selling.

I come before you and assume the presidency at a moment rich with promise. We live in a peaceful, prosperous time, but we can make it better. For a new breeze is blowing, and a world refreshed by freedom seems reborn; for in Man's heart, if not in fact, the day of the dictator is over. The totalitarian era is passing, its old ideas blown away like leaves from an ancient lifeless tree.

There are times when the future seems thick as a fog; you sit and wait, hoping the mists will lift and reveal the right path. But this is a time when the future seems as a door you can walk right through – into a room called tomorrow. Great nations of the world are moving toward democracy – through the door to freedom.

We know what works; freedom works. We know what's right; freedom is right. We know how to secure a more just and prosperous life for Man on Earth – through free markets, free speech, free elections and the exercise of free will unhampered by the state.

America today is a proud, free nation, decent and civil – a place we cannot help but love. We know in our hearts, not loudly and proudly, but as a simple fact, that this country has meaning beyond what we see and that our strength is a force for good. But have we changed as a nation even in our time? Are we enthralled with material things, less appreciative of the nobility of work and sacrifice?

My friends, we are not the sum of our possessions. They are not the measure of our lives. In our hearts we know what matters. We cannot hope only to leave our children a bigger car, a bigger bank account. We must hope to give them a sense of what it means to be a loyal friend, a loving parent, a citizen who leaves his home, his neighbourhood and town better than he found it.

No president, no government can teach us to remember what is best in what we are. But if the man you have chosen to lead this government can help to make a difference; if he can celebrate the quieter, deeper successes that are made not of gold and silk, but of better hearts and finer souls. If he can do these things, then he must.

George Bush

71

You ask, What is our policy? I will say: It is to wage war, by sea, land, and air, with all our might and with all the strength that God can give us: to wage war against a monstrous tyranny, never surpassed in the dark, lamentable catalogue of human crime. That is our policy. You ask, What is our aim? I can answer in one word: Victory – victory at all costs, victory in spite of all terror; victory, however long and hard the road may be; for without victory there is no survival. Let that be realized: no survival for the British Empire; no survival for all that the British Empire has stood for, no survival for the urge and impulse of the ages, that mankind will move forward towards its goal. But I take up my task with buoyancy and hope. I feel sure that our cause will not be suffered to fail among men. At this time I feel entitled to claim the aid of all, and I say, "Come, then, let us go forward together with our united strength."

Winston Churchill, 13th May, 1940

Dear Friend,

This time of year is a special time for most of us. A time when, however busy and harassed we have felt throughout the year, the thought of Christmas brightens the dark winter evenings. It's a time to rejoice at the special brightness in a child's eyes ... to show family and friends how much they mean to us ... and to prepare to extend the spirit of Christmas to others over the next months.

I would like to take this opportunity to wish you and your family just such a Christmas, and to hope that you share in all the peace and goodwill of this special season.

But at the same time I'd like to ask you if you could spare a thought for all those for whom this is not a happy time at all. In fact, Christmas, for many people in desperate need increases their despair in their troubled lives.

A child suffering from neglect and unkindness is a terrible sight at any time in the year, but at Christmas, traditionally a time for children, their plight seems even more distressing. And for an elderly person whose family may be dead or scattered, this family time may make their loneliness even more unbearable.

The Salvation Army

Sonic Garden Guarder repels moles harmlessly

Moles or burrowing rodents can ruin your garden, but how do you repel them without having to resort to traps, harsh chemicals or causing them any harm? The ingenious answer is this sonic Garden Guarder, developed in America. Just push the water-resistant stake into the ground, switch on, and every 15 seconds it emits a deep vibrating sound (frequency 300 Hz) that's believed to scare off underground dwellers over an area of 710m. Garden Guarder is safe, highly effective, measures a discreet 11" x 4" x 2¼" and uses 4 x 1.5v batteries (not supplied).
Garden Guarder £29.95 SG379D

Chapter 8

Letting off steam
or Swearing is good for you
– words used for venting spleen

When people are angry they usually do one of two things: they hit out physically, or, with less immediate damage, they hit out verbally. One of the convenient things about being human is that you can convey your negative emotions, as well as the positive ones we talked about in Chapter 6, in words.

When the pressure builds up to an intolerable level, people let off steam by swearing and stamping their feet. They don't even require an audience. My sister-in-law, an extremely polite, rather quiet person, can often be heard chunnering when a sponge cake has stayed as flat as a pancake or a piece of steak has refused to tenderise 'Oh, sod it all!' My brother, sensible man that he is, keeps well out of the way until the swearing is done before going in to make helpful and reassuring noises.

We have all done it. Our terms vary, of course, depending which particular taboos we recognise. Some of us will strew bloodies around pretty freely, but avoid 'the f word' (except for really violent outbursts); others of us will use any swear word but jib at blaspheming because we or someone we care about believes in God. Even in swearing, most of us have our standards!

Nevertheless, the act of saying rude words seems to satisfy a human need and may therefore be socially and individually useful. Rude words can replace violent action, and therefore never permitting yourself the indulgence of a good curse is probably bad for you.

Aside from the emotional release which cursing provides, it is generally agreed that verbalising or talking things over helps us to sort out our problems. Those people who are unable to do this may well resort to violence. Many violent criminals are inarticulate and cannot express their anger and frustration verbally. So much the worse for their partner or child. Time and again the police hear statements such as 'She just kept nag, nag, nagging and I couldn't answer back.' 'He thinks he's clever, twisting everything – well, I showed him!' Humiliating verbally someone unable to articulate their feelings can be tempting, but you can pay a high price for the pleasure. Better, I'd argue to be on the receiving end of what Cockneys call 'a bit of verbal'. It isn't exactly pleasant having someone bawl 'I hate you!' at the top of their voice, but it's probably good for them and not life-threatening to you. Children say it quite often – they aren't as various in their spleen-venting epithets as we more mature types!

Part of the socialising process in every culture is learning which words and phrases are totally unacceptable, and which can be used in special circumstances. Swear words are an important part of the lexicon, which is why it seems a pity if they are used endlessly and gratuitously – not because it offends us but because, like any medicine, they lose their efficiency when overused. Everyone builds up a tolerance to them and they lose their impact. They cease to signal anything, except perhaps insensitivity. And what do constant swearers have recourse to when they *really* need to let go?

Like individuals, cultures build up a store bank of insults, depending on what matters in their social setting. Different groupings develop different ritual insults. In some countries the way to wind someone up is to be suggestive or rude about their mother; in others to doubt their gender or parentage; in yet others to compare them to a camel or donkey. We all know, by a certain age, what really hurts – how best to get the verbal boot in. It may not be nice, but it's a fact of life and language.

Of course, some people take it to extremes and become almost professional insulters: we all know people who have 'a really wicked tongue'. There are verbal, as well as physical bullies in schools – people who use their linguistic superiority for extremely dubious purposes. Quite a few of our leading politicians (I won't name names) have a good line in the snide insult, but then the world of politics is very much one of verbal warfare. The odd thing is that nobody seems unduly concerned about the verbal cruelty of politicians. Perhaps their insulting gets rid of some of our spleen vicariously. Certainly, most of us enjoy the verbal barrages of comedians like Rowan Atkinson, Joan Rivers and Ben Elton. A stock-in-trade of British and American humour is insulting the rich and famous.

Letters

The snag about spoken insults is that you are there to face the feedback. For those who want to sound off without getting any backlash, letters to the press represent a golden opportunity. You can say whatever you like and withhold your name and address or use false ones. Alternatively, you can try and contact people of like mind.

The following letter is from *Spare Rib*, and seems to us a fairly typical example of its kind.

Well, I think page three, pornographic magazines and programmes which show two people in sex scenes with all the woman's body on show are disgusting, perverted and totally degrading to women. It is no wonder that rape is on the increase when women are forever portrayed as free, willing and easy.

I am also against naturist beaches and topless beaches.

People say it is natural and they are right; it was natural millions of years ago when cavemen and dinosaurs roamed the Earth.

This is the twentieth century and we are supposed to be civilised human beings. If people want to do this sort of thing, they ought to do it in private and not in public.

I feel VERY strongly about this and am quite prepared to start my own organisation and I know there are millions of MEN and women who agree with me.

I am willing to hold meetings and organise protest marches until we, being the minority or majority are heard.

Spare Rib

Before you read our analysis, attempt one yourself.

❖ What can you deduce about the writer?
❖ What is her purpose?
❖ Does she achieve it?

The first thing you notice about this letter is the regularity with which the pronoun 'I' appears. It is very much an expression of strong, personal feeling, so we find 'I think', 'I know', 'I feel very strongly' and 'I am willing'.

The strength of feeling is made clear by the emotive, assertive, rather incoherent style of the letter. The emotive element comes through in the extreme, pejorative adjectives: 'sex scenes' (notice the alliteration for emphasis) are 'disgusting', 'perverted' and 'degrading'. Adverbs are used to underline the writer's abhorrence – thus such scenes are 'totally degrading' – and the writer is not only prepared to start an organisation, she is 'quite prepared'. In the same way she feels not just strongly but 'very strongly'. She is also sick of women being 'forever' portrayed as (another cluster of pejorative adjectives) 'free, willing and easy.' All a little hyperbolic you might say.

The writer seems to find the whole subject too distressing to be precise about. Thus nudity and copulation become the vague and euphemistic 'this sort of thing' and 'sex scenes'. She is equally vague about history: we have a glancing reference to 'millions of years ago' when cavemen and dinosaurs (surprisingly simultaneously) 'roamed the Earth'.

The writer clearly enjoys the largeness that 'millions' gives to her assertions, since she also insists that 'millions' of people agree with her. She 'knows'. Other people's views are disregarded with a quick 'people say'.

Like many letter-writers, this one lapses into cliché. She gives us the not exactly startling information that 'this is the twentieth century' when we are 'supposed' (nice loaded word) to be 'civilised' (even more loaded) – and not only civilised but 'civilised human beings'. Yet suitably imprecise 'people' say awful things and do them 'in public', which is even worse.

She states that 'It is no wonder' – another cliché – that 'rape is on the increase'. She doesn't give us any statistics to back up her assertion; instead she piles on the emotive adjectives. She uses not one but three words of very similar meaning: the aforementioned 'free, willing and easy'. One word is simply not enough to express her disgust.

The letter may not be a very persuasive, coherent or sophisticated document. That is not its aim. It is an outburst of emotion and a statement of strong belief. It does not attempt to convert those 'people' who are 'easy', but the 'millions' who share the writer's views will no doubt nod their heads sagely as they read it. She has chosen her outlet well: the readership of *Spare Rib* are scarcely likely to disagree with her. You could not easily imagine this letter gracing the pages of *Penthouse*. But, to be fair, we all seek a sympathetic audience when letting out emotions.

Re-write the letter in a more sophisticated, structured style in an attempt to make it more persuasive.

The next letter was written by a man. (Ask yourself when you have read it whether you could have guessed that without being told.) It appeared in *New Musical Express*.

❖ Jot down what you would expect this paper's audience to be like:
   Age group?
   Any specialisms?
   How well educated?
❖ If you were writing for such an audience what tone would you adopt?
   How formal?
   Would you use any technical terms?
   Would you be serious or flippant?

How would you try to win the audience over?

◈ Now look at the letter. When you have read it, look for features which make clear the writer's viewpoint and strength of feeling. These might include clichés, emotive lexis and use of 'I' + assertion. Look also for features which show awareness of audience. Has the writer employed an appropriate tone and used appropriate vocabulary?

By now you will be well on the way to a full analysis of the piece, its aim and audience. Feel free to judge, but base your judgements on linguistic evidence, not prejudice. Personally, I am fairly sympathetic to the stance of the *Spare Rib* correspondent, but an analysis of her letter which dubbed it convincing, cleverly articulated or persuasive would be difficult to justify from the text. With linguistic analysis it must always be the text you return to, not your own preferences and obsessions.

Here, at last, is the text for you to consider:

> I've just read Culture Vulture (N.M.E. July 2nd) on White Magic. In fact, I've read it eight times trying to decide if it was tongue in cheek or a gutter press Sun exposé slag-off because you had a page to fill. Where did Wells and Quantick do their supposed research? They cocked up straight away, not knowing the difference between religion and Christian faith. The latter being a commitment to Jesus Christ and God, who, I might point out, we all answer to eventually, regardless of beliefs.
>
> 'Foul goodness' was a term used to describe so-called 'God-rockers'. Well, apart from being a contradiction in terms, it borders on the moronic. What is wrong with being against drugs, and sleeping with anything in a skirt if she happens to stand still long enough? Having tried both, I can give you the answer. Nothing. Just because Christians don't want to sit with the filth that crawls in the gutter, is hardly a good enough reason to pay someone to write such one-sided and uneducated drivel.
>
> In closing, the article draws no conclusions and makes no statements except to condone drugs, illicit sex (irresponsible with the A.I.D.S. epidemic) and devil worship. For the record, I'm a Christian and an alternative rock-band player. I used to think Jimi Hendrix was God until I found Jesus.
>
> *New Musical Express*

Writing letters of protest is a popular option amongst A-level Language students in their original writing folders. Look at the one which follows on abortion.

> Dear Sir,
>
> I feel I must reply to the obnoxious letter which was printed in your newspaper on 4th May 1988. The letter concerning abortion seemed to be ignorant of the true and horrific facts which surround this part of the medical profession.
>
> Abortion is the result of an unwanted pregnancy. Most of the women who choose to have their child aborted do not even consider

other options. They could have their baby adopted or put into one of the many caring foster homes.

This thoughtlessness or lack of concern for the unborn baby was proven by a recent survey carried out by S.P.U.C. (The Society to Protect the Unborn Child). It was discoverd that seventy-seven per cent of the women asked 'WHY IT HAD TO BE AN ABORTION' said it was because they did not want the child so why should they go through the agony of childbirth?

It must be pointed out that many 'mothers to be' do not decide to have their child aborted at once. Many leave the decision so late that although the doctor performs the abortion the baby can be born alive. 'Doctors are supposed to save lives and not take them away.' But these poor innocent babies who are born alive are put into plastic containers, similar to buckets, and left to die.

These doctors are obviously oblivious to the fact that they are life savers. I believe that they are nothing short of murderers.

Many doctors go on to argue that the small child does not feel any pain during the operation but research has proven that the baby does suffer. The research is dubbed 'the silent scream'. A scanning machine is used to see into the mother's womb during the abortion. To their horror doctors saw the baby's mouth open as if screaming as the acidic salt solution reached the amniotic sac.

The baby's dead body is then ripped to pieces as a suction machine drags it out of its once safe, comforting and warm home. This suction method, also known as 'vacuum aspiration', can be and is also used to take the baby from the womb without the use of acidic salt solution.

I find it extremely difficult to comprehend how any mother to be could have her child murdered in this terrible way. Just as I find it difficult to understand how we as human beings can allow this to happen.

How can any sane person openly support this form of murder?

❖ Does this letter seem to you authentic?
❖ Is it the sort of thing which would appear in a newspaper?
❖ How sophisticated is it lexically?
❖ What is its intended audience?
❖ Does this letter contain a line of argument?
❖ Is there a coherent statement that you can follow?
❖ Are statements amplified and supported by evidence?
❖ In short, does it convince you either intellectually or emotionally?

It may seem to you that this writer is rather too close to her subject or does not have the space to develop her ideas. She also wrote a speech on the subject:

The Bill that all abortions should be made illegal

Madam Chairman, ladies and gentlemen, I am not here to lecture you, but to present the unpleasant facts concerning abortion and to support the Bill that 'all abortions should be made illegal'.

A human life begins at conception, not as some people think later in the pregnancy when the baby is fully formed, or actually after the birth. As the embryo grows, a human being grows, a human being who is equal to any other. A human being with rights, a human being with the right to live.

Investigations by doctors who do care have shown that the baby does feel pain during the abortion. By the use of a scanning machine, doctors looked into a woman's womb while an abortion was being performed. During this abortion, medically named Dilation and Curettage, the murderous instruments were shoved into the amniotic sac and the doctors saw the baby struggle and actually try and escape, but of course it couldn't. The investigation, dubbed 'the silent scream', converted the doctors who were present and many others, but sadly many doctors choose to ignore the fact that the baby feels terrible pain and opens its mouth in an attempt to scream. Because they cannot hear the scream they continue their murder of the child with a clear conscience.

After the woman who is up to twelve weeks pregnant has paid the doctor who is to murder her child the following will happen. A strong acidic salt solution is injected into the amniotic sac. The solution has a dual function: it burns the baby's skin while at the same time poisoning it – 'the wonders of modern medicine'! The doctor will then use a vacuum-like instrument which sucks the murdered body out of the womb.

There is another form of abortion quite similar to this, known as vacuum aspiration, the difference being that during this abortion the 'dual purpose solution' is not used. By use of a strong suction power the small child's body is cruelly ripped apart. A heartless nurse is left to piece the mutilated body back together so that the doctor can be sure he hasn't left any of the mother's child in her womb. I suppose it could be said that the nurse has a sort of jigsaw puzzle to do. I find their indifference to the situation sickening.

Abortions which are performed much later in the pregnancy are not only terrible but also murder which cannot be denied. This method of abortion, named 'Prostaglandin', makes the contractions that a woman usually experiences at the end of pregnancy come sooner. The baby is usually still born and the little body is then thrown into a bucket and left as medical rubbish, while the woman is wheeled off for the best medical attention. Well, she has paid for it after all!

Recent reports have shown that babies have actually survived this terrible ordeal. Unlike a baby which is born prematurely, the baby that does survive is not given the medical treatment it is entitled to as a human being. Doctors who are supposed to be life savers ignore the painful cries for help and leave the baby to die on the side of a sink or in a plastic bucket with the rest of the dead. The doctors involved are blatantly dismissing their medical ethics.

The twelve week abortion Bill put forward by David Alton was a step in the right direction but of course it has been ignored.

Madam Chairman, ladies and gentlemen, can you honestly say that killing an innocent baby is permissible? Do you enjoy living in a world where one human being can kill another without being convicted for his crime, as in abortion?

As I have said before, life begins at conception and not after twelve weeks. I will not be satisfied until abortion is made illegal and both healthy and handicapped unborn children are allowed their right to live.

* Which piece do you prefer?
* Which do you consider more hard-hitting?

You might like to do a comparative analysis of the two or write a commentary on the one you prefer. Whether you write an analysis or a commentary, always try to return from the detailed analysis with three main points clear in your mind:

1 Which audience was the text aimed at, and how can you tell?
2 What aim did the writer have and how can you tell?
3 How successful or not was the writer in adopting an appropriate and consistent tone for the aim and audience?

An example from literature

Before we move on to real, spoken language of anger, I'd like you to have a look at a literary, dramatic representation of it.

* How many of the genuine hallmarks of spleen-venting does it have? (Make sure you look at the stage directions as well as the script.)
* Is there anything here which you consider overly dramatic and thus unconvincing?
* What knowledge about the language of strong emotion is evident?

Looking at something like this is useful in two ways: first, it tells you something about how literary writers shape reality and second, if it's well done, it points out features of real language use. Needless to say, I think this particular extract is well done. It is taken from Arthur Miller's *Death of a Salesman*. In this scene Biff, Willy's eldest son, is trying to convince his father that both of them are insignificant, failed men. Willy cannot accept this and the scene is full of strong and varied emotion.

> BIFF: Dad, you're never going to see what I am, so what's the use of arguing? If I strike oil I'll send you a cheque. Meantime forget I'm alive.
> WILLY [*to* LINDA]: Spite, see?
> BIFF: Shake hands, Dad.
> WILLY: Not my hand.
> BIFF: I was hoping not to go this way.
> WILLY: Well, this is the way you're going. Good-bye.
> [BIFF *looks at him a moment, then turns sharply and goes to the stairs.*]
> WILLY [*stops him with*]: May you rot in hell if you leave this house!
> BIFF [*turning*]: Exactly what is it that you want from me?
> WILLY: I want you to know, on the train, in the mountains, in the valleys, wherever you go, that you cut down your life for spite!

BIFF: No, no.

WILLY: Spite, spite, is the word of your undoing! And when you're down and out, remember what did it. When you're rotting somewhere beside the railroad tracks, remember, and don't you dare blame it on me!

BIFF: I'm not blaming it on you!

WILLY: I won't take the rap for this, you hear?

[HAPPY *comes down the stairs and stands on the bottom step, watching.*]

BIFF: That's just what I'm telling you!

WILLY [*sinking into a chair at the table, with full accusation*]: You're trying to put a knife in me – don't think I don't know what you're doing!

BIFF: All right, phony! Then let's lay it on the line. [*He whips the rubber tube out of his pocket and puts it on the table.*]

HAPPY: You crazy –

LINDA: Biff! [*She moves to grab the hose, but BIFF holds it down with his hand.*]

BIFF: Leave it there! Don't move it!

WILLY [*not looking at it*]: What is that?

BIFF: You know goddam well what that is.

WILLY [*caged, wanting to escape*]: I never saw that.

BIFF: You saw it. The mice didn't bring it into the cellar! What is this supposed to do, make a hero out of you? This supposed to make me sorry for you?

WILLY: Never heard of it.

BIFF: There'll be no pity for you, you hear it? No pity!

WILLY [*to* LINDA]: You hear the spite!

BIFF: No, you're going to hear the truth – what you are and what I am!

LINDA: Stop it!

WILLY: Spite!

HAPPY [*coming down toward* BIFF]: You cut it now!

BIFF [*to* HAPPY]: The man don't know who we are! The man is gonna know! [*To* WILLY] We never told the truth for ten minutes in this house!

HAPPY: We always told the truth!

BIFF [*turning on him*]: You big blow, are you the assistant buyer? You're one of the two assistants to the assistant, aren't you?

HAPPY: Well, I'm practically ...

BIFF: You're practically full of it! We all are! And I'm through with it. [*To* WILLY] Now hear this, Willy, this is me.

WILLY: I know you!

BIFF: You know why I had no address for three months? I stole a suit in Kansas City and I was in jail. [*To* LINDA, *who is sobbing*] Stop crying, I'm through with it.

[LINDA *turns away from them, her hands covering her face.*]

WILLY: I suppose that's my fault!

BIFF: I stole myself out of every good job since high school!

WILLY: And whose fault is that?

BIFF: And I never got anywhere because you blew me so full of hot air I could never stand taking orders from anybody! That's whose fault it is!
WILLY: I hear that!
LINDA: Don't, Biff!
BIFF: It's goddam time you heard that! I had to be boss big shot in two weeks, and I'm through with it!
WILLY: Then hang yourself! For spite, hang yourself!
BIFF: No! Nobody's hanging himself, Willy! I ran down eleven flights with a pen in my hand today. And suddenly I stopped, you hear me? And in the middle of that office building, do you hear this? I stopped in the middle of that building and I saw – the sky. I saw the things that I love in this world. The work and the food and time to sit and smoke. And I looked at the pen and said to myself, what the hell am I grabbing this for? Why am I trying to become what I don't want to be? What am I doing in an office, making a contemptuous, begging fool of myself, when all I want is out there, waiting for me the minute I say I know who I am! Why can't I say that, Willy? [*He tries to make* WILLY *face him, but* WILLY *pulls away and moves to the left.*]
WILLY [*with hatred, threateningly*]: The door of your life is wide open!
BIFF: Pop! I'm a dime a dozen, and so are you!
WILLY [*turning on him now in an uncontrolled outburst*]: I am not a dime a dozen! I am Willy Loman, and you are Biff Loman!
[BIFF *starts for* WILLY, *but is blocked by* HAPPY. *In his fury,* BIFF *seems on the verge of attacking his father.*]
BIFF: I am not a leader of men, Willy, and neither are you. You were never anything but a hard-working drummer who landed in the ash can like all the rest of them! I'm one dollar an hour, Willy! I tried seven states and couldn't raise it. A buck an hour! Do you gather my meaning? I'm not bringing home any prizes any more, and you're going to stop waiting for me to bring them home!
WILLY [*directly to* BIFF]: You vengeful, spiteful mut!
[BIFF *breaks from* HAPPY. WILLY, *in fright, starts up the stairs.* BIFF *grabs him.*]
BIFF [*at the peak of his fury*]: Pop, I'm nothing! I'm nothing, Pop. Can't you understand that? There's no spite in it any more. I'm just what I am, that's all.
[BIFF'*s fury has spent itself, and he breaks down, sobbing, holding on to* WILLY, *who dumbly fumbles for* BIFF'*s face.*]

Arthur Miller: Death of a Salesman

Authentic disputes

Now I'd like you to look at an authentic, rather undramatic dispute. I will provide the context afterwards but I'd like you to try and decide certain things for yourself as you 'listen' to it:

❋ What would you guess the relationship between A and B to be?
❋ What are they arguing about? Most rows have a short-term catalyst and a long-term niggle: try to identify both here.

❖ Where do you think the row takes place? (Restraint or lack thereof is usually a good clue.)

❖ Does either seem dominant or more fluent or more angry? How can you tell?

Notice that here you are not just looking at how anger is expressed but taking into account your knowledge of the way conversation works, the effect that context has on people's speech and so on. All sorts of knowledge is available to you: try not to think in boxes too much. Look at what is there and say something intelligent about it rather than working your way through some notional list of features.

A Why did you buy that?

B We needed one.

A I haven't got money to throw down the drain. I don't need another double quilt – we're not having visitors already are we? Spend as much as you like on things for yourself, but when it comes to things for the house, where I insist everything is fifty-fifty you'd just better ask me first or it'll cause arguments.

B The only reason this is causing an argument is 'cos you're in a foul mood. You've been determined to have a go at me all day. So don't bother pretending it's anything to do with money.

A Here's my half. Only don't ever do it again.

B I don't want your bloody money! I won't have to pay for a month and I told you I'd buy it.

A And I'm telling you not to buy anything else till we can both afford it.

B Christ, I don't half pick 'em!

Well, what did you make of that? Here are the facts: a young couple, who are just setting up home together, are having a swift disagreement about the purchase one of them has just made. The language they use is informal and they use a lot of contractions. However, they are in the middle of a department store, so they can't really go to linguistic extremes. I'll leave the rest to you.

Finally, we have a full-blooded row in a private context. This extract from a much longer row shows the climax.

C I've put up with your bullshit for years and I'm not f–ing well putting up with any more.

D Don't you eff in front of my wife. Gerrout before I kick you out.

C You and whose army? Anyway, I didn't know it was her turn.

D Oh, that's typical of you, bloody smart-arse. Not man enough to fight fair ... no respect for your elders and betters. If I were ...

C Spare me the impotent man's futile threats. I'll leave when I'm ready.

D You'll leave now. This bloody minute. Christ, you've got a nerve.

You come in here; you swear like a trooper for all your fancy language and stuck-up accent. You think you're somebody but ...

C I think I'm wasting valuable time arguing with an ignoramus like you. You'll be telling me what I 'turned round and said' next.

D Southern bloody jessie!

C Well, I think we've plumbed the last depths of your ingenuity now, so I'll say goodnight. Are you coming, Ann?

D Our Annie's stayin 'ere where she belongs.

I think it's clear that the two people in this extract are of a different educational level and wage verbal warfare in different ways. Analyse the language use of each of them and then the interaction between them. If you were the unfortunate Ann, would you go or stay? Do you sympathise more with C or D? How does this transcription indicate accent? Does it matter? Attempt an analysis yourself before looking at my comments.

This argument took place between a working-class, relatively uneducated man of fifty-five and his middle-class graduate son-in-law of thirty-five. Was all that fairly obvious? If it wasn't, look back and see if you can tell, now you know.

The older man uses assertion and imperatives in an attempt to be forceful. He tells the younger man to 'Gerrout' (notice the non-standard accent.) His language, angry as he clearly is, is liberally sprinkled with taboo words like 'smart-arse', 'bloody' and 'Christ'. However, he does not use 'the f word' which, in his terms, is only acceptable when ladies aren't present.

His son-in-law's pun on 'in front of your wife' (he pretends his mother-in-law wanted to swear first) makes his contempt clear: he treats the older man's anger as a joke. He deliberately uses sophisticated words like 'ignoramus', 'impotent' and 'ingenuity' to wrong-foot his opponent. The opponent's only reply is abuse: 'Southern bloody jessie'.

There is little doubt that the younger man 'wins' the fight: he keeps cool enough to make sarcastic remarks, for example mocking the northern phrase 'turn round and say'; he interrupts the older man; he decides when to accelerate the row and when to stop it. Whether this is a good purpose to put a university education to is another question ...

Chapter 9

Contracts and promises
– words to close the loopholes

There are times when the seriousness of an occasion demands a special form of words. We want to make a fully binding promise and we do so publicly and in a set manner. The fact that we do not make up our own form of words is important: certain ritualised forms have developed over the centuries and use of them stresses the social as well as individual nature of the promise. However, some small allowance can be made for personal preference: for example, many women of the late twentieth century, though willing to promise to love and even honour their husbands, are not prepared to add 'obey'. However, it is important to keep most of the wording the same: the form of words derives its potency and conviction from being ritualised – it is almost like a charm.

When you think about it, most of the major watersheds in our lives are signalled and sealed by the use of these special, legal forms of language. Fairly soon after our entry into the world, we may be baptised, and some believe that a child cannot go to Heaven unless the words 'I baptise thee in the name of ... ' have been said. Others might not go that far, but they would certainly regard the ceremony as a statement of faith and intention on the part of the parents and godparents.

Later, the child has an opportunity to confirm or deny the promises made at a confirmation ceremony. Such ceremonies are linked to the church, although this would not be the case in other cultures. The important thing to notice is that language is the tool people use to commit themselves, whether to a relationship – 'I'll be your best friend'; 'I will' (take you as my husband/wife) – or a duty – 'You have my word I'll do it'; 'I promise to pay the bearer on demand the sum of £50.' None of us takes these assurances lightly, and keeping your word is highly valued: 'He's a man of his word' is praise anywhere in the world and 'He speaks with forked tongue', however expressed, is blame.

Returning to the ceremonies we go through ... an adult is likely to go through a wedding ceremony, whether in church or a registry office. It would not do to say in the middle of the ceremony 'Go on then, I'll have him', and a practical joker who butted in with a witticism after 'Does anyone know of any just cause or impediment why these two may not be joined together in holy matrimony?' would wreck the whole affair. Words matter because they can symbolically function as deeds. I suspect the much mentioned right a Muslim man has to say 'I divorce thee; I divorce thee; I divorce thee' and make it so is very rarely, if ever, exercised. However, we are all familiar with the bottle-smashing and 'I name this ship the ... May God bless her and all who sail in her.'

The last major occasion of our life – our funeral or cremation – again has very fixed formulae. We are not, of course, able to make a personal contribution, but by then we may have already made our feelings and wishes known in the very particular form of a Last Will and Testament:

I, JOHN SMITH, of 99 King's Road, Salford, in the Metropolitan County of Greater Manchester, company director, HEREBY REVOKE all wills and testamentary documents heretofore made by me and DECLARE this to be my LAST WILL AND TESTAMENT.

1. I APPOINT my wife Joan Smith, and my solicitor, Thomas Jones, to be jointly my executors of this my will.

2. I DEVISE my freehold cottage known as THE LILACS, at Coniston in the county of Cumbria, unto my son ROBERT SMITH in fee simple.

3. I BEQUEATH the following specific legacies:

(i)   to my son, Robert Smith, any motor-car I may own at the date of my death.
(ii) to my daughter, Jane Smith, all my shares in the company known as Imperial Chemical Industries.
(iii) To my said wife all my personal chattels not hereby bequeathed for her absolute use and benefit.

4. I BEQUEATH the following pecuniary legacies:

(i)   To my daughter Jill Smith, the sum of £3000
(ii) To my daughter Jenny Smith, the sum of £3000

5. I DEVISE AND BEQUEATH all the residue of my real and personal estate whatsoever and wheresoever not hereby or by any codicil hereto otherwise expressly disposed of as to my freeholds in fee simple and as to my personal estate absolutely unto my said wife, Joan Smith, for her own absolute use and benefit.

6. I DIRECT that any executor of this my Will being a solicitor or a person engaged in any profession or business, may be so employed and act and shall be entitled to make all proper professional charges for any work done by him or his firm in connection with my Estate including work done which an executor not being a solicitor or a person engaged as aforesaid could have done personally.

IN WITNESS whereof I, the said John Smith, the Testator have to this my LAST WILL set my hand this thirty first day of December One Thousand Nine Hundred and Ninety.

SIGNED AND ACKNOWLEDGED by the above-named John Smith, the Testator, as and for his LAST WILL in the presence of us both present at the same time who at this request in his presence and in the presence of each other have hereunto subscribed our names as witnesses:

Frank Ellis	Jeremy Goodall
6, The Crescent	2, High Street,
Salford	Bolton
Clerk	Chartered Accountant

The first thing to say about wills is that they are all written to the same recipe. Only the names are changed to benefit the fortunate survivors.

The reason why there are so many givens in legal language is not because solicitors are idle, but because a form of words has been found over the centuries which is as unambiguous and unforgeable as possible. To be of any legal value, a will must be precise. Thus you don't have 'I, John' but the testator's full name, address and occupation. This is to ensure that he is not confused with any other John Smith. Adjectival phrases are scattered throughout the document. 'My wife/son/daughter' will not do: all sorts of people might start claiming that John had fathered or married them. So all benefactors are named in full. Places are similarly specified: 'my cottage in the Lakes' might be meaningful to John and his family, but, to be watertight, its name and precise location are added. Legal language is an extreme example of elaborated variant: it may contain plenty of jargon but it eschews insider references.

The most vital element of any will is who gets what. The who, as already explained, is very exactly stated. The what is divided into set categories in a set order, which helps to avoid forgery or misunderstanding. First, we have specific legacies – i.e. things – then the pecuniary ones – the cash – and finally, to cover all eventualities, we have the catch-all clause (clause 5) which gives anything else not mentioned to one person, in this case John's wife. Such a clause makes argument well-nigh impossible.

More blatant thieving by alterations is also discouraged. The date – vital in the case of a will – is written in words since numbers are relatively easy to 'rearrange'. The very fixity of the form, the fact that everyone knows what should come where, also helps: tacking on a new paragraph or omitting one would be noticed immediately.

The standard running order is as follows: first, the testator states that he revokes all previous wills and that this is his last one. (You'll see now why the date matters.) Key words like 'hereby revoke' and 'last will and testament' are capitalised for emphasis. Next, two executors are appointed. One is normally a solicitor. This makes a lot of sense since the form of wills is very much written for a specialist audience – of solicitors!

Before the specific and pecuniary legacies we have the 'devising' of a freehold cottage 'in fee simple'. At this point you should all recognise that this document is indeed written for lawyers and not for the lay person. We may just have coped with the archaic 'hereby revoke', but we will not be familiar with this usage of 'devise' and I doubt whether any of us could hazard a guess as to what 'fee simple' means. I certainly couldn't! I know that it is from French, like much of the jargon of the legal trade, and I also know that many other legal words have been culled from Latin (declaration, habeas corpus for example), but to some extent I have to take it on trust that lawyers know their job and have good reasons for the usage of such words.

The next section of the will stretches our faith in solicitors to its limits. It is the clause which, with surprising vagueness, states how much money the 'solicitor or any person engaged in proper, professional business' will be entitled to. It doesn't give any maximum! Instead it promises to pay 'proper professional charges'. The person who decides what those proper charges might be will, presumably, be the solicitor!

At the end of the will we have another cluster of set features. The testator – now referred to as 'the said testator' – 'sets his hand to' (an archaic version of 'signs') this, his last will. Two others, both in the presence of the testator, also sign it. They, too, are specified with full names and addresses.

And there we have it: a document designed to be clear and incontrovertible. A document written with lawyers in mind – only they and vicars talk about chattels. It is not very lively to read, of course, because it is precisely designed to lack colour, personality and individuality: these would get in the way. John's being a Northerner, a keen amateur photographer and a working-class man do not shine through; legal language is not the place for dialect forms and colloquialisms.

Imagine that you are a solicitor. Wilf Woffler has come to consult you, bearing his stab at a last will. Rewrite it so that it is legal, i.e. clear and watertight. Don't forget the solicitor's payment clause!

19/8/90

I haven't got much but I want the house and most of the cash to go to Barry. Our Freda can have £500 so long as she looks after the cats. If the car passes its MOT our Jim can have it 'cos his Mam can't drive. He can have me cufflinks, too, if he'd like 'em.

I'd like me best mate, John, and Mr Clark on the High Street to do the business. I've got all me chairs at home.
Wilf Woffler

To complete your expertise in last wills and testaments perhaps you ought to write your own!

Legal language

We have already mentioned birth, marriage and death. Perhaps, since we live where and when we do, we ought also to give some time to the ending of marriages. Conveyancing and will-making aside, divorces create more work for solicitors than any other human activity. Legally ending a marriage is a complicated and time-consuming affair whatever the popular press say. It is also, sadly, often acrimonious with squabbles about custody of children and ownership of the matrimonial home. The only safe way to sort out the mess is to consult a solicitor, and there are those who specialise in the cut and thrust of divorce litigation.

The example we want you to look at is a written report but was actually spoken by a solicitor in court. This means that as well as employing the jargon of the trade and the necessary precision, the speaker is also being persuasive and slightly more personal. The text will probably seem to you a strange mixture of registers. One way in would be to sort out examples from the text under the following headings:

Legal lexis and structures
Structures introduced for clarity
Examples of detached, almost scientific, language use
Examples of more persuasive and personal language use.

If you sort out these elements you will be well on the way to the analysis that you should now attempt. Identify the purposes and target audience of the text. If it has more than one purpose or audience (it has!), make clear which are most centrally significant.

It was submitted on behalf of the wife that because the board in this case has consented to disclosure of certain company documents the court is entitled to draw the inference that other documents to the disclosure of which the board has objected are in the power of the husband. It was said that the board cannot pick and choose, and cannot approbate and reprobate. I do not accept that submission as a proposition of law. Every document or class of documents must be looked at separately, and because disclosures of certain classes of documents is not objected to, it does not follow that other classes of documents the disclosure of which is objected to, are within the power of the husband. In any event it has been made clear that in this case the objection in point of law extends to all documents in the possession of the company, although an ex gratia offer to disclose certain documents has been made. It was also submitted on behalf of the wife that the court was entitled to look at the way in which the husband had used the resources of the company for his private purposes over the years; and to the extent to which his business life and his personal life were intermingled. It was submitted that, if the evidence showed that the husband had lived off the company in the sense that the company had met all or substantially all his private expenditure in cash and kind, that was an additional fact from which it could be inferred that the husband in truth and in fact controlled the company and that the documents of the company were in his power. I am not prepared to say as a matter of law these factors are irrelevant, but the court will, however, consider them against the background of the share structure of the company, the institution of the board and other matters to which I have referred.

All England Law Reports

For a last bit of practice, it seems only fair to give you something a little more straightforward and which is typical legal language of a different sort. It seemed appropriate to finish the chapter on legal language working for 'the law'. This is the 'written rules and regulations' sort of legal language which has the very clear aim of conveying unambiguous information. Which of its features remind you of instructive and technical writing?

Jot down the striking features of this text. You need not write a full analysis since it ought to be clear to you by now what you would include.

A more useful and hopefully more interesting exercise might be to re-render this information as spoken instruction. Imagine that you are an instructor at the police training academy. You are to give a short talk explicating for your probationers the general conditions of arrest. It is vital that you do not mislead them; at the same time you ought to try not to bore them to death. Write your script!

General arrest conditions
25. – (1) Where a constable has reasonable grounds for suspecting that any offence which is not an arrestable offence has been committed or attempted, or is being committed or attempted, he may arrest the relevant person if it appears to him that service of a summons is impracticable or inappropriate because any of the general arrest conditions is satisfied.

(2) In this section, "the relevant person" means any person whom the constable has reasonable grounds to suspect of having committed

or having attempted to commit the offence or of being in the course of committing or attempting to commit it.

(3) The general arrest conditions are

(a) that the name of the relevant person is unknown to, and cannot be readily ascertained by, the constable;

(b) that the constable has reasonable grounds for doubting whether a name furnished by the relevant person as his name is his real name;

(c) that –
   (i) the relevant person has failed to furnish a satisfactory address for service; or
   (ii) the constable has reasonable grounds for doubting] whether an address furnished by the relevant person is a satisfactory address for service;

(d) that the constable has reasonable grounds for believing that arrest is necessary to prevent the relevant person –
   (i) causing physical harm to himself or any other person;
   (ii) suffering physical injury;
   (iii) causing loss of or damage to property;
   (iv) committing an offence against public decency; or
   (v) causing an unlawful obstruction of the highway;

(e) that the constable has reasonable grounds for believing that arrest is necessary to protect a child or other vulnerable person from the relevant person.

(4) For the purposes of subsection (3) above an address is a satisfactory address for service if it appears to the constable –

(a) that the relevant person will be at it for a sufficiently long period for it to be possible to serve him with a summons; or

(b) that some other person specified by the relevant person will accept service of a summons for the relevant person at it.

(5) Nothing in subsection (3) (*d*) above authorises the arrest of a person under sub-paragraph (iv) of that paragraph except where members of the public going about their normal business cannot reasonably be expected to avoid the person to be arrested.

(6) This section shall not prejudice any power of arrest conferred apart from this section.

Harris: Criminal Law

Contracts and promises: P.S.

As a final thought, perhaps we could look at some rather different legal language which is empowering a people instead of limiting them. The United States' Declaration of Independence was just that. Its introduction asserts that

We the people of the United States, in order to form a more perfect Union, establish Justice, insure domestic Tranquillity, provide for the common defense, promote the general Welfare, and secure the Blessings of Liberty to ourselves and our Posterity, do ordain and establish this Constitution for the United States of America.

It would clearly be impossible for you to analyse all of this lengthy document, but it did seem to us inherently interesting as well as an unusual example of legal language. First look at some of the rights given to the States:

> 1. No State shall enter into any treaty, alliance, or confederation, grant letters of marque and reprisal, coin money, emit bills of credit, make anything but gold and silver coin a tender in payment of debts, pass any Bill of Attainder, *ex post facto* law, or law impairing the obligation of contracts or grant any title of nobility.

> 2. No State shall, without the consent of the Congress, lay any impost or duties on imports or exports, except what may be absolutely necessary for executing its inspection laws, and the net produce of all duties and imposts, laid by any State on imports or exports, shall be for the use of the Treasury of the United States; and all such laws shall be subject to the revision and control of the Congress.

> 3. No State shall, without the consent of Congress, lay any duty of tonnage, keep troops, or ships of war in time of peace, enter into any agreement or compact with another State, or with a foreign power, or engage in war, unless actually invaded, or in such imminent danger as will not admit of delay.

❖ In what ways is the language framed to avoid confusion and be exhaustive?
❖ Are there any examples of legal jargon in this document? (Think about foreign terms, compound words and specialist lexis.)
❖ Are the structures typical of legal language or not? (Consider sentence types and structures and look at the clauses.)

Most people, if asked about the rights of American citizens, would vaguely remember – if only from Hollywood films – 'I plead the Fifth Amendment.' Do you know what the Fifth Amendment is? If not, here is your chance to find out:

> No person shall be held to answer for a capital, or other infamous crime, unless on a presentment or indictment of a Grand Jury, except in cases arising in the land or naval forces, or in the militia, when in actual service, in time of war or public danger; nor shall any person be subject for the same offence to be twice put in jeopardy of life or limb; nor shall be compelled in any criminal case to be a witness against himself; nor be deprived of his life, liberty, or property, without due process of law; nor shall private property be taken for public use without just compensation.

Imagine that you have to explain this article to a child of, say, ten. Translate this formal, legal language into a colloquial, easily-comprehended version.

Chapter 10

Jargon – words to baffle the uninitiated

When does necessarily specialist language, which communicates effectively, become jargon – that is, unnecessarily bewildering terms designed to exclude non-specialists? I may as well begin with the million-dollar question!

I think the answer lies in another question: has the language user adopted agreed-by-all-interested-parties labels to simplify matters, or needlessly elaborated the simple to boost his ego and trample yours?

This question is usually relatively easy to answer. I am not offended if a mechanic refers to camshafts and tick-overs – such terms are clearly the shorthand of his trade. If I chose to, I could make the effort and learn the basic vocabulary needed to talk about car engines, but I prefer not to. It is a different matter, I suspect, if a doctor tells me to exercise my cardio-vascular system when he means get my heart beat going: it is less clear, it is liable to be misunderstood and it is unhelpful. He is using jargon, and his main purpose seems to be to remind me that he understands these things and I don't. He wishes to preserve the mystique of his profession. Clearly, this is not what we, as contributors to the National Health Service, are paying our doctors for: we'd prefer to be enlightened and reassured, not baffled and put down.

Doctors are an obvious example, but most professionals can, and on occasion do, play the same game. The average parent is bewildered by talk of objective assessment, unit accreditation and profiling. What is worse, the teacher who is glibly trotting out these formulae is well aware of the fact; and since he is paid to be a good communicator, such linguistic tactlessness is even more unforgivable. So why does he do it?

The first and most charitable construction that we can place on his behaviour is that he does not know that he's doing it: the specialist terminology has become so familiar that he fails to notice that he's using it. He has the same problem, arguably, that any adult has when talking to a child: how do you recognise the hard bits when to you it's all easy? Predicting which parts of your everyday language will be bewildering or offensive to others can be genuinely problematic.

All of us belong to several speech communities (that is, groups of people who talk in the same way because they're all Mancunians or teenagers or lawyers.) We switch styles in different company so as to fit in, just as surely as we change our dress. Certain specialists such as civil servants, lawyers and doctors seem to find the quick verbal change difficult. However, if specialists are to interact successfully with the rest of humanity, they need to recognise the common core of their language and keep their specialist vocabulary strictly separated from it.

The sad truth is that some specialists are not prepared to go to this trouble, in the first place because they are lazy and do not want to sieve what they say to check its appropriateness; in the second place because knowing fancy, specialist terms makes them feel good. They haven't studied their subject for donkey's years in order never to display their esoteric knowledge! Words are valuable social weapons and it is only human not to want to yield a hard-won advantage.

What jargon users need to recognise is that their stunning array of abstruse terms is not an advantage in the human game of communication: the little they gain on the 'cleverness' scale is more than outweighed by the loss on the 'sensitivity' one. I suppose that if they wanted to have their cake and eat it they could use the specialist term (subtext 'Look how clever I am') but then translate it for you (subtext 'Look how considerate I am'). However, having to express everything you say twice is rather time-consuming and, one suspects, would rapidly become very irritating.

Many of the readers of this book, consisting as they do of an educational elite, are the potential specialists – and jargon users – of the future. Perhaps you ought to reach a decision now, on both a practical and human basis, that jargon, if used to the general public, is not 'worth what it does cost the keeping.' You can bully, but not persuade those whom you make to feel inadequate; you might inspire awe but not affection and co-operation. So ask yourself very seriously, is it worth it? Isn't language supposed to be a bridge builder, not destroyer?

In case anyone remains unclear what jargon looks and sounds like, we are going to look at some prime examples. But before we do, it might be an idea to isolate certain elements of jargon in a more systematic way.

Features of jargon

Words are often long and needlessly confusing. Additions to words are often Latin or Greek prefixes and suffixes.

Euphemisms abound! Governments don't bomb, they give 'air support'; you aren't promiscuous, you 'practise distributive sex', and you don't become pregnant you're 'in an interesting condition'.

Certain **vogue words** which are trendy are oft-used by jargonauts. Thus 'interfaces', 'facilities' and 'situations' 'co-exist'; 'facilitators' 'enable' and 'share'.

Tricks for **stretching language** are used: nouns become noun phrases, so that a canteen is now a 'refreshment facility', a dustman is a 'refuse disposal operative' and the blind are 'visually challenged'.

Empty phrases and fillers are also used. Some favourites include 'at this point in time', 'from where I stand' and 'it seems to me'.

Needless verbs are added: for example, we now 'perform an investigation' rather than investigating. This makes for a rather pompous, re-stating the obvious style.

This pomposity often issues in **stock phrases**, which politicians seem especially fond of. They tell us 'It must be understood/noted/remembered' and 'cannot be stressed/emphasised too strongly'. Towards the end of their speeches (and far too often, towards the end of English essays) we find 'in conclusion'/'to sum up'/'to summarise'.

Redundant features (i.e. extra words that add nothing to meaning) are merely an irritation; other features of jargon are more sinister. The **use of the passive** is a case in point. This is a well-known ploy for avoiding responsibility: jargonauts don't like to be quoted! Jargon can also be used to fudge and positively mislead.

Our first example splendidly fulfils two of the three aims of jargon: it is very much for insiders and it is certainly out to impress. Before you are told anything about the passage, see what you make of it. When you have read it, try using the analysis guidelines from Section One of this book. Decide upon the purpose of the writer, the intended audience and thus the tone adopted. With this particular type of writing, audience is a good starting point. Another approach is to see whether the text has any of the hallmarks of jargon which were specified. Do try not to use our guide as a 'shopping list', though.

Whichever system you adopt, try to decide two things:

1 What is there, and
2 Why it is there.

GUIDELINES FOR INITIAL DISTRICT CONSIDERATIONS

The enclosed (blue) documents are included to assist Districts in their deliberations regarding TVEI (E). The process can be seen in six stages.

1. <u>A Consideration and Definition of the District Consortium</u>
The large chart has been designed to illustrate to colleagues that districts already provide a considerable service to young people. What is perhaps not readily available at present is an overview, both to individual providers and more importantly to young people. The initial task is therefore to take stock in the form of a

2. <u>District Audit</u> This is not intended solely as a paper exercise but as an opportunity to bring together the various agencies at District level to more fully understand and appreciate the variety of provision available and the role of education, training, industry and the community in the lives of young people. It is anticipated that this process will form the basis for a cohesive approach to policy and planning between education, training, industry and the community, the first stage of which will be

3. <u>Establishing Aims and Objectives for the District</u> This is an essential criterion in establishing TVEI (E) consortia at the District level and affords the opportunity for continuing, or establishing, working relationships on a sound footing. To achieve this degree of commonality of purpose it will be necessary to establish a

4. <u>Consultation Programme</u> This may be seen in three stages:

i) March/April 1987 – initial district response to meet the April 10th deadline

ii) April-July 1987 – detailed district response

iii) September 1987-August 1988 – the proposed consultation/ TVEI (E) lead-in year

5. <u>The District Management Structure</u> is to be indicated on the pro forma. Particular attention may be drawn to the representative and cohesive nature of such a structure to reflect the multiplicity of interests in the proposal as outlined in Part A, Review.

6. <u>Further Consultations</u> between April 1987 and August 1988 will focus upon possible delivery mechanisms e.g. cluster arrangements; defining specific curriculum developments; determining support strategies and presenting individual institution curriculum responses.

You might end up with notes along the lines of the following:

Approach 1

Audience
Specialist: 'TVEI', 'facilitators', 'curriculum response' (insider references)
Sophisticated: 'criterion', 'provision'; abstract nouns: 'arrangement', 'approach', 'mechanisms'

Tone
Euphemistic – 'young people'
Pompous – lots of tautology, long noun phrases
Detached – passives, abstracts

Purpose
Informative
Layout – numbered and underlined sub-headings, dates and deadlines

Approach 2

Specific features of jargon
Latinate words: 'consortia', 'criterion', 'pro forma'
Euphemisms: 'young people', 'facilitators'
Vogue words: 'overview', 'providers'
Noun phrases: 'commonality of purpose', 'possible delivery mechanisms'
Needless repetition: 'aims and objectives', 'understand and appreciate', 'continuing and establishing'
Fillers: 'on a sound footing'

As you will have noticed, the two approaches both elicit many of the same points. The important thing is that you do have *some* system, otherwise your answer could crumble into waffle.

Now you have your notes and ours, try to write an analysis of the piece. It comes, by the way, from an educational manager to his staff. It ought to fill your heart with pity for teachers!

This passage purports to inform – sorry! – pretends to tell you something. The six numbered points give a veneer of organisation, but try to summarise what it says. Difficult, isn't it? Let's look at why.

First of all, there is no honest statement of opinion. This would be appropriate if the document were totally objective yet in fact it is not. A point of view is implicit in 'overview' (someone has to provide it) and 'commonality of purpose' (someone has decided that this is desirable.) The writer seems to have made decisions which he is unwilling to take responsibility for, hence the passive form of the verbs: 'the chart has been designed', 'the process can be seen' and 'documents are included.' Thus also the total absence of first person pronouns, which are replaced by demonstratives: 'This is' and 'This is not'.

Next we are struck by the vagueness of so many of the words. Look at the title: 'Guidelines for Initial District Considerations'. Of these words, only 'district' is a concrete noun with precise meaning; the rest make no firm promises. These guidelines provide an 'opportunity' and 'may be seen': again no quotable commitment. This feeling we have of vagueness derives from all the abstract nouns. No-one can pin down what a 'cohesive approach' and 'possible delivery mechanisms' are. The latter expression is a high-faluting noun phrase replacing the more straightforward 'ways to deliver' (noun + verb). There are very many long nominal phrases in this text. Two particularly extended ones are 'The basis for a cohesive approach to policy and planning between education, training, industry and the community' and 'The representative and cohesive nature of such a structure.'

The elaborate, formal nature of the language disguises the fact that there is little content. This writer prefers to employ formulae and avoid simple lexis, so we have 'commonality of purpose' and not 'same aim', and 'support strategies' rather than 'help'. There are many more!

In this document, we never find a small word where a larger one will do. Thus 'institution' is used for 'centre', 'initial' for 'first' and 'solely' for 'only'. All these words are used to assure the reader that the writer knows his stuff. For good measure he throws in a few educational vogue words: teachers become 'providers', basis 'criterion' and groups 'consortia'. Jargon writers love Latinate words: they sound so much more impressive!

It is easy to mock, but in fact it's very easy to slip into jargon yourself in the misguided belief that it's the appropriate register. If people are really unaware of doing it, this is very worrying. It is even more disturbing when politicians, the forces and lawyers, amongst others, use jargon with a deliberate euphemistic purpose so that the unpalatable becomes acceptable: a leading politician keeps the president in the dark to provide a 'plausible deniability situation'; a bombing raid is re-christened a 'pre-emptive strike' and a jail is a 'total incarceration facility'.

As far as using language to fudge goes, estate agents probably take the gold medal. Having recently bought a house, I am now able to offer the world

A receiver's guide to the language of estate agents

Terraced houses become 'cottages' or 'quasi-semis' which are not cramped but 'deceptively spacious', not falling apart but 'offering plenty of scope for flair and personalisation'. 'Ideal for first time buyer' means cheap and probably nasty; 'ideal for professional couple' indicates that it has one bedroom, a tiny kitchen and no garden. The 'low overheads' which sound so attractive turn out to mean that the house is cheap to heat because it is minuscule.

Translating is fun for me but it's no joke for those innocent first-time buyers seeking their dream home – they are often shamefully misled and inevitably disappointed.

There follows a detailed description of a house which is interesting not only as jargon but also as a text which clearly has a target audience. Decide as you read it who it is trying to impress as well as noticing the jargon. A consideration of vagueness and euphemism will be particularly useful in this case.

> This outstanding and substantial residence is situated in one of the finest parts of Bowdon close to Dunham Park and overlooking National Trust land at the rear. The original part of the house, built about fifty years ago, was designed by Herbert J. Rowse. Within the last twelve years a substantial additional wing has been added.
>
> 'Levenot' therefore provides a splendid family residence with the added facilities of what is virtually an additional self-contained house with its own separate entrance and services which would be ideal for accommodating dependent relatives or simply part of the family. We should point out that whilst the additional wing is almost a separate

entity in itself it does connect directly with the main residence therefore achieving flexibility of use.

'Levenot' stands in its own grounds of approximately 1 acre which includes a former tennis lawn and a small copse. The gardens at the rear face almost due south overlooking National Trust farmland. The property has the benefit of a double driveway and there is a large double garage and a former small stables at the east side of the property.

There are two independent gas-fired central heating systems installed to heat the main house and extension.

Charcoal Road is considered to be one of the most sought after and highly regarded roads in Bowdon and the property lies within just a few minutes walking distance of the well known Dunham Park. The property lies in a very rural atmosphere and yet both Hale village and Altrincham town centre are jut a few minutes by car. Altrincham contains many of the well known multiples such as House of Fraser, Boots, W. H. Smith etc. The local train station offers a regular commuter link with many of the surrounding business centres. Wilmslow station, which is some 5 miles distant offers a direct inter city link with Euston station in London. The access point to the motorway network and Manchester Airport are both within a matter of minutes by car.

❖ To whom is this passage trying to appeal? (Why mention House of Fraser and not Woolworths?)
❖ How much factual information does it give? What sort of feature does it emphasise?
❖ Which words and phrases seem to you vague or misleading?
❖ Which words and phrases are estate agents' language?

Academic jargon

The jargon of estate agents is mainly a matter of imprecision and exaggeration. Very different is that of the academic. This sort of language, whether it intends to or not, tends to exclude and intimidate the outsider. Here is an example from a field we are all interested in – Linguistics:

> These quasi-physical aspects of technical organisation – time, physical shape, sound pattern – have all been regarded as less important in the novel (and in prose generally.) Novels are generally less punctuated in space, the printed lines reach regularly to the margin, encouraging fast, unbroken reading. But is is clear that the conventions of spatio-temporal attention and reading speed, applied to two different genres differ relatively not absolutely.

Well? What did you make of that? Let me translate it into plainer English:

> People normally notice the look of and sound of words in a novel less than in a poem. This is because the words aren't chopped up into lines and so you read them quickly. In fact, attention to detail and

speed of reading are only less noticeable when reading prose, not unnecessary.

I think that is what the writer meant. I can't pretend to be certain what 'the conventions of spatio-temporal attention' are – and this despite the fact that linguistics is my discipline.

Here are some more examples. Try to translate the first one into simpler English. Get rid of unnecessarily long or meaningless words. Avoid the passive where you can. Look at repetition of nouns and verbs. See if you can reduce sentence length.

> It is precisely and only because it is in this and other ways possible to assess philosophical expertise independently of any judgement of the truth or falsity of some particular position that we are able to conduct university examinations which set questions in philosophy as opposed to questions asking what some philosopher as a matter of fact said.
>
> Nevertheless, although generally distinctions can be seen as relevant or irrelevant and arguments to be valid or invalid independent of any categorical assessment of the truth or falsity of premises or conclusions in a particular case, a collection of premises may be known to be true, and then, given also suitable arguments we may claim to know the conclusions derived from those statements.

Having flexed your muscles on that text, have a look at two more. These are from a Trade Union booklet and a police training book respectively. For each, try to make sense of it, try to summarise it and analyse it.

Legal and Professional Services

> The review of legal services was concluded with positive decisions in line with the development of a structure of regional delivery. The ready and prompt availability of efficient and effective legal services was reaffirmed as a crucial feature of union benefit. Problems in established practice were quickly identified by the review. There has been an enormous increase in the volume of law affecting teachers and the education service. This had the effect of narrowing the delivery of legal services to those members who are sensitive to the fact that they have problems which they need to have addressed. Many others have faced the fact that legal changes have been interpreted to their disadvantage.
>
> Combined with this has been a massive escalation in legal costs expended through the established use of the Union's local Solicitor system – a figure of 1987 over two and a half times the 1983 figure. This represents an expenditure on casework problem-solving rather than problem prevention involving delivery to only a narrow section of the membership.

National Union of Teachers

Principal differences between felonies and misdemeanours:

1 The distinction between principals and accessories is recognised in felonies

2 To compound a felony is a criminal offence

3 The powers of arrest without warrant are wider in felonies than in misdemeanours

4 In felony the prisoner must be tried at the bar, he is given in charge to the jury and must be in the dock throughout the proceedings. The form of the oath taken by the jury varies therefore in felonies and misdemeanours.

5 A person convicted of felony may be ordered to pay compensation not exceeding £100 for loss of property caused by the felony.

6 Conviction of some felonies involves a disqualification for certain offices.

Harris: Criminal Law

You will, we hope, by now be aware that jargon does exist and can exist in many forms with several possible purposes.

Chapter 11

Just gimme the facts
– words used by journalists

In this country, newspapers contain a gamut of styles and viewpoints. In order to analyse them intelligently, you need to make certain decisions about the article in front of you. We return to our old friends purpose and audience.

It might seem incontrovertible that newspaper reporters report the news, i.e. give information. However, assuming that reports in the popular press are mainly about giving information is about as sensible as assuming that page three girls are there to give us a lesson in female physiology. The intention of most popular newspaper reports is to give pleasure – to entertain. The 'stories' are mainly of a 'human interest' kind; the focus is feeling.

The intentions of the quality press – by which I mean, reading from left to right politically, *The Guardian*, *The Independent*, *The Times*, the *Financial Times* and *The Daily Telegraph* – is more akin to reportage, the transmission of information. The content of a quality paper is more factual, the analysis more detailed because they are appealing to a more educated audience.

This is not to say that the quality press only informs or the popular press only entertains: quality journalists also want to keep their readership interested and the popular journalists know what they are writing about. The difference is in emphasis and priority. It is also vital to remember that both types of paper persuade as well as informing and entertaining. So there's plenty going on to talk about.

Do also bear in mind that a newspaper has more than one sort of article. There are the main 'news' stories: those on the front page ought to fall into this category. These news items are expected to be reports and not comment, whereas other articles which are headed Editorial or Comment or have a named writer discussing a topic are perfectly entitled to present a view.

Overleaf is an example of a 'comment' article followed by a straight news story. Look at the language of each. Can you see that their purposes are not the same? They are both from *The Guardian*, so presumably their audience is identical. However, they are not doing the same job.

❖ Of the quality papers *The Guardian* is the most left wing. Armed with that knowledge can you identify the bias in the first article?
❖ How is the Balfour Declaration criticised?
❖ Does the paper seem more in sympathy with the Jews or the Palestinians?
❖ What would you say the writer's intention was in writing the article?
❖ What could you deduce about the readership of *The Guardian*?
❖ Attempt a full analysis of the text, bearing in mind our three main guidelines, purpose, audience and tone.

MICHAEL ADAMS on the 70th anniversary of the Balfour Declaration

Equal shares for Palestine

SINCE the late summer, the Gulf has elbowed Palestine out of the headlines as the focal point for anxiety about the Middle East. Destroyers and helicopter gunships provide more vivid material for newspapers and television than an apparently static and insoluble political crisis.

The two situations differ in another way. Nobody understands what the Americans are up to in the Gulf or how the crisis began or what anybody can do about it. With the Arab-Israeli conflict over Palestine, the opposite is true. The objectives of the parties are clear and so is the only desirable outcome.

It began 70 years ago, when the British foreign secretary, Arthur Balfour, signed a letter to Lord Rothschild. It was a short letter, only 118 words in all but it acquired the title of "the Balfour Declaration" – in which, as Arthur Koestler put it, "one nation solemnly promised to a second nation the country of a third."

Koestler's epigram was neat but not quite accurate. What the declaration promised was Britain's support for the creation in Palestine of "a national home for the Jewish people."

But there was a difficulty. Palestine was already the home of a settled community, as even Mr Balfour (notoriously careless in matters of detail) was made aware. Its members were not consulted; but to reassure them, a condition – a categorical condition – was written into the declaration. It was to be "clearly understood that nothing shall be done that may prejudice the civil and religious rights of existing non-Jewish communities in Palestine."

That must have seemed reassuring enough, even if the phrase "existing non-Jewish communities" was a curious euphemism with which to describe the Palestinians, who constituted the overwhelming majority of the population and outnumbered the Jews in Palestine by nine to one.

And yet it is because that promise was broken that today 5 million Palestinians are scattered in resentful exile or else are held in subjection by a Jewish army of occupation in their own homeland.

Of course, much has happened and many mistakes have been made along the way. But it was Mr Balfour who wrote the overture to the tragedy and who set the tone for what was to follow. In November 1947, after the British had acknowledged their failure to resolve the problem which they had themselves created, the UN General Assembly "recommended" the partition of Palestine into two states, one Arab, the other Jewish.

The Palestinians protested that the UN had no more right than Mr Balfour to take half of their country and hand it over to alien immigrants – and they were right. Not even the Security Council (and certainly not the General

Assembly) had any such authority. But once again a decision which dramatically affected the destiny of the Palestinians was taken without their consent.

Forty years on from the partition resolution, and 70 years on from the Balfour Declaration, is it enough to dismiss all this as just water under the bridge? To be sure, nothing can undo those two decisions, whose effect was to pave the way for the dismemberment of Palestine and the dispersal of its indigenous population.

Neither the British Government in 1917 nor the UN General Assembly in 1947 was acting with true even-handedness. Each was subjected to energetic lobbying by the Zionists. Yet both felt the need to give their decisions the appearance of being evenhanded, and so – on paper – they were.

The Balfour Declaration incorporated the firm condition that the rights of the Palestinians must be secured. The General Assembly's partition scheme called for the establishment in Palestine not of one state, but of two, of which one was to be for the Palestinians. In other words, the principle was enshrined in both decisions that Palestine was to be shared, and shared on equal terms.

It is just conceivable that this might have been the outcome, had either side willed it to be so. Instead, they fought to prevent it and the Zionists won – and this time the international community, which could and should have intervened to prevent the distortion of its design for Palestine, stood aside and allowed events to take their course.

Israel's rulers were faced at the outset with a choice. They could seek a reconciliation with the Palestinians, which would mean giving up some of the territory they had won in 1948, and allowing back at least some of the refugees they had driven out. Or they could try by force to consolidate if possible extend their triumph at the expense of the Palestinians.

There were advocates in Israel for both alternatives, but they were unevenly matched. The hard men gained the upper hand and have never been seriously challenged – until now. For the only piece of good news to come out of the Middle East in the past three months is that a move has been initiated inside Israel to return to that neglected principle of a Palestine shared between its two claimants.

The initiative has come from the International Centre for Peace in the Middle East, which claims the support of several hundred leading figures in Israel, including 10 former cabinet ministers and 65 present and former members of the Knesset, as well as judges, reserve generals, writers, artists and rabbis.

They have appealed publicly for an end to "terror and violence ... and to the rule of one people over another." Instead, they urge, "the time has come to establish a peace of mutual recognition, based on territorial compromise and self-determination," which alone can guarantee " the security of Israel, the realisation of Palestinian aspirations and regional stability."

There is no sign that Israel's prime minister is ready to take up their challenge to "open negotiations without preconditions;" and the Palestinians will look with scepticism for the small print. And yet, who knows what might happen if the outside world took a hand again, but constructively, and if everyone, Jew and gentile, Russian and American – even Mrs Thatcher perhaps – were to lend their support? It would be a fine way to celebrate the anniversary of the Balfour Declaration.

Benefit rules tightened for unemployed

Simon Beavis
Labour Correspondent

THE Government is to tighten its scrutiny of people claiming unemployment benefit and scrap the UB40 claim form as part of a package of measures announced yesterday by Michael Howard, the Employment Secretary.

Under new rules which take immediate effect, claimants will have to attend interviews with counsellors after three months rather than six months and there will be more intense counselling and checking of how a claimant is going about finding work. This will be done by a designated counsellor.

The UB40 – which became a youth culture symbol of the era of mass unemployment in the 1980s, spawning a successful band of the same name – is to be replaced by a Back to Work plan and a booklet, entitled Helping You Back to Work and incorporating an attendance card as well as job hunting tips. All new claimants will begin receiving the booklet immediately.

The measures are part of the new Employment Services Agency which was uncoupled from the direct control of the Department of Employment this week and launched as a semi-autonomous body run by its own chief executive, Mike Fogden. All unemployment benefit offices are to be integrated with jobcentres to provide a one-stop benefit and job advice service.

The agency has been set rigorous targets to achieve in getting people back to work or into training. Among these is a requirement to place 1.65 million unemployed people into jobs this year.

The new five-point plan was announced yesterday by Mr Howard in written reply to a parliamentary question and places a greater emphasis on individual counselling than is currently the case, particularly for the long-term unemployed. "These changes will be of particular benefit to those who have been unemployed for over six months," he said.

The tougher measures to check on claimants follow last autumn's introduction of the actively-seeking-work ruling under which claimants had to prove what steps they were taking to find work or ultimately face disqualification.

Claimants will now be called in after 13 weeks for advice and counselling, and will stay with the same counsellor throughout. Further interviews will take place after six, 12 and 18 months and there will be intense counselling for people out of work for more than two years.

Do beware of thinking that a news article is a news article is a news article. The personalised one that you have just analysed is, quite legitimately, giving opinion. So is this article from *The Sun*:

THE SUN SPEAKS ITS MIND

TAME TEHRAN'S TWERPS

IN modern times there have been two states openly dedicated to the murder of British citizens.

First Libya and then Iran.

Libya's Gaddafi was effectively subdued by U.S. bombers launched from bases in Britain.

Now we have the infamous threats from Ali Rafsanjani, speaker of the Tehran Parliament, and most likely successor to the Ayatollah as the leader of Iran.

He has openly urged Palestinians to murder five Britons, Americans or Frenchmen for every one of their countrymen killed by Israel.

These are the words of a blood-crazed madman. Unfortunately, they have to be taken seriously because Iran is under the sway of criminality.

We have no quarrel with the Iranian people themselves. We would like to have friendly relations and to trade with them.

Regime

But in control in Tehran are fanatical creatures devoid of reason, compassion and every human quality. They cannot possibly be allowed to go on like this.

In the past, they have connived at the seizure, torture and sometimes deaths of British people in the Lebanon. They have ordered the execution of one British citizen, Salman Rushdie, for the crime of writing a novel of which they disapprove.

The civilized world cannot conceivably have dealings with Iran, for ANY purpose.

Our first measure should be to expel from this country all Iranians who are not proven enemies of the Khomeini regime and who may face danger at home.

And beyond this?

Reason

Foreign Secretary Sir Geoffrey Howe is asking for the support of our Common Market partners.

Fat chance! Last time we sought their help, several withdrew their diplomatic missions from Tehran. But then, one by one, they sidled back.

The Japanese, who always put trade before inconvenient principle, never left.

This time, the French are also in the firing line. Our suspicion, on past form, is that they will find some convenient trench for cover.

This leaves Britain and America. George Bush is a more cautious president than Ronald Reagan.

Old Ron's first impulse, we are sure, would have been to bomb the hell out of Tehran as he did to Tripoli.

Together our two countries could target devastating power against Tehran.

What if we told them that the very first time harm was done to a single British or American citizen, the next victims would be military targets in Tehran?

Protest

Were this to happen, we do not believe there would be any protest from the Muslim world, except perhaps Libya which does not matter any more.

The Arabs sided with Iraq in the Gulf War. There is a world surplus of oil and they know that they need the West more than we need them. Besides they must be as fearful of Iran as the rest of us.

In the end, a mad dog has no friends. No one knows whom he will bite next.

For the mad dogs in Tehran, the time has surely arrived for a final showdown.

- You will notice that there is a very different tone adopted in *The Sun*'s piece from that in *The Guardian*. Start by looking at its headline. What could you say about it?
- Next look at the lexis employed in the text: the fourth paragraph starting 'But those in charge' will give you the flavour. Which words are most loaded?
- How does the writer's viewpoint come through?
- The structures are also worth considering. Does this writer prefer assertion, question or command?
- How long are sentences and paragraphs?
- How complex in terms of clauses?
- What can you deduce about the readership of *The Sun* and about its political stance?

If it's in the paper it must be true ...

Whether or not we agree with them, such articles as you have just looked at do not mislead the reader; others, it is our contention, do. It is always a good idea to look carefully at those articles which pretend to be news reporting. Not all of these are in fact unbiased. Recognising bias in the press is a life skill as well as an exam one. It involves not only what adjectives and adverbs are used to describe people's characters and actions, but also which of the characters in the drama a paper chooses to quote, how flattering the picture of them is – verbal and photographic – and which facts are being given or withheld. It is an educational experience to read the same 'story' in several papers. Especially fruitful are those relating to politics.

An example was the reporting of a by-election in which the Conservatives won with a greatly reduced majority; the SLD/SDP polled between them far more votes than the Conservatives, and Labour lost their deposit. Accounts given and details emphasised in various newspapers were very different. The *Daily Mirror* (left-wing popular) stressed the 'disaster for the Tories' and failed to mention that the Labour candidate lost his deposit. The *Daily Express* (right-wing up-market popular) stressed the 'division at the centre of British politics', thus emphasising the Tories' invincibility. *The Guardian* (quality left) also discussed the centre ground, but to make the point that most people did not vote Conservative and that the centre parties were in disarray. They talked at length about David Owen's personal popularity. The poor showing by the Labour candidate was mentioned, but far more time was then spent on another by-election which Labour had won.

It is clearly naïve to believe everything that you read in the papers, yet people persist in doing so. What is perhaps worse is that we tend to read the paper closest in political viewpoint to our own, thus guaranteeing that we keep reinforcing all our prejudices and reading the statistics we want to see. Reading at least two quality papers' versions of a story is one way to be genuinely well informed. But of course being well informed is not what everyone wants from their paper.

Never mind the quality: read all about the bonking*

(*The word 'bonk' has just been included in the new Oxford English Dictionary as a verb and noun: a tribute to the power of the popular press.)

If it is true that we get the press we deserve, the eighties are a fairly depressing decade. Those papers that have the highest circulation seem to pedal competitions, gossip and soft porn – not necessarily in that order. They have very little to do with the news, yet people read them in their millions. What is the appeal of the popular press? Ease of reading would seem to be vital. The recipe goes something like this:

Content: royals, vicars or teachers – negative stories
Sports personalities and pop stars
Sex, violence and sentimentality
Outrageous, memorable headlines to grab the attention; mild swear words, abbreviated names and colloquialisms
Brief and juicy narrative; paragraphs no longer than two sentences
Mentions of the age and appearance of female characters and the occupations and comments of males
Mouth-watering subheadings of the 'Heartbreak', 'Kinky Fun' or 'Stunned' variety
Few words of three syllables or more; emotive words and plenty of adjectives
Use of alliteration and onomatopoeia
Puns and double entendres
'Exclusives' and 'World Exclusives'
Dickens' golden rules: 'make 'em laugh, make 'em cry, make 'em wait'.

Perhaps you think we are being grossly unfair and hyperbolic. Take a look at the front-page news story from *The Sun* on page 106 overleaf and see if you still think so.
Attempt an analysis of the article:

❖ **Is it news or titillation?**
❖ **How does it seek to interest and entertain?**
❖ **How many of the guidelines we wrote above can you see being followed? You could at least quickly do the following:**
❖ **Underline the emotive and hyperbolic lexis.**
❖ **Circle the colloquialisms.**
❖ **Asterisk the humorous touches.**
❖ **Decide why the story would interest and how graphics and photographs might be used.**

Another way into news reports and a good way to check how well you've grasped the style of a genre is to do a re-write or continuation. You could re-write this story from a different viewpoint – perhaps the wife's.

❖ **What would make a good headline?**
❖ **What would the heartbroken wife's view of 'pixie-faced Sally' be?**
❖ **How would you describe the wife in order to gain the readers' sympathy?**
❖ **Whom would you quote?**
❖ **What photos might you use?**

If you preferred, you could give the story a very different tone. You might like to sound shocked and morally outraged instead of treating the story as rather amusing.

❖ **How would you make the Head sound evil instead of foolish? Or even menacing?**
❖ **Who would you now quote – anxious parents?**
❖ **What would your final paragraph focus on?**

Whilst getting the subtler things right, think carefully about expression and content. Remember it is not only a matter of finding a subject that will interest your

HEAD'S LOVE FOR GIRL, 15

INSIDE OUR FIFTH FORM LOVE-NEST

A SCHOOL head carried on a passionate two-year affair after falling in love with a girl pupil aged only 15.

Donald Stevenson, 55, cuddled pixie-faced Sally Jones behind the closed doors of his office.

And 12 days after her 16th birthday he took her home for the first of a string of sex sessions while his wife was playing bowls.

Sally, now 17, said the sizzling sir gave her a torrid lesson in sex in his bed – when they did "everything else" but make love.

He even set her up in a flat and promised to move in with her.

But when the crunch came, he refused to leave his wife Janet.

Scorned Sally stormed to the headmaster's house and shouted: "Mrs Stevenson, I have been to bed with your husband!"

Sally said yesterday: "She told me I might as well announce it to the world. So I did."

The affair began when Sally was in the fifth form.

Mr Stevenson was assistant head until he retired early last term.

Sally, who says she is still a virgin, said:

'He would be very affectionate, but only when the door of his office was closed. My friends never noticed a thing.

He first took me home on a Monday night, just after my 16th birthday.

I knew what might happen, but I wasn't scared. As soon as we got inside he grabbed me and we ended up kissing and cuddling on the settee.

After that we would meet regularly on a Monday because his wife went to her ladies' bowls club then. He would meet me down on the beach. We'd go for long walks together and he'd take me back home.

PASSIONATE

We'd sometimes meet up in his lunchtime too.

Then his wife went away for a week and I stayed the night. I was very much in love and I found him very attractive.

Not so much the way he looks, more his personality. He made me laugh.

In bed he was very passionate. He knew everything about foreplay and I was very turned on.

But although we went to bed together he never made love to me. We did everything else and it was very passionate, but he said he wanted to wait until we could be together properly, when he had left his wife.'

Mr Stevenson set Sally up in a £28-a-week flat near his home in Dundee.

He left some of his clothes there and paid a deposit of four weeks rent, even though Sally had by now left school and was working as a shop assistant.

Sally said: "He gave me a gold ring and told me he would move in on August 12."

But he stayed with his wife – leaving Sally alone in a flat she says she can't afford.

STORY

Mr Stevenson said the relationship was nothing more than a schoolgirl crush.

Standing beside his wife as he spoke, he added: "I have been trying to finish it for a long time.

"This girl has been pestering me. She's a nice girl and I was trying to get her a job."

He admitted paying the deposit for the flat.

And he hung his head as he added: "Is it impossible to like somebody in this world?"

Love letters he wrote to Sally tell a more passionate story.

One read: "You have never pestered me, rather I pestered you. I fell in love with you and wanted to be with you all the time.

Another said: "I have never loved anyone the way I love you."

Mrs Stevenson stood by her husband yesterday.

ANGRY

She said: "I understand that the girl is hurt and angry. I'd have been the same at her age if my boyfriend wanted to finish it.

"But this is a teenage crush on an older man."

Sally denied being a "tease". She said: "I never lead him on. Now I wish he had left me alone."

selected audience, it is also a matter of 'speaking their language'. Without wishing to give a recipe, bearing some of the following points in mind might help you write a more convincing article.

Popular press

Headlines

Purpose: to attract attention
Style: colloquial and preferably using monosyllabic words
Tone: emotional – either humorous and punning or shocked and stunned
Layout: bold!

Lexical choice

Purpose: to move (emotive lexis) and to describe/narrate (adjectives and adverbials are very important)
Style: simple and colloquial, often hyperbolic
Tone: emotional

Structures

Purpose: to narrate, sequence material
Style: short, often simple sentences – making few demands on the reader. Compound sentences are often divided into two simple sentences for greater drama and simplicity. Thus many sentences begin with 'and', 'or' or 'but'.
Paragraphs are also short: two sentences is their average length.
Tone: akin to the spoken. Many inessential elements such as the verb 'to be' or the definite and indefinite article are omitted.
Layout and Phonology: graphics attract attention and can indicate bias. Often emotive in purpose.
Subheadings within the text maintain interest and provide a thumbnail sketch of the story.
Alliteration adds drama and memorability.

Quality press

Headlines

Purpose: often informative rather than sensational.
Style: more formal with fewer deleted elements (missing words)
Tone: factual
Layout: smaller than in the popular press

Lexical choice

Purpose: varied: sometimes to move, sometimes to inform
Style: not very colloquial. Very rarely include taboo words. Latinate words are acceptable as is some jargon.
Structures: complex sentences are needed because explanations and analyses require subordinate clauses beginning with 'unless' or 'meanwhile' or 'since'. More complex thought needs more complex structures of language.
Paragraphs and sentences are longer because more information is included.
Layout and phonology: graphics can be informative – for example maps. They need not be very large.
Subheadings would be an insult to the intelligence of the readership.
Sound effects can include puns and antithesis for effect.

Look at this article from *The Independent* about the Zeebrugge ferry disaster:

At least 26 reported dead, 240 missing, 300
Cross-Channel

AT LEAST 26 people were reported to have died after a British ferry capsized in near-freezing water about a mile outside the Belgian harbour of Zeebrugge.

Dover coastguards said early today that 240 people were still unaccounted for after the worst peacetime Channel disaster. Three hundred passengers and crew had been rescued from the ferry, the Herald of Free Enterprise, which was sailing from Zeebrugge to Dover.

The ferry capsized so quickly that there was no time for it to send out an SOS, a coastguard official said.

Differing reports put the number of passengers and crew at between 540 and 650.

Divers and an armada of small boats battled through the night to save hundreds of passengers trapped inside the ferry which capsized just outside Zeebrugge harbour on its way to Dover.

Jan van Moerbeke, a male nurse who boarded the stricken vessel, told reporters that he had found six people dead on top of the boat and that there were at least another 20 people dead inside. Dover coastguards also said 26 were dead.

Nearly 100 people were reported to have been injured, some badly.

All the survivors were wet and very cold, a Zeebrugge port spokesman said.

British survivor Rosina Summerfield said there was no question of women and children first when the ferry capsized.

"Everybody just scrambled," she said through her tears. "This ain't the Titanic, you know."

Children screamed and shouted as the ferry began to capsize. A lorry driver who escaped from the ship said he had thought he was doomed to death.

A 15-year-old boy from Hastings, Sussex, wrapped in blankets on the harbour, said: "I've lost my Mum. I don't know what has happened to her."

By **David Usborne** in Zeebrugge, **Peter Dunn** and **Anne Spackman**

"The lights went out and all you could hear was the water coming in the side that sunk," Ms Summerfield said, "Everywhere there were people floating about."

Nearly 40 ships from four nations – Britain, Belgium, Holland and France – joined a massive rescue operation.

The air over Zeebrugge was filled with helicopters hovering in the night sky to pluck survivors from the water.

A fleet of ambulances on the quayside took survivors to hospitals at special crisis centres throughout Belgium.

A spokesman at the Dover coastguards said: "The fact that people are missing just means they haven't been accounted for. It doesn't mean they have been written off."

The 7,951-ton ferry, carrying 84 cars and 36 lorries, was reported to have hit the harbour wall or a pier 45 minutes after setting sail from Zeebrugge to Dover. Other reports said it hit a sandbank.

The ferry capsized at 6.46 pm London time after a bow door burst open and water cascaded into the car deck, Townsend Thoresen said.

Dover coastguards said it was on its port side.

One report late last night said divers had seen people inside the vessel through portholes. They apparently had air.

But, early this morning, a Belgian coastguard said: "There is a slim possibility that there might be enough air inside the ship for people to survive, but it is only a slim possibility."

A salvage expert said late last night that there was air inside the ferry and it did not appear to be sinking any further into the water.

- This is potentially a very emotive subject. Would you say *The Independent* has treated it emotionally? Or is the report more factual? Justify your view.
- Rewrite the first three paragraphs and headline of the story as it might appear in the popular press. (Remember to bring in political bias as well as emotion.)

rescued, as ship hits Zeebrugge harbour wall

ferry disaster

Rescuers made their way into the ship through doors in the hull, using ladders, ropes, safety harnesses and other equipment.

To escape, people inside had to climb up vertically to reach doors and windows. Some were brought out through portholes.

Passengers were seen walking on the starboard side of the vessel as tugs tried to drag the roll-on roll-off ferry into shallower water.

One survivor said he did not feel an impact – "The boat just started to tilt."

Captain William Budd, of one rescue ship, the Taymar, said late last night that the ferry's propellers were out of the water.

'There is panic and confusion everywhere," he added.

The ferry carries four lifeboats and rafts to accommodate everyone likely to be aboard. But about half the emergency equipment would probably have been unusable after the accident, trapped below the water level on the port side.

Some passengers on the 132-metre (495-feet) ferry were understood to be readers of The Sun returning from a promotional day trip to Zeebrugge for £1 a head.

The Zeebrugge-Dover route is also popular with British military personnel going on leave from bases in West Germany.

"The ship took in some water and capsized," a spokesman for Townsend Thoresen in Zeebrugge said. The weather was calm but sea temperatures were very cold – 4 or 5 degrees centigrade. Waves round the stricken ship were about two feet high. Winds were blowing at 12 to 18 mph.

Among the helicopters scrambled for the rescue operation were two Royal Navy Sea Kings with divers from RAF Culdrose. Four RAF helicopters stood by at Manston, near Dover.

The Ministry of Defence said the frigate Diomede was sent to the scene. A Royal Navy diving team from HMS Vernon, Portsmouth, was flown out by RAF helicopter from Manston, Kent.

At least eight Dutch Navy divers went to Zeebrugge, Ostend radio appealed for more divers to go to the scene.

The Free Enterprise, a British ferry built in 1979, can carry 1,300 passengers and 350 cars. Launched in Bremerhaven, West Germany, it has a top speed of 23 knots.

The rescue was being coordinated from Koksjide in Belgium.

A Department of Transport surveyor travelled to Zeebrugge last night to conduct an on-the-spot investigation.

Mrs Thatcher was being kept informed of developments.

Mr John Moore, the Transport Secretary, will almost certainly make a statement in the Commons on Monday.

The ferry normally operates on the Dover-Calais route, but, because of refits to other vessels and winter timetables, it had been switched to the Zeebrugge service. It is one of the biggest in the Townsend Thoresen fleet, although larger vessels are due to be introduced.

The stricken vessel is one of the company's Blue Riband ships.

It has two stacked car decks. Passenger accommodation above them includes bars, cafeterias, shops and saloons.

The Herald of Free Enterprise is equipped with triple propellers aft. Forward, it has another propeller and a bow rudder to allow it to manoeuvre in tight spaces in crowded harbours.

A company spokesman denied a suggestion by a spokesman for the National Union of Seamen that the ferry was too big for the Zeebrugge port.

The last major ferry accident in the Channel was in December, 1982, when six people were killed after two ferries collided off Felixstowe, Suffolk, and one sank.

Bias

Look at the following extracts and see if there is anything which strikes you as you read them. Make a note of anything irrelevant or offensive.

> He was cleared of rape after telling the jury that the 23-year-old divorcee consented to intercourse.

> Mrs Thatcher and her bold policies are the only hope for our country. But confidence in her and her policies is being undermined by unemployment figures that seem frightening but in fact are phoney. Out of 2.1 million unemployed no less than 659,000, or just over a third, are women.

> Her hair neatly done, Mrs Thatcher had no apology for her war on public spending.

Well? Do you think the victim's age and marital status were relevant? Or that you're only really unemployed if you're a man (and thus 'the breadwinner')? Or that the state of Mrs Thatcher's hair is of national importance? It is all too easy not to notice such elements in the press, especially if you skim-read. Don't!

In case we should seem to be knocking only the right-wing press, let's take a detailed look at the article opposite from a left-wing paper which makes no bones about being propagandist and biased: *The Militant*. Before reading our analysis, try a paragraph-by-paragraph jotting down of key words and facts. Then check if we've mentioned anything you've missed, or vice versa.

Both headlines use emotive and dramatic lexis. Mortgages don't merely rise, they 'soar'. We do not have a problem but a 'crisis' and homelessness is at an all-time high judging by the word 'record'. And whose fault is it? Well, beside this article appeared a picture of Nigel Lawson, Chancellor of the Exchequer at the time, which maximised his least attractive features. He also seemed to be smiling in the face of all this suffering.

The first paragraph sets the tone for the rest of the article. It uses immediately comprehensible but emotionally effective cliché – the basic right of 'a roof over their heads'. It suggests there's a war on by using words like 'battle' and stating that the opposition don't mind using torture: 'tightening screws' are mentioned. The tone is fairly informal, so contractions such as 'they'd' and 'he's' are present. It subtly misleads: 'The Tory Chancellor says he's quite prepared to tighten the interest rate screws' suggests that they are quoting, but a moment's thought tells us that Nigel Lawson could not possibly have said that. The same moment's thought makes us feel that 'millions of home-owners' sounds dreadful, but is rather vague.

The second paragraph is also rather imprecise. The homeless have 'more than doubled' and we have estimations not facts, though the figures give a veneer of actuality. The 'desperate' and 'homeless' are constantly focussed on and an anonymous South London Advice centre worker is quoted. Would other workers agree? And how close to the truth is 'ABOUT a 50% rise IN SUCH CASES in the LAST FEW MONTHS' (my capitals)? He sympathetically says that 'these people stretched themselves to the limit'. Another commentator might judge that they had foolishly over-borrowed or left no margin for possible increases.

Record homelessness ... Mortgages soar ...

Housing crisis

A ROOF over their heads is the most basic right for any family. But keeping that right looks like an almost unwinnable battle to millions of home-owners as the year begins. Mortgage rate increases mean hardships they never dreamt they'd face. And Tory Chancellor Nigel Lawson says he's quite prepared to tighten the interest rate screws again.

By Tony Cross

While the Tories have been in power the number of homeless has more than doubled. The housing charity Shelter estimates that it is now well over a million. The soaring cost of housing means a new kind of client at agencies set up to help the desperate.

"They come in because the banks or the building societies are repossessing their homes," a South London advice centre worker told Militant.

"These are people who stretched themselves to the limit to get a mortgage. Now the mortgage rate increase takes them beyond that limit. There's been about a 50 per cent increase in such cases over the last few months."

Three million home-owners whose payments are adjusted annually will get a nasty New Year's gift from Chancellor Lawson. Some of them will have to pay 25 per cent more for their homes.

The Tories bribed and bullied people into buying their own homes. Taking out a mortgage bought you into their "property-owning democracy", they claimed. Lawson and Thatcher basked in the sunshine of a phoney boom based on borrowing and made the most of it in their election propaganda.

House prices have gone through the roof, rising four times as fast as incomes. Now home-owners are paying the price of Tory policies, as Lawson jacks up mortgage rates to try to stop inflation.

Shelter has reported suicides by home-owners faced with repossession and unable to tell their families the awful truth. The building societies admit to repossessing 23,000 homes in 1987. Other estimates put the figure even higher. In the year Thatcher's wrecking crew came into office the figure was 2,500.

And where will they go when they've lost their homes? Most families who apply to local authorities for homeless status get refused. Some councils are even claiming that someone who's been evicted by a building society is intentionally homeless.

The Tories have blitzed council housing. They want estates sold off to property developers or turned over to their dictatorial Housing Action Trusts.

They've slashed funding to councils so that they have next to nothing to spend on repairs and house-building. Less than 29,000 public sector houses are likely to be built next year, compared to 174,000 in 1975.

There's a housing crisis and it's going to get worse in 1989. Surely a home at a price they can afford is the least anyone can expect. The Labour leaders should launch a campaign against the mortgage rate increases and attacks on council housing and for a programme to build the homes we need.

* Homes for all at prices we can afford!
* Build a million homes a year!
* Restore the cuts in council rate support grants to 1979 levels!
* Freeze council rents!
* Stop the mortgage rate rises – nationalise the banks and building societies!

The placing of 'three million' straight after 'such cases' suggests that the former refers back to the latter. However, it doesn't. Careful reading also notices such things as the 'some of them' before the '25 per cent', but a quick flick through would certainly give the wrong impression. This is not so much to criticise the writer as to point out the importance of reading news reports properly and not skimming through them over the cornflakes.

The article becomes more colloquial and emotive as it goes on. Tories alliteratively 'bribed and bullied' with their propaganda. (Am I alone in collocating the word 'propaganda' with Hitler? Just a thought.) The Tories made false claims and were thus able to 'bask' with all its connotations of idleness and luxury. They are not graced with their first names: 'Lawson and Thatcher' sound far more threatening and inhuman. They later become the yet more unpleasant 'members of Thatcher's wrecking crew.' They colloquially 'jack up' mortgage rates which punningly go 'through the roof'.

Human interest is added by the mention of suicides. The effect of the word order is to permit suitable vagueness: if the people attempting suicide rather than the reporters of same were placed as the subject of the sentence, we would be more likely to notice that we are told very little about these unfortunate people. They are mentioned purely for passing effect. A more major focus (and therefore subject status) is placed upon the building societies who 'admit' (understood collocation 'their guilt in') repossessing homes.

The persuasion becomes yet more overt as we have an example of question and answer technique: 'Where will they go when they've lost their homes?' (So much more touching than 'houses'.) Not to council houses: with continuing war imagery these have been 'blitzed' by the Tories and not merely sold but 'sold off' (cheap?) to 'dictatorial' (boo!) Housing Action Trusts. Note that funds are viciously 'slashed' and that councils have the somewhat vague but memorable 'next to nothing' to spend.

The voice of doom says 'it's going to get worse in 1989.' 'Surely' suggests that we must all agree that 'all have a right to a home at a price they can afford.' Finally, *The Militant* tells us what must be done – with imperatives and plenty of exclamation marks for emphasis: 'Build', 'Restore', 'Freeze', 'Stop'.

The Militant is overtly propagandist, so analysing its purpose is not too problematic. Take a look now at the article opposite, from a paper which is not overtly a 'political' one, the *Daily Express*. Are there any comparisons to be made between it and *The Militant*? How contrasting are the views and how similar the techniques?

Audiences within audiences

We would like to make one last point before leaving the press. It is useful to remember when looking at news writing that the readership of most papers is very mixed and that few people read a paper from cover to cover. Some articles in a paper are certainly targetted at groups within the readership: such groupings could include businessmen, undergraduates, career women or children.

It might be a useful exercise to go through an entire edition of a paper attempting to decide who exactly the features, adverts and cartoons, for example, are aimed at. There are readerships within readerships.

Archbishop's moral mess

THE Archbishop of Canterbury, Dr George Carey, proclaims that we should not label the Newcastle rioters "sinners".

Well, I suppose he must be the best judge of what sin is so we'll leave that to him, though I'm suspicious of his judgement on anything intellectual.

Poverty

There can be no doubt, however, that what happened on the Meadow Well Estate was wrong, criminal, wicked and evil.

Who could say otherwise? Only a desperate-to-please, anxious to be loved, equivocating cleric who is looking for the approval of the liberal establishment while forgetting the victims of the carnage.

Nothing of what happened in Newcastle, Oxford, Cardiff or elsewhere can be explained away or excused by announcing as he did that "wrong-doing is inextricably linked to social deprivation, poverty, poor housing and illiteracy". Only a sociological simpleton could believe that to be true.

Besides providing an authoritative justification and excuse for all criminal activity, the priest has cast a slur on all law-abiding, deprived, poor and unemployed people everywhere.

The good doctor pleads in justification that he had been urged to give a moral lead, and that was all that he was doing. The Church of England wouldn't recognise a moral lead if it sauntered up to, and knocked on, the usually locked gates of the luxurious Lambeth Palace. It has sold the pass on every moral issue and ducked every major challenge to Christian values for over a decade.

Silly man. Giving a moral lead means knowing the difference between right and wrong and saying so, loud and clear.

Criminals

It is not taking a moral lead to say of the young criminals in designer clothes who steal cars; loots shops; petrol bomb the police, fire and ambulance officers; destroy property; terrorise old people; and beat up young women, that they are not sinners, that they cannot help it, they are just deprived, poor, illiterate.

That's called moral cowardice.

Have a look at the text on pages 114-115.

❖ Who do you think it is written for?
❖ What is its purpose?
❖ What is its tone?
❖ Rewrite this as it might appear if written for another group or in a different sort of paper.

This piece was actually written by an A-level Language candidate. We don't feel it suffers by comparison with professional work. Do you?

Give Opera a Go

"Opera?" you protest. "What? Enormously fat men and women, screaming away tunelessly in an incomprehensible foreign language about some impossibly melodramatic tragedy! No thanks! And anyway, people like me don't go to opera. The seats cost a fortune. It's only rich snobs who can afford the tickets and who got to somewhere like Covent Garden to get all dressed up for the evening."

Now hold on a minute! Have you ever actually been to an opera? I thought not. A lot of these ideas are completely wrongheaded, and obviously come from people who don't really know what opera is like.

Screaming away tunelessly

Well, this is just rubbish. Actually, opera is full of wonderful tunes, and a lot of people know them without realising it. Take many of the commercials on television. Bailey's Irish Cream, Galaxy chocolate, Kleenex tissues, Ragu tomato sauce, British Airways, Pirelli tyres all use great tunes, borrowed from opera. Yes, there are a lot of high notes in the soprano and tenor parts. But these are the very parts that are most exciting. Did you know that psychologists believe we respond to the high notes because they echo the primeval scream – the first expression of feeling man was capable of – and that something in us responds in a deeply primitive way? In fact, opera lovers get the biggest kicks as the singers soar to impossible heights. It's like watching someone take the high jump – will he make it?

Fat men and women

Well, yes, I have to admit that some of the greatest opera singers, particularly the Italian ones, are pretty large. They say that if they lose weight they lose the power in their voices. (Wish I had that excuse!) But more and more nowadays singers are expected to sound good and look good, so that the audience no longer has to put up with a fifty year-old, fifteen stone Madam Butterfly. The last time I went to the opera, to see 'The Pearl Fishers', the young men on stage were absolute hunks!

Incomprehensible

The foreign language does not have to be a problem. Our English National Opera, the ENO, always sings in English. And when Glyndebourne Opera sing the operas in their original tongue, they use what are called Supertitles. These are like the subtitles you get in foreign films, but they are shown on a screen above the stage. Failing these, there are always the programme notes. And as you get into the habit of going to operas, you get to know the stories anyway and are happy to go just for the music.

Melodramatic

Many operatic heroes and heroines come to a sticky end: Aida and

Rhadames entombed in a rock prison; Tosca throwing herself off the city walls; Don Giovanni carried off to hell; Mimi singing lustily while dying of TB and so on and so on. Personally, I think this is wonderful stuff! But people seem to be prepared to accept melodrama in soap operas like Dallas, whereas in grand opera they think it is going OTT. Another thing that people say is "If things were that bad you wouldn't be singing about it!" But wouldn't it be wonderful if, at moments of greatest joy or deepest sadness, we could actually open our mouths and let it all pour out? Opera is a beautiful expression of those emotions which we all feel so strongly at some time in our lives, yet are too inarticulate to express.

Opera can be fun!

Not all operas are tragic. There are many comic operas with funny stories and very catchy tunes. Try Mozart's 'The Marriage of Figaro', Strauss's 'Die Fledermaus' or Smetana's 'The Bartered Bride'. Modern operas too can have very different themes. I bet you didn't know that there is an opera called 'The Electrification of the Soviet Union'!

People like me don't go to opera

All types of people go to opera. There are lots of young people in the audience and they dress exactly as they please. The older people probably will be dressed up, but that isn't because it's opera, it's just a feature of the generation gap!

I can't afford the ticket

The best seats in the centre circle or stalls are very expensive – about £15 in Manchester, much more in London. But not all the seats are so pricey. If you want to give opera a try without breaking the bank, get a seat in the 'Gods'. This is the name given to the very highest balcony – nearest to heaven but farthest from the stage. Take along the Biology department's binoculars, or borrow your great grandmother's opera glasses – don't waste 20p on the little opera glasses provided in the theatre. They actually make the stage look farther away! The important thing about going in the Gods is that the sound is the same, and it won't cost you any more than going to a club or to a cinema in town. You might be lucky and get a seat on Standby. At a certain time on the day of the performance, any tickets unsold are released at a fraction of their full price, so these are a really good bargain.

How about an operatif?

Don't close your mind and say "Opera is not for me" until you have at least given it a chance. Choose your first opera carefully, perhaps according to your own temperament. One of the great romantic Italian operas might suit you: 'La Bohème' by Puccini, for example, is about students living on the Left Bank in Paris. Or, if you prefer a good laugh, Mozart's 'The Magic Flute' was originally written for the music hall.

So don't do a hatchet job on the operating theatre! Be adventurous! Give opera a go!

Chapter 12

House style to sell life style
– words used to foster group identity

Many magazines and periodicals are published each week or each month to help us to decide what to wear, what to cook, what to listen to, what to watch and how to decorate and furnish our homes. Insofar as the advertising they attract is usually in keeping with their choice of featured goods, personalities and music, we can say that they exist partly to sell style. Such publications cater for a wide range of ages, tastes and income brackets, from (at the time of writing) *Jackie* and *Smash Hits* through *Q* and *Vogue* to *My Weekly* and *Good Housekeeping*. Their success depends on identifying a 'target' readership and appealing successfully to it. Many are lavishly illustrated and several aspects of newspaper layout are employed. They make money for writers, publishers and the manufacturers whose products are featured, but they do not succeed unless they entertain their readers at the same time.

It is vital, therefore, that the language used by each magazine strikes the right note. It must create a sense of rapport with the readership. It would be no use at all to address the readers of *Kerrang* (heavy metal fans) in the manner expected by readers of *Woman's Own* (women of twenty-five and upwards, usually with a family). Particularly at the youth end of the market, any inappropriate or old-fashioned terms would affect the magazine's credibility (unless used tongue-in-cheek). Some of the magazines clearly see themselves as style-setters who create taste, but they must also reflect style. How can language reflect 'style' in its wider sense? What is style anyway?

Style

'Style' is a difficult word to define. Most words are capable of carrying various interpretations, but this is a particularly slippery one. In its most 'neutral' sense it is impossible not to display style in the same way as it is impossible not to communicate. This is true of visual or audio style as well as style in speech or writing. Whenever we select clothes or words and put them together we will be exhibiting some sort of style, maybe unique to ourselves.

In another more widely accepted meaning of the word, style is 'a coherent, recurring set of expected features' which identify the style of an individual or a larger recognisable group. This could be punk, yuppie or hippy in clothes, or a 'legal' or 'formal' style in writing.

Yet another way the word 'style' is used is to imply something desirable in itself: 'She has real style' or 'Your essays so far lack a sense of style.' In this sense, whether applied to language or to appearance, it is a term of approbation.

The way the word 'style' is used in this chapter is bound to slide about between these various meanings. This shouldn't cause any problem, as it doesn't in real life (that is, outside the pages of this book). We will know from the context what is meant. A definition which holds good in all situations is impossible to achieve. What we are interested in looking at is how magazines which exist to inform us about styles in other areas of life try to create a language style (as in 'set of recurring features') which appeals to and suits their audience and is therefore 'appropriate'.

When any publication strives to achieve this appropriate style or specific voice for itself, it has to aim for consistency throughout. Many different writers may contribute to it, but somehow the style has to be recognisable as that of that particular publication. In order to do this it creates a 'house style'. In order to accomplish this many newspapers, magazines and periodicals produce guidelines for their writers in the form of style sheets which outline the features they hope will identify their particular house style. Here are a couple of hints from the style-sheet of *The Economist*, which is aimed at an educated audience interested in current affairs:

> Do not be stuffy or pompous. Use the language of everyday speech, not that of spokesmen, lawyers or bureaucrats. (So prefer let to permit, people to persons, colleague to peer, way out to exit, present to gift, rich to wealthy.) You can avoid offending women without using chairperson, humankind and Ms. Prefer chairman (for a man) or in the chair, mankind, so long as the context is not offensive, and the precision of Mrs. and Miss whenever you can.
>
> Do not be too chatty. The sentence 'So far, so good' neither informs nor amuses. It irritates. So do 'Surprise, surprise' 'Ho ho' etc.
>
> *The Economist*

Perhaps on the basis of these guidelines alone you could make some further assumptions about the audience of *The Economist*. As language students you should be able to make some comments on the attitude to language shown.

A style to suit the audience

Many different sorts of magazines and periodicals produce style sheets. It would be particularly interesting to find those issued by publications in which a conscious effort appears to have been made to produce a house style for a very specific audience in terms of age. Here is an example:

> DON'T MENTION TIFFANY ...
>
> If you saw The Chart Show a few weeks back you might have spotted an extremely pretty young American lady called Tracie Spencer warbling a splendid ditty called Symptoms Of True Love. Apart from having a v. good voice and writing her own songs, there's another astounding fact about young Trace – she is only 12!!! And what's more it drives her a bit potty when people go on about her age. It also drives her a bit potty when people ask her what she thinks of Tiff 'n' Debs. She always wanted to sing. "I realised when I was three. I used to sing with the record player, especially to Billie Holliday records. Yeah, I guess that was kinda sophisticated for a three-year-old." She shot to fame in her native USA when she won the finals of a telly programme called Star Search which is rather like Bob Says Opportunity Knocks. "I was 11 at the time, and I sang How Will I Know? by Whitney Houston. The other finalist was only five." Tracie's dad is a singer and he started at the age of 12 too. She plans to carry on her studies so she can go to college to study drama. "I'd

really like to act when I'm older. I'd either like to be in something like The Cosby Show, or a horror film, like A Nightmare On Elm Street – they're my favourites." Her favourite singer is Whitney Houston, her favourite film star is Patrick Swayze. She collects Cabbage Patch and Barbie dolls and likes going to the movies and swimming.

Just Seventeen

At a glance it can be seen that this is aimed at a different audience from that of *The Economist*! The readership of this magazine is clearly young. Its title is *Just Seventeen*, although we suspect the average age of the readers is lower. This particular item is taken from a double-page spread which contained eight such 'news' pieces giving information about pop stars (sic), films and fashion. Much of this information probably arrived at the *Just Seventeen* offices in the form of press information handouts or other publicity material. The house style of the magazine must be imposed upon it, and this is a fairly typical example.

So, what are the distinctive features of *Just Seventeen* house style as revealed in this short extract? (By the time you are reading this you will probably need scholarly 'footnote' style information to inform you that Tiffany and Debbie Gibson were young American singers who were high in the charts in summer 1988. They were part of a wave of mid-teenage female solo vocal artists and obviously Tracie Spencer aspires to join them.) We'll submit this text to the basic questions:

Who is this written for?
Audience: young people interested in pop music

What is it written for?
Purpose(s): to inform (about Tracie Spencer) – 'to publicise her' might be more specific.
To entertain – the subject of the piece is not so well known that you would read on regardless.

How does the writer sound?
Tone: apparently direct and chatty, but also rather amused and detached (patronising?)

What we now have to show is how this tone is created. There is a direct, conversational approach achieved in several ways: the reader is directly addressed in the second person: 'Don't mention Tiffany', 'If you saw … ' There is an appeal to a shared frame of reference: the writer expects the reader to know who 'Tiff 'n' Debs' are. There is an attempt to establish the immediacy of a conversational tone through speech rhythms: 'And what's more', 'Tiff 'n' Debs'. There are colloquial expressions such as 'spotted' and 'telly' and abbreviations which appear in speech: 'Trace', 'Tiff' and 'Debs'. There is one other abbreviation though, which only appears in writing, and that is 'v. good', usually only to be found in school exercise books, which might strike a chord with the teenage readership and emphasise that 'Trace' herself is only a schoolgirl.

These points show some of the ways in which the familiar, chatty, direct tone is established. But there is something else going on here. There is a detachment in the style which shows that the writer of this piece is not exactly convinced of Tracie's talents, and is having a laugh ('giggle' might be more precise) at her expense. How is this conveyed?

The answer to this seems to be that it is done mainly through the lexis (word choice). There are several words and phrases here which do not belong to a familiar, chatty, colloquial register. When did you last hear anyone say 'warbling a splendid ditty' (more typical of Edwardian music hall) or anyone under thirty say 'drives her potty', which is from altogether another generation's slang?

The clichés in this extract also come thick and fast: 'shot to fame', 'native USA', 'astounding fact'. There is liberal use of exclamation marks and of intensifiers and positive modifiers: 'extremely', 'splendid', 'astounding'. These are used so close together that a tone of sarcasm or irony is established. Irony operates by making the readers aware that the writer's real point of view is not the same as the apparent one.

Surely the effect of this self-conscious exaggeration is to alert the reader that the writer – and possibly *Just Seventeen* – does not take 'young Trace' very seriously. Certainly not as seriously as she takes herself – listening to Billie Holliday at the age of three!

You will probably have noticed that about half-way through this piece the features that mark the house style seem to fade and what we are left with is a relatively unadorned, directly informative series of statements: 'Tracie's dad is a singer', 'She plans to carry on', 'Her favourite singer is ... ', 'She collects ... ' These sound much more like a straight 'lift' from a press handout, but there is so little attempt to disguise it that the effect is to add to the generally amused air the piece maintains towards its subject. It rather implies that 'young Trace' is being manufactured, packaged and then sold. *Just Seventeen* is part of this process, so it cannot afford to be too directly critical. The selection of items which are chosen to be included in this final section emphasises her youth and possibly a certain British detachment from the American scene: 'The other finalist was only five', 'She collects Cabbage Patch and Barbie dolls.'

Just how is this style, which uses a mixture of outdated phrases and old slang terms, features of teenage writing such as 'v. good' and '!!!' and obvious show-biz cliché, going to appeal to the readers of *Just Seventeen*? Some of it is hardly the language they themselves would use, but that is probably the point. Teenage current slang varies from group to group and region to region and is 'in' and 'out' of the vocabulary so quickly that to try to reproduce it accurately would be impossible and produce more discordant notes. Nothing is worse than trying to sound trendy and failing. Therefore the magazine creates a style which is lively and rather disconcerting in its switches of tone but which very quickly becomes recognisable to regular readers. It changes its 'in' words frequently but they are particular to the magazine, and in its self-conscious use of slang terms which are so obviously out of date it avoids looking as if it is trying to keep up.

A glance at another issue of the same magazine produces these similarly 'fossilised' expressions: 'chinwag', 'slightly squiffy', 'give you a tinkle', 'girlies', 'chappie', 'easy-peasy', 'jammy young lass', 'silly old sausage' and 'ne'er do well kind of chap'. Mixed in with these dated terms are some coinings (made-up words): 'hunkster', 'songstrel' (in the phrase 'crinkly old songstrel', applied to Barbra Streisand.) There are also some conscious archaisms – 'simple, is it not?' – and abbreviations – 'list of celebs' – or even elongations – 'sperlendid' – again mirroring speech.

Sometimes this mix is funny, sometimes it seems formulaic, as it possibly is in the case of the item we looked at, where it may have been employed to 'customise' an information or press handout. If it appeals to you, you probably find the mix of styles lively and amusing; if it doesn't, you probably find it irritating and mannered. That is part of style – you like it or you don't. At the time of writing this is a very successful magazine. This is of course because of its photographs of and interviews with famous stars as well as its written style, but that is true of most magazines of this type. They use the popular stars as much as they are used by them. At the time of writing, anything with Kylie Minogue or Jason Donovan on the cover is guaranteed a large sale. At the time of reading you may well be saying 'Jason who?' But *Just Seventeen*'s success suggests that they have – for the moment – got the style right.

Try to produce a style sheet, along the lines of the one for *The Economist*, which would help writers to achieve this 'right style'.

The next extract is also about pop (or rock) musicians. It is the opening of a longer, feature article from a magazine called *Q* aimed at an older, richer, altogether more sophisticated audience than that of *Just Seventeen*. It is a signed article by a particular writer (who is also associate director of the magazine). The introduction, however, is apparently anonymous. It is the 'voice' of the magazine setting the scene:

I'm with the band ...

The lights are bright and there are muffled sounds of merriment. Large, hairy creatures are carrying amplifiers. People in satin jackets are quaffing free drinks. There are men in suits with metal briefcases and girls with very long legs. And Bowie's in there, apparently. And George Michael and someone who used to be in the Belle Stars. Quick, the door's open – and Paul Du Noyer has one of those cards that says Access All Areas ...

In a sense it's like The Lion, The Witch And The Wardrobe. On this side is Reality, the world as we know it. Whereas on that side, through a small, obscure opening ... there lies an enchanted land. Outside of time, in another dimension. On that side is a country with its own traditions, customs and history; with its own hierarchies and intrigues, special pleasures and mysterious terrors. There you will find gardens of delight, and dungeons that have never known daylight. Kingly courts, there are, with courtiers and courtesans, loyal lieutenants and knavish ne'er-do-wells, hireling armies, and powerful wizards whose gifts can only be guessed at. There are serfs who toil, and parasites who do not; there are beggars at the gates, and strangers with elixirs for purchase. There is bustle and there is leisure, preening pomp and humiliating self-abasement.

All human life is there, and other kinds as well.

Step, if you will, through the rear of the Wardrobe. Let us enter that place that travellers have come to call ... Backstage.

This seems to be a rather different piece of writing. Let's look more closely:

◆ What does the title of the piece refer to? How does it help to set the scene?
◆ We noticed that the (anonymous) writer of the *Just Seventeen* item made his/her (the magazine's?) view of 'young Trace' pretty clear: a distance was kept between the writer and subject. Do you think a similar stance is being taken here in the introduction to this article? Are any words being used in a comparable fashion to 'warbling a ditty' for instance?
◆ How much do you already have to know about the 'rock scene' for this to make much sense, and what is the effect of this appeal to shared references, particularly at the beginning of a text?
◆ Why do you think the writer has chosen the tense he has for the verbs in the introduction? (Which tense is it?)
◆ Are there any attempts to adopt a chatty, speech-like tone?

When we come to the article itself, there is a noticeable change in style. There seems to be a distinct shift in tone to something more sophisticated, although the abruptness of this is masked by a conversational opening: 'In a sense'. After this it becomes clear that this is written for a different audience from *Just Seventeen*'s. Again the reader has to understand the references, but they are no longer to the world of rock music. The opening is an extended metaphor based on a famous children's book, and also perhaps to the world of fantasy games which might be familiar to many of the magazine's readers. How important is it that the reader shares these references?

The first thing to comment on is word choice. There are a lot of pre-modified nouns. Do these nominal groups fall into any particular groupings?

Then there's word order to consider. Occasionally this is not what you'd expect from a piece of modern journalistic prose. What do the inversions remind you of? There are other expressions which give the extract a rather old-fashioned, formal tone at times. Which are they?

Rhythm is important in this piece. Sentences (both major and minor) have been very carefully constructed. Find as many examples as you can of balance in a sentence, where there appear to be two equal parts (the technical term for this is antithesis). You might then look for a similar balancing within each half. What effects does this careful patterning produce?

Overall, the impression is literary. But let's not lose sight of what is actually being described here, albeit metaphorically. The article is really about what it's like to be backstage at a rock concert. These 'mythical' creatures are actually rock stars and their various hangers-on. Where is this reality most clearly hinted at? The contrast between this grand fantastical opening and what we sense Paul Du Noyer is going on to describe is humorous, but also has the effect of distancing him from the world of the superstars he's describing. He's not over-awed, he can put them in their place with words: the writer's power. Perhaps the techniques are not so different from *Just Seventeen*'s after all; it's the different audiences which make for the apparent contrast.

Different audiences

Both the previous texts were concerned with rock/pop music, and were from magazines which devote a lot of space to this area. The next piece is from a magazine with different concerns, and aimed at a different audience. It is from *Woman's World*, whose title clearly indicates the section of the population it is aimed at (more than can be said for a journal called *Q.*) Within this section it appears to be fairly middle of the road. It is not as stylish or sophisticated as *Cosmopolitan*, for example, but its shiny pages and general presentation (and its price) suggest that it does not see itself at the bottom end of the market either. The article we are going to look at is the one which almost literally establishes the 'voice' of the magazine. It comes right at the beginning, and is a message from the editor.

Welcome to our world!

Well, what a summer this has turned out to be. I expect you're as pale as I am, wondering how it is that the rest of the world appears to be permanently bronzed. No? I didn't think so, really. If, as I suspect, you're one of *them*, you will (I hope) be pleased to observe that this month I've selflessly included a post-tan plan, written by Jackie King, on page 23, so you can continue to swan around for as long as possible making people like me more envious.

Some of us, you see, haven't even planned a holiday yet, and have finally felt compelled – oh, the shame of it – to resort to a sunbed. I always swore nothing short of relocation to Siberia would induce me to use one of these things, but this year the yearning to have brown legs finally got to me.

So it was with some trepidation that I went along, handed over my money, and lay on a Perspex slab in a cramped little room, convinced I'd just paid to get cancer. I was relieved to note that the overhead canopy was a good three feet above me, and assumed this to be a very sensible precaution taken by the people who install them.

After three sessions I had to admit to no visible difference, as they say, so I gave up this particular sunbed centre and moved to another, grumbling to anyone who would listen about inefficient, clapped-out-equipment. This time I booked a whole course, had my first session in another matchbox-size cubicle – and still resembled a block of lard at the end of it.

Thinking by now that a long weekend in Trinidad would be cheaper, I nonetheless persevered, and this time shared a double cubicle.

Undressed, lay on slab, put card in slot, awaited results. "Excuse me," enquired my companion, "have you used a sunbed before? Do you know you're supposed to press the button marked 'down' – it will lower the canopy for maximum effect."

Ever felt a dumbo? My one consolation is that I could have spent the entire course in the single cubicle and been none the wiser – or browner – at the end of it.

I was going to draw your attention in greater detail to this month's feature *Could You Own Up To The Lies You Tell?* but, as I seem to have run out of space, can I just say I would love to hear from you about any whoppers you've ever told/been told. I'll publish the best (anonymously, if you prefer). Have a fun month!

Woman's World

Having read that, do you have any clearer notion of who this magazine expects its readers to be? Invent a possible contents page, including the articles you think it might contain.

One of the words which may come most readily to mind to describe this style is 'chatty'. It may not be a very technical term, but it describes one of the effects the writer is aiming for. How is she trying to give the impression that this is a spoken conversation between herself and her readers? There are several features to look at in relation to this:

Types of sentence A mainly informative piece would consist largely of statements. An attempt to create a feeling of interaction, of speaker/listener rather than writer/reader usually involves varying the sentence types. What variation do we have here?

Pronouns Large parts of conversation are usually conducted in the first and second person. We refer to ourselves a lot (I/we) and address the other person directly (you). There is no danger that it will not be clear who these pronouns are referring to. Of course the writer doesn't know exactly whom she is addressing here, but addressing the audience directly always creates some kind of relationship between addresser and addressee. How are pronouns used in this piece? What is the effect of the italicised 'them' in the first paragraph?

Anecdote Telling personal stories is characteristic of talk. As we tell our audience what happened to us we tend to embroider our narrative. We select and shape events, we exaggerate to make an immediate impact. We make attempts to be funny. Can you find examples of these here? In connection with this storytelling element you could also look at the verbs, and consider the mixture of tenses.

Slang and colloquial expressions These are more common in informal speech. We tend to use slang expressions with people we feel comfortable with. In many cases using the same expressions as our friends creates a sense of group identity. Of course, as we have already seen, these words are often used in written English, but usually to give the impression of informality. What slang phrases are used here? Do they come from a particular type or generation of slang? Are they in current use?

But of course, this is not an example of direct speech. Having employed some of these techniques to create the impression of direct formal address, are there any elements in the language which strike you as coming from a different register? More formal vocabulary perhaps? Are there examples within the passage of a more literary style? Or to forms which only occur in writing? If so, how do they affect the predominant air of informality? Do they clash, or are they a predictable and familiar mix? Despite the attempts at chattiness, could this only be an example of written language? All in all, how successful do you think this article is in establishing a personal voice, a familiarity of approach? If this sets the tone for the magazine, what do you think will follow?

On page 124 is another example taken from a different type of magazine. Write a description of the ways language is being used in it, taking as your starting points the basic questions

What is language being used for?   and
Who is it addressing?

As you can see, we have cheated a bit: there are two very distinct styles ... or perhaps they aren't so distinct. You might look to see if attempts have been made to integrate the two.

TRAVEL TIPS

HANDY HINTS FOR OVERSEAS TRAVELLERS

KIDS ON HOLIDAY-
TIME OFF
WITHOUT TEARS

BY CAROLINE BUCHANAN

YOU'VE BEEN AND GONE AND DONE IT. YOU'VE TAKEN THE BOLD, BRAVE STEP OF BOOKING A HOLIDAY WITH YOUR SMALL CHILDREN. AND YOU CAN'T HELP FEELING YOU MUST HAVE GONE OFF YOUR ROCKER - PROOF THAT A BREAK IS DESPERATELY NEEDED! YOU KNOW THAT THE KIDS, EVEN THE BABY, ARE GOING TO HAVE A WONDERFUL TIME WITH BUCKETS AND SPADES, AND FIZZY LEMONADES, BUT SUDDENLY THE PANIC SETS IN. HOW ON EARTH ARE YOU GOING TO MANAGE TO TAKE VERY YOUNG CHILDREN ABROAD? WELL, HAVE NO FEAR, FOR WHEN YOU'VE READ OUR TIPS FOR TIME OFF WITHOUT TEARS, YOU CAN SIGH WITH RELIEF AND START TO LOOK FORWARD TO IT ALL.

PLANNING AHEAD

1. At least two months before departure date, check with your doctor on any vaccinations you and your family may need. Immunisations against typhoid, cholera and yellow fever aren't recommended for babies under 12 months, so unless they've all had their first birthday, avoid any countries requiring them. Hopefully your youngest has already started a course of immunisation against diptheria, tetanus and polio.

2. Make sure the kids either have a passport of their own, or are firmly installed in yours.

3. Organise medical insurance. It's not expensive, and is worth every single penny. Don't try and do without – it's madness. Try to make sure the policy will include somebody who can talk to you in English.

4. Talk to your GP about any specialist needs your children may have. And find out the CHEMICAL, rather than the brand name of any prescription drugs you and your family use in case you need to get extra supplies while away.

5. Keep a notepad and pen handy, so any urgent holiday needs that spring to mind from now on can be written down immediately.

6. Don't forget your own needs. I've heard many a story of families who arrive at their destination with all their requirements organised brilliantly by Mum – only to find that in the supreme care of her family, she's forgotten to pack all her own clothes.

7. A trip to the dentist is a very good idea. You don't want anyone to be suffering with toothache on the beach.

More pieces of rock

Finally, because they're so outrageous, and to make it easy for you, we return to the world of magazines aimed at young people interested in popular music and include some extracts for you to analyse on your own. As we said at the beginning, all journals and magazines deliberately adopt a style they feel is appropriate to their audience, and to the image they wish to project. Some styles appear more discreet, more neutral, more formal than others, but the style will be deliberately chosen and sustained just as much as the sort which shouts from the page. Discreet and formal these examples aren't. A more technical way of putting it might be to say that 'language is foregrounded'. Have fun!

Yes, snorkellers, it's quite a sensation! Freddie and Monserrat Caballé have now made a whole LP of snoot "opera" tunes! And they've even invited *Bitz* over to Barcelona to watch them "perform" for the King of Spain! Its quite an occasion …

Buenos dias viewers! *Bitz* is in Barcelona! Yes! Barcelona, the city that never sleeps! The city of cathedrals! Of moustaches! Of Flamenco! Of lots of chubby opera singers! And today it is the very nerve centre of the universe because it is today that the Olympic flag arrives from Seoul to symbolise the beginning of the "build up" to 1992 – when the next Olympics will be held in this very place! Which is precisely why all of Barcelona's inhabitants have gone absolutely stark staring mad! They're also rather excited for tonight there is to be an open air "live" extravaganza, appropriately dubbed "La Nit"(!), the likes of which has never been seen before. And His Royal Highness Lord Lucan of Mercury, undoubtedly the most famous person ever in the history of rock will be "topping" the "bill" along with his portly chum Monserrat Caballé. And, of course, being a regular visitor to *Bitz*'s domain he was most anxious that *Bitz* should be there to witness him in his hour of glory.

In actual fact it's all rather a cunning wheeze because "Barcelona" by happy coincidence also happens to be the title of Freddie and Monserrat's new LP (hence the name). What a clever notion it is! And how very fortunate! And the people of Spain have not missed the importance of this sentiment because practically the whole city (i.e. 150,000 people) including His Majesty Juan Carlos The King Of Spain who is only marginally less famous than Freddie, has gathered in this glorious site that is Montjiuch Park to pay homage to this newly coupled singing sensation.

It's all a bit boring for a while. First of all there's a snoozesome "classical" bit featuring an 80-"piece" orchestra and about 80 million choir persons. Then Eddy Grant arrives and announces that it's "time to partee!!" at which point The King and his good lady wife (i.e. the queen) promptly leave. Then there's all sorts of second-raters such as Spandau Ballet and Suzanne Vega and then at long last comes the moment the whole of Spain has been waiting for!

"*Ledeez hand gentlemans, Monserrat Caballé and Lord Lucan of Mercury!!!!!*" Without further a "do" His Freddiness and the stout trout flounce onto the stage, holding hands and grinning from ear to ear. It is truly a sight. Together, with the aid of a 36-piece orchestra and 300 (or thereabouts) backing singers they storm the very barricades of rock! They bluster their way through a selection of "tracks" from their half pop/half opera LP concluding with a furiously patriotic rendition of their new single "Barcelona" quite a lot and it's suddenly all over ...

But not for long, because the very next day in London *Bitz* is invited to attend a v. exclusive and swank lunch with Freddie and Sir Monserrat. Perhaps *Bitz* could perchance to nibble upon a tender morsel at the same table as them! But wait! *Bitz* can hardly believe it's luck for here comes Sir Freddie making his way purposefully towards *Bitz* all of his own accord! This is not to be taken lightly for it is a once in a lifetime happener! And here is that historic conversation in "full" ...

Smash Hits

Having parted company with the Mary Chain, ALAN MCGEE has spent the last few months regenerating his Creation label, launching a new, major-monied, outlet, Elevation, and flying yet again in the face of indie orthodoxy by raiding the Virgin Megastore for the personnel of his latest brainwave. Baby Amphetamine. DANNY KELLY helps keep the fanzine hordes at bay.

"Right now, the whole of pop, Creation included, needs a good kick up the arse! And that's what Baby Amphetamine is – a good kick up the arse for Creation buyers, for Radio One producers, for everyone."

In a taproom near his Clerkenwell command bunker, Alan McGee's face is threatening to match the natural blood-orange tint of his hair. Lager is partly responsible for this evening's fetching facial hue, but mostly it's the stir caused by the 41st single released by his brainchild and passion, Creation Records.

Being poppy hip-hop (as opposed to acne angst jangle) and credited to a group flagrantly and artificially cobbled together by McGee himself, the record has left the self-appointed guardians of indie pop grasping for the six-pack of smelling salts.

Like the man said – 'Chernobyl Baby (Who Needs The Government)', by Baby Amphetamine, is a good kick up the arse! ...

Controversy, a nose for a good scam, and a thirst for new ways out of the indie poverty trap have been Alan McGee's edges.

It was those qualities that caused him to demonstrate, with his early Creation releases, that vivid independent life was possible outside the increasingly institutionalised walls of Rough Trade, Factory and Mute; it was those instincts that persuaded him to nurture the confrontatory sulk-rock of four zitty Glasgow youths 'till it was ready to be unleashed on the world as the awesome sonic barrage of The Jesus And Mary Chain; and it's those impulses that enable him to once again be setting the pace. Not just with the Baby Amphetamine hoopla, but with the WEA-funded setting up of Elevation Records.

New Musical Express

Chapter 13
Literature

What is literature?

What oft was thought but ne'er so well expressed

Organised violence done on language

The best words in the best order

Language at full stretch

A selection of language really used by men

The promotion of human awareness; awareness of the possibilities of life

Of all the varieties of language use, the most difficult to define is literature. Most attempts to arrive at a watertight definition fail miserably. In doing so, they cover certain well-worn territory. The following dialogue – like literature, based on reality but newly created – attempts to go over this ground at breakneck speed:

> 'What's so special about literature?'
> 'It's written by the best and most serious writers.'
> 'Who says? And what are they using their skill for anyway?'
> 'To express what we all feel.'
> 'Just like pop songs!'
> 'No; literature is much more flexible and unpredictable.'
> 'Oh, then it's more like adverts – original, amusing?'
> 'Well, no ... ads are limited in purpose – they just want to sell something.'
> 'Don't writers want to sell their books?'
> 'Yes, but unless they're Jeffrey Archer, they want to do more than that. They want to persuade, inform, entertain, move you ... '
> 'If they do so many things, what on earth do they have in common?'
> 'That they do it well!'
> 'I've heard that one before. If no-one can tell me exactly what it is, how can you expect me to tackle it?'

Well, clearly the medium of literature is language, so it can be analysed using the methods we have suggested. However, it seems also to be something more, or different; at once ordinary and extraordinary. It is because of this that descriptions as various as 'organised violence done on ordinary speech' and 'what oft was thought but ne'er so well expressed' can both be seen as valid.

Which description would best fit the following examples?

> As Gregor Samsa awoke one morning from uneasy dreams, he found himself transformed in his bed into a gigantic insect.
>
> *Franz Kafka*

If they be so, they are two so
As stiff twin compasses are two,
Thy soul the fixed foot makes no show
To move, but doth it th'other do.

John Donne

Her husband's tastes rubbed off on her soft, moist moral
surface and the couple lived in an atmosphere of novelty in
which, occasionally, the accommodating wife encountered the
fresh sensation of being in want of her dinner.

Henry James

Darkling I listen; and for many a time
I have been half in love with easeful Death,
Called him soft names in many a mused rhyme,
To take into the air my quiet breath.

John Keats

Watchwords

watch the words
watch words the
watchword is
watch words are
sly as boots
ifyoutakeyoureyesoffthemforaminute

                                  up
and   they're   and
    away
                              allover
       the
                                place

Roger McGough

That's my last Duchess painted on the wall,
Looking as if she were alive. I call
That piece a wonder, now, Fra Pandolf's hands
Worked busily a day, and there she stands
Will't please you sit and look at her? I said.

Robert Browning

Know then thyself, presume not God to scan,
The proper study of mankind is man.
Placed on this isthmus of a middle state,
A being darkly wise and rudely great.

Alexander Pope

Looking at these, we might well sympathise with the bewilderment of 'Baffled' on page 127! Why are all these under the umbrella of literature? What is distinctive about literature?

Clearly, all literary works do not have the same, easily identifiable aim: they are not reporting news, or informing experts, or selling baked beans. They do not relate to the world in those functional sorts of ways, because they create their own world. Each is a unique entity. Just as a painter uses paint to create a new image, a writer uses words to create a text. It may well relate to reality (the model landscape/ situation), but it is a new thing.

This new thing has not been created randomly or pointlessly. An important thing to recognise about literary works is just how carefully and consciously they are crafted. Words are the raw material of literature and literary writers stretch them to their limits.

Some writers are overtly experimental: others less obviously so, but all are selecting and shaping language. Some write within a familiar traditional form, such as the sonnet or rhyming couplet in poetry, or the epistolary form of the novel (one which is mainly composed of letters between the characters). Others aim for a more naturalistic style, closer to 'a selection of language really used by men.' For example, a playwright or novelist may write a dialogue which is naturalistic – i.e. it employs colloquialism, dialect words and so on – but this dialogue is very different from spontaneous speech. It will contain no non-fluency features, it will probably be less repetitious and more dramatic than ordinary speech. The art is in making the unnatural appear natural.

Look at this example of dialogue from a recent novel. In what ways is it like and unlike spontaneous conversation?

'Red cabbage?' asked Shirley.

'Red cabbage? Red cabbage? I thought it was sprouts. We always have sprouts.' An angry interjection from the oldest Mrs Harper.

'It's sprouts as well,' said Shirley. 'I thought I'd do some red cabbage too. As a change.'

'He won't like it. He won't want any. He likes his red cabbage pickled.' So pursued the oldest Mrs Harper. Her husband smiled and nodded.

'Yes,' mused Uncle Fred, 'families aren't what they were. It's all this moving around the country. Thank you, Shirley, that's grand. By the way, Brian asked me to London again, but I thought I'd wait till the weather's better.'

'All what moving about the country?' asked Cliff, largely to avert further discussion of sprouts and red cabbage, which he could see was imminent from the suspicious manner in which his mother was turning over the vegetables on her heaped plate.

'Oh, all this moving around for work.'

'Go on,' said Steve. 'No one moves round here. They stick fast, round here. Never been south of Nottingham, half the folks round here.'

'I think it's nice for the young folks to get out,' said Fred. 'I always encouraged my Brian. I didn't want to stand in his way.'

Margaret Drabble: The Radiant Way

Other forms of literature make no attempt to appear natural – in fact they deliberately surprise the readers' expectations. They might use familiar words in unfamiliar ways as e. e. cummings does, or they might coin new words as Gerard Manley Hopkins does. Perhaps we expect poets to use deviant language, but prose writers like James Joyce do it too.

This sort of literature draws attention to (or foregrounds) its language use, so it's probably easier to talk about. Nevertheless, other styles of literature, whose features of language are less immediately striking, are no less considered. A similar process of word choice and structuring will have been gone through. Jane Austen redrafted her novels every bit as scrupulously as William Blake did his poems. These, like all writers, selected the form of words most appropriate to their purposes.

What is the purpose of a literary text?

The answer to this question is that it is not as immediately identifiable as the purposes of some other types of text. Claims that all literary texts have the same purpose in the way that all advertisements do, are untenable. What it is often possible to do, within any one literary text, is to recognise a primary aim.

Every analysis of a literary text needs to try to decide how it affects the reader. Start with your subjective response. Ask yourself whether this text

- – seems to be affecting your emotions. Which ones?
- – seems to be telling you what to think.
- – seems to be making you laugh.
- – seems to be drawing a picture – evoking an atmosphere.

These are just some possibilities. Whatever your impression is, jot it down.

Now ask yourself, as you look again at the text, how the writer has made you feel/think/laugh/see. It is doing the writer less than justice if you assume that the effect is a happy accident. A literary writer's skill in finding the right words with the right connotations, the right sounds in the right combinations are what enables them to fuse meaning and form, when they are successful. Try very hard not to regard literary forms and language use as something in your way but rather as the writer's tools for making you, the reader, respond.

Since it is not feasible to analyse a complete novel or play in all its complexity, you are only likely to look at a representative passage. Similarly, you are more likely to be given a short poem than an epic one. What you need to do, whatever text you are presented with, is, as always, to see what is there and deduce something intelligent about why it is there. Your response is your best clue to the why.

We have decided, for the sake of clarity, that it might be best to look one by one at some of the major effects that literature provokes. Our list is a long way from being all-inclusive but some simplification is necessary for the sake of making sense of literary texts. We have decided to look at the following:

Establishing a voice/point of view
Evoking an atmosphere
Sending a message
Making people laugh and cry.

Chapter 14

Establishing voice and point of view

A good place to look for the establishment of voice is at the beginning of a novel. Look at the opening of *Midnight's Children* by Salman Rushdie, which we referred to in Section One:

> I was born in the city of Bombay once upon a time. No, that won't do, there's no getting away from the date: I was born in Dr. Narlikar's nursing home on August 15th 1947. And the time?
>
> The time matters too. Well then, at night. No, it's important to be more ... On the stroke of midnight as a matter of fact. Clock hands joined hands in respectful greeting as I came. Oh, spell it out, spell it out: at the precise instant of India's arrival at independence, I tumbled forth into the world. There were gasps. And, outside the window, fireworks and crowds. A few seconds later, my father broke his big toe; but his accident was a mere trifle when set beside what had befallen me in that benighted moment, because thanks to the occult tyrannies of those blandly saluting clocks, I had been mysteriously handcuffed to history, my destinies indissolubly chained to those of my country. For the next three decades there was to be no escape. Soothsayers had prophesied me; newspapers celebrated my arrival; politicos ratified my authenticity. I was left entirely without a say in the matter. I, Salleem Sinai, later variously called Snotnose, Stainface, Baldy, Sniffer, Buddha and even Piece-of-the-Moon had become heavily embroiled in Fate – at the best of times a dangerous sort of involvement. And I couldn't even wipe my own nose at the time.
>
> *Salman Rushdie: Midnight's Children*

❖ Who is telling the story?
❖ What are you able to deduce about the narrator so far? For example, would you regard him as a reliable informant? Does he strike you as modest or conceited?
❖ Is his tone consistent throughout? If not, where do the shifts occur?
❖ Is the passage amusing?
❖ Is it metaphorical?

Having considered the passage yourself, look at our analysis:

The writer of this opening clearly wishes to establish his central character, who is also the narrator, very strongly from the outset. He also wishes to stress the coincidence of the character's birth with the birth of a new nation: the moment of India's independence. This coincidence profoundly affected the rest of his life. The interplay of the personal and the historical perspectives is evident in the language of the whole paragraph.

There is an obvious attempt, almost literally, to establish the character's voice. Of the first three sentences, three are minor or incomplete, which in this context suggests speech. They read like utterances in one half of a conversation, two beginning with 'No' and one with 'Well then'. One, a question, appears to be an answer to a question. There are other expressions which sound as if he's talking to himself, 'spell it out, spell it out'. Gradually the 'I' becomes more specific as if the information is reluctantly given – so the evasive story-telling technique 'once upon a time' in sentence one finally becomes 'at the precise instant' in sentence nine. The birth is referred to four times; 'I was born' (twice), 'I came', and 'I tumbled forth'. Details of time and place are added, although the metaphorical 'clock hands joined hands ... ' seems like further prevarication, and the final announcement is delayed by a long adverbial phrase 'at the precise instant'.

Having established a rather colloquial tone in the opening sentences, the tenth builds on the note hinted at in the 'clock hands ... respectful greeting'. The first part of the sentence is the incongruous and rather ridiculous information that his father broke his toe, but the second, much longer section after the semi-colon includes the unusual collocations of 'occult tyrannies', and 'blandly saluting clocks' alongside the more familiar, hyperbolic idiom of 'benighted moment' and the mixed metaphor 'destinies indissolubly chained'. The magical and political significance of the stroke of midnight is suggested by 'soothsayers had prophesied me', and 'politicoes ratified'. The moment was important, as further emphasised by words such as 'decades', 'destinies', and 'embroiled in fate' – but perhaps rather consciously important. Alongside this, the pathetic individual who 'couldn't even wipe [his] own nose', also came into existence. The contrast between the two is exploited for humour, and also for irony. The writer has established a central character (and narrator) who is humorous, self-conscious, articulate and reflective.

Here is another first person opening, from Doris Lessing's *The Diaries of Jane Somers*:

> The first part is a summing-up of about four years. I was not keeping a diary. I wish I had. All I know is that I see everything differently now from how I did while I was living through it.
>
> My life until Freddie started to die was one thing, afterwards another. Until then I thought of myself as a nice person. Like everyone, just about, that I know. The people I work with, mainly. I know now that I did not ask myself what I was really like, but thought only about how other people judged me.
>
> When Freddie began to be so ill my first idea was: this is unfair. Unfair to me, I thought secretly. I partly knew he was dying, but went on as if he wasn't. That was not kind. He must have been lonely. I was proud of myself because I went on working through it all, "kept the money coming in" – well, I had to do that, with him not working. But I was thankful I was working because I had an excuse not to be with him in that *awfulness*. We did not have the sort of marriage where we talked about real things. I see that now. We were not really married. It was the marriage most people have these days, both sides trying for advantage. I always saw Freddie as one up.
>
> The word cancer was mentioned once. The doctors said to me, cancer, and *now* I see my reaction meant they would not go on to talk

about whether to tell him or not. I don't know if they told him. Whether he knew. I think he did. When they took him into hospital I went every day, but I sat there with a smile, how are you feeling? He looked dreadful. Yellow. Sharp bones under yellow skin. Like a boiling fowl. He was protecting me. *Now*, I can see it. Because I could not take it. Child-wife.

Doris Lessing: The Diaries of Jane Somers

❖ What can you tell about this person from the words she uses?
❖ What reason do you think the character had for writing her story?
❖ From what perspective is she telling her story? (Looking at the verbs might be helpful with both these questions.)
❖ This is written in the form of a diary entry. Is it convincing as diary style? What, if any, elements in it remind you of a diary?
❖ Of course, the fact is that this is the opening to a novel – what advantages does the diary form have?
❖ What have you learnt so far about the character, her attitudes and life?

By the time you have answered all these questions you should feel able to write a full analysis of the text.

A *different person*

The most straightforward way to establish a voice and point of view is to use the first person. However, narratives written in the third person can also stress one viewpoint or focus our attention upon one character. Omniscient narrators are not always objective. Consider the opening from the novel *The Life and Times of Michael K*:

> The first thing the midwife noticed about Michael K. when she helped him out of his mother into the world, was that he had a hare lip. The lip curled like a snail's foot, the nostril gaped. Obscuring the child for a moment from its mother, she prodded open the tiny bud of the mouth and was thankful to find the palate whole.
>
> To his mother she said, 'You should be happy, they bring good luck to the household.' But from the first Anna K. did not like the mouth that would not close and the living, pink flesh it bade to her. She shivered to think of what had been growing inside her all these months. The child could not suck from the breast and cried with hunger. She tried a bottle; when it could not suck from the bottle, she fed it with a tea-spoon, fretting with impatience when it coughed and spluttered and cried.
>
> 'It will close up as he gets older,' the midwife promised. However, the lip did not close, or did not close enough, nor did the nose come straight.

J. M. Coetzee: The Life and Times of Michael K

Now look at another passage about a mother and child:

> Daylight began to seep through the faded curtains. In the corner of the room a baby was crying. It made a thin, continuous bleating noise. A shape on the bed moved and a girl heaved herself up on one elbow. She remained still for a time, listening. At last she disentangled herself from the bed and crossed the room to the cot. She shook it viciously. The crying stopped. The girl stood still, staring down into the shadows in the cot. The room was cold, the light a matching harsh, watery grey. The backs of her skinny legs and arms glinted fish-belly white.
>
> The crying began again. She lifted the baby, holding it over her shoulder and began to pace the room. The noise stopped but she continued to pace mechanically, patting the baby's back rhythmically as she walked. She was very young, her body still thin and gawky as an adolescent's but with something pinched about it. She had not been allowed to flesh out into maturity. In the relentless dawn light her head was more of a skull than a face, the dark hollowness of eye sockets intensified by the dull glaze of her eyes and the smeared black mascara around them. Thin white skin was stretched taut over cheek and jawbone. She walked with face raised, like someone blind.

Jane Rogers: Separate Tracks

❖ How is the child presented? Compare this passage with the previous one.
❖ Consider the mother. Is she presented sympathetically? Look at adjectives and adverbs. The voice of verbs might also help.
❖ What effect does the description of the surroundings have? How does it relate to the characters? Look at the articles at the start of the text. Also, it might be helpful to notice the subjects of the verbs: are they objects, people or sounds?
❖ How is the relationship between mother and child portrayed?

Viewpoint in poetry

Presenting a viewpoint is not only achieved in prose. Many poems present the view/story and attitudes of a central character or persona. Some of them obviously establish a voice which is not the poet's own. Such a poem is the following:

An Irish Airman Foresees His Death

> I know that I shall meet my fate
> Somewhere among the clouds above;
> Those that I fight I do not hate,
> Those that I guard I do not love;
> My country is Kiltartan Cross,
> My countrymen Kiltartan's poor,
> No likely end could bring them loss
> Or leave them happier than before.
> Nor law, nor duty bade me fight,
> Nor public men, nor cheering crowds,
> A lonely impulse of delight

> Drove to this tumult in the clouds;
> I balanced all, brought all to mind,
> The years to come seemed waste of breath,
> A waste of breath the years behind
> In balance with this life, this death.

William Butler Yeats

Given that this is the voice of a man in wartime facing inevitable death, the tone of this poem is remarkably detached and matter of fact. How is this achieved?

There are a lot of statements which are brief and appear factual rather than subjective. The opening line 'I know that I shall meet my fate' is very different in emphasis from 'I expect that I ...', let alone 'I fear'. There then follows a series of one line statements offering no pause for argument, qualification of explanation. This voice knows his own mind!

He states that he has 'balanced all' and no hint is given in the poem that his balance is lost – surprisingly in view of his situation. The title and topic would lead us to anticipate an emotional, perhaps patriotic, perhaps heroic voice but as is often the case with poetry our expectations are confounded. With the striking exception of the lines in which he speaks of the 'impulse' which 'drove' him, the lexis is as neutral as possible. A more emotive voice could have employed 'protect' rather than 'guard'; 'home' rather than 'country', and both friends and enemies are reduced to the pronoun 'those'. Words such as 'hate', 'love' and 'duty', which in other contexts might seem highly charged, are here all preceded by negatives which bring them down to earth. The prospect of victory or defeat is coolly referred to as the 'likely end'.

He is equally unconcerned about his own end: his past and future are both dismissed as 'a waste of breath' and thus his death or survival is a matter of indifference to him. This indifference makes it difficult to pity or admire the airman – two emotions which most war poetry evokes in its readers.

One of the reasons why we do not engage with the airman is that his voice is not individualised. There are no colloquialisms, indications of accent or speech rhythms. Instead the voice is regular, formal – clipped even. A surprising number of the words are monosyllables and metre and rhyme are very regular. This creates an unemphatic, almost monotonous effect which is only disrupted by the stress on the first syllable of a line – 'Drove' – rather than the usual second. The repetition of phrases like 'Those that I' and 'waste of breath' and words like 'Kiltartan' and 'country' also contribute to the unremarkable sameness of the way he sees his life.

In sharp contrast to these impersonal descriptions are the more precise and emotive lines

> A lonely impulse of delight
> Drove to this tumult in the clouds;

'impulse' is not something we would associate with the man who 'balanced all', and although the impulse is a 'lonely' one the word 'lonely' also attaches itself to the airman himself. It is one of the very few adjectives in the poem, and certainly the only emotive one. Similarly, the abstract noun 'delight' is the only noun with unequivocally positive connotations. The word 'tumult' is unexpected, and unexpectedly precise. It is almost the exact opposite of 'balance', and yet this tumult was what attracted him.

We are intrigued by this individual, but he remains something of a mystery. In seeking for reasons to explain his lack of involvement with the conflict in which he is taking part we look again at the title of the poem. Perhaps the significant clue is the word 'Irish'. The reference to place is taken up again, this time more specifically, in line five, and reinforced by repetition in line six. In these lines his country and people are explicitly dissociated from any interest in the outcome of the war, and the connotations of words such as 'poor' and 'loss' imply that their lives are bleak and hopeless. This was his life too, until offered the chance of this one moment of 'delight', which is almost certain to be his last. There is irony in this, but also a deep sense of hopelessness.

Before we leave voice and viewpoint, we'd like you to look at two more poems. The first of these, *Porphyria's Lover* by Robert Browning, dramatically presents one viewpoint; the other, *Not Waving But Drowning* by Stevie Smith, switches from one voice to another for effect.

Porphyria's Lover

The rain set early in to-night,
The sullen wind was soon awake,
It tore the elm-tops down for spits,
And did its worst to vex the lake;
I listened with heart fit to break.
When glided in Porphyria; straight
She shut the cold out and the storm,
And kneeled and made the cheerless grate
Blaze up, and all the cottage warm;
Which done, she rose, and from her form
Withdrew the dripping cloak and shawl,
And laid her soiled gloves by, untied
Her hat and let the damp hair fall,
And, last, she sat down by my side
And called me. When no voice replied,
She put my arm about her waist,
And made her smooth white shoulder bare,
And all her yellow hair displaced,
And, stooping, made my cheek lie there,
And spread, o'er all, her yellow hair,
Murmuring how she loved me – she
Too weak, for all her heart's endeavour,
To set its struggling passions free
From pride, and vainer ties dissever,
And give herself to me forever.
But passion sometimes would prevail
Nor could to-night's gay feast restrain
A sudden though of one so pale
For love of her, and all in vain:
So, she was come through wind and rain.
Be sure I looked up at her eyes
Happy and proud; at last I knew
Porphyria worshipped me: surprise

Made my heart swell, and still it grew
While I debated what to do.
That moment she was mine, mine, fair,
Perfectly pure and good: I found
A thing to do, and all her hair
In one long yellow string I wound
Three times her little throat around,
And strangled her. No pain felt she;
I am quite sure she felt no pain.
As a shut bud that holds a bee,
I warily oped her lids: again
Laughed the blue eyes without a stain.
And I untightened next the tress
About her neck; her cheeks once more
Blushed bright beneath my burning kiss:
I propped her head up as before,
Only, this time my shoulder bore
Her head, which droops upon it still:
The smiling rosy little head
So glad it has its utmost will,
That all it scored at once is fled,
And I, its love, am gained instead!
Porphyria's love: she guessed not how
Her darling one wish would be heard.
And thus we sit together now,
And all night long we have not stirred,
And yet God has not said a word!

Robert Browning

◆ Who is telling the story, and can you follow the narrative?
◆ Is the narrator a sympathetic character?
◆ Is the narrator interesting or unusual in any way?
◆ How does the narrator's language use (e.g. word choice and order) help establish the character?
◆ Consider sound in the poem. Is it striking in any way?
◆ How effective do you consider the poem as a story, and as a presentation of a world view?

Not Waving But Drowning

Nobody heard him, the dead man,
But still he lay moaning:
I was much further out than you thought
And not waving but drowning.

Poor chap, he always loved larking
And now he's dead
It must have been too cold for him his heart gave way,
They said.

Oh, no no no, it was too cold always
(Still the dead one lay moaning)
I was much too far out all my life
And not waving but drowning.

Stevie Smith

The narrative and message of this poem are perhaps easier to decode. They deal with an individual who has never been able to connect with other people, who has spent a lifetime being ignored or ill-understood. His final, desperate flounderings as he drowns are misinterpreted as a cheery wave!

❖ How does the poet enable us to 'know' this man – to connect with him in fact?
❖ Separate out his lines. What does he communicate to you?
❖ Now decide who else speaks and what impression you get of them.
❖ Does the switching from voice to voice add to the poem's effect or merely confuse?

In this section we have been concerned with the writer's voice, the human voice. But characters don't exist in a vacuum; they exist in relation to place and time. The place and time may be an approximation of reality, or may be wholly fantastic. In either case the place needs establishing, and that is what we are going to look at in the next chapter.

Chapter 15

Creating a sense of place

A sense of place or atmosphere is obviously important to many different types of writing, from travel writing to ghost stories, from ballads to landscape poetry. We are going to look at two main approaches writers can adopt when seeking to evoke place. They can either use clusters of words within semantic fields to create atmosphere – in the way that an impressionist picture suggests poppies rather than delineating them – or they can give a lot of detailed information which enables the reader to see the scene in the mind's eye. This is a more realist, photographic approach. Each approach has its advantages, and in the hands of a talented writer will do the job. Which particular approach you prefer is mainly a matter of individual taste; which approach a writer uses may well be influenced by the sort of text he is writing. Details of exactly what is where are useful knowledge in a whodunnit, but useless clutter in a novel about relationships, where the mood of a place may match the personality of the central protaganist.

One of the most famous creators of mood through place is Thomas Hardy, so we will begin with a passage from *Tess of the D'Urbervilles*. When you have read it, jot down what impressions you receive of the places described.

❖ **What mood do you think is being evoked?**
❖ **Which of the words are carrying the emotional load – the modifiers, the verbs or the nouns?**

> There had not been such a winter for years. It came on in stealthy and measured glides, like the moves of a chess-player. One morning the few lonely trees and the thorns of the hedgerows appeared as if they had put off a vegetable for an animal integument. Every twig was covered with a white nap as of fur grown from the rind during the night, giving it four times its usual stoutness; the whole bush or tree forming a staring sketch in white lines on the mournful grey of the sky and horizon. Cobwebs revealed their presence on sheds and walls where none had ever been observed till brought out into visibility by the crystallizing atmosphere, hanging like loops of white worsted from salient points of the out-houses, posts, and gates.
>
> After this season of congealed dampness came a spell of dry frost, when strange birds from behind the North Pole began to arrive silently on the upland of Flintcomb-Ash; gaunt spectral creatures with tragical eyes – eyes which had witnessed scenes of cataclysmal horror in inaccessible polar regions of a magnitude such as no human being had ever conceived, in curdling temperatures that no man could endure; which had beheld the crash of icebergs and the slide of snow-hills by the shooting light of the Aurora; been half blinded by the whirl of colossal storms and terraqueous distortions; and retained the expression of feature that such scenes had engendered. These nameless birds came quite near to Tess and Marian, but of all they

had seen which humanity would never see, they brought no account. The traveller's ambition to tell was not theirs, and, with dumb impassivity, they dismissed experiences which they did not value for the immediate incidents of this homely upland – the trivial movements of the two girls in disturbing the clods with their hackers so as to uncover something or other that these visitants relished as food.

Then one day a peculiar quality invaded the air of this open country. There came a moisture which was not of rain, and a cold which was not of frost. It chilled the eye-balls of the twain, made their brows ache, penetrated to their skeletons, affecting the surface of the body less than its core. They knew that it meant snow, and in the night the snow came.

Thomas Hardy: Tess of the D'Urbervilles

So, what adjectives have you written down to describe this place at this time? 'Cold' would be an obvious one, since winter and snow are mentioned. Are there any subtler indications of cold? Is it a 'happy cold' or have you jotted down something like 'dreary' or 'bleak'? If your feelings about the place are being directed there is every chance that adjectives are the culprits. Have a look for some which add to the dismalness of the scene.

But even 'cold and bleak' doesn't explain the unpleasant, fearful emotions this passage awakens. Many of you (we hope!) will also have felt that there is a threatening, sinister quality to this place, these 'silent' birds, this winter which 'comes on' (relentlessly?) Have another read through the passage and seek to discover where the disquiet comes from. It might well be worth looking at verbs and their modifiers. You should now have a clear enough sense of the passage to read our analysis actively rather than passively.

In the opening paragraph, a sense of sinister purpose is attributed to the natural world. Somewhat paradoxically, the winter is bringing the world to life. This is explicitly stated in 'put off a vegetable for an animal integument' but is also implicit in the verbs 'came on', 'appeared' 'fur grown from the rind' and 'cobwebs revealed'. All these verbs would normally have animate subjects. In other words we have deviant collocation or personification. The simile 'like the moves of a chess player' reinforces this sense of a person – and a subtle one! The twigs have 'four times [their] usual stoutness' which makes them sound powerful, and the bushes form a 'staring sketch'. Like 'crystallizing' later in the passage, 'staring', since it is formed from a verb, sounds active and purposeful. Nor does the purpose sound friendly: staring is usually regarded as an act of hostility – and being 'crystallized' – frozen solid – scarcely sounds a good experience.

All this sinister action is taking place in an appropriate setting. The trees are 'lonely', there are spiky 'thorns' and the sky is 'mournful grey'.

Things don't improve in the second paragraph. The 'dampness', bad enough in itself, is made worse by the verbal adjective 'congealed'. The birds arrive 'silently'. (Like the 'stealthy and measured glide' of the winter in the paragraph before, the modifier suggests sinister intentions.) They are more than mere birds; they are a dark presence, 'dumb' and 'nameless'. They are connected to death, being 'gaunt and spectral', and have 'tragical eyes' which have seen unspecified (and therefore more frightening) horrors. These horrors are 'cataclysmal' and unimaginable, 'such as no human being had ever conceived.'

At this point the language becomes hyperbolic, and this hyperbole is associated with the almost surreal landscape which is the birds' natural home. In contrast with the winter landscape, the 'polar regions' are described in dramatic, but generalised terms. We have 'curdling temperatures', the 'crash of icebergs and the slide of snow-hills'. There is also the 'whirl of colossal storms'. This seems a far noisier world. This supernatural-seeming world seems to taint the natural one so that in the third paragraph the 'moisture' is 'not of rain' and the 'cold' 'not of frost'. Again, the cold and damp seem purposeful and malevolent: they 'penetrate' to the 'skeletons', the 'core'. The reader is bound to pity the hapless Tess and Marian caught in such a place and season.

The next place we would like you to look at is very far removed from the world of *Tess*. Here we are in the industrial North and with a modern writer, Alan Sillitoe. We want you to consider two short extracts; the first shows the 'hero' Arthur at play, the second at work. Read the two passages.

He stood in the parlour while she fastened the locks and bolts, smelling faint odours of rubber and oil coming from Jack's bicycle leaning against a big dresser that took up nearly one whole side of the room. It was a small dark area of isolation, long familiar with another man's collection of worldly goods: old-fashioned chairs and a settee, fireplace, clock ticking on the mantelpiece, a smell of brown paper, soil from a plant-pot, ordinary aged dust, soot in the chimney left over from last winter's fires, and mustiness of rugs laid down under the table and by the fireplace. Brenda had known this room for seven married years, yet could not have become more intimate with it than did Arthur in the ten seconds while she fumbled with the key.

He knocked his leg on the bicycle pedal, swearing at the pain, complaining at Jack's barminess for leaving it in such an exposed position. 'How does he think I'm going to get in with that thing stuck there?' he joked. 'Tell him I said to leave it in the back-yard next week, out of 'arm's way.'

Brenda hissed and told him to be quiet, and they crept like two thieves into the living-room, where the electric light showed the supper things – teacups, plates, jam-pot, bread – still on the table. A howl of cats came from a nearby yard, and a dustbin lid clattered on to cobblestones.

'Oh well,' he said in a normal voice, standing up tall and straight, 'it's no use whisperin' when all that racket's going on.'

They stood between the table and firegrate, and Brenda put her arms around him. While kissing her he turned his head so that his own face stared back at him from an oval mirror above the shelf. His eyes grew large in looking at himself from such an angle, noticing his short disordered hair sticking out like the bristles of a blond porcupine, and the mark of an old pimple healing on his cheek.

'Don't let's stay down here long, Arthur,' she said softly.

He released her and, knowing every corner of the house and acting as if it belonged to him, stripped off his coat and shirt and went into the scullery to wash the tiredness from his eyes. Once in bed, they would not go to sleep at once: he wanted to be fresh for an hour before floating endlessly down into the warm bed beside Brenda's soft body.

Arthur walked into a huge corridor, searching an inside pocket for his clocking-in card and noticing, as on every morning since he was fifteen – except for a two-year break in the army – the factory smell of oil-suds, machinery, and shaved steel that surrounded you with an air in which pimples grew and prospered on your face and shoulders, that would have turned you into one big pimple if you did not spend half an hour over the scullery sink every night getting rid of the biggest bastards. What a life, he thought. Hard work and good wages, and a smell all day that turns your guts.

The bright Monday-morning ring of the clocking-in machine made a jarring note, different from the tune that played inside Arthur. It was dead on half-past seven. Once in the shop he allowed himself to be swallowed by its diverse noises, walked along lanes of capstan lathes and millers, drills and polishers and hand-presses, worked by a multiplicity of belts and pulleys turning and twisting and slapping on heavy well-oiled wheels overhead, dependent for power on a motor stooping at the far end of the hall like the black shining bulk of a stranded whale. Machines with their own small motors started with a jerk and a whine under the shadows of their operators, increasing a noise that made the brain reel and ache because the weekend had been too tranquil by contrast, a weekend that had terminated for Arthur in fishing for trout in the cool shade of a willow-sleeved canal near the Balloon Houses, miles away from the city. Motor-trolleys moved up and down the main gangways carrying boxes of work – pedals, hubs, nuts and bolts – from one part of the shop to another. Robboe the foreman bent over a stack of new time-sheets behind his glass partition; women and girls wearing turbans and hair-nets and men and boys in clean blue overalls, settled down to their work, eager to get a good start on their day's stint; while sweepers and cleaners at everybody's beck and call already patrolled the gangways and looked busy.

Arthur reached his capstan lathe and took off his jacket, hanging it on a nearby nail so that he could keep an eye on his belongings. He pressed the starter button, and his motor came to life with a gentle thump. Looking around, it did not seem, despite the infernal noise of hurrying machinery, that anyone was working with particular speed. He smiled to himself and picked up a glittering steel cylinder from the top box of a pile beside him, and fixed it into the spindle. He jettisoned his cigarette into the sud-pan, drew back the capstan, and swung the turret on to its broadest drill. Two minutes passed while he contemplated the precise position of tools and cylinder; finally he spat on to both hands and rubbed them together, then switched on the sud-tap from the movable brass pipe, pressed a button that set the spindle running, and ran in the drill to a neat chamfer. Monday morning had lost its terror.

Alan Sillitoe: Saturday Night and Sunday Morning

- Which style of description, the impressionistic or the photographic, would you say predominates here?
- There is a lot of detail in Sillitoe's descriptions. How, and using which particular parts of speech, is this precision achieved?
- Place descriptions make appeals to different senses. Which senses are appealed to here, and through whom are we experiencing them?
- What class and region are these characters from, and how can you tell? Find some examples of significant word choice. How formal or informal is the tone?
- Is the tone consistent throughout each passage?

Now attempt a comparative assessment of these passages with the extract from *Tess of the D'Urbervilles*.

Places in poetry

Though we've considered prose so far, many people, if asked to think of memorable descriptions of place, would think of a poem such as Wordsworth's *Daffodils* or Gray's *Elegy*. Whereas in prose, place is often a background or context for events and characters, in poetry it may conventionally be the subject of a whole poem.

Here are two brief examples by the same poet, Douglas Dunn, of word picture poems. Read them both carefully.

On Roofs of Terry Street

Television aerials, Chinese characters
In the lower sky, wave gently in the smoke.

Nest-building sparrows peck at moss,
Urban flora and fauna, soft, unscrupulous.

Rain drying on the slates shines sometimes.
A builder is repairing someone's leaking roof.

He kneels upright to rest his back.
His trowel catches the light and becomes precious.

A Removal from Terry Street

On a squeaking cart, they push the usual stuff,
A mattress, bed ends, cups, carpets, chairs,
Four paperback westerns. Two whistling youths
In surplus U.S. Army battle-jackets
Remove their sister's goods. Her husband
Follows, carrying on his shoulders the son
Whose mischief we are glad to see removed,
And pushing, of all things, a lawnmower.
There is no grass in Terry Street. The worms
Come up cracks in concrete yards in moonlight.
That man, I wish him well. I wish him grass.

Douglas Dunn

The first of the poems, *On Roofs of Terry Street*, could hardly appear simpler. Only the second couplet presents any difficulty. What are these 'urban flora and fauna' and in what way are they 'unscrupulous'? Once this problem has been resolved, the poem appears to be a sequence of snapshots.

❖ How many separate pictures can you see?
❖ What is the effect of the total absence of linking words? In order to test this you could re-write the poem as three sentences. How is the impact altered?
❖ One way in which the impact will be different will be visually. Why do you think the poet chose to write in two-line stanzas?
❖ Do you see any connection between the poem's subject and its form?

The form of *A Removal from Terry Street* is different. Compare the placing of full stops in these two poems. What effect does the run-on of lines in *A Removal* have? Unlike the snapshots of the other poem, we now seem to have a procession passing through the frame.

❖ Which words are most significant in adding to the movement of the poem?
❖ How is it suggested in the first part of the poem that this is a familiar scene and at what point in the poem does the frame freeze – the general become particular?
❖ Consider the way in which people are referred to. As the poem progresses how do we get a clearer sense of them and their relations to each other – and to the poet?
❖ At what point do we become aware of the presence of the poet?
❖ In the last three lines we move away from pure description. What is the effect of this?

We have looked at a couple of poems where place was very much dominant. Next we are going to look at a poem which sets a person in their context. In this respect it is more akin to the passage from *Tess of the D'Urbervilles*. This is an extract from a long poem called *The Borough* written by George Crabbe in 1810, in which he describes an East Anglian fishing town and its inhabitants. One section of the poem tells the story of Peter Grimes, a fisherman ostracised by the community for ill-treating his apprentices. Here Peter, compelled to live alone, is placed in appropriately dismal surroundings. Read the extract aloud.

> Thus by himself compell'd to live each day,
> To wait for certain hours the tide's delay;
> At the same time the same dull views to see,
> The bounding marsh-bank and the blighted tree;
> The water only, when the tides were high,
> When low, the mud half-cover'd and half-dry;
> The sun-burnt tar that blisters on the planks,
> And bank-side stakes in their uneven ranks;
> Heaps of entangled weeds that slowly float,
> As the tide rolls by the impeded boat.
>
> When tides were neap, and, in the sultry day,
> Through the tall bounding mud-banks made their way,

Which on each side rose swelling, and below
The dark warm flood ran silently and slow;
There anchoring, Peter chose from man to hide,
There hang his head, and view the lazy tide
In its hot slimy channel slowly glide;
Where the small eels that left the deeper way
For the warm shore, within the shallows play;
Where gaping muscles, left upon the mud,
Slope their slow passage to the fallen flood; –
Here dull and hopeless he'd lie down and trace
How sidelong crabs had scrawl'd their crooked race;
Or sadly listen to the tuneless cry
Of fishing gull or clanging golden-eye;
What time the sea-birds to the marsh would come,
And the loud bittern, from the bull-rush home.
Gave from the salt-ditch side the bellowing boom:
He nursed the feelings these dull scenes produce,
And loved to stop beside the opening sluice;
Where the small stream, confined in narrow bound,
Ran with a dull, unvaried, sadd'ning sound;
Where all, presented to the eye or ear,
Oppress'd the soul with misery, grief, and fear.

George Crabbe

❖ Does anything strike you about the sounds in the poem?
❖ What pace did you choose to read at? We'd be surprised if you read this rapidly. Why?

First of all, look at the length of the vowel sounds. Pick out a couple of lines which contain striking clusters of long vowels. Are there in fact examples of assonance (the recurrence, systematic or not, of a vowel sound throughout a passage)?

Now consider consonants. Which consonants seem to be repeated most often? The recurrence of a consonant throughout a passage is called consonance; if the consonant is repeated at the beginning of words it is called alliteration. Which of these sound effects can you find examples of?

The sense of slowness in this passage is not affected only by choosing sounds which take some time to say. The length and ordering of words within sentences is also important. There are several examples of sentences in which the subject is on one line, the main verb on another. One example would be the 'gaping muscles' which only 'slope' a line later. Can you find a couple more examples?

Although the rhythm and rhyme scheme of this poem are very regular, the regular units are broken down and the sense carried over by such methods as separating subjects from their verbs. Another way in which the sense of length and slowness is achieved is the use of numerous conjunctions, both co-ordinating ('and', 'or') and subordinating ('which', 'where'). Although the rhyme is at the end of lines, the sense is often carried over and the sentence extended by use of subordinate clauses:

Through the tall bounding mud-banks made their way,
Which on each side rose swelling.

145

Prepositions, which place one thing in relation to another, are similarly placed at the beginning of lines, and mean that the sense unit is carried over from one to the other and the line runs on:

> There hang his head, and view the lazy tide
> In its hot slimy channel slowly glide

It might be expected that the avoidance of commas and full stops at line ends would increase the pace of the verse; however, the effect is to create a longer unit of sense, and thus a slower pace. The use of frequent full stops to make shorter sentences results in a rapid, staccato rhythm which increases the speed, and this is true of verse as well as prose. We have dealt at some length with features of sound in this poem because they are a prominent aspect of the verse.

Summarise the main points we have made about sound effects in this poem, illustrating them with your own examples. Then go on to describe other techniques Crabbe uses to achieve his effects.

The next poem we'd like you to take a look at is from a similar period to the one by Crabbe. It is *This Lime-Tree Bower My Prison* by Coleridge. Although the poem is not rhymed, it is, in several ways, more overtly 'literary' than the Crabbe.

This Lime-Tree Bower My Prison

> Well they are gone, and here must I remain,
> This lime-tree bower my prison! I have lost
> Beauties and feelings, such as would have been
> Most sweet to my remembrance even when age
> Had dimm'd mine eyes to blindness! They, meanwhile,
> Friends, whom I never more may meet again,
> On springy heath, along the hill-top edge,
> Wander in gladness, and wind down, perchance,
> To that still roaring dell, of which I told;
> The roaring dell, o'erwooded, narrow, deep,
> And only speckled by the mid-day sun;
> Where its slim trunk the ash from rock to rock
> Flings arching like a bridge; – that branchless ash,
> Unsunn'd and damp, whose few poor yellow leaves
> Ne'er tremble in the gale, yet tremble still,
> Fann'd by the waterfall! and there my friends
> Behold the dark green file of long lank weeds,
> That all at once (a most fantastic sight!)
> Still nod and drip beneath the dripping edge
> Of the blue clay-stone. Now, my friends emerge
> Beneath the wide wide Heaven – and view again
> The many-steepled tract magnificent
> Of hilly fields and meadows, and the sea,
> With some fair bark, perhaps, whose sails light up
> The slip of smooth clear blue betwixt two Isles
> Of purple shadow! Yes! they wander on
> In gladness all; but thou, methinks, most glad,
> My gentle-hearted Charles! For thou hast pined
> And hunger'd after Nature, many a year,

In the great City pent, winning thy way
With sad yet patient soul, through evil and pain
And strange calamity! Ah! slowly sink
Behind the western ridge, thou glorious Sun!
Shine in the slant beams of the sinking orb,
Ye purple heath-flowers! richlier burn, ye clouds!

Samuel Taylor Coleridge

Look at the lexis. Would you say that there were examples of literary and archaic lexis? If you would (and, to be frank you should!), find a few examples.

Literariness is not only a matter of individual words, however. Word order is also significant. If you look at the first line, the inversion of 'here must I remain' is immediately striking. Can you find other examples of this technique?

Ask yourself if the style is formal/literary throughout or whether there is not also a less formal, spoken element. (Looking at punctuation marks may help you here.)

Given that elements of this poem are very literary (some commentators would call it 'poetic diction') there is also a voice in the poem which is personal, emotional and spontaneous. Check which person this is written in and which references seem personal and emotional.

Once you have established that there is a person, a voice in this poem, ask yourself what the voice is up to. Is he merely describing a place he knows well or is there more to it than that? Why, for example, if he is describing a place he has seen is he using the present tense? Write down what you would say the poet is doing in this extract.

We would argue that he is imagining (and the Romantic poets were very keen on the faculty of imagination) making this journey with his friends by recalling every tiny detail of their pathway and thus reliving it with and through them. The reader certainly gets a clear notion of their movements. Take a look at the verbs of motion in this poem – in fact list them. Now consider Coleridge's use of prepositions which enable us to know not only how they are travelling but in what direction.

❋ **The poet takes the reader from scene to scene. Identify the different stages of the journey. How is each scene conveyed?**
❋ **Are modifiers important here?**
❋ **Is a visual scene only being described or are any other senses engaged?**

As this poem continues you will notice that the poet's tone becomes more philosophical; he is not merely comparing the city and the country in terms of appearance but almost morally. What is the poet's attitude to the city and how can you tell? (Be precise please; it is pointless answering 'By what he says.')

At the end of this section of the poem there are three imperative forms. Find them and then ask yourself why they are there. What is their effect?

Finally, we would like you to look at one more prose piece and one more poem. Since so far in this section we have dealt only with England we felt it was high time other countries were represented. The poem is relatively close to home – Wales; the prose a little further away in all senses – Persia. Attempt a full analysis of each without any help from us. By now you ought to be asking yourselves the appropriate questions.

It is winter. A narrow, muddy street, flanked by low mud-brick walls beneath a cloudless steely sky. The ground rutted deep by cartwheels, pock-marked with mule and donkey hooves, covered with a thin layer of ice that crunches underfoot. Dirty patches of snow linger here and there at the base of walls. At the end of the street the embrasure of a door in front of which hangs an indigo-blue patched curtain, like a single spot of colour on a fawn canvas. From behind it comes a regular, monotonous muffled thud, like a distant hammer, followed by a whining screech.

This is my first memory – I must have been two or three years old. An inquisitive child, I stop and lift a corner of the curtain apprehensively: a pungent, spicy smell wafts across the street; inside is a small, dark room filled with clouds of yellow dust; in the middle a huge circular stone with a mast at its centre is being dragged round and round by a large, emaciated horse on bending spindly legs. His eyes are blindfolded with a black cloth and, as he rotates the stone, a mustardy-yellow flour pours from under it into the surrounding gutter. The scene is lit by a single glass eye in the domed ceiling far above, which shoots a diagonal shaft of light and illuminates a column of dust whose yellow specks dance as if to the rhythm of the horse's hooves on the stony floor.

'Come along, child, we must hurry.' My mother. She takes me by the hand and pulls me away. I cling to the door, mesmerised, as the blindfold horse pulls round and round, its yoke screeching, its hooves thudding, its nostrils puffing jets of steam into the icy yellow air – turning, turning.

'Why are his eyes covered, Mother?'

'So that he doesn't see where he is, otherwise he would get dizzy going round in a circle all day, and he would balk. Blindfold, he can imagine he is walking in a straight line, in a field. But don't worry, at the end of the day they take off the cloth from his eyes and give him some lovely oats to eat. He is quite happy, really ... '

Shusha Guppy: The Blindfold Horse

Hay-making

You know the hay's in
when gates hang slack
in the lanes. These hot nights
the fallen fields lie open
under the moon's clean sheets.

The homebound road is
sweet with the liquors
of the grasses, air
green with the pastels
of stirred hayfields.

Down at Fron Felen
in the loaded barn

new bales displace
stale darknesses. Breathe.
Remember finding
first kittens, first love
in the scratch of the hay,
our sandals filled with seeds.

Gillian Clarke

Chapter 16

Sending a message

One of the purposes of literature is to change people's attitudes. It is most unlikely that any writer would create only to practise iambic pentameters or metaphorical use of language. He is far more likely to have a statement or world view embedded in his text. Most readers approach a text wondering what it will have to say rather than how it's said, although we find the style of some writers more to our taste than others. We read for sense not form, but we would hate to suggest that the two are separable.

Wilfred Owen, who wrote poems from and about the trenches in the First World War, obviously had a message about war that he desperately wanted to send to his readers. The way he put it was that 'the poetry is in the pity'. In other words the feelings evoked by the words were more important than the words themselves. Without the effect, the poetry would be pointless.

Let us start our look at didactic writing by considering Owen's poem *Anthem For Doomed Youth*. To focus your attention upon the precision of his language use, consider alongside it an earlier draft, *Anthem For Dead Youth*.

Anthem for Dead Youth

What passing bells for you who die in herds?
– Only the monstrous anger of the guns!
– Only the stuttering rifles' rattled words
Can patter out your hasty orisons.
No chants for you, nor balms, nor wreaths, nor bells,
Nor any voice of mourning, save the choirs,
And long-drawn sighs of wailing shells;
And bugles calling for you from sad shires.
What candles may we hold to speed you all?
Not in the hands of boys, but in their eyes
Shall shine the holy lights of our goodbyes.
The pallor of girls' brows must be your pall.
Your flowers, the tenderness of comrades' minds,
And each slow dusk, a drawing-room of blinds.

Anthem for Doomed Youth

What passing bells for these who die as cattle?
– Only the monstrous anger of the guns.
– Only the stuttering rifles' rapid rattle
Can patter out their hasty orisons.
No mockeries now for them, no prayers nor bells,
Nor any voice of mourning, save the choirs,
The shrill, demented choirs of wailing shells;
And bugles calling for them from sad shires.
What candles may be held to speed them all?
Not in the hands of boys, but in their eyes

Shall shine the holy glimmers of goodbyes.
The pallor of girls' brows shall be their pall;
Their flowers the tenderness of patient minds,
And each slow dusk a drawing-down of blinds.

Wilfred Owen

Read both versions in their entirety – you cannot look at the trees before the wood. Remember that poems are an entity, not a jumble of lines. Which, if either do you prefer, find clearer, find more moving or amusing?

Presumably the writer preferred the final draft and made quite conscious decisions about the effect he wished to achieve. You may not agree with him, but at least try to see what his intentions were.

Identify the changes that have been made. A systematic differentiation of types of change e.g. lexical, phonological, syntactic may well help you later. Colour coding might be useful – or straight and wiggly lines!

Try to group the changes: it is dull and pointless to start at the beginning and wade through till you reach the end. You are likely to be repetitive and unclear. Possible groupings might include for these two versions:

1 writing for a different audience
2 altering to a more emotive lexical style
3 gaining impact through sound, e.g. alliteration.

Next, prioritise your groups. Which clutch of changes seem to you most significant? You should deal with these first. Then go on to another group which is similar in effect. Then do the rest. If this sounds very mechanical we can only insist that people's personalities and talents do enable the same system to come up with very different results.

You should be in a position by now to see not only Owen's message in the poem but also how he is going about conveying it. Attempt a detailed comparison and evaluation of the two versions.

Now look at our students' answers. Which seems to you more thorough? Convincing? Linguistic? Give each answer a grade.

1 *The changes that have been made to the early draft significantly alter the intentions and impact of the final draft in a variety of ways. The changes can be divided into three main elements. Firstly the changes made to the early draft result in the final draft being aimed at a different audience, consequently resulting in an alteration of the aims which the poem conveys. The changes result in an 'emotional shift', i.e. the final draft conveys much more emotion than the early draft. The third main element of change is evident in the manipulation of sounds which occurs to give the final draft much more drama and emphasis.*

Upon reading the early draft, it is evident that the poem is slow and emotive, yet the final draft is much more emotive and slower in pace. The presence of a much more emotional impact in the final draft is brought about mainly through a variety of lexical changes to the earlier draft. The first noticeable word change is apparent in the title of the poems, the title of the early draft being 'Anthem for Dead Youth' and the title of the final draft 'Anthem for Doomed Youth'. The word 'dead' is an extremely final word, whereas 'doomed' is connotatively associated with something which has not yet happened, but which is ultimately inevitable and conveys a sense of expectation. ('Dead' = it's over, final, nothing more can happen whereas 'doomed' = what can happen before the inevitable; expectations.) 'Doomed' is much more dramatic and emotive than 'dead'. 'In herds' (early draft) is amended to 'as cattle' in the final draft, thus giving the poem a greater emotional impact to its audience. 'In herds' conveys numbers, but it is not very precise or descriptive as to how the soldiers died. 'As cattle', portrays not only numbers, but places much more emphasis on the way in which the soldiers died. 'As cattle' conjures up negative connotations to the audience. It is a simile, likening the death of soldiers to the death of cattle i.e. cattle are slaughtered thus dying without dignity — inferring that humans were to be slaughtered. 'As cattle' is much more precise and clarifies the poet's intention of describing the terrible inhuman way the soldiers met their deaths.

'Mockeries' replaced 'chants' in the final draft as 'mockeries' is a much stronger and more emotive word than 'chants'. 'Chants' could have positive connotations i.e.: chants of encouragement for example whereas 'mockeries' has definite negative connotations i.e: to mock someone is jeering at and making fun of them. This lexical change again helps the poet to clarify his point to the audience. 'We hold' in the early draft conveys a sense of 'here and now', i.e. the present tense, whereas 'be held' is much more generalised and portrays the idea of forever and expands into the future. Thus by this lexical change the poem can be for an audience of any era and is not just directed at an audience of the era when the poem was written i.e. World War I, 1914-1918.

The use of 'comrades' in the early draft conveys the idea that other people care, whereas 'patient' in the final draft conveys the idea of those at home waiting for their loved one to return. Again this is much more emotive.

The final draft is directed at a different audience than that of the early draft. By amending the pronouns 'you' and 'your' to 'these', 'their' and 'them' in the final draft the poem is not only directed at a different audience, but a much broader audience also. The early draft is directed at those fighting in the war i.e. the soldiers, yet the final draft is directed at a general audience and conveys the idea that war is the responsibility of everyone, not just the soldiers. In the final draft the poet is perhaps trying to change/influence public opinion at home whereas in the early draft he is conveying the obvious to the audience i.e. the soldiers.

By manipulating the sounds of the early draft, the final draft is far more dramatic, emotive and emphatic. 'Rapid rattle' is rhythmic, portraying the sound of a gun shooting. The alliteration of the r's and the assonance of the a's are effective in impact to the reader of the final draft. However, in the early draft 'rattled words', which is not as phonological or as descriptive in expressing the rhythm of a gun shooting, was used instead. By using 'rapid rattle', Owen helps the audience to gain a greater feel of the mood of the poem. 'Rapid rattle' has far more impact than 'rattled words'.

Although the early draft has a slow pace, the final draft contains a far slower pace. In the early draft 'nor balms, nor wreaths, nor bells' was changed to 'no prayers nor bells' in the final draft, as the previous line read like a list, thus losing some of its emotional impact. By reducing the words in the line in the final draft, the emotional impact is retained. The semi-colon before 'no prayers nor bells' gives a much longer pause and is much more rhetorical in effect. 'Shrill demented choirs' in the final draft is quicker in pace and is more emotive than 'long drawn sighs'. It infers the screams of dying people in phonology and connotations, having a greater, more frightening impact on the audience. 'Shrill demented choirs' has far shorter vowels than 'long drawn sighs', whose vowels are long and drawn out.

'Glimmer' is similar to an onomatopoeia (i.e. glimmer is a faint hope, a flickering light) in its word effect. It is much more rhythmic in sound than 'light'. 'Light' connotates a great hope, burning brightly, which is wrong for the context of the poem, as the poem is about the 'doomed' i.e. those awaiting death, and here 'glimmer' is much more suitable in connotation. By replacing 'drawing-room' with 'drawing-down' Owen includes alliteration of the d's which are extremely final in sound – tying in with the theme of the poem. It is an action word and symbolises literally the death of a person (curtains drawn when in mourning). 'Drawing-down' is very final. It conveys the idea that now all will be dark and that the aforementioned 'glimmer' has now died.

The changes made to the early draft result in a much more meaningful, emotive and dramatic final version of Owen's poem, 'Anthem for Doomed Youth'.

2 The first obvious difference that we notice between the first and final drafts of the poem is that the first is directed at one soldier in particular and that the final draft is directed at all the soldiers.

The poet has a pessimistic view of the soldiers. The final version is not as pessimistic as the first one. The first version contains words such as 'mourning', 'wreaths', 'long-drawn'. These words would normally be associated with sad occasions such as a funeral. They have been omitted from the final version.

The title of the first draft has a more angry tone to it than the final draft. It is changed from 'Anthem for Dead Youth' to 'Anthem for Doomed Youth'. The first gives the impression that the soldiers have already been killed and that it is all over whereas the second gives the impression that the soldiers are still in the process of being killed, that it is happening at present.

In the final draft the word 'cattle' is used instead of 'herds'. The poet is being more specific by stressing exactly what he means but the word 'cattle' also has a callous meaning to it. Because cattle are used as meat the reader would associate this with cattle being carted off to the slaughterhouse to be killed. It is as if the poet is implying that the soldiers don't have a chance, that they are walking into death.

Alliteration is used in the poem, for example, 'rifles' rapid rattle'. There is repetition of the letter r. If the words are said they sound like the rifle being fired. This is also an example of onomatopoeia.

The line that read 'No chants for you, nor balms, nor wreaths, nor bells' has been changed to 'No mocking now for them, no prayers nor bells'.

The new line is quicker to say and has a much smoother rhythm. It has a sarcastic tone whereas the first draft has a bumpy rhythm and is drawn out.

Personification is used throughout the poem, for example, 'And bugles calling for you ...'. Here it is as if the bugles are people calling after the soldiers as they go to war.

'Wailing shells' as if the bullets from the rifles are screaming as they are fired. There is a sequence in how the lines rhyme.

The last line of the poem has a very emotional and morbid tone: 'A drawing down of blinds.' The drawing of a blind/curtains is used as a mark of respect when somebody dies. It is a symbol of death. This ties in with the theme of the poem – which is the death of the soldiers.

Out of interest, we gave these answers a B+ and a D+. If you strongly disagreed with us, perhaps you ought to have another look.

If you feel you need to do more work on double drafts – and they are excellent practice – take a look at these two versions of *London* by William Blake. Try an analysis of it using our suggested method. When you have completed yours, turn to the end of the chapter and look at ours.

London (early draft)

I wander thro' each dirty street,
Near where the dirty Thames does flow,
And mark in every face I meet
Marks of weakness, marks of woe.

In every cry of every man
In every voice of every child
In every voice, in every ban
The german mind forg'd links I hear.

But most the Chimney-sweeper's cry
Blackens o'er the churches' walls,
And the hapless Soldier's sigh
Runs in blood down Palace walls.

From every wintry street I hear
How the midnight Harlot's curse
Blasts the new born Infant's tear
And hangs with plagues the marriage hearse.

London (final version)

I wander thro' each charter'd street,
Near where the charter'd Thames does flow,
And mark in every face I meet
Marks of weakness, marks of woe.

In every cry of every Man,
In every Infant's cry of fear,
In every voice, in every ban,
The mind-forged manacles I hear.

How the Chimney-sweeper's cry
Every black'ning Church appalls;
And the hapless Soldier's sigh
Runs in blood down Palace walls.

But most thro' midnight streets I hear
How the youthful Harlot's curse
Blasts the new born Infant's tear,
And blights with plagues the Marriage hearse.

William Blake

Poetry for the people

Owen and Blake wrote poetry with the general public as their audience; they were trying to prick the conscience of a nation, not entertain the literary few. Something we would wish to convey strongly is that literature is not for the elite by the elite. This is an accusation often levelled at it, especially at poetry. Poets themselves are aware of the danger of becoming part of a Standard English cultural heritage: indeed they write about the problem.

We would like you to take a look at *Them and* [uz] by Tony Harrison. It is a poem which strenuously argues that poetry does not belong to 'them' ('them' being the middle class, middle brow, middle-aged 'haves'.)

Them & [uz]

for Professors Richard Hoggart & Leon Cortez

I

αίαῖ, ay, ay! ... stutterer Demosthenes
gob full of pebbles outshouting seas –

4 words only of *mi 'art aches* and ... 'Mine's broken,
you barbarian, T.W.!' *He* was nicely spoken.
'Can't have our glorious heritage done to death!'

I played the Drunken Porter in *Macbeth*.

'Poetry's the speech of kings. You're one of those
Shakespeare gives the comic bits to: prose!
All poetry (even Cockney Keats?) you see
's been dubbed by [ʌs] into RP,
Received Pronunciation, please believe [ʌs]
your speech is in the hands of the Receivers.'

'We say [ʌs] not [uz], T.W.!' That shut my trap.
I doffed my flat a's (as in 'flat cap')
my mouth all stuffed with glottals, great
lumps to hawk up and spit out ... *E-nun-ci-ate*!

II

So right, yer buggers, then! We'll occupy
your lousy leasehold Poetry.

I chewed up Littererchewer and spat the bones
into the lap of dozing Daniel Jones,
dropped the initials I'd been harried as
and used my *name* and own voice: [uz] [uz] [uz],
ended sentences with by, with, from,
and spoke the language that I spoke at home.
RIP RP, RIP T.W.
I'm *Tony* Harrison no longer you!

You can tell the Receivers where to go
(and not aspirate it) once you know
Wordsworth's *matter / water* are full rhymes,
[uz] can be loving as well as funny.

My first mention in the *Times*
automatically made Tony Anthony!

Tony Harrison

❖ Start your consideration of the poem by looking at the title. Why do you think [uz] is written in phonetic script?
❖ Any idea who 'we' might be?

Don't be put off by the Greek at the beginning; it is a reference to Greek comedy and tragedy. Demosthenes was a great orator despite the fact that he had a stutter. Before we discuss the poem, think about a few questions:

❖ The first section deals with part of Harrison's life. Which part?
❖ Do you recognise '*mi 'art aches*'?
❖ Who says 'Mine's broken' and why does he call Tony Harrison T.W.?
❖ How is this picked up on in the second section?
❖ There are quite a few linguistic jokes in both sections. Find them and decide how they work.
❖ There are also a lot of humorous and striking sound effects. Are there any you particularly like?
❖ Harrison clearly feels that *The Times* belongs to 'them'. Do you feel that his tone is too belligerent? Or do you sympathise with him?
❖ Would this poem only really strike a chord with Northerners?

Now let's look at the poem in a bit more detail. The title neatly emphasises the gap and hostility between two worlds; not only are the halves of the divided nation economically and geographically separate, they even talk differently. 'They' don't call people by the same names as we do – they reduce them to anonymous, offensive initials or smarten Tony up to Anthony. They don't let people choose their name (and we discussed in Section One how important names are.)

The poem discusses the tendency of educated, middle class, RP speakers to take 'literature' over – a nice pun being coined on the word 'Receivers'. Poetry, which is written in individual, different voices (Cockney Keats, Cumbrian Wordsworth who pronounced 'water' to rhyme with 'matter') get tidied up and dubbed into RP; [uz] becomes [ʌs], which removes its reality and its charm. As Harrison points out, '[uz] can be loving as well as funny', and why should only the comic lines in Shakespeare be spoken in a regional accent? Don't RP speakers get drunk?

As well as pointing out the importance of accent and sound in speech, and therefore in poetry, Harrison deliberately uses dialect words for emphasis and precision. A 'gob full of pebbles' sounds far more undignified than a 'mouthful'; 'hawk' is far more onomatopoeic and descriptive of those long, rattling spits than 'spit' could ever be. Words are carefully selected for their effect when spoken with a Northern accent: 'yer buggers' needs a Northern *u* to sound aggressively humorous, and the man-in-the-street version of 'Littererchewer' brings it down a peg or two.

Spelling makes an important contribution to the poem's effect.

So does sound. The rhyming couplets give the poem a jaunty fluency. Asides are set out to be just that: 'I played the drunken porter in Macbeth.'

Alliteration reinforces the anger of 'lousy leasehold Poetry' – with a capital *p* and therefore not 'our' sort! Also 'home' is placed deliberately to rhyme – it does in Yorkshire – with 'from'.

The voices of the poem come across very clearly and dramatically. As the poem continues, the spokesman, the I, becomes more and more confident, till he feels able to say

> You can tell the Receivers where to go
> (and not aspirate it)

The colloquialisms and the jokey asides don't stop the message coming across loud, clear and sincere.

We thought we would finish the 'sending a message in poetry' section with another poem which is not in Standard English. It is *Sonny's Lettah* by Linton Kwesi Johnson. As language students you will probably have done some work on patwa so you shouldn't have many difficulties of comprehension.

Sonny's Lettah

(*Anti-Sus poem*)

> Dear Mama,
> Good Day.
> I hope dat wen
> deze few lines reach y'u,
> they may find y'u in di bes' af helt.
>
> Mama,
> I really doan know how fi tell y'u dis,
> cause I did mek a salim pramis
> fi tek care a lickle Jim
> an' try mi bes' fi look out fi him.
>
> Mama,
> Ah really did try mi bes',
> but none-di-les',
> mi sarry fi tell y'u seh
> poor lickle Jim get arres'.
>
> It woz di miggle a di rush howah
> wen everybady jus' a hus'le an' a bus'le
> fi goh home fi dem evenin' showah;
> mi an' Jim stan-up
> waitin' pan a bus,
> nat causin' no fus',
> wen all an a sudden
> a police van pull-up.

Out jump t'ree policeman,
di 'hole a dem carryin' batan.
Dem waak straight up to mi an' Jim.
One a dem hol' an to Jim
seh him tekin him in;
Jim tell him fi let goh a him
far him noh dhu not'n',
an him naw t'ief,
nat even a but'n.
Jim start to wriggle.
Di police start to giggle.

Mama,
mek Ah tell y'u whey dem dhu to Jim;
Mama,
mek Ah tell y'u whey dem dhu to him:

dem t'ump him in him belly
an' it turn to jelly
dem lick him pan him back
an' him rib get pap
dem lick him pan him he'd
but it tuff like le'd
dem kick him in him seed
an' it started to bleed

Mama,
Ah jus' could'n' stan-up deh
an' noh dhu not'n':
soh mi jook one in him eye
an' him started to cry;
mi t'ump one in him mout'
an' him started to shout
mi kick one pan him shin
an' him started to spin
mi t'ump him pan him chin
an' him drap pan a bin.

an' crash
an de'd.

Mama,
more policeman come dung
an' beat mi to di grung;
dem charge Jim fi sus;
dem charge mi fi murdah.

Mama,
doan fret,
doan get depres'

an' doun-hearted
Be af good courage
till I hear fram you.

I remain,
your son,
Sonny

Linton Kwesi Johnson

❖ Try to summarise the story of the poem – it is narrative as well as didactic; literature isn't that watertight.
❖ Do you find the story credible? Do you find it moving?
❖ How does the poet convey Sonny's voice and what impression do you get of him?
❖ We would classify this as social protest poetry. Do you think it works as such?
❖ Look at the opening and the closing of the letter. What could you say about them?
❖ In the course of the poem there are several changes in tone and emotional content. Could you divide the poem up into sections?
❖ Which section do you consider the most effective?

You now have enough material to write an analysis of the poem, as a poem and as persuasion.

Didactic prose

Of course it is not only poetry writers who use literature didactically. Prose writers are every bit as committed and usually have more space in which to persuade you. Some authors are renowned for their strong feelings and clear expression of them: try reading Charles Dickens or George Eliot! For a rather easier start than their prose style represents, take a look at this passage from D.H. Lawrence's book *Nottingham and The Mining Country*.

The great city means beauty, dignity and a certain splendour, but England is a mean and petty scrabble of paltry dwellings called homes.

The promoter of industry, a hundred years ago dared to perpetrate the ugliness of my native village. And still more monstrous, promoters of industry today are scrabbling over the face of England with miles and square miles of red-brick 'homes' like horrible scabs. And the men inside these little red rat-traps get more and more helpless, being more and more humiliated, more and more dissatisfied, like trapped rats.

Do away with it all then. At no matter what cost, start in to alter it. Never mind about wages and industrial squabbling. Turn the attention elsewhere. Pull down my native village to the last brick. Plan a nucleus. Fix the focus. Make a handsome gesture of radiation from the focus. And then put up big buildings, handsome, that sweep to a civic centre. And furnish them with beauty. And make an absolute clean start. Do it place by place. Make a new England. Away with little homes! Away with scrabbling pettiness and paltriness. Look at the contours of the land, and build up from these, with a sufficient nobility. The English may be mentally or spiritually developed. But as citizens of splendid cities they are more ignominious than rabbits. And they nag, nag, nag all the time about politics and wages and all that, like mean narrow housewives.

D. H. Lawrence: Nottingham and the Mining Country

One read of this passage ought to be enough to tell you that it a rhetorical piece of writing. Before you look at our analysis, jot down the answers to these questions and attempt an analysis of your own:

❖ Why is this text split into three paragraphs?
❖ What is the content of each?
❖ Does anything strike you about verb forms in the final paragraph?
❖ Look at the nouns. Are they abstract or concrete? What difference does it make?
❖ What sort of connotations – positive or negative – do they have?
❖ Look at modifiers. Is the writer directing us or informing us? Which are the key words?
❖ Does this literary writer employ imagistic, metaphorical language? Does it work?
❖ Are there any sound effects in this passage?

Here is our analysis:

Lawrence's aim here is to point out a state of affairs as emphatically as possible and then provide the cure. He uses extreme, pejorative modifiers to describe our cities and homes like 'mean', 'petty' and 'paltry' ('petty' and 'paltry' are further emphasised by an alliterative effect.) The city is essentially 'great': it is what men have 'dared to perpetrate' upon it which is so dreadful. Their conduct is described as 'monstrous', a very extreme term. They have taken something with great abstract qualities – 'dignity', 'beauty' and 'splendour' – and reduced it to a cluster of 'rat-traps'. This is clearly not literally true. The passage uses language metaphorically to gain maximum emotional impact. The red-brick homes are seen as 'scabs' – the outward sign of damage to the body surface. The village is seen as damaged and broken as well as ugly.

The writer seems to feel the more strongly because what he is describing is not any old village but his own: 'my', the possessive pronoun, adds emphasis and personalises the issue. In turn, the place's ugliness affects those who live in it; they become 'humiliated' and 'dissatisfied'. They are the rats in the rat-trap.

Having identified how damaging the ugliness and soullessness of the village is, Lawrence uses a string of imperatives in the final paragraph to insist on what can be done. Adopting a more spoken, colloquial tone, he tells the reader 'Do away with it all, then.' The verbs are no longer stative, but dynamic. They must 'start in to alter', 'pull down', 'plan' and 'fix'. In short, do something! More positive evaluative adjectives are now used. Gestures and buildings alike will be 'handsome'. It will be a 'clean' – with all its connotations of purity – start. A new beginning is to be made, leading to 'a new England'. The vision is thus widened from the one village; it is seen as representative. The readers are told not only what to build but what to destroy:

'Away with little homes!' Lawrence exclaims. He has no patience with the thrice repeated nagging or the squabbling over pay. He insists that they must address themselves instead to creation – and creation of something of beauty. Not for them the timidity of rabbits, or the little-mindedness of housewives (not a phrase likely to endear Lawrence to feminists, I feel!) They must build the new Jerusalem.

Having cut your teeth on that, perhaps you could now have a look at the Victorian novelists in their full intensity. Here are two extracts, one from Charlotte Brontë's *Jane Eyre* and one from George Eliot's *Middlemarch*. Both seem to us to be fairly blatant in their message-sending. Look at each and ask yourself the following questions:

❖ What point, broadly, is each trying to make?
❖ What are the main structural devices employed by each of the writers?
❖ Which word classes carry the major emotional meaning?
❖ Does this show some of the features you might expect in poetry such as deviant syntax, unusual collocations and densely figurative language?
❖ Which of the two do you consider the more effective?

'Her size is small; what is her age?'

'Ten years.'

'So much?' was the doubtful answer; and he prolonged his scrutiny for some minutes. Presently he addressed me –

'Your name, little girl?'

'Jane Eyre, sir.'

In uttering these words I looked up: he seemed to me a tall gentleman, but then I was very little; his features were large, and they and all the lines of his frame were equally harsh and prim.

'Well, Jane Eyre, and are you a good child?'

Impossible to reply to this in the affirmative: my little world held a contrary opinion: I was silent. Mrs Reed answered for me by an expressive shake of the head, adding soon, 'Perhaps the less said on that subject the better, Mr Brocklehurst.'

'Sorry indeed to hear it! She and I must have some talk'; and bending from the perpendicular, he installed his person in the arm-chair, opposite Mrs Reed's. 'Come here,' he said.

I stepped across the rug: he placed me square and straight before him. What a face he had, now that it was almost on a level with mine! what a great nose! and what a mouth! and what large, prominent teeth!

'No sight so sad as that of a naughty child,' he began, 'especially a naughty little girl. Do you know where the wicked go after death?'

'They go to hell,' was my ready and orthodox answer.

'And what is hell? Can you tell me that?'

'A pit full of fire.'

'And should you like to fall into that pit, and to be burning there for ever?'

'No, sir.'

'What must you do to avoid it?'

I deliberated a moment: my answer, when it did come, was objectionable: 'I must keep in good health, and not die.'

'How can you keep in good health? Children younger than you die daily. I buried a little child of five years old only a day or two since – a good little child, whose soul is now in heaven. It is to be feared the same could not be said of you, were you to be called thence.'

Not being in a condition to remove his doubt, I only cast my eyes down on the two large feet planted on the rug, and sighed, wishing myself far enough away.

'I hope that sigh is from the heart, and that you repent of ever having been the occasion of discomfort to your excellent benefactress.'

'Benefactress! benefactress!' said I inwardly: 'they all call Mrs Reed my benefactress; if so, a benefactress is a disagreeable thing.'

'Do you say your prayers night and morning?' continued my interrogator.

'Yes, sir.'

'Do you read your Bible?'

'Sometimes.'

'With pleasure? Are you fond of it?'

'I like Revelations, and the Book of Daniel, and Genesis, and Samuel, and a little bit of Exodus, and some parts of Kings and Chronicles, and Job and Jonah.'

'And the Psalms? I hope you like them?'

'No, sir.'

'No? Oh, shocking! I have a little boy, younger than you, who knows six Psalms by heart: and when you ask him which he would rather have, a ginger-bread-nut to eat, or a verse of a Psalm to learn, he says: "Oh! the verse of a Psalm! angels sing Psalms," says he; "I wish to be a little angel here below." He then gets two nuts in recompense for his infant piety.'

'Psalms are not interesting,' I remarked.

'That proves you to have a wicked heart; and you must pray to God to change it: to give you a new and clean one; to take away your heart of stone and give you a heart of flesh.'

Charlotte Brontë: Jane Eyre

One morning, some weeks after her arrival at Lowick, Dorothea – but why always Dorothea? Was her point of view the only possible one with regard to this marriage? I protest against all our interest, all our effort at understanding being given to the young skins that look blooming in spite of trouble; for these too will get faded, and will know the older and more eating griefs which we are helping to neglect. In spite of the blinking eyes and white moles objectionable to Celia, and the want of muscular curve which was morally painful to Sir James, Mr Casaubon had an intense consciousness within him, and was spiritually a-hungered like the rest of us. He had done nothing exceptional in marring – nothing but what society sanctions, and considers an occasion for wreaths and bouquets. It had occurred to him that he must not any longer defer his intention of matrimony, and he had reflected that in taking a wife, a man of good position should expect and carefully choose a blooming young lady – the younger the better, because more educable and submissive – of a rank equal to his own, of religious principles, virtuous disposition, and good understanding. On such a young lady he would make handsome settlements, and he would neglect no arrangement for her happiness; in return, he should receive family pleasures and leave behind him that copy of himself which seemed so urgently required of a man – to the sonneters of the sixteenth century. Times had altered since then, and no sonneteer had insisted on Mr Casaubon's leaving a copy of himself; moreover, he had not yet succeeded in issuing copies of his mythological key; but he had always intended to acquit himself by marriage, and the sense that he was fast leaving the years behind him, that the world was getting dimmer and that he felt lonely, was a reason to him for losing no more time in overtaking domestic delights before they too were left behind by the years.

And when he had seen Dorothea he believed that he had found even more than he demanded: she might really be such a help-mate to him as would enable him to dispense with a hired secretary, an aid which Mr Casaubon had never yet employed and had a suspicious dread of. (Mr Casaubon was nervously conscious that he was expected to manifest a powerful mind.) Providence, in its kindness, had supplied him with the wife he needed. A wife, a modest young lady, with the purely appreciative, unambitious abilities of her sex, is sure to think her husband's mind powerful. Whether Providence had taken equal care of Miss Brooke in presenting her with Mr Casaubon was an idea which could hardly occur to him. Society never made the preposterous demand that a man should think as much about his own qualifications for making a charming girl happy as he thinks of hers for making himself happy. As if a man could choose not only his wife but his wife's husband! Or as if a man could choose not only his wife but his wife's husband! Or as if he were bound to provide charms for his posterity in his own person! – When Dorothea accepted him with effusion, that was only natural; and Mr Casaubon believed that his happiness was going to begin.

He had not had much foretaste of happiness in his previous life. To know intense joy without a strong bodily frame, one must have an enthusiastic soul. Mr Casaubon had never had a strong bodily frame, and his soul was sensitive without being enthusiastic: it was too languid to thrill out of self-consciousness into passionate delight; it went on fluttering in the swampy ground where it was hatched, thinking of its wings and never flying. His experience was of that pitiable kind which shrinks from pity, and fears most of all that it should be known; it was that proud narrow sensitiveness which has not mass enough to spare for transformation into sympathy, and quivers thread-like in small currents of self-preoccupation or at best of an egoistic scrupulosity. And Mr Casaubon had many scruples: he was capable of a severe self-restraint; he was resolute in being a man of honour according to the code; he would be unimpeachable by any recognized opinion. In conduct these ends had been attained; but the difficulty of making his Key to all Mythologies unimpeachable weighed like lead upon his mind; and the pamphlets – or 'Parerga' as he called them – by which he tested his public and deposited small monumental records of his march, were far from having been seen in all their significance. He suspected the Archdeacon of not having read them; he was in painful doubt as to what was really though of them by the leading minds of Brasenose, and bitterly convinced that his old acquaintance Carp had been the writer of that depreciatory recension which was kept locked in a small drawer of Mr Casaubon's desk, and also in a dark closet of his verbal memory. These were heavy impressions to struggle against, and brought that melancholy embitterment which is the consequence of all excessive claim: even his religious faith wavered with his wavering trust in his own authorship, and the consolations of the Christian hope in immortality seemed to lean on the immortality of the still unwritten Key to all Mythologies. For my part I am very sorry for him. It is an uneasy lot at best, to be what we call highly taught and yet not to enjoy: to be present at this great spectacle of life and never to be liberated from a small hungry shivering self – never to be fully possessed by the glory we behold, never to have our consciousness rapturously transformed into the vividness of a thought, the ardour of a passion, the energy of an action, but always to be scholarly and uninspired, ambitious and timid, scrupulous and dim-sighted. Becoming a dean or even a bishop would make little difference, I fear, to Mr Casaubon's uneasiness. Doubtless some ancient Greek has observed that behind the big mask and the speaking-trumpet, there must always be our poor little eyes peeping as usual and our timorous lips more or less under anxious control.

George Eliot: Middlemarch

Before you leave the area of literature to persuade, perhaps a group of you could put together an anthology of pieces of writing which made you think or feel differently. This will also give you an opportunity to 'sell' your favourite writers.

Our analysis of Blake's London

The alterations which immediately strike one are lexical. In the first two lines of the poem 'dirty' has been replaced by 'charter'd'; in terms of sound effect these are very similar, both being bi-syllabic and containing the fluid, alliterative r. However, their emotional impact is very different: 'dirty' is a word collocated with disapproval (its value is pejorative), whereas 'charter'd', whose signification is 'mapped out', is far more factual in tone. The lexical change in the third line is even more significantl. Not only does the elision of the word 'mark' avoid an unnecessary and ineffective repetition but 'see', which replaces it, has two values: to see physically and to understand. 'Mark' has only the value 'notice', and is thus implying less sympathy. The choice of 'infant' in line six has a similar effect. Unlike 'child' it is collocated with the infant Jesus and thus has connotations of innocence and purity. 'Cry' is clearly more emotive than the factually descriptive 'voice'. The same emotional shift is evident in the change in the second line of the last stanza from 'midnight' with its overtones of darkness, loneliness and sinister activities to 'youthful' with overtones of innocence and freshness. 'Youthful' is a far more shocking, oxymoronic adjective with which to modify 'harlot' since one would expect a prostitute to be corrupt.

Sometimes, not wishing to lose the impact of an individual word, Blake has transposed it rather than omitting it. Thus he retains 'midnight' but places it in the first line modifying 'streets' instead of the second. He also moves 'But most' to the opening of the final stanza rather than the third one. This clearly makes more sense, since 'But most' would normally introduce a climax. Putting the climax at the end gives a feeling of build-up.

The final lexical alteration is in the final line of the poem, and has a dual purpose. 'Blights' not only achieves an alliterative and thus emphatic effect with 'blasts', but is also inherently more dramatic. 'Blights' could never be collocated with happy endings!

Often in the poem the need to alter one word has necessitated the entire re-wording of a line. For example, in the eighth line Blake has excluded 'german'. Perhaps he realised that it might offend some readers or simply felt that its value was unclear. (Blake would seem to be collocating 'german' with cold and ruthless; this would not be the case for many readers.) The omission of 'german' affects the rhythm of the line, leaving it two syllables short. The change from 'links' to 'manacles' rectifies this, and at the same time it creates an alliterative effect in combination with 'mind-forg'd' and collocates more closely in the reader's mind with imprisonment.

Not every alteration in the poem is purely lexical. If we consider the second stanza we can see that whereas in the first draft a parallel structure (preposition, adjective, noun) has been used to divide up units of meaning and have repetitive force, in the later draft the parallel structure is abandoned and thus the commas are needed to separate the units. The structure has been altered to allow the inclusion of the more emotive lexical items 'cry of fear' and 'infant'.

Another line which has been altered radically is the second one of the third stanza. The tense change from 'blackens' (present simple) to 'black'ning' (present continuous) suggests that the process is ongoing – is happening continually and cannot be stopped. The use of 'black'ning' as an adjectival modifier links it more closely to the church. 'Every ... church' is far more emphatic than 'churches', meaning as it does churches without exception rather than simply more than one church. 'Church' (singular) also has the value of the institution, and thus the entire institution of the church is seen as being undermined, not just individual buildings. The use of 'appalls' is also interesting. An emotive verb usually collocated with animate objects, it is here used to emphasise that the church has feelings, is almost human. This is akin to personification.

To summarise, we can see that by altering lexical items, introducing more emotion, by changing phonological items to gain alliterative, emphatic effects and by careful use of punctuation and verb forms Blake has achieved a more persuasive, dramatic whole.

Chapter 17

Make 'em cry

We will now move on to that other aim of literature closely linked to message-sending: its ability to move us. No-one is suggesting that we all weep buckets when we read; many would consider this self-indulgent and superficial. However, one of the legitimate functions of literature is catharsis – the releasing of negative emotions. We will start with poetry, since it is easier to see the effect of the whole of a short poem than of a prose extract.

We have chosen the first poem because, despite the fact that it is about an incredibly emotional subject – the death of an infant son who, judging by the subheading, was brain-damaged – is not melodramatic or sentimental. Read it now and see if you agree with us. All readers respond personally, and for some of you it may be more upsetting or offensive than it is to us. If that is the case, adopt every reader's right and skip this bit of text. If, on the other hand, you agree with us that it is a moving, effective, interesting poem, think about it a little before you read our analysis.

Death of a Son

(who died in a mental hospital, aged one)

Something has ceased to come along with me.
Something like a person: something very like one.
And there was no nobility in it
Or anything like that.

Something was there like a one-year-
Old house, dumb as stone. While the near buildings
Sang like birds and laughed
Understanding the pact

They were to have with silence. But he
Neither sang nor laughed. He did not bless silence
Like bread, with words.
He did not forsake silence.

But rather, like a house in mourning
Kept the eye turned in to watch the silence while
The other houses like birds
Sang around him.

And the breathing silence neither
Moved nor was still.

I have seen stones: I have seen brick

But this house was made up of neither bricks nor stone
But a house of flesh and blood
With flesh of stone

And bricks for blood. A house
Of stones and blood in breathing silence with the other
Birds singing crazy on its chimneys.
But this was silence,

This was something else, this was
Hearing and speaking though he was a house drawn
Into silence, this was
Something religious in his silence,

Something shining in his quiet,
This was different this was altogether something else:
Though he never spoke, this
Was something to do with death.

And then slowly the eye stopped looking
Inward. The silence rose and became still.

The look turned to the outer place and stopped,
With the birds still shrilling around him.
And as if he could speak

He turned over on his side with this one year
Red as a wound
He turned over as if he could be sorry for this
And out of his eyes two great tears rolled, like stones, and he died.

Jon Silkin

❖ How is sentimentality avoided in this poem?
❖ What emotions does the description of the child evoke?
❖ Is the poem restricted to this one death or does it seem to have a wider relevance?
❖ Does the poem seem at all self-indulgent or mawkish?

What we were struck by most on a first reading of this poem was the almost shocking apparent detachment of the writer. The very title *Death of a Son* sounds so matter-of-fact. Why the indefinite article 'a' rather than the possessive pronoun 'my'? (That might be worth seriously considering.) The description of the child as 'some*thing*' which is very '*like*' a person' is distressing, and the bald statement 'there was no nobility in *it*' (notice the neuter pronoun) is candid and clear. The last line of the stanza, the more colloquial, imprecise 'Or anything like that' is striking. The writer seems vague – indeed much of the poem conveys a seeking after understanding of the child and what he represented. His father compares him to things: 'like a one-year-/Old house'. He emphasises and re-emphasises the child's silence. At first this is seen negatively – 'dumb as stone' suggests lack of feeling and lack of intellect. In contradistinction the other children are animated: sing, laugh, are normal. The attitude of the writer to his son seems negative: he stresses what he did *not* do, that he 'Neither sang nor laughed', that 'he did not forsake silence and 'did not bless silence ... with words.'

At this stage an alert reader notices a lexical shift and a different emphasis. The choice of words suggests a religious context, almost a Christ-like peace. Later on this is made more blatant in the phrase 'Something religious in his silence'. His silence begins to seem less and less passive and uninterested; it is 'breathing' – alive and yet dead-seeming. The child is described as 'a house of flesh and blood'. The 'flesh' here may well connote with God made flesh; again the link with Christ.

As the poem progresses, the words describing the child become more and more positive. There is 'Something shining in his quiet'. Nor is he selfish or callous: he stops 'looking inward'. He has made a choice, it seems, not to speak (not to complain?) It is as if he could speak (the modal auxiliary is vital here) and could be sorry for himself and mankind, but he will not utter a word. However, his pain and humanity are conveyed by the 'two great tears' which roll from his eyes. 'Great' would seem to have the meaning 'noble' as well as 'large' here. They are his final, human statement.

Just as the attitude to this child shifts, so does that towards the other children. At first, they are seen positively: they 'sang ... and laughed'. At the next mention, they 'sang' only. Then, interestingly, they are described as 'singing crazy'. (Is this a reminder that they, too, are mentally handicapped but they take refuge in sound rather than silence?) Their noise is not normal or joyful. This is most clearly conveyed in the final reference to them – 'the birds still shrilling' – which sounds most unattractive.

Indeed, sound is an important element in the poem's impact. The line division of 'one-year-' from 'Old house' makes the reader recognise the incongruity of 'one-year-old' as a collocation. The expression is a standard one but the writer adds to its meaning by the pause between the lines. He makes us aware that the child encompasses both extreme youth and ancient wisdom. The fact that 'Old' is placed initially gives greater emphasis to the child's 'age' than to his youth.

Rhyme also has a part to play. The rhyme linking 'laughed' and 'pact' accelerates the pace of the stanza and makes the other 'buildings' sound brighter and more active and jolly. The caesura before 'But he' gives it full emphasis and slows the pace down, conveying a more serious tone. The short, bald statement utilises long, slow vowels because the tone is contemplative and the poet is trying to puzzle out why. This explains the 'But rather' which has the flavour of a spoken voice explicating or re-expressing and searching for the right words. Part of this search necessitates similes. He is 'like a house in mourning' metaphorically as well as literally. He is also a 'breathing silence' and 'a house of flesh'.

Many vital words are placed initially after a run-on line. One example would be

> **And then slowly the eye stopped looking**
> **Inward.**

Line length and layout also emphasise important parts of the text. Thus

> **And the breathing silence neither**
> **Moved nor was still**

is a two-line stanza standing out from the other four-line ones. The line 'Red as a wound' with its four monosyllables is noticeably short. The last line is the longest and mirrors the slow, painful yielding up of the child's life.

The next poem we'd like you to look at is also about loss, but this time the separation is between man and wife and voluntary – at least on the wife's part.

Song for Last Year's Wife

Alice, this is my first winter
of waking without you, of knowing
that you, dressed in familiar clothes
are elsewhere, perhaps not even
conscious of our anniversary. Have
you noticed? The earth's still as hard,
the same empty gardens exist; it is
as if nothing special had changed.
I wake with another mouth feeding
from me, yet still feel as if
Love had not the right
to walk out of me. A year now. So
what? you say. I send out my spies
to discover what you are doing. They smile,
return, tell me your body's as firm,
you are as alive, as warm and inviting
as when I knew you first. ... Perhaps it is
the winter, its isolation from other seasons,
that sends me your ghost to witness
when I wake. Somebody came here today, asked
how you were keeping, what
you were doing. I imagine you
waking in another city, touched
by this same hour. So ordinary
a thing as loss comes now and touches me.

Brian Patten

❖ Look at the title and the first word of the first line. What is their effect?
❖ Who is the audience of the poem?
❖ Look at the layout of the poem. Is it a poem?
❖ Why is it less overtly 'poetical' than most poems?
❖ Is the poem metaphorical or figurative at all?
❖ What sort of tone does it have?
❖ How would you describe the attitude of the writer (or his persona) to his wife?
❖ How effective do you consider the last sentence of the poem to be?
❖ Do you find the totality moving or not?
❖ Finally, select three lines or images which you feel work well, and try to explain their effect.

The final poem we would like you to consider in this chapter returns to the theme of loss by death. It is a very well known poem by a writer far more literary and overtly 'poetical' than Patten – Dylan Thomas. The poem is directly addressed to another person.

◆ Decide to whom the poem is addressed.

◆ Look carefully at repetition in the poem. Is it emphatic and effective or merely tedious?

◆ Some have regarded Thomas' verse as 'sound and fury signifying nothing'. Write a full analysis of the poem which includes a judgement on its manner as well as its matter.

Do Not Go Gentle Into That Good Night

Do not go gentle into that good night,
Old age should burn and rave at close of day;
Rage, rage against the dying of the light.

Though wise men at their end know dark is right,
Because their words have forked no lightning they
Do not go gentle into that good night.

Good men, the last wave by, crying how bright
Their frail deeds might have danced in a green bay,
Rage, rage against the dying of the light.

Wild men who caught and sang the sun in flight,
And learn, too late, they grieved it on its way,
Do not go gentle into the good night.

Grave men, near death, who see the blinding sight
Blind eyes could blaze like meteors and be gay,
Rage, rage against the dying of the light.

And you, my father, there on the sad height,
Curse, bless me now with your fierce tears, I pray.
Do not go gentle into that good night.
Rage, rage against the dying of the light.

Dylan Thomas

Prose

It is rather more difficult to find prose passages which have an immediate impact upon the reader because prose is so much more context-dependent. What we will do is to provide an introductory statement about each of the passages so as to put you in a better position to judge the passage's effect.

The first extract is from Paul Scott's novel *Staying On*. The novel concerns an elderly, superficially unattractive couple who decide to 'stay on' in India after their retirement. Tusker, the husband, is irascible, seemingly selfish and by no means a model husband. The extract is a letter from Tusker to his wife, Lucy, explaining what her position will be in the event of his death. In the context of the novel, it is in many ways a shock, because it allows us to see a very different side to Tusker's character. At the same time it contains many elements which are in line with Tusker as we have come to know him. At the end of the chapter, the letter is described as 'the only love letter she had had in all the years she had lived'.

Read the extract and do three things:

❖ Decide whether you would describe it as a love letter. What evidence is there to support such a claim?
❖ Attempt a character sketch of Tusker on the basis of the letter. How much do you learn about him?
❖ How much can you deduce about the thematic content of this novel? Do you think the Indian element is important? Or the fact of the central characters being old?

While the kettle was boiling she read Tusker's note again:

'You asked for a clear statement of yr posn if widowed. Far as I can see y'd get from IMWOF about £900 pa plus a RW supplt of maybe £600. Say £1500 in all, adjustable from time to time to cost of living index. The Smalley Estate income dries up on my death but y've always known that, Luce, and for the past ten years quite apart from the fall in value of the capital investment it's also yielded less interest because some bloody fool at Coyne Coyne persuaded the trustee to reinvest some of it in so-called Blue Chip equities (young Coyne, I reckon). Been getting less than £200 a year out of it since about 1964. Always tried to keep some of that money back in London but gradually had to have it all transferred as it came in to the Bank in Bombay. Present bank balance here approx £500, maybe £200 in London. Life Insurance only £2000 but the policy's with profits and been going long enough maybe to double that value at maturity. What it all comes to Luce is you've enough to take you home if that's what you want though in yr posn I'd prefer to stay here, considering the sort of income you'll have. At home you can't starve really, what with supplementary benefits, and things like Distressed Gentlefolk (Ha!). Also they've got the Nat Health and Old People's Homes. Perhaps for a white person being poor in England's better than being poor in India, though by average Indian standards we're rich if not by the standards of the Indians we mix with. I'm sorry, Luce, if I seem to have made a mess of things. You'll be wondering where some of the money we've occasionally managed to get our hands on went and I don't really know. It was never much anyway. About £3000 compensation when my army career petered out with Independence and I was too old to transfer to British service. We spent a lot of that on that trip home for Smith Brown & McKintosh (because they only paid my expenses) but I'm not making that an excuse. I know I was a fool, Luce. The profit I made on the car we brought back from the UK and sold to old Grabbitwallah as I used to call him, in the days when that sort of gimmick was still legal was really no profit because it was paid for in black money, in one hundred rupee notes which I couldn't very well bank, and nothing goes quicker than hundred rupee notes. Some of them quick on the Bombay racetrack, as you know. In those days nearly everybody was bringing cars out from home free of UK tax because they were being exported and then selling them to Indians who couldn't get cars any other way except by waiting years. But I was playing out of my league because I thought of money like

171

that as fairy gold whereas to people with a real instinct for turning a fast buck it was plain solid cash. Some of my separation pay from Smith Brown & McKintosh went on paying up arrears on my contributions to IMWOF, I'd got a bit behind, but I never mucked about with that, Luce, because I knew it would be your mainstay. Most of the rest went on that round-India trip before settling here. I know for years you've thought I was a damn' fool to have stayed on, but I was forty-six when Independence came, which is bloody early in life for a man to retire but too old to start afresh somewhere you don't know. I didn't fancy my chances back home, at that age, and I knew the pension would go further in India than in England. I still think we were right to stay on, though I don't think of it any longer as staying on, but just as hanging on, which people of our age and upbringing and limited talents, people who have never been really poor but never had any real money, never inherited real money, never made real money, have to do, wherever they happen to be, when they can't work any more. I'm happier hanging on in India, not for India as India but because I can't just merely think of it as a place where I drew my pay for the first 25 years of my working life, which is a hell of a long time anyway, though by rights it should have been longer. But there you are. Suddenly the powers that be say, Right, Smalley, we're not wanted here any more, we've all got to bugger off, too bad you're not ten years younger or ten years older. I thought about this a lot at the time and it seemed to me I'd invested in India, not money which I've never had, not talent (Ha!) which I've only had a limited amount of, nothing India needed or needs or has been one jot the better for, but was all I had to invest in anything. *Me*. Where I went wrong was in thinking of it that way and expecting a return on the investment in the end, and anticipating the profits. When they didn't turn up I know I acted like an idiot, Luce, for years and years. The longest male menopause on record. One long Holi. Can't talk about these things face to face, you know. Difficult to write them. Brought up that way. No need ever to answer. Don't want you to. Prefer not. You've been a good woman to me, Luce. Sorry I've not made it clear I think so. I'm not going to read all this rigmarole through when I've finished – if I did I'd tear it up. So I'll just stick it in the envelope and forget it. Don't want to discuss it. If you do I'll only say something that will hurt you. No doubt will anyway. It's my nature. Love, Tusker.'

Paul Scott: Staying On

It probably required quite an imaginative leap for you to empathise with a couple of retired Anglo-Indians. If you did, so much more credit to Scott. One of the things many would claim for literature is that it widens our sympathies.

The following extract will probably make yet greater demands upon your abilities to empathise. It comes from a novel called *Walter*. Like the poem we looked at earlier it deals with the potentially mawkish subject of a brain-damaged person. What is interesting and daring about the novel is that it gives Walter a voice; an opportunity to express his point of view. The narrative often switches from his point of view to his mother's. The first extract we shall look at is from the mother's viewpoint.

> Sleeping. He always slept well. She stood, watching him sleep, had risen earlier from her own bed than was necessary, in order to stand over him while he slept. Sleeping, she could bear him. If he slept for ever, she would be content.
>
> Yet the face on the pillow never ceased to make her angry. She herself had been pretty, and had been told so, more than once. His father had looked – not handsome, not even passably good-looking, since his neck had been long and thin like a bird's neck, but at least alright: Eric had looked alright. But Walter, sleeping, Witless Walter, was a mistake made by nature, and God had chosen not to correct it. The heavy hooded eyelids, closed now over bulging eyes. The hooked nose, which resembled a joke nose one might buy at the seaside, with an elastic band to hold it over one's real nose. The large pointed jaw, and protruding teeth, yellow and green where they stuck out sharply from the gums. The oily sallow skin and tiny white-headed pimples.
>
> Leaning over him, close to his sleeping face, she whispered, 'You must be the ugliest person in this town, and you spent nine months inside me.' His breath was foul. 'Constipated. Must be. Never thinks to tell me these things.'
>
> She moved away, and sat against the wall on a straight-backed chair to watch him. There was plenty of time. She spoke to God, as she had spoken many times before. 'Why has my life been so ill arranged, Lord? Why allow me only one child, and that an ill-put-together, foul-smelling, dribbling lump of ugliness?' God might have replied that she had never tried to make another, that although matrimony was a holy state and sanctified for the procreation of children, she had denied her husband access to her womb after it had once been filled, so that He, God, could hardly be held responsible for any subsequent barrenness. But God was old and wise and knew well the futility of argument with a complaining woman. He permitted her to continue.
>
> 'I won't mince words with you, Lord. Not now; I'm too old.' She never had minced words, God sighed, and wondered whether a sparrow somewhere might be falling, to distract His attention. 'I've visited Your chapel twice every Sunday, since I was taken there, at five years old, to Sunday School. Almost sixty years, multiplied by fifty-two, then doubled. I can't begin to count the hours I've sat on hard benches or knelt on a prayer-stool to Your greater glory, and tried to cast everything from my mind but Your face.' It would be the face of Christ she meant; the other two persons of the Trinity didn't have a face. The Face composed itself in patience, and continued to listen. 'I never believed those pictures with the halo. Not like that. Not You. You had to be more beautiful in my mind, more masculine than any of those. Man was made in Your likeness.' She looked across at the sleeping figure. 'Is this what You look like? Is Walter made in Your likeness? Is that Your likeness, a physically grotesque man of twenty-seven, with the brain of an infant? Why?'

Why the years of soiled blankets and sheets, the crying, shouting, screaming? Why the hope that he would improve, would learn, that with age he would change, would become at least less of an embarrassment? God had made that hope, had allowed it to persist, kept Sarah at it. Had His intention been to punish? If so, for what? 'Everybody has thoughts. Thoughts they shouldn't have. Unnatural.' Everybody must have those thoughts sometimes, the shameful, unnatural thoughts, which slipped into her mind and clung, like spiders clinging to the side of the bath. You might wish to wash them away down the dark plug-hole, and clean yourself, but there would be no hole in your mind down which to wash them, so they would persist.

But everyone would have such thoughts: it was unfair to punish her. God was unfair and heartless. She had complained to Him so often, and He never took any notice. Walter's mother wiped the tears from her face with a small lace handkerchief which smelt of lavender. She returned the handkerchief to the pocket of her apron, and went over to the bed. It was time to wake her son.

David Cook: Walter

A very striking aspect of this passage is the mother's attitude to her son. She is distressingly negative about her child: 'Sleeping, she could bear him. If he slept for ever, she would be content.' Not only is the surface statement here upsetting, the fact is that she did literally bear him, so her callousness seems unnatural and frightening in its intensity. The wish that he might sleep forever is tantamount to wishing him dead.

The mother is not merely indifferent; she is positively repelled. The words used to describe Walter as she looks at him make this clear. He has 'heavy, hooded eyelids', 'bulging eyes', a 'hooked nose' and a 'large pointed jaw' with 'protruding teeth', both 'yellow and green'. 'Oily, sallow skin' dotted with 'tiny white-headed pimples' completes the dreadful picture. She seems utterly relentless – cruel to the point of spitefulness – yet she has 'risen earlier than was necessary, in order to stand over him while he slept.' Was it only to indulge in a two-minute hate?

Look at the passage again. How does it make you feel about the mother, the son and their relationship? Try to pick out the key words.

Now look at Walter's description of his mother and reference to himself in the following extract:

The first thing he saw every morning was her face.

Sleeping was like being dead. She would shake him out of sleep at half past seven every morning. He didn't like it. He was drowned, and she would pull him to the surface with a long rope. He would struggle, but the rope would only become tighter. The water round him would bubble, pulling him down, water up his nostrils and inside his head, hair flattened over his eyes.

He would come up slowly, gulping at the air when he reached the top.

'Come on, Walter. You can't lie there forever.'

That's what she always said, every morning. The water was warm.

He liked it above his head. Not having to think. You can't ever go backwards. Even when you remember last week, you can't go there. The clock keeps ticking, moving you on. When you're in a pleasant bit of time, why can't you just stop there?

She shook him. He nodded. Alive, there was time to pass, things to remember, other people asking questions. Rules.

She watched him all the time. All the time, his mother watching. She said they were tied together by a rope he couldn't see. He always did as he was told now, yet she got no pleasure, not even when he was good. She used to like him to remember things. Now she liked nothing. Smile, he had seen her smile. But he could no longer remember her smile.

The first thing he saw every morning was her face. It was not like his own. Her face was small, round and shiny. She did not wear make-up like the Counter Girls. It was dirty stuff; she did not hold with it. 'Come on! Out you get!' He closed his eyes, remembering the warmth of the water, and she shook him.

Her eyes were not hooded like his. 'Move, will you?' He sat up, blinking. His mother's eyes did not stick out, but fitted with the rest of her face. They were red this morning, because she cried for him.

She took his ankles, and swung them round so that his feet were off the bed and touching the cold linoleum.

Her nose was not like the top half of a parrot's beak. He did not go to school any more; he was too old now to go to school. They had called him names, 'Parrot Face' and 'Witless Walter'.

Her teeth did not stick out. They were false now, because she was old; he had seen them out of her mouth.

She stood back from the bed, and watched him. She would remain to make sure that he stood up, his body entirely leaving the bed. She would not leave the room until he had taken his pyjamas off. He could tell her he was alright now, but she would stand there; she would not go. He would whine, but she would wait.

He took off his pyjama jacket. She should know now that he had grown out of messing himself, it was a subject no longer mentioned. He dropped his pyjama trousers to the floor, and turned round on the spot. No need for words now. Looks were enough.

She left him, and went into the bathroom. He heard the sound of water running, wrapped a towel around his waist, and sat on the bed until she called for him.

He sat on the toilet, while she waited outside the door, listening. He made water, but nothing else.

'I'll give you something this morning to make your bowels move. And if you have to go while you're at work, remember to clean yourself properly. And wash your hands.'

The sound of the toilet being flushed brought her into the bathroom. He sat in the lukewarm water, while she slid the lavender-scented soap all over his body. He didn't shout now, or scream, or make any noises to stop her. He didn't struggle. He just sat there.

She slid her soapy hands all over his chest, back and legs. She never touched his willy. She would point to that, and give him the soap. 'Do it some more. Come on. More soap. Between your legs.'

She was standing now, and she had the towel ready. As he stepped out of the bath, she turned her head away. 'You must be rotten inside, the way your breath smells.'

He stood there while she dried his back, legs and buttocks, rubbing them hard. 'If you can't do Number Twos in the morning, you must tell me. Alright?' He nodded. 'No sense in leaving it until you've got to smelling like a parrot's cage. What will they think at work?'

He didn't know what they would think.

'Don't know was made to know. If people complain about you, you'll be out of a job. Woolworth's customers don't want you breathing down their necks, not with that breath.'

She finished drying his face, neck, ears and feet. He did the rest. He had clean underwear every other day. She would watch to make sure he wore it.

As I get into my clothes, I tell myself aloud what I have to remember. 'Don't dawdle!' 'You're slouching, Walter. Stand up straight.' 'Pay attention.' 'You are a cross for my back, Walter, you really are.' All my socks are darned. She does them well. I won't wear nylon socks. I'd rather break things up than wear socks that squeak and crackle. She knows now not to buy them. I taught her. 'It's not worth the screaming fits, even though wool is more expensive.' I wear a navy-blue suit to go to work in. At work I wear an overall. Seventy-four bus, that's what I get. 'Not the Forty-seven, Walter. Silly blockhead! Seventy-four, not Forty-seven. Mill Hill, Chorlton, Flixstead. The number Six goes to Flixstead too. You don't want that.' I sit on my bed, rocking, taking time to dress. She watches. 'Number Two is a Special. Only bring it out at holiday times. Always clean, Number Two.' I laugh because she has to wait for me. No, Forty-seven's not my bus, not for going home on. Seventy-four. 'There you are, you see. You're alright, Walter. Walter's alright. Only eleven pence to the shilling, but he knows what it's about.'

'Are you ready?'

I look at her and laugh, rocking backwards and forwards as I sit on the bed. She shakes her head, and looks at the linoleum on my bedroom floor. I stop laughing, and try to see what she is looking at. But there's nothing there, only the pattern.

'Li No Lee Um. Not lino, Walter. Linoleum.'

Breakfast was on the table. She would lay it out the night before, and come down before she woke him, to cook the rest. She couldn't sleep.

She sat beside him, not facing him. She had the view out of the window to look at, and did not have to look at him. He swung his legs backwards and forwards as he ate. Whenever she heard them bang against the chair, she shouted at him to stop.

She wouldn't eat until after he had left the house.

She stared out of the window. She only looked at him to see whether he had finished.

She could feel him looking at her with those bulging eyes. The hooded lids blinked as he grinned and chortled to himself. How could she know what he was thinking?

If anyone looks at me, I point my finger at them, and start to laugh. I throw my head back, and laugh until they turn away. She taught me. At school, they would do that to me, and when I told her she said, 'Do it to them back, then,' but if I waited for them to do it first, I felt sad inside, and couldn't laugh. So I started to laugh at them before they had time to laugh at me. I put my hand over my mouth, and pointed, and laughed. It made them angry, and they called me names. Then they stopped laughing at me. They would pretend I was not there. Then I would laugh to myself. I started laughing a lot then. I keep myself ready in case somebody who doesn't know me should point at me and laugh. I'm laughing to myself now. It annoys her.

She woke me up.

David Cook: Walter

❖ How realistic is Walter about himself?
❖ How does he feel about his mother?
❖ How does he describe her and her actions?
❖ With whom do we sympathise in these passages?
❖ What emotions do they evoke?
❖ Are they in 'good taste'?

You will have noticed that when discussing the second passage we talked a lot about voice – which is where we began. It isn't really possible to divide up the aims or effects of literature into watertight compartments.

Chapter 18

Make 'em laugh – Humour

In the final part of this literature section we are hoping to end on a cheerful note by looking at some of the ways writers attempt to make us laugh.

Writing to make a reader laugh can of course be an end in itself, but frequently humour is harnessed to other purposes as well. It is rarely possible to say that a stretch of writing, still less a whole work, is written simply to make us laugh, or just to entertain, to teach, to illuminate the human condition or any other of the clichés pressed into service to explain what a piece of literature is 'for'. We have already touched on the virtual impossibility of answering this question, so let's just accept that a lot of stories, poems or plays make us laugh, and look at how writers use words to amuse.

Sometimes the humour is closely involved with something we've just been looking at, the establishment of a 'voice'. The tone adopted by the writer is itself amusing, full of witty asides and comments, or it can be amusing by virtue of its inappropriateness, in which case we laugh at rather than with the narrator.

Sometimes the events and characters described are themselves fantastic or ridiculous, the literary equivalent of slapstick humour. By exaggerating characters and situations which are similar to those of 'real life' (if there is such a thing) humour can be used to comment on injustice, cruelty or evil. One of the most 'literary' forms of humorous writing is when one writer imitates, but exaggerates, the style of another, usually in relation to totally inappropriate subject matter. This is parody. Lastly, words themselves become the source of humour, as in puns, riddles, rhyme and word-play.

This is far from being an exhaustive list, but it does include some of the techniques used by the writers we are going to look at. The range of styles in humorous writing and the uses it can be put to, are many and varied. Let's look at our first example.

This is an extract from a book called *Lake Wobegon Days* by an American, Garrison Keillor, who is usually described as a 'humorous writer'. The book is not a novel: it has no continuous narrative. Instead, Keillor creates a fictional small town in the middle of America and describes the characters who live there, its history and the main events of the year. He appears to be drawing on memories of his own childhood, and some of the humour comes from the fact that Lake Wobegon resembles real small towns in mid-America. This extract is fairly representative.

> What's special about here isn't special enough to draw a major crowd, though Flag Day – you could drive a long way on June 14 to find another like it.
> Flag Day, as we know it, was the idea of Herman Hochstetter, Rollie's dad, who ran the dry goods store and ran Armistice Day, the Fourth of July, and Flag Day. For the Fourth, he organized a double-loop parade around the block which allowed people to take turns marching and watching. On Armistice Day, everyone stepped outside

at 11 A.M. and stood in silence for two minutes as Our Lady's bell tolled eleven times.

Flag Day was his favorite. For a modest price, he would install a bracket on your house to hold a pole to hang your flag on, or he would drill a hole in the sidewalk in front of your store with his drill gun powered by a .22 shell. *Bam!* And in went the flag. On patriotic days, flags flew all over; there were flags on the tall poles, flags on the short, flags in the brackets on the pillars and the porches, and if you were flagless you could expect to hear from Herman. His hairy arm around your shoulder, his poochlike face close to yours, he would say how proud he was that so many people were proud of their country, leaving you to see the obvious, that you were a gap in the ranks.

In June 1944, the day after D-Day, a salesman from Fisher Hat called on Herman and offered a good deal on red and blue baseball caps. "Do you have white also?" Herman asked. The salesman thought that white caps could be had for the same wonderful price. Herman ordered two hundred red, two hundred white, and one hundred blue. By the end of the year, he still had four hundred and eighty-six caps. The inspiration of the Living Flag was born from that overstock.

On June 14, 1945, a month after V-E Day, a good crowd assembled in front of the Central Building in response to Herman's ad in the paper:

> Honor "AMERICA" June 14 at 4 p.m. Be
> proud of "Our Land & People". Be part of
> the "LIVING FLAG". Don't let it be said
> that Lake Wobegon was "Too Busy". Be on
> time. 4 p.m. "Sharp".

His wife Louise handed out the caps, and Herman stood on a stepladder and told people where to stand. He lined up the reds and whites into stripes, then got the blues into their square. Mr. Hanson climbed up on the roof of the Central Building and took a photograph, they sang the national anthem, and then the Living Flag dispersed. The photograph appeared in the paper the next week. Herman kept the caps.

In the flush of victory, people were happy to do as told and stand in place, but in 1946 and 1947, dissension cropped up in the ranks: people complained about the heat and about Herman – what gave *him* the idea he could order *them* around? "People! Please! I need your attention! You blue people, keep your hats on! Please! Stripe No. 4, you're sagging! You reds, you're up here! We got too many white people, we need more red ones! Let's do this without talking, people! I can't get you straight if you keep moving around! Some of you are not paying attention! Everybody shut up! Please!"

One cause of resentment was the fact that none of them got to see the Flag they were in; the picture in the paper was black and white. Only Herman and Mr. Hanson got to see the real Flag, and some boys too short to be needed down below. People wanted a chance to go up to the roof and witness the spectacle for themselves.

"How can you go up there if you're supposed to be down here?" Herman said. "You go up there to look, you got nothing to look at. Isn't it enough to know that you're doing your part?"

On Flag Day, 1949, just as Herman said, "That's it! Hold it now!" one of the reds made a break for it – dashed up four flights of stairs to the roof and leaned over and had a long look. Even with the hole he left behind, it was a magnificent sight. The Living Flag filled the street below. A perfect Flag! The reds so brilliant! He couldn't take his eyes off it. "Get down here! We need a picture!" Herman yelled up to him. "How does it look?" people yelled up to him. "Unbelievable! I can't describe it!" he said.

So then everyone had to have a look. "No!" Herman said, but they took a vote and it was unanimous. One by one, members of the Living Flag went up to the roof and admired it. It *was* marvelous! It brought tears to the eyes, it made one reflect on this great country and on Lake Wobegon's place in it. One wanted to stand up there all afternoon and just drink it in. So, as the first hour passed, and only forty of the five hundred had been to the top, the others got more and more restless. "Hurry up! Quit dawdling! *You've* seen it! Get down here and give someone else a chance!" Herman sent people up in groups of four, and then ten, but after two hours, the Living Flag became the Sitting Flag and then began to erode, as the members who had had a look thought about heading home to supper, which infuriated the ones who hadn't. "Ten more minutes!" Herman cried, but ten minutes became twenty and thirty, and people snuck off and the Flag that remained for the last viewer was a Flag shot through by cannon fire.

In 1950, the Sons of Knute took over Flag Day. Herman gave them the boxes of caps. Since then, the Knutes have achieved several good Flags, though most years the attendance was poor. You need at least four hundred to make a good one. Some years the Knutes made a "no-look" rule, other years they held a lottery. One year they experimented with a large mirror held by two men over the edge of the roof, but when people leaned back and looked up, the Flag disappeared, of course.

Garrison Keillor: Lake Wobegon Days

The comic effect of this passage relies on the interplay between the ridiculous, yet just plausible nature of the situation which is described, and the 'deadpan' tone in which the events are recounted. The narrator doesn't explicitly point to, or comment on, the humour of what is happening until the 'of course' in the final sentence.

It is important for the plausibility that the reader accepts the 'reality' of this place and these people and the authenticity of these events. How is this achieved?

Although the author does not represent himself as an actual participant in the 'living flag', which enables him to keep his detached, distant perspective on the scene, he does establish himself as a member of the community through such expressions as 'as we know it' (the inclusive first person plural), 'What's special about here' (not 'there'), and the description of Herman as 'Rollie's Dad' which carries no explanation of who Rollie might be. 'If you were flagless, you could expect to hear from Herman' he says conversationally, as if he'd seen it happen. He's clearly in the know: 'You need at least four hundred to make a good one.'

By such means the reader accepts the reality of the event and is drawn into it. Events become progressively more ridiculous and the final punch-line is built up to in a gradual and believable fashion. Did you see it coming?

Something else which contributes to the impression that the writer is not describing this because it's funny, but because it's 'real' is the unadorned and factual nature of the prose. The narrative itself, as opposed to the direct speech, consists mainly of statements. There are relatively few adjectives, though Herman's 'hairy arm' and 'poochlike face' are obvious exceptions. The paragraph which begins 'His wife Louise handed out the caps' contains eleven statements, all with the same, simple subject-verb structure. The sentences are often linked by the co-ordinating conjunction 'and'. The final short sentence of the paragraph, 'Herman kept the caps', is just the sort of straightforward detail that confirms the authenticity. The effect of this apparent 'artlessness' is to make the reader feel she is not being led or manipulated by a lot of literary trickery, but is being told real events by a real voice.

This final sentence is funny because by this time we feel we know Herman and we know what he would do. His patriotic fervour and his entrepreneurial talents have formed a happy combination. Herman's character is important to the humour. He is a serious organiser, a bit of a 'wheeler-dealer' who, despite his earnest attempts, is defeated by human nature.

Herman's defeat is best shown in the verbs used in the passage. In the early part, Herman is the subject of most of the verbs: he 'ran', 'organized', 'would drill', 'would say', 'asked', 'ordered' and so on. He is still there at the end: he 'cried', he 'gave them the box of caps' (as opposed to selling them!); but in the latter part of the piece, the Flag (note the capital) is taking over. As you would expect, either the Flag collectively or its constituent parts become the subject of many of the verbs: 'The Living Flag filled the street'; 'The Living Flag became the Sitting Flag'; 'everyone had to have a look.' The Flag has won. Herman is no longer in charge.

There are other humorous touches in the piece, such as the way the participants are referred to by their function in the flag: 'Stripe No. 4, you're sagging', 'one of the reds made a break for it'. Capitalisation of the Living Flag gives it an importance which is comic, as do the recurring military references: 'dissension cropped up in the ranks', 'a Flag shot through by cannon fire.' The event is apparently treated very seriously by the people involved, by the narrator at first and above all by Herman; but by the end it has become ridiculous.

The next extract is from Charles Dickens' novel *Bleak House*, and in it he describes tea-time with the Smallweed family. This follows a passage in which he has introduced old Grandfather and Grandmother Smallweed, a particularly dry and joyless couple, like most other members of the family. Dickens conveys the most representative family trait, lack of imagination, in an extended metaphor:

> Everything that Mr. Smallweed's grandfather ever put away in his mind was a grub at first, and is a grub at last. In all his life he has never bred a single butterfly.

All the Smallweeds are 'lean and anxious-minded', and never seem to have displayed or enjoyed the fun, irresponsibilities and imaginative pleasures of childhood. They all appear to have been born 'complete little men and women' until 'Mr Smallweed's grandmother, now living, became weak in her intellect and fell (for the first time) into a childish state.' Having thus had the family characterised fairly explicitly for us, we join the Smallweed grandparents waiting for their tea:

At the present time, in the dark little parlour certain feet below the level of the street – a grim, hard, uncouth parlour, only ornamented with the coarsest of baize table-covers, and the hardest of sheet-iron tea-trays, and offering in its decorative character no bad allegorical representation of Grandfather Smallweed's mind – seated in two black horse-hair porter's chairs, one on each side of the fire-place, the superannuated Mr. and Mrs. Smallweed while away the rosy hours. On the stove are a couple of trivets for the pots and kettles which it is Grandfather Smallweed's usual occupation to watch, and projecting from the chimney-piece between them is a sort of brass gallows for roasting, which he also superintends when it is in action. Under the venerable Mr. Smallweed's seat and guarded by his spindle legs is a drawer in his chair, reported to contain property to a fabulous amount. Beside him is a spare cushion with which he is always provided in order that he may have something to throw at the venerable partner of his respected age whenever she makes an allusion to money – a subject on which he is particularly sensitive.

"And where's Bart?" Grandfather Smallweed inquires of Judy, Bart's twin sister.

"He an't come in yet," says Judy.

"It's his tea-time, isn't it?"

"No."

"How much do you mean to say it wants then?"

"Ten minutes."

"Hey?"

"Ten minutes." (Loud on the part of Judy.)

"Ho!" says Grandfather Smallweed. "Ten minutes."

Grandmother Smallweed, who has been mumbling and shaking her head at the trivets, hearing figures mentioned, connects them with money and screeches like a horrible old parrot without any plumage, "Ten ten-pound notes!"

Grandfather Smallweed immediately throws the cushion at her.

"Drat you, be quiet!" says the good old man.

The effect of this act of jaculation is twofold. It not only doubles up Mrs. Smallweed's head against the side of her porter's chair and causes her to present, when extricated by her granddaughter, a highly unbecoming state of cap, but the necessary exertion recoils on Mr. Smallweed himself, whom it throws back into his porter's chair like a broken puppet. The excellent old gentleman being at these times a mere clothes-bag with a black skull-cap on the top of it, does not present a very animated appearance until he has undergone the two operations at the hands of his granddaughter of being shaken up like a great bottle and poked and punched like a great bolster. Some indication of a neck being developed in him by these means, he and the sharer of his life's evening again fronting one another in their two porter's chairs, like a couple of sentinels long forgotten on their post by the Black Serjeant, Death.

Judy the twin is worthy company for these associates. She is so undubitably sister to Mr. Smallweed the younger that the two kneaded into one would hardly make a young person of average proportions, while she so happily exemplifies the before-mentioned family likeness to the monkey tribe that attired in a spangled robe and cap she might walk about the table-land on the top of a barrel-organ without exciting much remark as an unusual specimen. Under existing circumstances, however, she is dressed in a plain, spare gown of brown stuff.

Judy never owned a doll, never heard of Cinderella, never played at any game. She once or twice fell into children's company when she was about ten years old, but the children couldn't get on with Judy, and Judy couldn't get on with them. She seemed like an animal of another species, and there was instinctive repugnance on both sides. It is very doubtful whether Judy knows how to laugh. She has so rarely seen the thing done that the probabilities are strong the other way. Of anything like a youthful laugh, she certainly can have no conception. If she were to try one, she would find her teeth in her way, modelling that action of her face, as she has unconsciously modelled all its other expressions, on her pattern of sordid age. Such is Judy.

Charles Dickens: Bleak House

This could hardly present a greater contrast to the *Lake Wobegon Days* piece. In that, we noticed a lack of adjectives and little figurative language. Here, there is a lot of premodification, mainly in the form of adjectives, and post-modification in the form of similes. The reader's responses are quite clearly being directed by Dickens. It would be an obtuse reader who identified or sympathised with the Smallweeds. The humour depends on our being aware of the writer's perspective and laughing at these characters with him.

Yet on the face of it, Dickens uses some complimentary phrases to describe the family. List all the words and phrases with positive associations used to describe the three Smallweeds. There are a fair number, aren't there? Words such as 'venerable', 'good old'. If we include other expressions associated with them such as 'while away the rosy hours', this list would imply that this is a sentimental description of lovable Darby and Joan in contented retirement. But of course it isn't.

Now list all the words and phrases with negative connotations used to describe the Smallweeds. There are just as many of those: words such as 'spindle', 'horrible old parrot'. You might notice that the word 'old' had positive connotations when collocated with 'good', but negative ones when linked to 'horrible' and 'parrot', an example of how words are coloured by those surrounding them.

Yet there really aren't any problems for the reader in this mix of positive and negative descriptions of the same characters. Nor do we feel ambivalent towards the Smallweeds. This is because we recognise that the 'positive' description is not to be taken at face value. In other words we recognise irony, the gap between what the writer is apparently saying and what we know he means. Irony is a frequent feature of humorous writing. In this passage it is easy to spot because Dickens has already made his opinions of the characters he has created quite clear.

Now let's consider the way Dickens presents the events, which are themselves the source of much of the humour, concentrating on the paragraph which begins 'The effect of this jaculation'.

Look first at that word 'jaculation', which actually means 'the action of darting, hurling or throwing'. Its main interest lies in the fact that it is rather obscure. If you look it up in the Shorter Oxford Dictionary, it actually says that it is 'rare'. It is a word of Latin derivation, not in common use.

Can you find other examples in this paragraph of Dickens choosing to use rather elevated words or phrases instead of more common or direct expressions? Words of Latin derivation are often associated with higher levels of formality, so you could note any of those too.

There are several examples of both elevated formal lexis, and of using a group of words where one might have done (technically this is called periphrasis), such as 'does not present a very animated appearance' instead of 'lifeless' or 'necessary exertion' instead of 'effort'. What is the effect of this, and does it add anything to the humour of the passage? The contrast between the sordid, undignified events and the formal elaborate way they are described certainly needs commenting on. The mismatch of tone and subject matter is seen throughout the passage, but is most noticeable in this paragraph.

Easier to comment on, possibly, is the contribution made by the use of figurative language to the comedy of the piece. Pick out four examples of this, two similes and two instances of metaphorical usage.

If one of the examples you have chosen is 'shaken up like a bottle and poked and punched like a great bolster', perhaps we should stop and consider why anyone might find it funny to imagine an old person being treated in this way. But this isn't the place for a lengthy disquisition on taste. If it is funny, the humour is in the ingenuity of the comparison, in creating incongruous, exaggerated pictures in words. After all, Grandfather Smallweed isn't real, although in depicting the life-denying constrictions of the Smallweed personality Dickens is clearly making serious comment. The humour of this piece is a mixture of the slapstick and the grotesque, but harnessed to a serious moral purpose. The 'pattern of sordid age' which has moulded Judy is not really anything to laugh at. No irony here, but maybe we take the point more seriously because of the previous laughter.

The next passage, which we'd like you to do the work on, is the opening of a short story by the contemporary writer Fay Weldon. Like Dickens, Weldon is using humour to make a serious point, and as with *Bleak House*, we are in little doubt about the author's perspective on her characters. However, she uses rather different methods. Here is the opening of Fay Weldon's story *Weekend*:

> By seven-thirty they were ready to go. Martha had everything packed into the car and the three children appropriately dressed and in the back seat, complete with educational games and wholewheat biscuits. When everything was ready in the car Martin would switch off the television, come downstairs, lock up the house, front and back, and take the wheel.
>
> Weekend! Only two hours' drive down to the cottage on Friday evenings: three hours' drive back on Sunday nights. The pleasures of greenery and guests in between. They reckoned themselves fortunate, how fortunate!
>
> On Fridays Martha would get home on the bus at six-twelve and prepare tea and sandwiches for the family: then she would strip four

beds and put the sheets and quilt covers in the washing machine for
Monday: take the country bedding from the airing basket, plus the
books and the games, plus the weekend food – acquired at intervals
throughout the week, to lessen the load – plus her own folder of work
from the office, plus Martin's drawing materials (she was a market
researcher in an advertising agency, he a freelance designer) plus
hairbrushes, jeans, spare T-shirts, Jolyon's antibiotics (he suffered
from sore throats), Jenny's recorder, Jasper's cassette player and so
on – ah, the so on! – and would pack them all, skilfully and quickly,
into the boot. Very little could be left in the cottage during the week.
("An open invitation to burglars": Martin.) Then Martha would run
round the house tidying and wiping, doing this and that, finding the
cat at one neighbour's and delivering it to another, while the others
ate their tea; and would usually, proudly, have everything finished by
the time they had eaten their fill. Martin would just catch the BBC2
news, while Martha cleared away the tea table, and the children
tossed up for the best positions in the car. "Martha," said Martin,
tonight, "you ought to get Mrs Hodder to do more. She takes
advantage of you."

Mrs Hodder came in twice a week to clean. She was over seventy.
She charged two pounds an hour. Martha paid her out of her own
wages: well, the running of the house was Martha's concern. If
Martha chose to go out to work – as was her perfect right, Martin
allowed, even though it wasn't the best thing for the children, but
that must be Martha's moral responsibililty – Martha must surely
pay her domestic stand-in. An evident truth, heard loud and clear
and frequent in Martin's mouth and Martha's heart.

"I expect you're right," said Martha. She did not want to argue.
Martin had had a long hard week, and now had to drive. Martha
couldn't. Martha's licence had been suspended four months back for
drunken driving. Everyone agreed that the suspension was unfair:
Martha seldom drank to excess: she was for one thing usually too
busy pouring drinks for other people or washing other people's
glasses to get much inside herself. But Martin had taken her out to
dinner on her birthday, as was his custom, and exhaustion and
excitement mixed had made her imprudent, and before she knew
where she was, why there she was, in the dock, with a distorted
lamp-post to pay for and a new bonnet for the car and six months'
suspension.

So now Martin had to drive her car down to the cottage, and he
was always tired on Fridays, and hot and sleepy on Sundays, and
every rattle and clank and bump in the engine she felt to be somehow
her fault.

Martin had a little sports car for London and work: it could nip in
and out of the traffic nicely: Martha's was an old estate car, with
room for the children, picnic baskets, bedding, food, games, plants,
drink, portable television and all the things required by the middle
classes for weekends in the country. It lumbered rather than zipped
and made Martin angry. He seldom spoke a harsh word, but Martha,
after the fashion of wives, could detect his mood from what he did not

say rather than what he did, and from the tilt of his head, and the way his crinkly, merry eyes seemed crinklier and merrier still – and of course from the way he addressed Martha's car.

"Come along, you old banger you! Can't you do better than that? You're too old, that's your trouble. Stop complaining. Always complaining, it's only a hill. You're too wide about the hips. You'll never get through there."

Fay Weldon: Weekend

Look first at the opening three paragraphs. They end with Martin saying 'She takes advantage of you.' What was your reaction when you read that? If it was the same as ours, a hollow laugh and a 'she's not the only one', then Fay Weldon has made her point without any explicit statement. How? To answer this we suggest you look for a few specific things:

Verbs: who are the subjects of them? Count them.
What sort of verbs are they?
Lists
Repetition of structures
Punctuation
Frequency and placing of names (as opposed to pronouns)

Of course, seeing how point of view is created need have nothing to do with humour, but in this case it does. The predictable nature of this family's behaviour is important to the comedy. We 'see it coming' and the unrelenting pattern which is set up, like knowing which clown at the circus is going to get the bucket of water in his face, is part of what makes us smile. It's a form of exaggeration, but the exaggerated picture is in the selection and accumulation of detail, rather than the details themselves.

The relationship between Martha and Martin is not the only comic subject here. There is also social satire on the customs and lives of a particular class. How and where is this best conveyed?

As the passage continues, a different sort of vocabulary enters for the first time. What sort of words are 'right', 'responsibility' and 'truth'? Does the introduction of this judgemental attitude affect our reaction to the situation?

Interestingly, the one person who does not have critical terms applied to him is Martin. Even when he gets angry he is described in positive terms: 'merrier still'. How do we receive his final remarks to the car?

Our final passage, for you to analyse, is another satire on (almost) contemporary life. It is from a novel by Tom Sharpe called *Wilt*. In it, the 'hero' Wilt, a teacher in a further education college, is 'teaching' a class of apprentice butchers with little enthusiasm. Describe how language is used to produce comic effects in this extract.

At five to two, none the wiser, he went down to Room 752 to extend the sensibilities of fifteen apprentice butchers, designated on the timetable as Meat One. As usual they were late and drunk.

'We've been drinking Bill's health,' they told him when they drifted in at ten past two.

'Really?' said Wilt, handing out copies of *The Lord of the Flies*. 'And how is he?'

'Bloody awful,' said a large youth with 'Stuff Off' painted across the back of his leather jacket. 'He's puking his guts out. It's his birthday and he had four Vodkas and a Babycham ...'

'We'd got to the part where Piggy is in the forest,' said Wilt, heading them off a discussion of what Bill had drunk for his birthday. He reached for a board duster and rubbed a drawing of a Dutch Cap off the blackboard.

'That's Mr Sedgwick's trademark,' said one of the butchers, 'he's always going on about contraceptives and things. He's got a thing about them.'

'A thing about them?' said Wilt loyally.

'You know, birth control. Well, he used to be a Catholic, didn't he? And now he's not, he's making up for lost time,' said a small pale-faced youth unwrapping a Mars Bar.

'Someone should tell him about the pill,' said another youth lifting his head somnolently from the desk. 'You can't feel a thing with a Frenchie. You get more thrill with the pill.'

'I suppose you do,' said Wilt, 'but I understood there were side-effects.'

'Depends which side you want it,' said a lad with sideburns.

Wilt turned back to *The Lord of the Flies* reluctantly. He had read the thing two hundred times already.

'Now Piggy goes into the forest ...' he began, only to be stopped by another butcher, who evidently shared his distaste for the misfortunes of Piggy.

'You only get bad effects with the pill if you use ones that are high in oestrogen.'

'That's very interesting,' said Wilt. 'Oestrogen? You seem to know a lot about it.'

'Old girl down our street got a bloodclot in her leg ...'

'Silly old clot,' said the Mars Bar.

'Listen,' said Wilt. 'Either we hear what Peter has to tell us about the effects of the pill or we get on and read about Piggy.'

'F– Piggy,' said the sideburns.

'Right,' said Wilt heartily, 'then keep quiet.'

'Well,' said Peter, 'this old girl, well she wasn't all that old, maybe thirty, she was on the pill and she got this bloodclot and the doctor told my auntie it was the oestrogen and she'd better take a different sort of pill just in case and the old girl down the street, her old man had to go and have a vasectomy so's she wouldn't have another bloodclot.'

'Buggered if anyone's going to get me to have a vasectomy,' said the Mars Bar, 'I want to know I'm all there.'

'We all have ambitions,' said Wilt.

'Nobody's going to hack away at my knackers with a bloody great knife,' said the sideburns.

'Nobody'd want to,' said someone else.

'What about the bloke whose missus you banged,' said the Mars Bar. 'I bet he wouldn't mind having a go.'

Wilt applied the sanction of Piggy again and got them back on to vasectomy.

'Anyway, it's not irreversible any more,' said Peter. 'They can put a tiny little gold tap in and you can turn it on when you want a nipper.'

'Go on! That's not true.'

'Well, not on the National Health you can't, but if you pay they can. I read about it in a magazine. They've been doing experiments in America.'

'What happens if the washer goes wrong?' asked the Mars Bar.

'I suppose they call a plumber in.'

Tom Sharpe: Wilt

Much of the humour of Wilt's rather desultory conversation with Meat One is the humour of speech. It does somewhat dignify the exchange

'Old girl down our street got a bloodclot in her leg ... '
'Silly old clot,' said the Mars Bar.

to call it wordplay, but it is wordplay of a crude and obvious kind. This passage is full of attempted jokes and asides at other people's expense, of bawdy and insulting comment, and of the sort of random connections between one subject and another which crop up in everyday talk.

Humorous verse

These and other qualities of spoken language are often exploited in humorous verse, which delights in puns, rhymes, alliteration and the melody and stress patterns of speech. Some instances of such verse just have to be recited out loud for full effect. They are written to be performed, often in a particular accent and/or dialect, in which pronunciation adds to the humour. Examples of these would be *Albert and the Lion* (Lancashire), *Ilkla Moor Baht 'at* (Yorkshire) or many of the poems of John Betjeman (Southern RP).

There is a distinct satisfaction in verse with a regular rhyme and rhythm which lends itself to humour. Think of limericks you know, where the amusement is in spotting the final rhyme; or the familiar patterns of traditional pantomime, in which either the predictability or the ingenuity of the rhymes contributes a lot to the fun.

Here is a poem by the Jamaican poet, Valerie Bloom. The basic joke is the puzzlement a newcomer to England experiences when she hears the variety of words which English people use for meals. As language students you will probably have discussed this question yourselves. Why is the same meal 'tea' for some people, but 'dinner' for others? To the native speaker, this can be a clear marker of class or region; to the stranger, it's just confusion.

Wha Fe Call I'

Miss Ivy, tell mi supmn,
An mi wan' yuh ansa good.
When yuh eat roun 12 o'clock,
Wassit yuh call yuh food?

For fram mi come yah mi confuse,
An mi noh know which is right,
Weddah dinnah a de food yuh eat midday,
Or de one yuh eat a night.

Mi know sey breakfus a de mawnin one
But cyan tell ef suppa a six or t'ree,
An one ting mi wi nebba undastan,
Is when yuh hab yuh tea.

Miss A dung a London ha lunch 12 o'clock,
An dinnah she hab bout t'ree,
Suppa she hab bout six o'clock,
But she noh hab noh tea.

Den mi go a Cambridge todda day,
Wi hab dinnah roun' bout two,
T'ree hour later mi frien she sey,
Mi hungry, how bout yuh?

Joe sey im tink a suppa time,
An mi sey yes, mi agree,
She halla, Suppa? a five o'clock,
Missis yuh mussa mean tea!

Den Sunday mi employer get up late,
Soh she noh hab breakfus nor lunch,
But mi hear she a talk bout 'Elevenses',
An one sinting dem call 'Brunch'.

Breakfus, elevenses, an brunch,
lunch, dinnah, suppa, tea,
Mi brain cyan wuk out which is which,
An when a de time fc hab i'.

For jus' when mi mek headway,
Sinting dreadful set mi back,
An dis when mi tink mi know dem all,
Mi hear bout one name snack.

Mi noh tink mi a badda wid no name,
Mi dis a nyam when time mi hungry,
For doah mi 'tomach wi glad fe de food,
I' couldn care less whey mi call i'.

Valerie Bloom

In this poem the rhythm is not absolutely regular. Lines vary between three and five stresses, although the majority are three; but what is consistent is that the final line of each verse always has three stresses and rhymes more or less exactly with the second line, rounding off each verse neatly and making the poem a series of minor jokes within the framework of the one which runs throughout.

By the end of the second verse we know what this basic joke is, and what we are waiting for, especially in performance, is to see what the next permutation is going to be. The structure tells us when the punchline is coming, and we know there's a limit to the number of terms the poet has to play with, so we try to anticipate what she will come up with this time. Because she is more ingenious than us, and because, although it works best in performance, this is written and cleverly crafted, Valerie Bloom delivers better lines than the ones we had anticipated.

The dialect contributes to the humour in other ways. It helps establish the character's perspective. It is often funny to look at something very familiar through a stranger's eyes. The poet Craig Raine does the same thing in his 'Martian' poems, in which ordinary objects and events are described by a visitor from outer space. In this case, the difficulty experienced by a visitor from another country in understanding our language customs has the effect of making us wonder why they are so curious and inconsistent. There is an explicit reference to the speaker's visitor status: 'For fram mi come yah ... ', but it is reinforced throughout mainly by the dialect.

Something of the speaker's character is conveyed through the 'voice'. There is a genuine sense of puzzlement throughout verse three, for instance: 'An one ting mi wi nebba undastan'; and finally we recognise that this is an outsider with a lot of common sense:

> For doah mi 'tomach wi glad fe de food,
> I' couldn care less whey mi call i'.

We can do little but agree that we are a rather odd lot to have constructed so many social hurdles around the simple subject of food. The joke is on us.

But it is a fairly gentle joke. Humour can be used in verse, as in prose, for more serious purposes. Alexander Pope, in the eighteenth century, wrote a long poem called *The Rape of the Lock*, in which he ridicules the 'high society' of his day by mocking the importance attached to fashion and social etiquette to the neglect of virtue and true morality. Much of the humour of this poem comes from his descriptions of minor social events such as card games, in the style traditionally associated in classical poetry with epic events like battles. In this short extract the sylphs whose job it is to preserve the appearance of fashionable young women as they go about their social round, explain the difficulties of their task:

> "Our humbler province is to tend the fair,
> Not a less pleasing, though less glorious care;
> To save the powder from too rude a gale,
> Nor let the imprison'd essences exhale;
> To draw fresh colours from the vernal flowers;
> To steal from rainbows, ere they drop in showers,
> A brighter wash; to curl their waving hairs,
> Assist their blushes and inspire their airs;
> Nay, oft, in dreams, invention we bestow,
> To change a flounce, or add a furbelow.
>
> "This day, black omens threat the brightest fair
> That e'er deserved a watchful spirit's care;
> Some dire disaster, or by force, or flight;

But what, or where, the Fates have wrapp'd in night.
Whether the nymph shall break Diana's law,
Or some frail china-jar receive a flaw;
Or stain her honour or her new brocade;
Forget her prayers, or miss a masquerade;
Or lose her heart, or necklace, at a ball;
Or whether Heaven has doom'd that Shock must fall.

Alexander Pope

Here the rhyme scheme, and the rhythm, are absolutely regular. The lexis is elevated: 'humbler province', 'imprison'd essences exhale', 'invention we bestow'; but the task is mundane: 'save the powder', 'curl their waving hairs' or 'change a flounce'. The contrast between the language and the events is the source of the fun. At first it seems harmless: vanity might be a sin, but as manifested in these pretty young women, it hardly seems a deadly one.

The sting, however, is in the second part. The spirits are troubled by a sense of foreboding; something dreadful is about to happen. As they speculate on what this might be, they consider, in lines fifteen to nineteen of the extract, the worst things that could happen to a young woman.

The rhythm and rhyme scheme here balance the alternatives: she may lose her virginity ('break Diana's law') or crack a favourite ornament. The two things are equated in the verse, just as they are in the mind of the young woman. This disturbs us: it's funny, but it's shocking. Pope goes on to list other 'calamities' whose juxtaposition has the same effect as the first. Is a vanity which equates the loss of a necklace with the loss of a heart really so harmless? Pope's humour is harnessed to serious purpose here, as in the poem as a whole.

The next poem for you to look at, by the contemporary poet Adrian Mitchell, does not use its humour for any purpose other than to call attention to itself in the exuberance of its language.

Watch Your Step – I'm Drenched

In Manchester there are a thousand puddles.
Bus-queue puddles poised on slanting paving stones,
Railway puddles slouching outside stations,
Cinema puddles in ambush at the exits,
Zebra-crossing puddles in dips of the dark stripes –
They lurk in the murk
Of the north-western evening
For the sake of their notorious joke,
Their only joke – to soak
The tights or trousers of the citizens.
Each splash and consequent curse is echoed by
One thousand dark Mancunian puddle chuckles.

In Manchester there lives the King of Puddles,
Master of Miniature Muck Lakes,
The Shah of Slosh, Splendifero of Splash,
Prince, Pasha and Pope of Puddledom.
Where? Somewhere. The rain-headed ruler

Lies doggo, incognito,
Disguised as an average, accidental mini-pool.
He is as scared as any other emperor,
For one night, all his soiled and soggy victims
Might storm his streets, assassination in their minds,
A thousand rolls of blotting paper in their hands,
And drink his shadowed, one-joke life away.

Adrian Mitchell

What is the 'one joke' on which this poem is based? If any of you come from Manchester you may consider this just another addition to the tired old jokes which stereotype your city as somewhere it's always raining, but there's a lot of variety in this wetness, isn't there?

❖ List the different ways the puddles are characterised.
❖ How has Adrian Mitchell employed the language to imply that they have a sense of purpose?
❖ Look at the titles he gives to the King of Puddles. What language devices are being used here? Can you invent some more titles of your own in the same vein?
❖ Where else in the poem does playing with the sounds of words add to the humour?
❖ How are the tables turned in the last five lines? Is there anything about these lines which makes you wonder for a moment whether Mitchell might have a serious purpose after all?
❖ There is no regular rhythm or rhyme scheme, but both rhyme and rhythm are exploited for comic effect. Where and how?

Parody

Finally, we are going to ask you to look at an example of one of the most literary forms of humour – parody.

To write a parody, you must have a model. In your parody, you imitate the style of the model, but introduce inappropriate subject matter, or words from a different register. In a sense, Alexander Pope was writing a parody of the epic style in the example we looked at from *The Rape of the Lock*. He used the grand style for inappropriate subject matter, and we laugh at both the style and the society whose pretensions he was ridiculing.

Sometimes the purpose of parody is to ridicule, but just as often it's primarily to amuse. To show what we mean, here is an example of parody at its simplest, in an example you may well be familiar with:

Hark! the jelly babies sing,
Beecham's pills are just the thing,
They are gentle, meek and mild,
Two for a man and one for a child.
If you want to go to heaven
You must take a dose of seven,
If you want to go to hell
Take the blinking box as well.

Obviously, this is a children's parody of the carol *Hark! the Herald Angels Sing*, in which the usual words have been replaced by mildly irreverent ones. Literary parodies, in which one writer mimics the style of another are usually a bit more sophisticated, but the principle is the same. We leave you to make a detailed comparison of the following two poems.

Hawk Roosting

I sit in the top of the wood, my eyes closed.
Inaction, no falsifying dream
Between my hooked head and hooked feet:
Or in sleep rehearse perfect kills and eat.

The convenience of the high trees!
The air's buoyancy and the sun's ray
Are of advantage to me;
And the earth's face upward for my inspection.

My feet are locked upon the rough bank.
It took the whole of Creation
To produce my foot, my each feather:
Now I hold Creation in my foot

Or fly up, and revolve it all slowly –
I kill where I please because it is all mine.
There is no sophistry in my body:
My manners are tearing off heads –

The allotment of death.
For the one path of my flight is direct
Through the bones of the living.
No arguments assert my right:

The sun is behind me.
Nothing has changed since I began.
My eye has permitted no change.
I am going to keep things like this.

Ted Hughes

Crow Resting

I sit at the top of the tree,
My mouth closed. I have been sitting here
Since the beginning of Time.
I am going to carry on sitting here
And if anybody tries to stop me sitting here
I will remove his head;
A single-mind-sized bite will do it.
I will eat his head and with a stab, a jerk
A bounce I'll have his bowels, balls,

Big toes, his colon and his semi-colon.
I will drink his blood from the goblet
Of his skull, his thin giblets
From the platter of his pelvic bone. And
I will spread his shit with generosity.
In other words forget it.
I was here first, I was here long ago.
I was here before you. And I will be here
Long after you have gone. What superbard says
Goes. I am going to keep things like this.

Edward Pygge

• SECTION THREE •

LANGUAGE INVESTIGATION

This section provides advice on conducting your language project.

Chapter 19: What can I look at?
– the collection and recording of good and honest data.

Chapter 20: What can I look for?
– how to ask questions of your data.

Chapter 21: How should I present my findings?
– hints on how to submit your investigation in its final form.

Chapter 22: Inside a marker's head
– examples of good and bad practice

Chapter 23: Your own words
– the link with creative writing

Chapter 19

What can I look at?
– the collection and recording of data

So far in this book you have been looking at varieties of English which have been provided for you. The third section of *Your Own Words* aims to help you choose your own examples of language, spoken or written, to investigate yourself – a personal investigation.

As your curiosity and knowledge about language have been increasing alongside your skill in describing it, you will have become more sensitive to interesting features in language use you come into contact with every day, such as intriguing differences between one speaker and another, or the way a single speaker's language varies from one situation to another. You may have noticed significant distinctive features in the style of a newspaper or magazine you read, or a type of novel you enjoy. You might wonder why particular occupation or interest groups develop their own vocabulary and style, or notice the way particular 'slang' expressions come into and out of English and mark off one group from another. You might be fortunate enough to be in regular contact with a young child who is just learning to speak, or to read or to write, and be able to investigate their progress. In fact, the possibilities are endless, and any of these topics and many, many more could provide you with material for project work.

A language project is a personal investigation into a variety of English, spoken or written. It might be quite a small scale one to begin with – just noting and recording the forms of address used by or to you in one day, for example, and suggesting what these might reveal about your social relationships. It could be a contribution to a larger group investigation into swearing, or telephone manners. If there is a project as part of your course you will then have to undertake a thorough, well-defined investigation which is presented clearly in a formal fashion.

However large or small your project the same systematic and objective approach is necessary. Your project should not be a collection of random observations, it needs to be well planned and researched. Investigating language for project purposes enables you to apply your knowledge and understanding of it in greater depth to a relatively small area. You will be discovering things for yourself. In the process you will become quite an expert on your particular topic and sharpen the skills which develop your confidence in discussing language generally.

Although there is an enormous range of subjects which are suitable for investigation, all good language projects have a few basic features in common:

They all have as their basis/starting point good and 'honest' raw material – **data**.
They all have a focus for the investigation – a question, a theory or hypothesis to 'test' in relation to the data.
The findings are clearly presented in readable fashion.

The next three chapters explore project work in relation to these features. They answer the questions

What can I look at? – which gives some ideas for project work and suggestions about how to obtain useful data, spoken and written.

What should I look for? – which examines ways in which you can focus your investigation, and how to test your hypothesis.

How should I present my findings? – which gives advice on how to write a project in its final form, in itself quite a challenging exercise.

As a summary, this section gives hints on what makes a good and a bad project, and considers some examples.

There is one other feature which all good investigations must have in common and, although it is not treated separately, it underlies all the hints and advice in the next three chapters. It is most important of all that any findings which emerge as a result of your hard look at the evidence arise from the data itself and are not imposed by you. In other words, although you should have a hunch about what your investigation might come up with, you must see what is there, and not only what you expect to see. Your intuition might be the starting point, but, like a good detective, you must assume nothing, and take nothing on trust. You may miss the vital clue if you start with too many preconceived notions. You must be prepared to discover that the language of the *Daily Star* newspaper is more complex and sophisticated than the language of *The Guardian*, even if your instincts tell you it isn't. You must start with an open mind. A project which discovers the opposite of what it expected is just as valid as one which finds what was anticipated, provided that in both cases the findings emerge from an objective and systematic look at the evidence. And it would be no disgrace for a project conducted along these lines to come up with no hard or fast conclusions. The process of investigation is the crucial factor.

What can I look at?

The answer to this is anything – any use of language you hear or see around you. Provided that the focus of your investigation is a question concerning language, the world (or in this case, word) is your oyster!

In practice, of course, although some language investigations do look at a new area in a totally original way, most fall into certain categories, and similar questions get asked in relation to different data. For instance, an investigation of the language development of a two year-old child will be unique because that child's language will be unique, but it will also probably discover that it shows many of the features you would expect of other two year-olds. In the same way, an examination of the way the same news story is presented by different newspapers with different readerships or political standpoints will be original because the news stories are new, but it will probably discover similar stylistic features as other such investigations. But these projects might also discover something new – something particular. Whether they do or not, however, is not crucial.

Take a good look at yourself

It is crucial that you choose your own area of investigation and formulate your own project title. You are much more likely to feel committed to and involved in an investigation in which you have found the evidence and posed the questions, rather than one which has been given to you by a (despairing?) teacher! By all means seek advice, from teachers and from books, but choose your general area yourself. Draw on areas of interest, use your strengths and avoid drawing attention to any areas of weakness. This is possible if you are finding the material and narrowing down the focus. You are in control. This is possibly more important when deciding what to look for (in the next section) but should influence your choice of topic too.

Strengths: Familiarity

Let's be positive first: is there any area of language of which you have a particularly close knowledge or experience? This might be related to your life outside school or college or to your other subject areas. Do you know a lot about computer language? Do you read a lot of science fiction, romance, or fantasy novels? Perhaps your other subjects bring you into contact with specialist magazines or forms of specialist language – legal, business or scientific. Do you speak a particular form of colloquial English or possibly patwa, or are you bilingual? Do you watch a lot of soap operas, have a part-time job which uses occupational jargon, listen to a lot of local radio? Are you involved in a pressure group or interested in politics? The list is endless. A familiarity with a particular variety of English means you probably already know quite a lot about it and have an ear for its subtleties. You can build on and exploit this in an investigation, provided that you can step back and view it objectively.

Interest

You will probably be choosing your topic for investigation about half way through the course. Which areas of study have interested you most so far? You are going to spend a long time looking very hard at a fairly small amount of data, so choose something you find interesting, or you could end up merely going through the motions. Perhaps you have become particularly engaged with certain topics: whether men and women use the same language, or recent changes in language use you have discussed, or the differences between spoken and written forms, or what you have learned about interaction and discourse anlaysis. Choose an area which intrigues and stimulates you, rather than something which seems straightforward (or even easy).

Access

Something else which might influence your choice is whether or not you have easy and natural access to any varieties of language which would provide you with good project material. Do you look after or live with a small child whose language is developing fast? Do you have a relative, friend or neighbour who speaks with a pronounced accent or dialect? At college, home or work is there anyone whose use of language interests you and can you observe them easily in particular or different situations? Perhaps your family speak a language other than English at home, or a mixture of English and mother tongue. Do you have letters from a foreign penfriend, all your school exercise books, old diaries or letters, an exhaustive collection of Manchester United football programmes or copies of *The Beano*? Again, the list is endless.

Of course, you can set out to search and find data by research and use of libraries, archives or by writing letters requesting access to observe and visit primary schools, old people's homes, magistrates' courts – anywhere you like – and we discuss these later. But look at your immediate environment first to exploit all possibilities. After all, why make problems for yourself?

Skills

What are you particularly good at? Do you have any special skills that you could draw on for your project? Do you have a particularly good ear for the sounds of language? If so, a project on spoken English which looked at accent, pitch and stress features might be a good idea. Are you developing skills related to other subjects which would be useful – for instance, Sociology (drawing up questionnaires, sampling techniques); Computing (handling and analysing a lot of data); Literature (this gives you a head start on stylistic analysis); another language (an insight into translation problems and comparing languages); Psychology (group interaction)?

All projects demand that you analyse language, but you might know that you are better at some aspects of this than others. For example, are you particularly sensitive to the meanings and associations of words? You might consider looking at news reporting or some project which concentrates on point of view. Draw on your particular area of strength, and avoid

Weaknesses

Be honest. If you have strengths then you probably have some areas of weakness too. If phonetics remain a bit of a mystery, avoid projects on accent. If syntax is still something of a blind spot, then don't choose a topic which exposes this, such as most areas of close stylistic analysis.

Fortunately, with almost any stretch of data, you can formulate different questions to focus on, so perhaps it is in the 'what should I look for' section that we need to consider this more fully. It's important to set yourself a challenge with your project, but there's no need to be foolhardy. In choosing your topic, then, you need to balance interest, knowledge, realistic access to data and strengths and weaknesses. None of these should dictate your topic area, but a balanced and honest look at yourself is a good place to start when you are deciding what to do.

Next you must decide on your approach.

Scientist or detective?

It cannot be too strongly stressed that the vital pre-requisite for a good project is an open-minded investigator. Good projects must reveal what is there – present in the language – not what you, the investigator, would like to see. You start with your 'specimen' of language – your data – and work outwards rather than looking at the evidence in the light of preconceived ideas. Like a good scientist or detective, you don't impose your conclusions, you come to them only after close and sceptical scrutiny. So whether you prefer to see yourself as a scientist or as a detective, you must question and look closely. But before any of this objective research can take place you need something to work with, so that's where we will start. Scientific principles are as important in the collection of data as they are in the actual investigation.

First catch your specimen

Just as in the laboratory, unless the raw material you are working with is pure and uncontaminated, you are never going to reach accurate conclusions. The data must be as genuine, as honest as possible. What does this mean?

First of all, what does 'data' mean? It's an awkward word. Is it singular or plural? Is the first *a* pronounced as in 'date' or as in 'dart'? Turning to that useful research tool for any language investigator, an etymological dictionary, does provide us with some answers: 'data' is the plural form of 'datum' and is pronounced 'dayta'. The most useful meaning which is given for our purposes is 'something known or assumed as fact and made the basis of reasoning or calculation.'

Well ... yes, but this doesn't accurately reflect common usage. Most people use the singular verb with this plural form, as in 'my data was hard to collect', and would extend the meaning to include not only facts, but things – in our case words or sounds in combination. So the working definition of data for our purposes is the stretch of language in recorded, transcribed or written form that we are looking at.

Finding such data may on the face of it seem easy: after all, we have said you can look at anything. However, there can be pitfalls in the collection and assemblage of data. As well as suggesting what you might look at, this chapter aims to help you to avoid these problems. Before you start collecting your specimen, you need to be aware of certain basic principles.

Be fair to your data

The only way to know what you're working with is to collect the data yourself. Perhaps this is best illustrated by examples. If, for instance, you wish to look at a particular form of regional accent or dialect as it is currently spoken, you must try to record speakers in as natural a situation as possible. Don't rely on actors' versions of the same dialect and don't ask the speakers to say particular words directly. This will make them self-conscious and distort the results. Don't use secondary sources, such as glossaries of how to talk 'proper Lancashire'. You would probably be looking at an outdated version of the dialect. If your project is on graffiti or slang, don't work with examples from books on the topic. You don't know where they are from. The authors might even have made them up, in which case they're not graffiti at all.

This is not to say that you could not do a project on actors' attempts to reproduce regional dialects in television dramas, provided that it was very clear that you knew you were not looking at the real thing; or that you could not write a project on dialect verse, again provided that you show all the way through that you were looking at a particular literary version of dialect, not spontaneous speech. Know what you want to look at and what to call it.

Compare like with like

There are particular aspects to bear in mind in different project areas to ensure that you are fair to your data. If you are making any kind of detailed comparison between or within varieties for instance, you must try to ensure that you are comparing like with like and reducing the number of irrelevant variables. Is there any point in comparing the lyrics of a song by Cole Porter with those from one by Led Zeppelin? Just possibly, if they're on the same theme, or use a similar structure, but it seems unlikely. There must be some kind of framework for comparison. Comparing lager advertisements on television, the radio and in the press might similarly present too many variables in the media themselves – linked only by subject – unless you can think of a tight focus.

Investigation – not essay

And one last general principle before we go on to consider specific topics. If you are in the fortunate position of having too much data, or if the variety of language you wish to look at is readily available, don't select the actual material you eventually look at because it supports your thesis best, and don't select from within your data only those examples which suit you. You must not ignore evidence which you find inconvenient. If, for example, your hunch is that a particular newspaper presents images of women in a certain way, don't only choose those articles which prove your point and discard any which don't. If you did, you would not have undertaken an investigation but written an essay putting forward a particular point of view with illustrations to support your argument.

So, before you even begin to collect material and certainly as you collect it, you must bear the following points in mind in order to be fair to your data:

Have a fairly clear idea of what you want to look at.
Don't select examples which are already beginning to prove your point and ignore those which are inconvenient.

Suggestions

On the following pages you will see examples of possible project areas. They are presented to give you some ideas and they do not aim to be exhaustive: that would be impossible and undesirable. You will choose your own area of language to investigate, which may or may not be prompted by the ideas presented here. It is important that you do choose your own topic and don't have one 'given' to you. Follow your own interests and observations. You're going to become very familiar with your own particular subject as your investigation proceeds and it is much better to be working with material you find intrinsically fascinating – even entertaining!

The suggestions which follow have been divided into three broad sections:

1 those where the data involved is primarily spoken English
2 those where the data is primarily written English
3 those where the data could be either speech or writing, or both.

We have deliberately not tried to match the focus of the investigation to the possible topics because there is a variety of questions to be asked of any stretch of language. We'll discuss what to look for in the next chapter. The remainder of this one is concerned with particular aspects of data collection in relation to particular areas.

Working with spoken data

If data collecting had tariff ratings like highboard dives at the Olympics, the gathering and transcribing of spoken data would carry a very high one. Some forms, such as working from recordings of radio or television chat shows, 'phone-ins or sports commentaries aren't too problematic. However, recording a discussion, conversation or argument in real life is very difficult, and achieving a good, accurate transcription of what was said is no mean feat in itself, before you even go on to anlysis.

Some points to bear in mind before embarking on an investigation into forms of spoken English are:

Yourself You need a fair degree of patience and perseverance to collect data in this area. You must be prepared to make several attempts at achieving a good, clear recording. When you have obtained a taping which is good enough it will take you a long time to transcribe it into written form before you can start work on describing and analysing it. Just transposing the sounds into words in written form with no pronunciation or stress features marked can take a long time on its own. A good detailed phonetic transcription of ten minutes of tape could take you up to four hours to transcribe. Producing an accurate transcription is a challenging but rewarding task, and in the process of it you will learn a lot more about spoken language – but it will take time.

Good equipment Different types of tape recorder are available and you should try to obtain the use of one which best suits your purposes. But whether it is a large, visible piece of equipment or one small enough to conceal in your pocket, it will have to be a good one – especially if you are taping a subject against a fair amount of background noise. It must have a good microphone, whether separate or inbuilt. If you want to make your equipment less noticeable, the small pocket dictaphones designed for the dictation of business messages are ideal. If it is less important that your subject is unaware of being taped, then the larger, more conventional tape recorders are fine.

Test the machine out in advance of any taping session. Don't set up that crucial encounter or interview and then realise that the equipment is unequal to the task. Familiarise yourself with it too. Don't have to fuss and fiddle with it too visibly. It will make your subject(s) even more self-conscious. Will electric sockets be readily available (with attendant trailing wires)? Or would a battery operated machine be better? If so, make sure the batteries won't run out.

Situation Try to choose a place for the taping session which is as free of background noise as possible, but still maintains the level of formality or informality which is consistent with obtaining authentic data. This, of course, is easier said than done. If you want to record an informal discussion in the cafeteria or a pub, then you might think it impossible, but even within these areas there are quieter times and places. Recording conversations in clubs and discos would surely defeat all but the most intrepid!

It's worth doing a bit of fieldwork in advance of any session. It might produce a technically better recording to interview a couple of four year-olds in the nursery teacher's office, but will they relax and talk as freely there as in the reading corner of the nursery itself? You must weigh up the pros and cons of the situation, taking into account how well they know you and each other, the inhibiting aspect of having their friends around, and what you want the data for. If it's pronunciation rather than interactive features it may not matter very much. Consider whether you need a framework for your taping session. Is it important that your subjects discuss certain topics or say certain sounds? If so, you may need to provide clues in the shape of pictures perhaps, or toys for children, or a script – something to read in which the particular pronunciation features you're looking for are bound to come up – or a 'plant' to steer the discussion along certain lines: someone who is your accomplice, who knows what you are doing but who is not themself crucial to your investigation. You shouldn't leave such matters purely to chance or the vital elements may be entirely missing from your data.

All or nothing – what to tell your subjects (victims?)

We are all self-conscious when we know someone is recording what we are saying, and this will affect the way we are speaking. It may make us more concerned to get things 'correct'. Accents may be modified to become closer to RP (there's a certain amount of evidence that this might be more true of women than men) and we may use less colloquial vocabulary. On the other hand we could become so nervous that there are many more false starts and long pauses than in our speech generally. The more accustomed we become to being recorded – if the session goes on a long time or happens frequently – the more we may become unconscious of the tape, but it is something anyone doing a project in spoken English needs to be aware of.

If you have decided that for your purposes it will make little difference whether your subjects know they are being taped, or if it is impossible for you to disguise the fact that you are recording, then you may decide to 'come clean'. You may need to ignore the early part of your recording when your subjects are most self-conscious, so it is a good idea not to start straight into the subjects and features you are most interested in. It may take several sessions before the subjects are relaxed enough to provide good data, but it is clearly possible. Think of all the 'fly on the wall' documentaries that you have seen on television, where people do seem to become oblivious to the cameras after a time. When examining your data or drawing conclusions from it you should, however, take into account that data may be distorted to a greater or lesser degree by the recording process.

If you want to tape people who are unaware of the fact they are being recorded you will have to choose unobtrusive equipment and set the situation up in advance. You may well need an accomplice who knows what is happening but whom you will ignore when you are drawing conclusions.

Recording people without their knowledge may seem rather sneaky or unethical, but it is the only way to obtain some types of conversation 'in the raw'. However, using the material afterwards without the subjects' consent is, we think, unacceptable. Most people do not object after the event, but sometimes they consider it to have been an invasion of their privacy. They might think that the material discussed or the way they spoke is not for 'outsiders' to hear. This has happened to students of ours whose families have objected to what they considered private subjects and intimate forms of expression being 'published'. If this does happen you should respect your subjects' wishes. It is something to be borne in mind before attempting such investigations. Sometimes offering anonymity overcomes the objections.

There is a middle way which might help with your project. With this method the subjects are aware that they are being taped, but think it is for a purpose different from the real one (i.e. looking at language features). If you tell someone that you're interested in their childhood memories, whereas really what interests you is dialect features, at least your subject will not be self-conscious about the very feature you're interested in. If you tell students that you are interested in their views on the state of the student common room when really you're interested in how they pronounce 'smoking', they won't be distorting their pronunciation of the word. This may seem rather devious but it's a well-worn research technique.

Recording children
    'Never work with children or animals.'

W. C. Fields

This might be sound advice for the acting profession, but children are frequently the targets of attention for linguists and students of language. Investigating stages of development, comparing children of the same or different ages, comparing 'normal children' with those with a language delay and charting the development of one child (takes long-term planning, this one) – all these and many more are productive topics for project work.

You are luckiest of all if you have a child of your own whose language you can record, or a younger brother or sister. If you have a young neighbour, or you babysit regularly for a child, you are fortunate too. In these situations you already have an established relationship to build on, and with frequent access can introduce the tape recorder naturally at a convenient time as part of play. Another advantage is that the child will be relaxed with you and likely to use language in a natural way. Depending on the focus of your project you may well have to structure the situation carefully and lead the conversation or exchange into areas you think will be productive. This may take some patience, but if you know the child you have a head-start.

If you're interested in this area, but don't know any young children well, don't despair. Playgroups, nurseries and infant classes are usually quite receptive to pleas for help, and are willing to co-operate. If you're interested in older children, try primary schools, Brownie and Cub packs, Sunday schools, even Youth Clubs.

Having established contact you need to decide what sort of role you are going to adopt when you meet the children. Are you going to be the outside expert with only one task in view (this may be appropriate if you are interested in language use in a fairly formal situation)? Or is it important to establish a more informal relationship, in which case you will probably have to make several visits and become involved in some other role – helper, story reader. Don't become too familiar – you won't be there for very long. Accept the advice and help of teachers and parents, who will almost certainly want to be present when you are recording. The presence of a familiar adult is usually a help.

Again, you will probably need a pretext for talking to the child, so consider what would be appropriate – books, toys, games or pictures. If your project is going to look at the way children interact with each other, or with teachers or parents, you will have to blend into the background and become as unobtrusive as possible. The co-operation and consent of the adult involved is vital. This is not an appropriate area for saying nothing. It is very important to give the impression that you know what you are doing and are prepared to explain it to people in as much detail as they require.

The accomplice

There are a few situations in which it might produce better data if you ask someone else to do your recording for you. This is not suggested as the coward's way out, but only in situations where it might be more appropriate for someone in a role other than researcher to do the taping.

An obvious example of this would be the classroom discussion, in which it would be more natural for the teacher to be taping the proceedings. S/he might even enter into the spirit of things and announce a reason for doing this which is nothing to do with your language research, but we do not suggest that you expect this co-operation, which is above and beyond the call of duty.

There may be other places or situations in which your presence would be obtrusive and automatically alter or affect the way people spoke. Social clubs might be somewhere where it would be better for a parent or friend who was already part of the scene to do your taping for you. We do not especially recommend this, as control of the recording process is out of your hands and it may be imposing on the goodwill of others, but there are a few situations where it might be appropriate and desirable.

Other practicalities

Tact, sensitivity and ingenuity (at least!) are needed to obtain good recordings, but in the euphoria of having finally achieved them, you must also remember to record

> the date, the time, the place
> the names of the participants (although you may use pseudonyms in the transcript if you or they wish)
> their ages – very precisely in the case of children; approximations may be preferred by adults
> their gender – even if this is not apparently of central concern
> other relevant information (e.g. places of birth and domicile in accent or dialect projects)

And of course, you must keep your tapes and submit them with the finished project. They are the proof of your hard work, and that your data was not faked!

Taping from radio and television

Radio and television can provide examples of spontaneous and scripted speech to translate into data, and with none of the problems of live recording. The additional factor to consider in this is the element of 'performance'. Even the most apparently relaxed and casual interview or talk-show programme, even members of the public being interviewed for news and documentary programmes, know that they are on television, and this affects their speech. Some of the most apparently natural television and radio performers are of course just that – performers – exhibiting a great deal of skill which in turn is probably based on much experience (if not rehearsal). Of course this does not invalidate transcripts of talk on radio and television shows as 'honest' data for projects, just as long as you know what you are looking at and bear in mind this element. You could choose to make it the focus of your investigation, if you wished, and examine how the constraints of the media affect talk. The requirement about recording dates, times, participants is exactly the same as for live recording.

How much should you transcribe?

Having obtained your recordings you now have to turn them into written data, which might seem a bit perverse. You have to make transcripts. Advice has been given about this in the first section of this book. Your first decision is how much of the tapes to transcribe. Listen carefully to your tape and decide which sections might be most useful to you. You do not need to transcribe every minute of every tape. You may well have an hour or more's recording, only a portion of which is relevant to the subject of your project.

In notes accompanying your transcript you should indicate the total length of the recording and give a brief description of the whole. If your project is focussing on interactive features there might, for example, be three extended exchanges which you wish to examine in detail. These should be transcribed and some indication given as to where they occurred in the exchange as a whole, but you do not need to transcribe sections to which you are not going to refer in detail. You could refer to the frequency of a specific feature in the entire conversation without transcribing everything. You have, after all, submitted the tape as evidence, so your claims can be checked.

If you are looking at a child's language development and have a lot of taped material you must choose substantial representative passages (or a single longer passage) to transcribe, and work from those, although again these could be supported by references to the frequency of these features in the rest of the recorded evidence.

It's a good idea to look at the problem of 'how much' from the reader's point of view. It should be possible to find parts of the transcript referred to in the body of your project easily. This will be harder to do if you have submitted pages and pages of transcript, not all of which is relevant. We talk about presentation in a later chapter, but it is always a good rule of thumb to consider your project from the point of view of those who might read it. Ease of reference is extremely important, more important than attempting to impress by sheer weight of material.

So, in answer to the question 'how much?' it seems that hard and fast rules are difficult to draw up. You must provide a substantial transcript of continuous discourse as the basis of a project on spoken English, and there may be more specific guidelines for different courses. You must consider the whole of your taped material, whether it's all transcribed or not. If your project consisted of a general commentary on the language of a two year-old, for example, with only isolated examples transcribed to prove points, you would be writing an illustrated essay, not an investigation. You must not pick your examples and ignore inconvenient evidence which does not support your general thesis.

Which features should be marked?

Pronunciation It is not necessary or desirable to attempt a full phonetic (or even phonemic) transcription of all your data with every feature of stress, intonation and pitch marked. It would only be a slight exaggeration to say that could prove to be a lifetime's work! Obviously if you are going to refer to pronunciation features you should represent those phonemically.

You cannot refer to accent features without doing this. You may not, however, need to transcribe whole utterances phonemically if what you are interested in is the pronunciation of single words or specific sounds. A phonemic transcription is usually adequate for describing broad differences in accent (RP and Wigan, for example), but to compare more similar accents (Wigan and Bury, for example) you would need an excellent ear and the ability to make a phonetic transcription. The scope of most A-level courses would not prepare you for this, and unless you are exceptionally skilled in this area it should not be attempted. However, when you are referring to pronunciation features you must represent them phonemically – a more personal ad-hoc approach (e.g. 'he pronounced the *oo* in "book" like the *oo* in "you"') is not acceptable, and could be meaningless or wrong in some areas of the country.

Stress and pitch If you are concentrating on interactive features it is more likely that you will want to mark pitch, stress and tone. Ways of doing this have been suggested in Chapter 4. There are many different systems for indicating these features, and it does not matter which you choose as long as it is consistent and is adequate for your purposes, and you include a key. Use the one you feel most familiar with. Again, it is not essential to mark all features in every stretch of transcript, but only those utterances you are referring to in detail, or where stress, pitch and/or tone are features you are going to comment on.

The Golden Rule

Consider your reader – you must make your points clear and readily understandable. If you have been unable to indicate through your transcript what the language actually sounded like, and sound is what you are commenting on, you will have failed. However, if the actual sounds of speech are not important to the points you are making, then it is not necessary, and might even be distracting, to mark them all.

Projects on spoken language which do not involve taping

It is possible to conduct an investigation into a specific area of speech which will not involve your making tape recordings, although it will necessitate recording your findings quickly and simply in another way.

One student, for example, who had a part-time job in a shoe shop, was interested in the different ways in which customers addressed him. He designed a simple form which would allow him quickly to record after each transaction the sex and approximate age of each customer and the manner in which he was addressed. He was only interested in one feature, so it was possible to do this.

The American language researcher Labov did something similar as part of his famous survey of accent and class in New York. Choosing different department stores which were known to cater for broadly different income groups (an English equivalent might be Harrods and Woolworths) he devised a question for his researchers to ask which in each case would require the response 'fourth floor'. He was interested in whether the *r* was sounded, and whether there were differences between stores. There was no need to tape responses, just to record on a form if the *r* was or was not sounded.

If you are interested in such a straightforward, isolated feature you may not need to tape. What you must do, though, is to keep meticulous records of the dates and places where your research was undertaken; firstly to make sense of your findings, but also to authenticate your data.

Projects which involve collection and transcription of spoken language are likely to gain credit for the time, care and skill you have put into assembling your data and making it clear and comprehensible to the reader. Obviously you have to put more effort into the initial stages of your project than a colleague who has chosen three versions of a newspaper story to compare. There is more challenge in the initial stages of a project in spoken language, but you know that the data (if it's good) is original, and many of the most interesting investigations are undertaken in this area.

Working with written data

If you decide to investigate a variety of written language you will obviously have fewer problems about collecting your data. However, if this area attracts you primarily for this reason, a word of warning: a policy of least effort is bound to show elsewhere in your project. Although you may have fewer difficulties with the initial assembling of data than your intrepid colleague, you must be equally scrupulous in your choice, research and presentation. Sloppiness shows. A remark such as 'I decided to make a random choice of story/contract/newspaper to make sure it was representative' is nonsense, and will readily be spotted as an attempt to excuse laziness.

We are surrounded by print – books, newspapers, magazines, circulars, forms, advertisement hoardings, greetings cards. We write a lot ourselves, either by hand or word processor – letters, notes, memos, essays, diaries. All this material, unlike speech, has to be consciously destroyed if it is to cease to exist, and forms a mountain of printed and written words all waiting to be investigated and analysed.

Where to look

As always, the starting point should be your own interests and observations. It may be helpful to consult lists of suitable topics or investigations already undertaken, or to listen to suggestions from teachers and fellow students. These could provide initial stimulation to get you thinking, but in the end the decision is yours. Here are a few suggestions which may help you to accumulate suitable data for your investigation.

Be a hoarder: save letters, circulars, interesting newspaper articles, diaries, exercise books, college prospectuses and official handouts. When people in the street are handing out leaflets for political causes, religious tracts, advertisements for new take-away restaurants or supermarket bargains, don't quicken your pace to avoid them, but accept them all. Some or all of this material might be just what you need. If you have your old files or exercise books from school (or a brother or sister does) these could provide the basis for an examination of developing style, or spelling difficulties. A collection of letters from a foreign penfriend could be the starting point for an investigation of the problems second language learners have with English. When you are filling in an application form for a passport or a driving licence, keep a copy. If Jehovah's Witnesses come to the door accept – even purchase – a copy of *The Watchtower*. Researching your next holiday? The glossy brochures in the travel agent are free, and are there to be taken. The same is true of estate agents' handouts. There are endless free examples of the written word around us, but it can be frustrating to have missed an opportunity to collect what you need through lack of foresight, so

Look ahead

You will know at which point in your course you will begin working on your project. Let's imagine for a moment it's June. If it occurs to you at that point that the language of political pamphlets and leaflets is worth looking at, and you've thrown away all the stuff that came free through the door in May, you are going to have to go to a lot of trouble to find it now. On Valentine's Day every year, the newspapers have taken to printing hundreds of messages and verses in their personal columns, which would make a fascinating topic for language investigation. Acquiring back copies of newspapers takes much more time and trouble than remembering to save them in the first place.

Be alert

At certain points in the year advertisers launch major new campaigns. Perhaps they are trying to change a product's image or to introduce a new product. The Government periodically makes vigorous attempts to stop us drinking and driving, or smoking, or to get us to adopt a healthier diet and to exercise. Are they using language in a particularly interesting way to do this? However, these moments may not be as predictable as election time or Valentine's Day, so you need to be alert and save the evidence.

If you know that you are interested in newspaper style or house style of magazines, you need to familiarise yourself in some depth with the field before finding the best examples to look at in detail. Major news stories covered at length by a variety of newspapers are few and far between, as popular and 'quality' papers have very different interests and readerships, so it's as well to be on the lookout for them if that is what interests you.

It's impossible to indicate the whole range of possibilities in the area of written language, and in some ways the most satisfying thing of all is to come up with an original idea, although this is difficult (increasingly so) to do. We are not suggesting that you hang on to any piece of paper with writing on it which passes through your hands: all those cardboard boxes full of canvassing material, *Reader's Digest* free offers, back copies of *Pigbreeders Monthly*, would constitute a fire hazard. But it does pay to be receptive, to be alert and to plan ahead if you are thinking of writing about some of the printed ephemera surrounding us.

If, however, you are interested in more 'permanent' printed material, here are a few more suggestions. You are not confined to Literature if you wish to work with the (permanently) printed word. Libraries and bookshops can be the source of all sorts of variety of written language.

Letters, diaries, notebooks

The letters, diaries and notebooks of the famous are often printed in book format. Writers, painters, politicians, civil servants, spies, criminals, royalty – anyone who achieves fame or notoriety – is likely to have their written output collected, anthologised or quoted extensively in biographies. These can provide a rich source of material for investigation. Of course, many of the great and good wrote diaries and letters during their lifetime with half an eye to the publisher, but equally much of the material here was not written in the belief that it would be collected and 'frozen' into print, and is more informal, more colloquial and unpredictable. If you are interested in language change these collections can provide examples of styles from different periods, or you may be interested in the way individuals use language to express themselves in the more private examples of their writing, freed – if we ever are – from the constraints of audience.

It is more difficult to find examples of non-celebrity documents. Most of us do not have our correspondence and private writing preserved and made publicly available. However it is not impossible to find the writing of 'ordinary' people in print in the Social History and Sociology sections of libraries. Compilations of first-hand accounts of the nineteenth-century factory system or the Great Fire of London can be found in abundance, if you know where to look. There is an obvious danger here in becoming more interested in what is being said than in the way it is being said – which should always be the focus of a language investigation – but provided you guard against this, projects in this area can be very worthwhile. More contemporary examples can be found in the material compiled by Mass-Observation, or the American writer and anthologist Studs Terkl, who compiles first hand accounts and interviews with an enormous variety of people. The Oral History sections of some universities and polytechnics can even provide you with ready-made transcripts.

Textbooks

Textbooks written for different age groups or levels of expertise can provide interesting data. Of course, you will only have a few in your possession, but there are probably some fairly ancient ones mouldering away in your college or school stockroom, or to be picked up cheaply in secondhand bookshops. These could provide the basis for a comparison of different styles from different periods, or an investigation of the 'textbook' style itself in the light of what textbooks are written for. Dare we suggest that grammar books from different periods might be interesting?

Children's books

The language of books written for children of different ages, sexes or periods is worth looking at – and most of us do keep our own favourites. Classic children's stories remain in print for a long time and provide accessible examples of how styles might have changed. Children's annuals – compilations of stories, articles and comic strips – from the past and present provide a range of writing within one volume, and comparisons of then and now in this area can be particularly illuminating. Ask friends or relatives if they have kept *Girl* or *Eagle* annuals from a previous generation.

If you are fortunate enough to know (or to be!) a genuine hoarder with a collection of, for example, comics, football programmes or Angela Brazil stories which stretches back for decades, you could really be lucky.

Popular fiction

The distinctive styles of popular genres, such as romance, crime, horror or science fiction, can provide good material for language projects. However, since you will need to narrow the scope of your investigation – four thousand words on 'The language of popular romantic fiction' could hardly fail to be a survey or an essay, not a project – it is important to pose a particular question or limit the focus of your project. We will discuss this in the next chapter. A knowledge of the genre beyond the text(s) you are looking at closely will help, so again the advice is to follow your interests. If you would find it tedious to read half a dozen novels by Stephen King in order to write a project on how the tension is created in Chapter 7 of one of them, don't undertake the project in the first place. Acquiring examples of popular fiction from fifty to a hundred years ago might be difficult – possible, but difficult. On the whole, much of this sort of writing does not remain in print as long as the classics. So don't set yourself a comparison of past and present unless you are sure you can obtain the evidence you want.

Literature with a capital L – an area for the enthusiast
There are few problems finding the data here. Your problem is more likely to be narrowing the focus or formulating a question related primarily to the language rather than writing a lit crit essay. However, there are some particularly suitable areas for language study in relation to literary texts, the most obvious being drafts of the same poem or passage, or changes between editions, and these can be difficult to come by. Here you would be looking hard at stylistic features. Comprehensive biographies are usually quite a good source of different drafts, libraries and second-hand bookshops of different editions. This is definitely an area for the enthusiast. You will have to have some knowledge of what you're looking for, some knowledge that these different versions exist and are interesting, before embarking on any wild goose chase.

Translations
Different translations into English of the same foreign work provide good material for language projects too, but here you must have a liking for very close language study, and preferably some understanding of the language the work was written in. If you are bilingual, or are studying another language however, translations – not only of 'great' works but of guide and tourist books, or instructions which seem to be rather literal renditions of some text clearly first written in the mother tongue – provide subjects which allow you to draw on your knowledge of language rather than English, and to compare different systems.

Grey areas: written or spoken? (or even sung!)

Are speeches, play and film scripts and scripted commentaries, not to mention song lyrics, examples of spoken or written language? Written originally, they were scripted to be spoken and, sometimes, to sound like naturalistic speech. In varying degrees they exhibit the features of written language, combined with the delivery of spoken. For these very reasons, they make interesting subjects for investigation, although they may not always be as easy to find in printed form as other species of written English. Significant political 'set' speeches are often printed at length in the 'quality' papers; political speeches are available in full in *Hansard*.

Most plays written to be performed in the theatre exist in published text form, unless they are brand new. Television and film scripts have not often been published, and to make transcripts would take a much longer time than you have at your disposal. You can make life easier for yourself by working only with scripts which have been published, or you can transcribe from video or audio cassette the sections of the script which you want to look at in detail, along with a description of the programme which puts them into context. It is not always readily obvious whether some shows are scripted or spontaneous. Watch out for this. As language students you should be particularly alert.

Song lyrics are usually published somewhere – most accessibly on LP covers and CD booklets. Famous and popular songwriters usually have their œuvres collected and printed in book form, as do those whose lyrics are most frequently referred to as 'poetry' (Bob Dylan, for example). Rock and teenage magazines often publish the lyrics of current hits. It is surprisingly difficult to transcribe lyrics from listening to songs, as you may have discovered. (What 'saving his life for the pork sausages' has to do with the rest of *Bohemian Rhapsody* has long puzzled Queen fans. Turn to the end of the chapter to solve the mystery, if you haven't already.)

A warning: your investigation should concentrate firmly on language features, but at the same time should be informed by an understanding of the immediate context of the language. You should steer a fine line between being distracted and side-tracked by the accompanying visual images (film/television drama) or music (song lyrics) and on the other hand ignoring these other elements completely and treating your material merely as words on a page.

Comparisons between written and spoken language

There are many possibilities for project work which involve a comparison between written and spoken language, and one of their advantages is that they provide you with an instant focus for your investigation – the differences between the two in terms of word choice and syntax. It is necessary to make sure that you are comparing two examples of language which are worth comparing. If, for example, you are looking at speech which is scripted to sound like spontaneous speech – whether in a Pinter play or *Emmerdale* – and comparing it with an example of conversation you have recorded and transcribed, try to ensure that the participants in the two have something in common. There would be little point in comparing the scripted speech of female pensioners in *EastEnders* with a conversation in a club in Widnes between two eighteen year-old youths (unless you make the case very clearly!) The grounds for comparison could be subject matter – a spoken commentary and written report on the same sporting event for instance; purpose – a political or promotional talk or speech compared with its written equivalent; participant(s) – a vicar's sermon compared with his parish newsletter. There are many possibilities, but the grounds for comparison should be made clear.

General points

Secondary sources

What are these, and why is reliance on them to be avoided at all costs? Firstly, this project is a personal investigation into an aspect of language. It is imperative that you find and select your own material. There may be a wonderful example of a conversation in patwa in one of your textbooks, but you must not extract it and use it as your own data even if you credit it (and if you didn't, of course, it would be unfair practice). That transcript is someone else's data, and you would be using it secondhand – as a secondary source.

You may refer to this transcript and the way in which it is described or analysed, perhaps to acknowledge where you found some of your ideas and methods; in fact this would be the correct way to proceed. Obviously we are stimulated by books we read, and there is no requirement that your project topic and method of procedure be totally original. However the material you work with must be what you have found for yourself.

It is easy to see how this is the case with spoken data. You must record and transcribe your own. But perhaps you want to look at literature, for example the creation of a new 'language' in Russell Hoban's *Riddley Walker*. You know this may have been done before and you may (should) have researched other work on the subject. How then can your data be fresh and original? Well, it can't be in the same way as a unique stretch of conversation is, but if you know that your selection of passages to analyse closely is entirely your own, and you think you have a new perspective on the material or you are going to approach it in a rigorous and systematic way, then that is perfectly acceptable. What you must not do is analyse the same passages in the same way as any other study you are aware of.

References

You must add a list of any books you have consulted at the end of your project, and if you quote from them within your investigation this must be clear and credited: that is accepted and expected academic practice. If you observe this there will be no suspicion that you are passing someone else's work off as your own.

Finally we come to a question which always worries students at the beginning of their work on projects: how much data is needed? The almost universal tendency is to take on too much. In fact the amount you will need varies from topic to topic. If you are working primarily with written language, there is a danger of merely providing a running commentary, or coming close to writing an illustrated essay. It is much more of a temptation, if you are working in an area where evidence is plentiful, to 'dip in' and use your examples to illustrate your argument rather than to allow your findings to emerge from a hard look at the evidence. If you do this you will have written an essay, not a project. So although you must start with a question, or a hunch about your material, you should not limit yourself to discussing only 'convenient' examples, but choose a large enough sample which will allow you to be fair to your data.

How much?

You may be interested in looking at a specific type of written language – for example the style of the language of pamphlets issued by the DSS for the information of benefit claimants. You might have a theory about it: perhaps it's impenetrable and you wish to look more closely at how and why. Or maybe you've discerned a welcome trend to simplify or to make plain. This would make an interesting area for project work, provided that it appeals to you.

Your first step would be to collect as much material as possible and to familiarise yourself with it. It would not be a good idea to pick up the first pamphlet you see and to analyse the language of that. Equally it would be inappropriate, not to say impossible, to try to do the same for every leaflet you pick off the rack in the local office ... but you do need to be familiar with a range of material in order to select from within it an example you consider typical, or particularly interesting.

Don't take on too much: your project probably has to be of a certain length, it isn't a life's work. You will be aware of the particular constraints within which you're working. The immediate reaction of most of us when faced with a word limit is not 'How will I keep within it?' but 'How on earth will I write that much?'

The solution to the *Bohemian Rhapsody* mystery is 'Spare him his life from this monstrosity'.

Chapter 20

What should I look for?
– how to ask questions of your data

It may seem strange to consider this question separately from 'What can I look at?' but in our experience students usually have an idea of the variety of English they wish to study before they have sharpened the focus into what within that large area they are going to look for. It's true that some work the other way round and start with a question – 'Why is the language of contracts so inpenetrable? Does it have to be?' – before finding examples to concentrate on, but this is relatively rare. More usually a student will say 'I've noticed that the way ... ' or 'I'd like a closer look at ... ', then after reading or listening closely within a chosen area and beginning to pick out features of language, will decide what to concentrate on.

There is usually a lot of accurate description within a good project – of identifying and collecting patterns of sounds, vocabulary and structures. Why then do you also need to ask a question in relation to your data? Wouldn't a good, thorough description be adequate on its own? The answer to this is that it is virtually impossible to write a good description without asking questions. The questions, which may start as pretty obvious and basic, provide a framework for your description. You have to begin making sense of a stretch of language somehow, and applying the fundamental questions to it is a good technique to adopt.

Questions to ask

Since in the end your finished project will be of limited length and scope, you will almost certainly choose to restrict yourself to one or two aspects of the text or transcript, and you will have refined your questions and answers accordingly. However, to start this process going here are some of the obvious questions to ask:

What is language being used for here? (functional focus)
Where is this language occurring? (situation; register)
When is/was this language occurring? (language change/development)
How is language being used here? (stylistic focus)
Who is using language here? (register)
To whom? (audience; interactional features)

These questions are too blunt on their own to make an effective project topic, but a combination of the 'how' with one or two of the others in relation to your specific area will probably help you to come up with a hypothesis. For example, let's suppose you are interested in the style of theatre reviews. You have conscientiously collected the reviews from five different publications – local, evening, 'popular' and 'quality' papers, and an 'alternative' listings magazine – of the same five productions, a total of twenty-five reviews in all. How are you going to shape your writing about them into a project?

If you apply the basic questions you see that you could end up with a different focus for your project:

What is language being used for? (The functional approach)	To inform To entertain To express an opinion To persuade	How do different reviewers combine these functions in their reviews?
Where is this language being used? (Register)	In journalistic publications, in expected position on the review pages	What are the features of this particular specialised example of journalism? (Look for similarities then differences.)
Who is using language here? (Establishment of point of view)	Anonymous reviewer Established reviewer	How are objective/ subjective views combined in these reviews?
To whom? (Audience)	Readership of newspaper (Research this!)	How do readership considerations affect the style of this particular species of journalism? (This might focus on differences, then on similarities.)
When is/was this language occurring?	Contemporary usage (This would only become an issue if you decided to introduce new material and compare your reviews with others from a previous era.)	
How is language being used? (Style)	Lexis Structures Layout Tone	What seem to be the major factors contributing to style? – audience, lexical and structural choice – house style: look at other articles from the same pa]per

It will be obvious that the questions overlap. You cannot consider any of them in isolation from the others. It's just that you have to decide where to put the emphasis of your investigation. If you look at all twenty-five reviews in relation to each question you won't really get to grips with any of them, you will never look closely at language – which is the point of the exercise – but skate over the surface illustrating general points with examples taken from here, there and everywhere. But once you have decided which focus interests you most, you can then make some decisions about the shape and scope of your project and how to use your data.

In the process of considering what your focus will be you may well decide not to use all the material. If you focus on how readership may be related to style, you may decide that popular/quality and alternative may well be enough, and that only a couple of examples of each will do for close analysis.

If you are interested in individual style and how reviewers develop their own, you may wish to concentrate on only two named writers, but look at all five of their reviews.

If you are interested in the functional features first and foremost, you will probably select the reviews which provide most contrast in emphasis – informative/ entertaining or informative/critical.

Whichever tack you take you will almost certainly not want to devote the same amount of close analysis to all twenty-five reviews, although you may wish to refer to most or all of them for some purposes – a count of the frequency of proper nouns, or sentence types and lengths if relevant. You should probably include them in your appendix to show that you have surveyed a range before making your final selection. Why waste work after all?

Let's look at another possible stretch of data, this time a transcript of spoken language.

You are interested in the language used in group discussion and have made a longish (twelve sides) transcript of a tape recording of your drama group – seven students (four female, three male) and your teacher (female) – discussing two projects for the end of year assessment. Each possible production has its supporters and at times the discussion becomes heated. At one point the teacher is called away and is absent for a few minutes. It is a good, clear transcript, full of interesting and varied language use, but you are uncertain about how to start analysing it. Look at it first in the light of the broad questions what, where, who, when and how.

Question	Overall purpose	Focus of investigation
What is language being used for here?	To attempt to reach a decision At different times during the transcript: to persuade, to inform, to insult	Interactive features of language Which utterances were constructive? Which prevented development of discussion and decision making process? Use discourse analysis features
Where?	In fairly structured classroom situation, although teacher absent for part of the time	If you wanted to see how this affected the language, you'd need to record some of same individuals in a more informal situation to compare, or, if there was enough, compare the discussion when the teacher was absent to when she was present.
Who?/To whom?	Participants: 5 females, 3 males	Again, you could focus on interactive features but with

	Issues of dominance/gender	different emphasis, concentrating on roles of individuals, number and length of utterances etc. If you think the age of the participants is important, this could be a possible area. What roles did individuals appear to adopt? Any significant differences between male and female speakers?
When?	Contemporary	This question has little relevance to this material unless you wish to focus on contemporary colloquial usage (but there probably won't be enough material). It's difficult to think of any way of getting similar language use from another time.
How is language being used?	Look at form and features of language	Look at the features of the spoken language itself. Does it change as participants become more involved? Incidence of fillers, false starts, minor sentences etc.

Again we see that there is overlap in all these areas – the 'where' and 'who' sections for example – and any investigation involves part of the 'how' answers, the features of the language. But if you tried to answer all these questions in that amount of detail in relation to the whole transcript you would either have to write at least twenty thousand words, or you would end up treating them all so superficially that you would not have space to look hard at the language. If you wished to look at interactive features – what, rather than who, helped the decision along or obstructed the decision-making process – you might choose to look in detail at certain passages you identify as key points in the discussion.

If you want to consider the part that gender might or might not play in the language of this mixed group, you would probably want to look at the transcript as a whole and to examine length of utterance, interruptions, use of supportive/destructive comments and questions, tentativeness etc. (a 'who' question).

If you are interested in the effect of the presence of the authority figure on the discussion you would want to concentrate on what happened when she left the room. If the answer to this is that there was very little change, then it's a non-starter unless you are prepared to record the same individuals in a less structured situation.

Focus

When you have found the focus for your investigation, you do not necessarily have a project title. It is the first step in finding the way into your material. What do we mean by this rather overused word 'focus' anyway? Just that it provides a direction for your investigation. You may be faced with a lot of data and somehow you have to narrow down the scope of your approach. You must look closely at language, and if you attempt to cover all aspects of it you won't look closely enough. 'Focus' is a useful metaphor, because when you are focussing on something you are not totally unaware of surrounding features: you realise that they impinge on what you are looking at, yet you see in most depth and clarity what you are concentrating on. If you're fortunate – or inspired – you might see something no-one else has seen!

There are some projects which provide their own framework by the nature of the task. The most straightforward of these are those which deal with comparisons or developments.

Comparisons

We have already discussed the importance of comparing like with like. There might be some point in comparing a live python with a stuffed koala bear, but on the face of it there seem to be so many differences that the task seems laughably easy. If you were to undertake it at all, your first challenge would be to convince your audience that the exercise had any validity. In order for there to be any purpose in comparing one thing with another there must first be some points of similarity. You will have to convince your readers of the validity of your undertaking.

Normally the rule about comparing one stretch of language with another is to reduce the number of features you are comparing to the few which form the core of your investigation. Thus, if you are comparing transcripts of two three-year-olds on the basis of gender, make sure the boy and girl have similar backgrounds, if possible are in the same position in the family, and that either both or neither attend playgroup regularly. You still will not be able confidently to attribute differences in language to gender alone nor make large conclusions about language acquisition on the basis of such a small sample, but you will be attempting to isolate the feature which most interests you. If, on the other hand, you are interested in the impact of playgroup attendance on language development you would limit the other variables and choose children of very similar age and background and of the same sex.

If you are comparing the styles of different newspapers, make certain you compare news items with news items, features with features and comment with comment. If you are comparing instruction manuals or guides, compare them describing the same or very similar processes or places. Don't take on too much. Comparing two, or at most three, different subjects is enough. By this we don't mean only look at two newspaper articles, one from each of your chosen papers: you can handle a bigger sample than that. But compare the *Daily Star* with *The Daily Telegraph* in news or features, not the styles of the *Daily Star*, the *Daily Mirror*, the *Daily Mail*, the *Daily Express*, *The Guardian* and *The Daily Telegraph* in news and features, or the finished product will be a survey not an investigation.

It will be obvious from these remarks that although a project which is a comparison provides you with a framework, you will still have to decide which features to concentrate on. You can't compare everything.

Development

Another approach which provides you with a structure but not necessarily a focus is to look at the development of a subject's language, or the language of a sequence of publications (such as a reading scheme). This usually takes forward planning, but not always. You could look at the progressive degrees of complexity in a reading scheme for example, and this would be fairly easily available.

If, however, you wish to study the language development of a two year-old over a period of six months it obviously takes a large commitment of time and a great deal of forethought. Another example of this might be to look at the changing language of a political or public information campaign as it responded to public opinion polls. This data would take more time to gather than an afternoon spent in the local reference library. However, time spent in data collection might be time saved in wondering how to structure your final project. What you would be looking for in your project is how the material changes, but within that large question you might very well have to narrow down the aspects you concentrate on.

Narrowing down – looking at the language

It is not possible to be endlessly specific about what you might start looking for when, having chosen your broad approach to the data, you begin to look in detail at the language. That will very much depend on what you're looking at, as well as the focus you've decided upon.

If you are looking at spoken language you may now be wishing to look at the phonological features of pronunciation, accent, stress, pitch and tone. On the other hand you may well have decided to minimise your reference to these and to concentrate on interactive features of a conversation, the dynamics of the exchange.

If you are working on journalism, news reporting or advertising, you may have decided to concentrate on semantic features, to classify and group together similar words and to discuss the effect of the choice of one word rather than another. Or you may be more interested in grammatical structures, the use of the passive, sentence types, major and minor sentences. Perhaps a combination of both is appropriate?

However, there are some approaches generally worth taking which would apply to most projects.

Patterns and repetitions

Do certain features – be they sounds, words, structures – recur, establishing the tone and coherence of the language? What is characteristic of this user's idiolect, or style of writing? There may be a preponderance of words from a particular register, or associated with a specific field. There may be a distinctive sentence pattern, a tendency to begin or end sentences in a certain way. There may be a particular way of pronouncing a vowel sound, or omitting consonants at the end of words. As you look harder at your material you are bound to see certain features recurring which may be attributable to an individual style or dictated by what the language is being used for – or a combination of the two. These are worth grouping together and examining further. The likelihood is, when you look a little harder, that within a group of features you thought were similar, there are some further groupings which could be made. If, for instance, looking at the style of a particular journalist, you have noticed that he often uses a form of direct address to the reader and you have collected all the examples of this in your data, you may find on closer examination that he does it for different effects – to sound familiar, to share references, to challenge his readers, to appear to attempt to dialogue. What you thought was going to be a fairly straightforward discussion of the use of one particular language 'trick', you now discover is more complex and varied than you first imagined. This is what should happen as you get further into your investigation. You discover much more than appeared at first sight. And that is why most students have no trouble in achieving the stipulated word length (if any).

Look for departures from the pattern. Once you've established what are the predominant features of language use within your data, you can examine variations from them. You won't have to look very hard for these, as they're probably some of the first things you noticed. Are there any sudden switches of tone or register, words used unexpectedly, departures from Standard English, or switches into it? Did that two year-old, just once, use a construction you weren't expecting? The list is endless and will depend very much on the variety of language you are working with. These features which draw attention to themselves are easy to spot, but why are they there? How do they fit into the overall patterns?

Don't lose sight of the wood for the trees. Don't forget the overall structure of the language you are investigating as you become involved in looking at the details. It is particularly easy in a piece of stylistic analysis to forget that the article or passage may have a beginning, a middle and an end, or at least some progression within it from unit to unit. The questions posed in the introduction to your project and returned to at the end should ensure that you don't get side-tracked or bogged down in feature-spotting for its own sake, but try to bear a sense of the data in its entirety in mind as you proceed with the description of small sections of it, and to relate the parts to the whole. Your data may not be an example of a 'whole'. It might be just a part of a transcription of a long conversation, lesson or lecture. Or your data could comprise several 'wholes' in that it is a collection of letters, or articles or sets of song lyrics. If you keep a sense at all times of what the language is being used for and relate your descriptive points to that you shouldn't go far wrong.

Don't make unsubstantiated claims. When you reach the end of your project, it can be a temptation to make larger claims for your findings than are justified by the scope of your investigation. You may have shown that in your sample of a hundred customers who address you at work, men are more likely to call you 'love' than women are, but you haven't proved that this is true of the male population of Britain as a whole. Your findings may well be affected by regional, class and age factors which you can only speculate about.

Similarly, you may have discovered that of the two-year-old twins whose language you have been observing, the girl has a larger active vocabulary than the boy. However, you have only observed and recorded this in relation to those children, and cannot go on to make more general claims about gender difference in relation to language development.

It is legitimate to indulge in a little speculation, and to refer to other, more comprehensive surveys in the same field if you are familiar with their findings, but you must bear in mind the limited nature of your own project. This is not always easy to do, especially if it has absorbed you day and night for months! However, your conclusions are not weakened but are stronger if they are based solely on your examination of the data, and are no less interesting for that.

Chapter 21

How should I present my findings?
– how to submit your investigation

Deciding on the best way to set out your project is much more than a cosmetic exercise. We are not going to discuss in this chapter whether you should have an illustration on the cover, or what sort of typeface to use. The major concern is that you say as directly as possible what you intend to say. Presenting your work clearly is an indication that you have a definite idea of what you are doing, and the process of working this out is as useful to you as it will be helpful to your readers.

Consider your reader

Your reader(s) should be your first concern. They should not have to work hard to puzzle out what you are trying to say, nor should they have to wade through pages of the appendix to find the sentence you are discussing in detail. Your project provides you with an opportunity to show that you can write, and that the time you have spent looking at other people's language has taught you a few lessons about how to improve your own.

Start in good time

You must be prepared to write several versions of your project, so make sure you leave yourself time to do this. Your first attempt will probably reveal omissions, non-sequiturs in your argument, technical errors and patches where the writing is less than clear. It may be too long and repetitive, or it may be too skimpy, with obvious gaps in coverage. The best way to discover these flaws is to give it to someone else to read, probably your teacher or a fellow student, although a non-specialist reader might have some interesting comments too – over-reliance on jargon or unclear use of technical terms perhaps? You will almost certainly be too involved with the material to view it dispassionately, although this can sometimes be overcome by leaving time between finishing a draft and coming back to read it. (We are speaking of the ideal world here. Time constraints may well prevent this.)

Another reason not to delay the actual writing of your project too long, however much preparation and research have been involved, is that the process of writing aids thinking. You do not have to have your project planned to the last detail before setting pen to paper, or fingers to keyboard. It is surprising how many students are reluctant to stop making notes and start writing the 'real thing'. Writing your thoughts, findings and analysis down can help to clarify things in your mind. This will help you to get to grips with the possibilities and limitations of what you will be able to say in the finished version.

Don't be defensive about your first attempt. Criticism is constructive in this case. You know your work isn't perfect – yet! Your most critical readers can be the ones who in the end provide the most help. However it is your project, and after due consideration you might decide to reject some of the critical remarks, but weigh them up carefully first. To soften the blow you can ask your readers to tell you what they like about your work as well – there's bound to be something even in the most tentative first draft.

Title

The logical place to start a section on presentation is with the title – but this does not mean that the title need be the first thing you write. The safest sort of title, which is perfectly adequate, if not inspired, is descriptive: 'The language of sports commentaries: An analysis of the Radio 2 commentary on the football game between England and Scotland on 21st May 1988.' The opening part of this title indicates the general field of the investigation, the second is more specific about the data it is based on. Don't make it too long and complicated – the title should definitely be shorter than the project itself!

If the project has set out to answer a question, then make that question the title. This arouses curiosity in the age-old 'read-on' tradition, and indicates the direction the project will take. Questions make good titles: 'Do men and women speak the same language? An analysis of three conversations: men only, women only and a mixed group.'

Of course this raises expectations that you will have answered the question by the end of your investigation, whereas your findings may be inconclusive. Don't worry about this. Don't force a conclusion if there isn't one.

Some students are inspired to produce short, snappy titles followed by a more explicit description. They may even attempt wit. An investigation into common spelling mistakes by fifteen-year-olds, for example, was called 'The error of our weighs, waze, ways'. One which investigated the idiosyncratic style of Salvador Dali's diaries had the title 'Painting by letters' and looked at whether the painter was trying to use words in the same unsettling way he used images. This approach is fine, if it works, but it is not necessary. The most important aspect of a title is that it gives a clear idea of what is to follow.

Style

Which style is appropriate to project writing? You have been studying language, and a project is a writing exercise in its finished form. It is important to get this right. Is it advisable to make your style lively, humorous or original in order to make your project easily readable? On the whole, the answer to this is no. It is not the primary purpose of your project to entertain your readers. On the other hand, you do not want to bore them. A direct, clear style is best. Try to write as simply as possible and to convey your meaning accurately. You do not have to use a lot of technical or jargon words to sound impressive, but only where they are necessary and the most straightforward way to make your point. Wit should be confined to section headings and sub-titles, and in any case used only if you are good at it. Accept the advice of others on this point.

It is a good idea to break up your text into sections. It makes it more 'digestible' for the reader and shows you have a plan and a structure. If used correctly, they also help to make your points more clearly: significant analysis or conclusions can easily get lost and be overlooked if the text is continuous. Structuring also makes reference back much easier. To make an obvious point, page numbers also help with this.

How to begin?

The best way to begin is with your hypothesis, the question you are asking of your data. This may be preceded or followed by some account of how you came to choose this topic and to formulate your approach. This is a personal investigation, and your reasons for choosing this area are interesting to the reader as well as relevant to your investigation. Describe the process by which you came to your general topic area, and to narrow down the focus of your project. By this we don't mean that you go into too much detail:

> Sitting on the top deck of the thirty nine bus on my way home
> from the pictures wondering whether or not to get off a stop early
> and get some chips, I heard a woman behind me say 'She's a strange
> woman, that Mrs Reynolds.' I began to wonder about the frequency of
> delayed naming in the Bradford dialect ...

(if there is such a phenomenon!) This would probably be including too much irrelevant personal detail. However, some indication of how you did decide on your topic is interesting to the reader and can convey some of your interest and enthusiasm. Was the source of your topic personal observation, or did it come from your reading? Did the general area or the question come first? How did you then refine your ideas to give you the shape of your project? Start with the beginning and describe the process.

If this is in fact your third project idea after two unrelated false starts, it is not necessary to describe your previous subjects. But if the area you began with was similar and it is as a direct result of a previous false start that you finally developed your current project, then it may well be relevant. It is part of the process.

Having introduced your topic and indicated the question you are asking of your data you can then outline how you are going to proceed and give your reader an idea of what to expect from your project and what the scope of it is. Like any good resumé or plot summary you should not give away the ending at this point. Don't arouse unreasonable expectations, but arouse some!

Explain your methods

Briefly explain how you collected your data, and the principles which underlay the collection of it. How did you make sure you were comparing like with like? How did you reduce variables which might have confused your findings? Did problems with data collection actually affect the subsequent direction of the project? Do you have reservations about the material you finally had to work with, or does it exactly serve your purposes? This is the place to explain this to your reader, although it is not necessary to include a blow-by-blow account.

Where should I present the data?

All the data which you have used and referred to should be submitted with your project, usually in the form of an appendix. However, when you are referring in detail to any part of your data within the body of your project you should include it at that point. The golden rule is to consider your reader. It should be easy for the reader to refer to the data you are analysing, and not to have to keep turning to the back.

You will probably have access to a photocopier, and it is useful to make several copies of your material, whether it is a transcript, newspaper articles, advertisements or poems, as a back-up in case you lose anything, as a copy you can scribble on, and as a spare copy you can cut up and insert whole in the main part of the project when you are considering that part in detail.

In some types of project the decision about how and where to display your data is crucial, and solving the problem is an important step in the development of the project. Consider an investigation which is comparing two different translations of a work in a foreign language. The whole point of the exercise is to make detailed comparisons of two texts. It is vital to display both texts, and probably the original, in a way which makes it easy for the reader, and for you, to make rapid reference from one to the other. You would have to decide what size 'chunks' of the text would be manageable – sentences or paragraphs? You might also wish to highlight certain features, such as lexical choice, to compare directly. Colour coding with highlighting pens can help here. A student of ours who was comparing two versions of Albert Camus's *L'Etranger* spent a long time evolving a consistent system which simplified data reference for the reader, but once she had, the whole method of procedure fell into place. Not all considerations of where to display data in your project are as complicated as this, but many do involve decisions about how much data to include at which points in the body of the text as well as the appendix. This is an element of presentation it is well worth spending time on. If your text is clear to the reader, the reader will assume it is clear in your head!

How should I present data?

If you are discussing a particular feature which recurs across the whole of your material, the easiest way to present your findings in a summarised, easily assimilable form, is to draw up a table.

Overleaf is an example from a student of ours who was looking at sex-stereotyping in the popular press. He was comparing the way men are described with the way women are described in one edition of *The Sun*. Having decided that people are usually described according to occupation, age, appearance and personality, he drew up two tables to see if there was a significant difference in the information that was given about male and female subjects. As you see, he shows pretty conclusively that there is (in this newspaper anyway!) He had started out with a hunch, but by this method he had confirmed it at a glance for the reader. The tables represent a lot of hard work on his part.

The data was not just presented in this form without comment. The student went on to discuss specific examples and groupings in more detail, having made it easier for himself and his reader to grasp the main point readily.

Female Labels

Label	Occupation/position in society	Age	Appearance	Personality
Gorgeous			X	
Girl			X	
Fiery				X
Model Agency Boss	X			
Sexy			X	
Blonde			X	
Delicious			X	
24-year-old		X		
Stripagram Girl	X			
Barmaid	X			
Beautiful			X	
21-year-old		X		
Lovely			X	
Archers Star	X			
Attractive			X	
Actress	X			
36-year-old		X		
Star	X			
Daughter	X			
Pop Singer	X			
Raunchy			X	
Pretty			X	
17-year-old		X		
School Girl	X			
Patient	X			
Widow	X			
Solicitor's Clerk	X			
Young		X		
Attractive			X	
Petite			X	
Raven Haired			X	
Star Stunna			X	
Brunette			X	
Bubbly			X	
Golden Girl			X	
Angelic			X	
Green-eyed			X	
Model	X			
Stunning			X	
Sexy			X	
Teaser			X	
Landlady	X			
Popular				X
42-year-old		X		
Smartly Dressed			X	
Total 45	14	6	23	2
%	33	13	48	6

Male Labels

Label	Occupation/ position in society	Age	Appearance	Personality
Pub Boss	X			
Cheeky				X
Fire-eater	X			
Tory chief	X			
Party Chairman	X			
Opponent of Loose Morals				X
Thatcher's Key Supporter				X
BBC Interviewer	X			
Straight-Talking				X
Top Tory	X			
Manager	X			
Mid 30's		X		
Co-star	X			
Dentist	X			
55-year-old		X		
Prosecutor	X			
61-year-old		X		
Husband	X			
Killer				X
Heathrow Porter	X			
46		X		
Total 21	**12**	**4**	**0**	**5**
%	57	15	0	24

Terminology

It is not necessary to use a lot of specialist terms in your investigation to make it read and sound impressive. Use technical vocabulary only where it is necessary and certainly only if you feel comfortable with it. Don't use any terms you are unsure about, instead try to think of another way of saying what you mean.

If you are using key terms or concepts regularly it is a good idea to explain what you mean by them. If you have invented any new terms or phrases to express what you mean, you should certainly make them clear. For example, a student of ours who was looking at the language of poetry written by English black poets repeatedly used the term 'language marriage' to express the blend of patwa and Standard English in the poems. This sounded good but was really rather an empty phrase until he inserted an explanation of the term. He wanted to express the sense of a new voice which was a single entity although it was still possible to talk of the individual 'components' which came together to create it. He felt it expressed exactly what he wanted to say. Suddenly it made sense.

Any technical, linguistic terms which you use in your investigation should be used because they are the most accurate ones, because they enable you to make points clearly and succinctly; and they must be used consistently. If register is an important term for you, explain the first time it is used what you take it to mean, and henceforth use it to mean only that.

Framework for analysis

The main body of your project will be given over to a description and analysis of your data. It is important that this proceeds in a systematic, logical fashion. The simplest way, but not necessarily the best, is to 'talk us through it', concentrating on various language features as you work your way through the data. The problem with this is that it can lead to a lot of repetition, as the same pattern is observed at different points in the data. This is a rather naïve approach and has the look of a first attempt. It probably is what you did when you first looked at the data, but by the time you reach the finished product you should be aiming to produce something rather more sophisticated. Having said this, it is just possible that you think this is the best way to proceed with your data – if it's a transcript of a conversation for example. If you are convinced, then do it this way. It is your project.

However, most projects gather together examples of one particular feature and discuss them together, as in the 'labelling' in *The Sun* articles mentioned above. Once you have decided what these clusters of features are, then your only problem is the order in which you discuss them. Do you look at the most prominent first? Do you keep what you regard as your most striking discovery and perceptive analysis until the end? Do you arrange your analysis along phonological/lexical/grammatical lines? It is up to you, but there must be some discernible organisation and system. This is the main part of the investigation and your project will stand or fall according to the quality of it. Display your hard work to best advantage.

The conclusion

Your conclusion should return to the question you asked of your data at the beginning. Have you answered it? You must be honest in your answer, which should be faithful to the analysis you have just undertaken in the main part of the investigation. It doesn't matter whether you are able to say 'My analysis of the evidence has indeed shown ... ' or 'I found to my surprise when I looked in detail ... ' or even 'Although this appears to bear out my hypothesis the sample is probably too small ... ' This is the part of the project you were aiming towards, but the process of the investigation is more important than the originality of your conclusion. The quality of your conclusion in that it arises directly from looking at the data is crucial, but don't force it.

Sources

At the end of your project you should acknowledge any books you have consulted which you have found useful in writing your project. You may have used the vocabulary and approach for discourse analysis which you read about in a specific volume, or you may have adapted it for your own purposes. Either way you should list the titles of any books which have given you ideas or inspiration, or which you have drawn on to improve your understanding of your topic area.

Presentation

How important is it to have your project presented in a professional manner? It is not vital to have your work typed. Perhaps you yourself can't type and you certainly can't afford to pay for someone else to do it. You will definitely not be penalised for this. However, your final version should be presented with care. It should be legible, clear and easy to read and follow. The quality of the work itself is the most important thing, but if you have not taken the trouble to consider your reader it may indicate that the whole process has been rushed and ill-thought-out. Leave yourself enough time to make sure that the final draft gives the impression that you have approached the whole enterprise with care and commitment.

You must not make greater claims for your investigation than the examination of the evidence can stand. You may have discovered that the language used in the sports section of a tabloid newspaper is more complex than that used in the news stories, as measured by sentence length and use of specialist terms. You will only have shown this to be the case for the edition(s) of the newspaper(s) you have looked at, not for all tabloid newspapers for all time; you may go on to speculate about why this difference exists, but you cannot say conclusively why it is so. You may have called your project 'The Language of Fantasy Literature', but you will certainly only have looked at a relatively small sample. You cannot make claims for the whole genre, and you would invalidate your conclusions if you did. You may believe that your findings hold good for a particular writer's entire œuvre, but unless you've looked at it all (highly unlikely!) you must not state that they do.

State clearly what you think you have discovered and don't be unduly modest, but don't make unrealistic claims which will weaken the whole enterprise. The time and words that are available to you inevitably limit the scale of your project, but if it is clear, original and it answers the questions it raised, you and your supervisor have every reason to be gratified.

Chapter 22

Inside a marker's head –
examples of good and bad practice

We have discussed at some length what goes to make a good project, what topics, approaches and modes of presentation seem most appropriate and fruitful. It now seems a good idea to exemplify the points we've made with extracts from genuine projects. All were produced under the supervision of the writers, so we know how much they represent a triumph or disaster.

We do recognise that the project represents a difficult task for many students, but given guidance, sense and determination the worst horrors can be avoided. No-one expects everyone to be a genius, full of original ideas and talented as a writer, but we can expect you to ask yourself basic questions like

Is this really a project rather than an essay?
Have I displayed some relevant knowledge?
Does this project have a structure?
Does it make sense?
Is it legible and as well written as I can make it?
Does it reach conclusions and prove something?

If the answer to any of these questions is no, do something about it!

First impressions

Clearly, presentation matters. No, it is not worth taking a course in word processing; yes, it is worth doing a genuinely neat final draft that looks as though someone cares about it. Your project ought to be the culmination of a lot of research, thought and writing – don't let yourself and your material down at the last hurdle. Why not put it in a plastic wallet at least so that it doesn't get dog-eared? Trite trivia will still be trite trivia even if beautifully typed and bound, but you do yourself no favours by assuming that your intellect will shine through illegible scrawl. It will not.

Every cover sheet tells a story

Is your title hopelessly vague? 'Television adverts', 'Comparing popular and quality newspapers' or 'Child language acquisition' immediately give the impression of a poorly focused, probably entirely unoriginal project. Some A-level language students manage to come up with witty, striking titles; at least ensure that yours sounds considered and personal. One project which had a first draft title 'Analysis of songs' (subtext 'I can't think what the hell to do but I like pop songs so I'll have a bash at them') became, by final draft 'A linguistic analysis of songwriting from the 1960s and 1970s commenting on difference, change and development.' The subtext of this is very different: 'This is not waffle, it is linguistic and I know exactly what I'm looking at.' The area still sounds rather large but the reader feels the writer is in control.

Your brief description of your project also speaks volumes. Does it actually say any more than the title? Notice the wording: 'outline of topic stud*ed* and sources consult*ed*'. You are expected to write some of it at least *after* you have written the rest. Your outline ought to give the marker a clear and positive impression of what is to follow. Don't miss your chance!

Your supervisor's remarks may well accompany your project. It is silly for you to think that these have nothing to do with you: 'X has still not produced her data', 'Y failed to consult me' and 'Z insisted on including this against my advice' help no-one. 'Excellent in every way' and 'I wish every language project were as easy to supervise as this one' paint a very different and more encouraging picture. Your teacher is an important resource – and probably a bad enemy to make!

What do you get marks for?

Examination boards recommend a loose marking scheme to their markers. The names for the different elements vary a little from board to board but the same virtues – knowledge, clarity and wit – are bound to be appreciated. Of these elements, knowledge is the most vital at this level. The JMB, for example, recommends its markers to give twenty of the available fifty marks for linguistic knowledge. This includes many possible aspects: grammar, phonetics, analytical skill and topic knowledge all come under the umbrella. As you prepare your project, ask yourself 'Where am I getting my linguistic knowledge marks from?' Have you proved that you can do discourse analysis or understand difficult theories of child language acquisition or transcribe phonetically or discuss morphemes or syntax convincingly, for example? Look at what you have done and try to be objective. Do you sound as if you know what you're talking about? Is your approach rigorous? Are your comments precise and accurate?

To show what I mean by precise and accurate let's look at a couple of examples of analysis from projects. Read each one yourself. Both are from projects whose main task is to analyse literature linguistically. Try for the moment to ignore my marginal remarks and ask yourself:

Is the writer knowledgeable?
Is she using specialist terms with confidence and appropriateness?
Is she precise?
Is she proving anything?

> Catherine also uses colloquial phrases in letter number six – 'Well I never' is an expression not authentic to Brontë's writing, or indeed to letter writing, especially at the beginning of a correspondence. Catherine is writing letters to Heathcliff, but the style of writing is almost like a dialogue. These examples show a complete lack of formality, the formality *stylish* inherent in letters written at that time. 'I don't know why I put up with you' is another modern phrase, as is 'How are you doing over there in New York?' (letters six and one respectively.)
>
> The reference to 'all that Wuthering on the moors' is a play on the title 'Wuthering Heights'. 'Wuthering' is an old dialect word used in Yorkshire to mean stormy or blustering. By re-collocating the word 'Wuthering', the *precise* connotation shifts from those suggesting something passionate and turbulent to something clearly disparaging. In the same letter (number

one), there is a reference to Golgotha – the Aramaic word for Calvary which is the place where Jesus Christ was crucified. Biblical allusions were quite widely used at the time when 'Wuthering Heights' was written. This use of a Biblical term suggests that Edgar's sister is a cross which Catherine must bear, but she expresses this in an indirect and sophisticated way.

knowledgeable

lucid

The writer does use some archaic lexis to emphasise that the theme of the story is a nineteenth-century novel. However, the letters contain a combination of lexis from the nineteenth century and the modern/late twentieth century. An example of the archaic lexis used to add to the humour can be seen in the third letter, 'Ah me alas, alackaday ... ' which are terms not in use today, neither would the archaic word for influenza – 'grippe' – be used in either speech or writing today. The writer uses the term 'New World' many times – this is an old word for America.

Not all of the lexis used is early nineteenth or late twentieth century. For example, in the first letter, Catherine says 'Edgar is sweet but a terrible stick.' 'Stick' is lexis most commonly found in the late nineteenth/early twentieth century. It is used in this context for humorous reasons; the connotations of 'stick' are highly inappropriate, and it creates a jar of registers which is characteristic of the humour of the story.

what & why

again, precise and technical

Catherine uses different terms to finish her letters such as 'Yours in ennui' (letter three) – a French word meaning boredom – and a Latin phrase more likely to have been used in previous centuries, 'Yours in extremis' – meaning at the point of death. The use of these words is characteristic of pastiche, the style of the piece is exaggerated for humour. 'Yours in extremis' conjures up an image of a girl pining away, but here it is used in a semi-joking way. In the novel, the characters do not dramatise themselves so much.

In the second letter, Catherine says 'We Yorkshire lasses are not so dumb as you think!' The use of 'dumb' in this context is to mean stupid. This is an example of an Americanism which would not have been used in the nineteenth century, as the American influence would not have infiltrated the English language at that time. Such usage of Americanisms is only a recent happening.

thorough and intelligent

The letters were obviously not written in the nineteenth century and they are not typical letters of any period. The letters are more like an actual conversation between Catherine and Heathcliff. The letters are accurate in that they contain questions, although most people would not begin to write a letter with a question (letters one and five), especially not during the period when 'Wuthering Heights' was written.

The letters are a cross between the original novel and a more up-to-date version. Certainly, a nineteenth century writer would not have begun a letter 'Dear Heathcliff, you Bastard ... ' as in letter number eleven, which is obviously a modern usage of the word.

1. Ground thoroughly covered – a clear line of argument
2. Assertions backed by precise and valid examples
3. Technical terms in abundance, appropriately used
4. Comments precise and convincing
5. An intelligent, perceptive analysis – impressive.

Analysis of 'Gulliver's Travels'

The tone of the passage at first strikes me as humorous and quite *[vague and unproven]* dramatic as it is so unusual. When reading the passage it is very easy to get into the atmosphere and you can imagine yourself actually being there. You can see the story from two sides, as Gulliver himself being attended *[chit-chat not linguistic]* to and what the Lilliputians must have seen and felt like. Swift therefore seems most concerned with the atmosphere, although Gulliver himself is setting the story. *[examples?]*

[repetitive] The language is formal, although Gulliver is telling the story himself it is not colloquial. All the responses are directed at the Lilliputians as Gulliver keeps mentioning what they are doing and what their lives are like. Nouns *[just a list, & not an impressive one]* are mainly concrete but some proper nouns are used for effect, to make the piece more realistic e.g. 'Burgundy'. Adjectives are very frequently to do with the senses and to describe the situation such as 'small' and 'universal'. Verbs are mainly in the past tense e.g. 'descended', and they are showing the situation and what everybody is doing. The infinite form of the verb is used e.g. 'to stand', 'to mount'. There are some fictional words *[coinages? oh for some technical terms!]* in the passage e.g. 'Hekinah Degul' and 'Borach Mivola'; this is supposed to be the language of Lilliput. *[this doesn't link together at all!]*

There is a semantic field in the passage to do with the meat which Gulliver was eating e.g. 'flesh of several animals – there were shoulders, legs and loins, shaped like those of mutton – very well dressed.' Collocation is used, e.g. 'half a pint'. *[what does this mean?]*

Personal pronouns are found frequently throughout the passage e.g. 'my sides', 'my mouth', 'my hand'. Demonstratives such as 'that hogshead' can be found and relative pronouns e.g. 'who durst venture', 'that several ladders', 'which I drank'.

Conjunctions which connect phrases together seem to be fairly frequent: 'and' is used a lot in the first sentence. Co-ordinating conjunctions can be found also, e.g. 'They slung up with great dexterity one of their largest hogsheads, then rolled it towards my hand.'

1. No line of argument – no overall statement
2. Assertions rarely borne out by evidence
3. Technical terms absent or ill-understood
4. Comments vague and unconvincing
5. This is analysing by rote – no evidence that she understands why features are there.

Now look at what I thought as I read them and at my summative remarks at the bottom. Did we agree? For your interest the first extract came from a grade A project, the second from one which failed – so I hope you could tell the difference.

Phonetic transcription

Doing this accurately is a skill in itself and will impress. However, it should also be serving a useful purpose. The most likely such purpose is to clarify exactly what someone sounds like in order to comment on their accent. This is the purpose to which this candidate is putting it. First he transcribes what they say – accurately:

Got up at quarter to seven this morning made myself a drink
gɒt ʊp æt kwortə tə sevən ðɪs mɒrnɪn meɪd mɪself æ drɪnk

of tea sat down for half an hour while I came round went
ov ti sæt daʊn fʌ haːf ən ɑə waɪl æ keɪm raʊnd went

upstairs got dressed came back down washed the breakfast pots
ʊpstɛəz gɒʔ drest keɪm bæk daʊn wɒʃd ðə brekfəst pɒts

Then he finds patterns within their speech in order to make specific points about their accent:

The Salford Accent

The Salford accent, or what is supposedly a Salford accent, has become familiar to many people around Britain through the programme 'Coronation Street'. Yet to many people unfamiliar with the area it is difficult to tell which of the accents on the programme most truly depicts the Salford one.

For example, Brian Tilsley seems to have more of a Geordie accent, Sally seems to have a Bolton/Bury accent, while Vera Duckworth has a very over-emphasised and exaggerated Salford accent, but someone unfamiliar with the area would find it difficult to tell the difference. Hopefully, my project will help to illustrate what is a true Salford accent.

1) The first feature I came across was the use of the 'schwa'. That is, instead of **/ɜ/** for the 'er' sound at the end of or middle of a word, the schwa **/ə/** sound is used.
e.g. in **/kwortə/**

2) The next feature is the dropping of the final consonant of a word, commonly the 'g'.
e.g. instead of **/lɪvɪŋ/** it is **/lɪvɪn/**

3) The dropped final consonant is a common feature of the Salford accent, as are the following vowel sounds:
The 'a' sound is **/æ/** for example in the word **/bæk/**. **/bæθ/** would have been a better example, but this was not used in the transcript. The **/æ/** sound is a typical Northern accent feature in comparison to Received Pronunciation which would be **/aː/**
Also the deep Northern **/ʊ/** was a common feature in words such as **/ʊp/**

4) Some vowel sounds were sounded in an unfamiliar way, for example, the **/ɪ/** in **/mɪself/**

Then he gives them a word list in order to check their pronunciation of certain, isolated phonemes against those of another speaker:

funny	/fʊnɪ/
book	/bʊk/
luck	/lʊk/
door	/dɔr/
butter	/bʊtə/

begin	/bɪɡ̃ɪn/
later	/leɪtə/
no	/nəʊ/
stay	/steɪ/
hanging	/haŋɪn/
birthday	/bəθdeɪ/
bus	/bus/
door	/dur/
tomatoes	/tɒmaːtəʊs/
potatoes	/pʌteɪtəʊs/
honour	/ɒnə/

The use of phonetic transcript has enabled this candidate to differentiate very clearly between the speakers. Without this system he would be reduced to saying things like 'The Bolton accent has much longer vowels.' This is far too vague to be of any linguistic value: precision is all when discussing vowels. It is far more helpful, in this case to say 'Whereas the Salford speaker has the pure vowel /ʊ/, the Bolton speaker has the diphthongised vowel /ʊə/.'

If you has to ask you ain't got it: rhythm

Many projects are written about songs, the analysis of which inevitably leads to discussion of rhythm: weak candidates waffle about a song being 'rhythmic' and 'lines being drawn out.' The candidate quoted below has ensured that she is rigorous by looking at stress and syllabic structure. She has also used phonetics to clarify how the lines are sung.

Rhythm

Rhythm plays an important part in the way a song appeals to its audience, but its analysis depends largely upon its stress and syllabic structure.

In song writing rules can be broken: words can be 'moulded' to fit the rhythm or mispronounced to fit the rhyme. Also music can be written to suit the lyrics. One can often tell by the use of lexis and rhyme, whether the music or the lyrics was written first. It was the case with many songs of the 1960s that the music was written first and the lyrics were made to 'fit', hence the occurrence and in fact re-occurrence of cliché and metaphorical language.

One usually finds that the songs containing the simpler lexis have a steadier rhythm. This is the case with the songs chosen for this section of the project. Both songs have a steady rhythm, but when the lexis is written on paper one wouldn't think that this was the case as the lines are of unequal length in terms of the number of syllables that they contain. This comes back to an earlier point I made about 'words being moulded to fit the lyrics.'

For example Song 1, Verse 1:

As I walk this land of broken dreams, (9)
I have visions of many things, (8)
And happiness is just an illusion (10)
Filled with sadness and confusion (8)

(The numbers in the brackets indicate the number of syllables in each line.)

Lines of random length are not very easily set to a 'fixed' rhythm, so to make things easier the verse is pronounced thus

'As I walk this land of broken /drɪ//ɪmz/ (10)
I have visions of /ə/ many /θɪ//ɪŋz/ (10)
And happiness is just an illusion (10)
Filled with sadness and confus- /ə//ən/ (9)

As you can see, certain vowels have been diphthongised i.e. (/drɪmz/ becomes /drɪ//ɪmz/) Now the first three lines are decasyllabic and fit into the rhythm. The last line has only nine syllables, but the introductory 'Now' which starts the chorus each time makes up the tenth.

It is worth mentioning, perhaps, that in the first draft this candidate found this aspect of analysis difficult. Here is her first attempt at analysis:

In this first verse, the first line has nine syllables, the second is octosyllabic, as is the last, and the third is decasyllabic. Lines of random length are much more complex and cannot be easily set to music. Therefore rules are broken and the lines are put into a much more simple form. This is where the steady rhythm enters. The verse therefore is pronounced thus:

As I walk this land of broken dre-eams
I have visions of a many thi-ings
And happiness is just an illusion
Filled with sadness and con-fu-usion

The first three lines become decasyllabic lines, due to lengthened vowels. The last line has nine syllables, which leads into the chorus which always begins 'Now ...' This could, of course be making up the extra vowel, as the line containing nine syllables runs straight into the 'Now'.

No-one expects you to get everything right at first or ever, unaided. It is vital that you are self-critical and listen to advice, though!

Can you manage your grammar?

Where weak candidates go wrong here is by feeling that they must include some comment about sentence structure or parts of speech, but being, in fact, incapable of saying anything constructive. It is pointless saying 'verbs include the future tense and the past tense: future "there would be" and past "you lived", "it struck him"'. What does this prove? Why did the writer employ these tenses? Was the past gaining detachment, the future predicting, or what? The 'whats' of language are of limited value unless you make some intelligent remarks about the 'whys'.

Similarly, it is of no value to state that 'There are 73 simple, 22 compound and 7 complex sentences in this extract' or 'Many of the sentences are long and hard.' What does 'hard' mean? And what does this preponderance of simple sentences tell us about audience? Much more sensible is the following approach:

As children of the age of approximately five get confused if word order other than standard is used, adjectival and adverbial phrases are not very common in the programme. This is because they would affect standard word order.

Sentences are mainly simple and compound. Simple sentences, for example 'Now have a look inside', 'You could use one of those um clothes drying racks.'

The compound sentences often use the simplest conjunction 'and'. Examples: 'And then I stuck bits of material for curtains, and here is the door and it's got a handle'; 'A piece of cardboard is stuck here to make an upstairs and a downstairs and the windows and door have been cut in.'

There are very few complex sentences such as 'There's a tasty looking carrot. It wouldn't be though because this carrot is made out of cardboard and paper.'

About an even number of short and long sentences are used. Some long sentences are often still simple.

The programme contains sentences that are mostly statements, informing the audience. There are only a few commands, imperative ones, for example, 'Have a look at these children playing' and 'Now have a look inside.'

There are also polite commands, for example, 'You could have a go at making this' and 'Perhaps you could make a toy shop for your toys.'

The few imperatives and questions are for the child's involvement in the programme, but the tone is predominantly informative.

This says a good deal about structures: their complexity, function and type. The same candidate deals in a helpful way with parts of speech:

Lots of nouns are used, mainly concrete nouns. These often refer to objects shown and used in the programme. For example, 'Big Ted has got cushions and even a box television, books, cup and saucer.'

Plenty of adjectives are present, mostly simple ones such as in 'Put a big curtain over the top of it all', 'This bit is a great big box.' The adjectives are informative.

There are lots of verbs, for example, 'Look at these children playing,' as lots of action takes place in the programme.

Here the writer is not merely feature-spotting: she is able to label what is there in order to explicate why it is there.

Is the knowledge displayed relevant?

A warning note: do resist the temptation to add in anything linguistic that you happen to know in a desperate bid to get some linguistic knowledge marks. It has to be relevant. If the purpose of the project is to compare two three-year-olds' language development, it is pointless to explain all the stages they've already gone through. In the first place, it is irrelevant; in the second place it looks like teacher's notes! You ought to be utilising your linguistic knowledge to shed light on your data, not wheeling out one more time half of an essay that once got you a good mark. Such stuff is useless padding and easily spotted as such by a marker.

Structure

Introductions

What about the rest of the marks? Something which is vital to a project is a good structure and line of argument. One of the most disastrous failures for a project is signalled by its looking and reading like an essay.

Your project will have an introduction in which you clarify for the reader what your hypothesis is and how you are going to test it. A good project ought, as we have said, to be seeking to discover something, not merely describing. Here is an introduction which, though brief, does its job:

Introduction

My aim in this project was to ascertain whether or not the language of romantic fiction differs in different women's magazines. I looked at a range of women's magazines, and having defined the differences between them, I chose the three magazines which most closely fitted my aims. The magazines I chose covered the range of women's papers – 'Cosmopolitan', 'Woman's Own' and 'The People's Friend'.

The Magazines

'Cosmopolitan' is published monthly. It is a glossy magazine, around two hundred pages in length. The style of the magazine tends to attract well educated readers and has a variety of features and articles which are of general interest, not purely for its female readers. 'Cosmopolitan' contains several fictional stories in each issue, which do not necessarily have happy endings, nor are they typical 'boy meets girl' romances as some magazine stories tend to be.

'Woman's Own', as its name suggests, is a magazine mostly for women. This weekly magazine has cookery articles and clothes features as well as articles of general interest. 'Woman's Own' features both weekly serials and short stories. The serials tend to be serialised books rather than stories written especially for the magazine, such as the novels 'Lace' or 'The Thorn Birds'. The short stories are generally light romantic fiction, and they would usually have happy endings.

'The People's Friend' is a Scottish magazine available throughout England. The style of the magazine tends to appeal to older ladies, containing clothes patterns and recipes every week. It has both serials and short stories. The serials tend to have a Scottish flavour and the short stories are light, romantic fiction which always have happy endings. 'The People's Friend' is published weekly.

Method

I took each magazine and read the short stories which I had chosen. Then I gave each story a full linguistic analysis, as for literary material.

Your introduction sets the tone for the test of your project. If it is derivative (i.e. reads as if it's been copied from a book), narrative or descriptive, it is setting the wrong tone. Look at this example and see if you agree with my remarks:

Introduction

The existence of the English Language as a seperate idiom began when Germanic tribes had occupied all the lowlands of Great Britain. When the invasions from the continent were discontinued, the settlers in their new homes were cut off from their continental relations which was an imperative condition of linguistic unity. The historical records of English do not go so far back as this, for the oldest written texts in the English Language (in Anglo Saxon) date from about 700 and are thus removed by three centuries from the beginnings of the language. Comparative philology is able to tell us something about the manner in which the ancestors of these settlers spoke centuries before that period, and to sketch the pre-historic development of what was to become the language of Chaucer and of Shakespeare. *copied*

There are more varieties of English in Britain than any other English speaking country. The diagram shows this and explains why this is the case. *point?*

The passages chosen to analyse are from Shakespeare's 'Hamlet', Jonathan Swift's 'Gulliver's Travels' and George Orwell's '1984', three very different books. *.!!!*

The analysis hopes to show why these pieces are different and give the reader some idea of the change in language structures.

Narrative, derivative & largely irrelevant

As you will have noticed, the data used is secondary. This makes it doubly important that the project has an interesting and clear focus. This introduction does not encourage us to believe this project has that. To say that the writer 'hopes' to give the reader 'some idea' of the change in language does not augur well: you are not rewarded for diffidence! It may seem unkind to give examples of bad practice, but we hope by raking up forgotten disasters to avoid your going down the same blind alleys.

To prove the point that we don't expect brilliance on all fronts, take a look at another introduction and my comments on it. Yes, it has its limitations; parts of it are irrelevant and the style is nothing spectacular, but it has many virtues, too. It shows thought, it is not derivative, it clearly means well and is the beginning of a voyage of discovery. This represents a middle range C-grade candidate doing their best. Your personal best – whatever that may be – is as much as anyone can ask of you.

Introduction

When thinking of a project title I decided to do my project on changes in written language. I was going to use Shakespeare's writing to study, but decided against this, as Shakespeare's literary writing was not a 'natural' look at English from this period of time, as like any literary piece, it has been changed and perfected to make a classic piece of writing. *honest and clear*

I wanted writing from the nineteenth century that showed how most people would have used English. I decided to analyse the informal language that can be found in personal letters. Letters often express a style of writing that is the nearest to spoken language. When writing to somebody with whom you share a relationship, true feelings can be thought about and written down, as a permanent record of spoken-style English. *good point*

I decided to use letters from the nineteenth century because this English is not too archaic, so that the lexis is totally different. I was not looking for the changes in spelling, which occurs in the seventeenth and eighteenth century, because the English language did not have a set mode. However I wanted to find differences between emotive language and how it is expressed, and the change in lexis and actual sentence structure. I expected to find some of the lexis to be different in context than it is today.

For example, the word 'nice' in the English language today is one of the most meaningless and corrupted words. We can use it for a variety of objects, like 'the *rather irrelevant* nice girl', 'the nice house', 'the nice little business' and 'a nice sum of money'. The word 'nice' almost becomes an approving noise. However, nice was not always so vague, and its meaning has undergone drastic changes. It derives from the Latin word nescius, which means 'ignorant'. In 1560 it meant foolish, stupid, in 1606 it was used to mean wanton and also in the sixteenth century it was sometimes used to signify rare or strange, difficult to please, fastidious and thus precise or particular.

By analysing letters rather than literature we may also find more colloquial language, and it is more likely to find slang, blasphemy and possibly swearing, since letter writing is a natural intimate form of communication and it is spontaneous and tells us a lot about how people spoke. *a little repetitious*

I have chosen to analyse two letters from the nineteenth century, and two letters from the early twentieth century. I will be looking for unusual sentence structures, colloquial lexis and also the individual style of writing people possess.

good In my study of informal English I will be studying letters written by men, both of whom are writing to two different people, and so their style of writing can be seen to change according to audience. By using men, rather than men and women, we can narrow the reasons for language change, as men and women do tend to write in different styles.

sensible and genuine if not scintillating!

Some candidates don't feel confident enough to tackle an entirely new field but at least have the sense to put the old wine in new bottles. An introduction can point out to the reader what the 'angle' is:

Hypothesis

My hypothesis is that I would expect the child from the middle class family to be ahead of the child from the working class family in stages of language acquisition. I would also expect to find that she has a wider vocabulary. The reason for this difference would be that her parents would probably be better educated and therefore they would have a much more varied lexis and they would talk to her in a more adult way using this wide lexis.

Method

I took a child from a working class family and taped her talking while playing. I then took a child from a middle class family of the same age and taped her also at play. These two children were chosen because they have only one major difference and that is that they belong to a different class.

Conclusions

Following the introduction, most projects have the 'sandwich filling' – very often of detailed analyses. It is important that these analyses are somehow brought together at the end rather than standing in splendid isolation. The industrious and sensible candidate whose introduction we read earlier worked through her four analyses and then wrote a fair conclusion:

When I first analysed the two letters by John Keats I was surprised at the sophisticated lexis that was used. Even today, formal letters written to people who we do not know would not contain the sort of lexis that Keats' letters did. Keats was writing to a good friend, Benjamin Bailey, and his girlfriend Fanny Brawne, so this elaborate lexis was quite unusual.

The letters written by 'Ed' were totally different and did not contain the formal, sophisticated tone of Keats' letters. Ed's writing was much more colloquial and chatty. The most striking feature I found about the four letters I analysed was that of the two, Ed seemed to be in the most depressive situation, being at war, and despite this, Ed's letter was far more chatty and colloquial than Keats'.

The different styles of writing that Keats and Ed possess were quite dramatic. Keats' writing was definitely longer in quantity and contained a lot of hyperbolic and emotive lexis. Ed's writing however was a lot shorter in length, had a lot of abbreviated words, and was generally more colloquial and friendly.

It could be said that if Keats writing is a good, fair look at typical written English of the nineteenth century, then we could say that letter writing may have been more of an 'art' or hobby, and this elaborate lexis may not have been a natural form of spoken language of this period. It seems that Keats has taken a lot of care and time when writing his letters, and his ideas in his writing to Fanny about his love for her are very expressive and provoke emotion:

'But if you fully love me, though there may be some fire, 'twill not be more than we can bear when moistened and bedewed with pleasures'.

We could say that Ed's writing is more like the style of letter writing we would read today. It contains the same sort of friendliness and colloquialism that is used today. Ed seems to use phrases that were probably popular at the time he writes the letter. 'Wind up': he uses this expression in both his letter to Jess and his mother. Ed also uses the word 'absolutely' which was also a popular word in this period. Today certain phrases and words are popular for limited periods, and then they often die out. It seems that the word 'absolutely' may have been an example of this.

Ed's writing is generally more factual than Keats' letters, which tend to contain more statements, especially in his letter to Fanny.

Keats writing was definitely more philosophical and hyperbolic, and contained less factual information even though the letters are longer than Ed's.

It is a little repetitive and the style is nothing remarkable but it does round the project off.

Some conclusions, of course, are rather too much to believe from the data given. On the basis of two children only, one candidate's assertion that 'The hypothesis that a middle class child would acquire language more rapidly than a child of the working class is correct and must be accepted' is not really on, is it? Tact and diplomacy do matter: don't fail to mention what your project has proven but don't exaggerate its importance.

It can be very difficult to avoid being repetitive in conclusions. If you have chosen to analyse two programmes/stories/poems to see how they are similar and how they are different you have little choice but to do each on its own and then the two together. A very talented candidate might manage to discuss both at once, in detail, and also make general points. However, this would be difficult and no reasonable marker would object to your doing it the other way – as the following one has:

A comparison of the radio programme and the television programme

When comparing the two programmes, the most obvious difference is that the television programme makes full use of visual aids, which the radio programme cannot use. The television programme is based on the audience <u>watching</u> what is going on. It doesn't give instructions to make the audience join in. The contents of the programme rely on the audience watching the screen. Firstly there is a film. The audience are instructed to '<u>Have a look</u> at these children playing.' If the film is on the screen, a song is sung by the narrator. The words of the song correspond to certain actions in the film.

Features in the studio use visual aids, which are talked about and pointed to. Songs are sung and actions to go with them are performed by the narrators. For example, the song about sailing has the man pictured in a pretend ship.

When the second film is watched, there are only occasional words from the narrator. This is an example of the programme's reliance on the audience watching the screen. The whole of the programme would be hard to understand without the visual side.

The lexis is slightly more complicated and colloquial. The speech is also more chatty, less carefully spoken and less clear than the radio programme's. This is because the visual side makes it easier to understand.

The radio programme concentrates on getting the audience to join in, as they have nothing to watch to keep them interested. Obviously, the radio programme has no films like in 'Playschool' but it does have songs sung by the narrators. The difference is the songs on the radio include parts for the audience to join in with.

The television programme makes full use of the visual side, while the radio makes full use of sound effects. The noises animals make are used instead of pictures of animals, short tunes signal the beginning or the end of a piece in the programme, whereas on the television, the changes in the topics can be <u>seen</u>.

Both programmes have a male and a female narrator. In the radio programme, different sections appear to be spoken by Tony and Janet. This gives the audience a change of voice to listen to and helps distinguish between the different areas in the programme.

My Conclusion

The radio programme appears to have more of an educational element to it, because of the 'teacher like' speech and instructions and the clearness of the speech.

Although both radio and television programmes contain many different sections such as songs, stories, etc. in the short time they are on, the radio stays to the theme of the farm. I favour this, because I think once the children get used to the theme of the programme, they may be able to relate some of their own knowledge of farms, either from television or real life experiences, to the programme. If they have no idea what a farm is about, they should have some knowledge by the end of the programme. I also think the radio programme is more stimulating for the children, because of the way they are made to join in.

Sarah's response backs up some of what I've said. She was mostly interested in the parts of 'Playschool' that showed some involvement for the audience. They were not actually allowed to join in there and then, but the ideas were there for them to use afterwards. The least appealing parts were the footages of film. These had very little narrated parts. The only thing to do was watch. Perhaps the topic of the film (children playing) was not very interesting to the audience.

Of the two, the radio programme was obviously the one which Sarah preferred. I think this is because the programme got the audience to join in.

I would conclude that the radio programme fulfils its aim more than the television programme. It succeeds in entertaining and involving the audience throughout. I think the audience like being involved in the programme and 'Playschool' did not provide much involvement.

Do try to keep your conclusion brief: one side of A4 typed ought to be enough.

The best candidates combine linguistic knowledge, a sense of direction in their writing and good style. A grade A conclusion will be stylishly expressed: 'Women no longer need to be carried off to harems by darkly handsome sheikhs' (in reference to the world of women's magazines.) Such a conclusion will also offer genuine insights into language, will make suggestions and display perception:

There are conclusions already made in each section of the project, so there is little point in repeating how the accents and dialects of Bolton and Salford differ.

The project has proved that, within six miles, two very different accents exist. Also, there is a marked dialectal variation.

The origins of the two areas may provide an explanation as to why there are such differences.

Bolton was one of the main centres of the industrial revolution, in particular the cotton industry. During this period many people will have migrated into Bolton from the surrounding countryside. These people perhaps had broad accents which were picked up and spread around the town.

Salford has always held an important position on the outskirts of Manchester, and at the head of the Manchester Ship Canal. It has perhaps been influenced by Merseyside or the Irish from the canal, or by the traders and immigrants who came into Manchester, again during the Industrial Revolution.

These origins may appear to be too recent to be valid reasons for the development of regional accents. Some may argue that accents and dialects have taken more than one hundred and fifty to two hundred years to develop.

Personally, I think that the Industrial Revolution has had a great deal to do with causing regional variations. Before this time, the population was much more spread around the country in very small settlements. An industry developed, towns and cities grew up and various separate regions and then conurbations could be identified. With this, a common accent and dialect may have developed, and even if there were other causes, this seems to have been a very important one.

Another theory is that of 'mee-mawing'. This is, during the Industrial Revolution, Bolton was one of the main centres. Therefore many people would work in the mills and would have to lip-read. To make themselves understood, they would have to exaggerate vowel sounds, and thus the accent would develop.

Hopefully, the work in this project has illustrated to you the variations in Salford and Bolton language.

I would like to thank both the subjects for their co-operation, and also my English teachers for their help.

Notice that this very good candidate does not go over the same ground in his conclusion. He also feels relaxed and confident enough to adopt a slightly more personal tone. For example, he writes

Comparing the Salford and Bolton Accents: the Similarity

The title is not a mistake: I could only find one!

A strong enough candidate can show a little more personality than a mediocre one could. However, bringing your personality into a project can be a dangerous thing. If in doubt, do as the following candidate who ended her project in a very clear, workmanlike way. It may not be exciting to read, but it's obviously intelligent and thorough!

Summary of results

Roman Catholic	Mormon
1 There is only one speaker throughout the sermon, the priest.	1 There can be a number of people speaking, which can be any of the members, not necessarily the bishop.
2 The sermon is more formal as it has been prepared.	2 The service is slightly informal as the speakers are sharing their own personal testimonies.
3 The priest uses formal modes of address but none which show any level of intimacy with any member of the congregation.	3 The speakers use formal modes of address but show intimacy with the congregation as specific names are used.
4 Uses the distinction between first and second person to create a sense of hierarchy.	4 There are frequent first person references as they are talking about personal experiences. Use of the third person plural only when the speaker is referring to the time when she wasn't a Mormon: she is distancing herself.
5 There is a progression from abstract nouns, when the priest begins by giving his spiritual message, to concrete nouns, as he tells the congregation how they should apply the message to their lives.	5 There is no progression from concrete nouns when the speaker is talking of personal experiences to abstract when she is relating her previous experience to how she feels now she is a member.
6 There is the use of proper nouns, who are considered to be holy figures of worship.	6 The proper nouns which are used are the names of the speakers' family.

7 There is a progression from active verbs in the syntactic sense but not not the semantic sense, towards slightly more active nouns. The pattern is not as distinct as those found previously, e.g. nouns.

7 There is a distinct progression from active verbs, when relating everyday experiences, to stative verbs to convey the spiritual level she has reached through her experiences.

8 Lexis begins formal and ends slightly colloquial.

8 Lexis begins colloquial and becomes slightly more formal.

9 Speech is prepared, therefore it will be more formal, fluent and clear.

9 Speech is not prepared as the speakers are relating past experiences, therefore disfluency will occur.

10 Pauses are planned for effect.

10 A lot of voiced and unvoiced pauses in this transcript.

11 As the speech has been prepared, rhetorical questions occur.

11 No rhetorical questions.

12 The priest doesn't use any biblical quotations.

12 The speakers use a lot of biblical quotations and back them up with one of their personal experiences that relate to them.

Conclusion

The language reflects the way in which the churches are organised, not simply in the kinds of language used but in the progressions which seem to occur within the extracts. All of which support the idea that the Roman Catholic sermon is more authoritarian and the Mormon services are egalitarian.

As any A-level language student knows, 'it ain't just what you say, it's the way that you say it': if your written style is unclear, vague or clumsy, if you can't spell for toffee or have no idea how to construct a sentence, it will have a decided impact upon your mark. Be prepared to redraft your project till it says something reasonably original, says it clearly and says it correctly if not stylishly. The writer who handed in

> The results show that Sophie as a very good command of the english language. The non-fluency features show however, that although she is well advanced she still requires to think before talking some of the time. She does not have any more stages to learn

was doing her valid and original data a disservice.

Summary

In a nutshell, here are the thoughts which most often go through a marker's mind:

Scope/data

Am I reading something fresh?
Have they taken on too much?
Is this authentic?
Oh no! not TV ads again!
Crystal and Davie (or other textbook) chapter five one more time!

Structure

This proves nothing!

Why is this here?

I read this in the introduction (when reading the conclusion)

This is not what the data shows.

Knowledge

This is just a list.

Why use phonetic script if you can't get it right?

I recognise this but they don't admit sources.

They don't know an adverb from an adjective!

This transcription is as clear as mud.

Style

The teacher might at least have corrected all these spelling errors.

All these subheadings are boggling my mind!

The pie charts are very pretty but what do they prove?

Get to the point!

If this seems very negative, it is only to stop you making anyone think such things. Most of the examples included in this section are of good, not bad practice. Good luck!

Chapter 23

Your own words
– the link with creative writing

It would seem obvious that once you have become expert in decoding other people's language, you will become a more tactful and skilful language user yourself. You will have brought a lot of your knowledge of language to the surface and this will enable you to approach written tasks with far more confidence.

Let us make one thing clear immediately. No-one is suggesting that you approach creative writing like a recipe: mix two rhetorical questions, three parallel structures and plenty of emotive lexis. Blend well. Add a pinch of sarcasm and humour to audience's taste. Result: persuasive writing. However, there is something to be said for a little conscious craft. Writing is work, not a matter of sitting awaiting inspiration or a visit from the muse. Yes, you should be committed to what you are writing about; yes, you should know what you're talking about; but there is nothing wrong with thinking about useful techniques and appropriate register. Indeed, if you cannot do that then the course has taught you little.

Your ultimate aim will be to find your own voice and those styles and forms which work best for you. However, this is not going to come without a lot of practice. One of the best ways to get started is to take other writers or texts as models.

Pastiche and parody

This is a genre of writing in which you deliberately write in the style of someone or something else. It might be that, having steeped yourself in popular newspapers for a month, you know you can capture their tone perfectly. Do it! The best way to check if you have really grasped the style of a writer or genre is to try to emulate it. Even if you eventually decide that you prefer to write something more original, it will have been a useful exercise. If you want to attempt something a little more light-hearted (and harder, if we're frank) try a parody.

This is a deliberate exaggeration of a style. It has to be over the top, but it also has to have the hallmarks of the original – or no-one will see the joke. We include at this point one student's parodied versions of a popular newspaper story. We have also included her commentary on her work. It is always a good idea to write a commentary to accompany your work, because it allows you to prove that your achievement is not a happy accident, but a carefully considered effect.

Read the material overleaf which this young writer has put together.

The Daily Sprite

"I DEFIED THE PICKETS"

EXCLUSIVE STORY

The Truth; The Passion; The Pain; The Heartbreak – Miner Reveals All!

34-year-old Jimmy Jones crossed the picket line today!

Despite insults and abuse from so-called "workmates", father of fourteen Jimmy, clocked on for the first time in over six months.

Heart-rending

Jimmy, who works at one of Yorkshire's largest collieries, agreed to tell us, your sizzling, sensational Sprite, his heart-rending saga of the strike and how it has affected him and his lovely family.

Poverty-stricken

It has been hard. For six long months they have had to endure an almost poverty-stricken lifestyle.

Said Jimmy, "I didn't want to go back to work, but me and my wife have had to struggle on next to nothing. The kids, I've got fourteen kids, have had to make do.

They have had to take it in turns to go to school; we've only got one pair of shoes, between fourteen of them that is. It's worrying, I don't want my kids to miss out on their education, not when jobs are so hard to come by."

" ... sake of my family."

What will Jimmy do when the strike is over?

"They probably won't talk to me," Jimmy said of his workmates, "But I don't care. I can take it. I returned to work for the sake of my family. They are the most important thing in my life."

Invalid mother

Not only does large-hearted Jimmy have a wife and fourteen children to support but has his invalid mother to support too.

Said Jimmy, "My mother, she's sixty-nine. She depends on me. She needs some new teeth and a heart transplant and she's got dry rot in her wooden leg ... that's why I've gone back to work."

Jimmy's mother, 69-year-old, silver haired Sarah Jones said "He's a good lad."

"Proud"

Jimmy's blonde, 38-24-36, 5'9" wife Sharon, aged 29, has been a great support to Jimmy.

Sharon said, "I'm so proud of my Jimmy, the kids are really proud of him and his mother, his poor old invalid mother, she's so proud of him."

"Scab"

Until the strike breaks up, Jimmy will have to put up with shouts of 'scab' each day as he crosses the picket line to do an honest days work.

"...old drinking mates..."

Even when the strike is over many of Jimmy's old drinking mates will not want to know him. How has this affected Jimmy?

Said Jimmy, "Obviously my social life has been stripped down to a minimum.

I can't go out to the pub anymore. Not that I could afford to go to the pub, not to drink anyway, but me and the lads used to go down to the Bull on a night, have a natter, a game of darts, play pool, have the odd 5 or 6 pints, you know. That's all in the past now.

None of them want anything to do with me now. But I am devoting my time to my wife and my children."

Said blonde, bubbly Sharon,

"Jimmy hasn't got very many friends left, well he hasn't any at all actually, but he's coping really well. He doesn't mind having to work on his own."

Return to work

But Jimmy won't be back on his own for long though!

Statistics show that thousands of miners are giving up the picket lines in return for work – and pay!

The N.C.B. revealed today that by next week, more than three-quarters of the striking miners will have returned to work and the whole Scargill saga will be over.

Talks

Talks between the N.C.B. and N.U.M. will take place today at a secret location at London's Hilton Hotel, away from the media.

" ... continue working ..."

And what will Jimmy do in the meantime?

"I'll continue working, I believe I'm doing the right thing. This strike has been going on for more than six months now. We can't win. The sooner Scargill realises that the better."

Encouraging

Sharon and their fourteen children have all been a great encouragement to Jimmy.

Said Sharon, "We are a family and we are all right behind Jimmy. The kids have been very understanding. They are terrific kids. I just hope all the others follow Jimmy's selfless example."

Jimmy said of his family "I couldn't have done it without them!"

On page 3 Jimmy poses with Samantha Fox.

No signs of agreement

The miners dispute, now into its tenth month, is showing no signs of ending.

Discussions between N.U.M. president Mr. Arthur Scargill and N.C.B. leader Mr. Ian Macgregor, have so far proved to be ineffectual. It was disclosed that further negotiations would take place later on this week.

The majority of mine workers are still out on strike but large numbers of men are returning to work each day.

Mr. Scargill said, "We can win this dispute if we stick together. The figures of men returning to work, as released by the N.C.B. are unrealistic. Hopelessy unrealistic."

It is believed that the high figures quoted by the N.C.B. are part of tactics currently being employed by the N.C.B. to dishearten the disputing miners.

Said Mr. Scargill, "They must not believe everything they hear."

Mining families are finding it progressively more difficult to cope with the rising cost of living.

Many families are going hungry and there is much concern, particuarly for the children of the miners.

An N.C.B. spokesman said "There is no way we are going to alter our decision to close uneconomic pits. These men will return to work sooner or later. We know that most families are suffering due to low finances and we are fairly confident that many will return to work if only for the sake of their families."

To close down collieries, in many areas, would be to take away the major, and in some cases the only, source of employment.

With already high unemployment figures, had the N.C.B. considered this aspect?

"Obviously we have considered this, but the decision, reached by us and the Government, is still withstanding. To keep open many pits would not prove beneficial to the economy of the country and at the end of the day, that is what we have to consider."

It has been alleged by the N.C.B. that the only reason why more men have not returned to work is because they fear that they will be victimised.

Mr. Scargill vehemently denies this allegation. "That is totally untrue, I find it hard to believe that even the N.C.B. could come up with a statement as incredible as that.

The reason these men are out on strike is because they value their jobs and value their whole way of life. Obviously the men would like to return, of course they are finding things hard, but I am not prepared to make any decisions concerning their future until the Government and N.C.B. are prepared to alter their plans to close the pits which they consider to be uneconomic."

The amount of picket line violence is creating a cause for concern.

It is thought that the disturbing amounts of excess violence, as witnessed on the picket lines, towards working miners and towards the police is undermining the very valid cause the miners have.

However, it is claimed by Mr. Scargill that many of the people responsible for the acts of violence are not mine workers but political agitators.

"Many of the picketers are merely agitators, not miners, who have come from all over the country. It is these people who arc causing the trouble, not the miners. This began as a peaceful dispute but has accelerated into something much more."

The N.C.B. and the Government have condemned the violence saying it is "disgusting and barbaric" and that the pickets behaved "like animals".

An N.C.B. spokesman said "We are not prepared to revoke any of our decisions; especially in the light of the uncivilised behaviour displayed by many of the picketers."

The N.C.B. chairman, Mr. Macgregor said, "I am not prepared to comment on the strike at this moment in time."

Negotiations will resume tomorrow and it is hoped that a compromise will be reached.

Mr. Scargill said, "I want this strike to be settled just as much as anyone else, but I want a secure future for my men guaranteed."

Commentary

The two articles are a pastiche cum parody of two newspaper styles.

The first article is written in the style of a 'gutter press' or popular newspaper such as 'The Sun'. The second article is written in the style of a quality press newspaper.

The primary function of a popular press newspaper is to entertain and appeal to emotions rather than to inform.

The aim of quality press newspapers is to inform and educate people.

The distinction of the two styles is achieved by the use of features which are typical of newspapers.

The first noticeable feature of the first article is the large bold print headline. This is a graphetic feature employed frequently by the popular press newspapers. It is intended to be eyecatching and to obtain a reader's interest. The headline is sensationalistic and contains a highly emotive word 'defied'. 'Defied' has connotations of a heroic, courageous figure and creates interest.

Following the main headline is a sub-headline 'Exclusive story' – this is a feature used frequently by the popular press with the main function of selling newspapers. The 'Exclusive story' is a tactic used by newspapers who would like to convince the public that they should buy this newspaper because they won't find this story anywhere else.

The sub-headline contains a series of highly emotive words e.g. 'the pain'; 'the passion'; 'the heartbreak'. These words are intended to gain the interest of the reader and create intrigue; 'pain' and 'passion' are also alliterative which is eyecatching.

In contrast to the outstanding and eyecatching headline of the popular press article, the second headline is much simpler and less eyecatching. The headline is more informative and contains no emotive words.

'No Signs of Agreement' is simply informative and does not appeal to the emotions or attempt to sell newspapers. The audience it is aimed at is a more educated audience, who don't need enticing to buy a newspaper.

Popular press newspapers often use sub-headings. The sub-headings highlight the content of that particular paragraph. The sub-headings tend to be highly emotive words. For example 'Heart-rending' 'Poverty stricken'; 'Invalid mother', 'Proud'. These emotive words are used to evoke pity and sympathy.

The subject of the story is one of human interest, as is common in the popular press, and is not an informative news story as the second article is intended to be.

The lexis in the first article is extreme. It is emotive and often hyperbolic. For example, words and phrases such as 'heart-rending saga', 'endure', 'struggle', 'honest day's work'.

As frequently appears in the popular press there is heavy pre-modification when referring to a person. This is often hyperbolic. For example 'Jimmy's blonde, 38-24-36, 5'9" wife Sharon, aged 29' and '69- year-old, silver haired Sarah Jones'; 'blonde, bubbly Sharon' and 'large-hearted Jimmy'.

There is use of alliteration in the popular press e.g. 'sizzling, sensational Sprite'; 'saga of the strike', 'Scargill saga' and 'blonde, bubbly'. The alliteration is eyecatching and sounds 'snappy' and is more entertaining.

The lexis in the second article is much more sophisticated. For example 'ineffectual', 'negotiations', 'vehemently denies this allegation'. These are not everyday words and are intended to appeal to a more educated audience.

There is a deviant collocation of the lexical item 'accelerated' in the second article: 'This began as a peaceful dispute but has accelerated into something much more'. 'Accelerated' is usually associated with the speed of a car but is used here to emphasise the speed with which the dispute has developed.

There is alliteration used: 'creating a cause for concern' – this is emphatic.

A syntactical deviance is common to both styles of newspaper. For example, the placing of the verb in the subject position 'Said Mr. Scargill' and 'Said Jimmy'. This is for purposes of emphasis.

Syntactical deviance also occurs in the first article on 'Despite insults and abuse from so called 'workmates' father of fourteen Jimmy clocked on for the first time in over six months'. Here the SV(C)A pattern is changed to A(C)SV. This is to bring emphasis onto the emotive word 'despite', which evokes sympathy.

The pre-modification 'father of fourteen' is alliterative and sounds entertaining. There is also post-modification: 'Jimmy, who works at one of Yorkshire's largest colleries, agreed ... '

The sentence structures in both articles are complex and compound. Very few simple sentences occur due to the pre- and post-modification.

The second article is informative and the complex and compound sentence structures are needed to allow the information to be successfully conveyed.

The subject of the miners strike, on which the articles were based, is treated in different ways by the two types of newspaper. The popular press has a tendency to take one man's story and create news out of nothing, making a plea to the heart of the nation. The quality press report the situation.

These differences are due to the difference in politics. Like many popular press newspapers, the first article has a political slant to the right and praises the miner's return to work and sympathises with him e.g. ' ... Jimmy Jones crossed the picket line today!' ' ... him and his lovely family.'

The second article has a left-wing political slant and does not sympathise with the miners who have returned to work. Though the slant is not so obvious, the newspaper sympathises with the miners who are still striking e.g. ' ... undermining the very valid cause the miners have' and ' ... tactics being employed by the N.C.B. to dishearten the disputing miners.'

The political slant of the articles is important to justify many of the comments made.

The truth of many popular press articles is often dubious, therefore there is deliberate hyperbole in the first article, for example, ''' ... The kids, I've got fourteen kids, have had to make do. They have had to take it in turns to go to school; we've only got one pair of shoes, between fourteen of them that is'''; and ''' ... She needs some new teeth and a heart transplant ... and she's got dry rot in her wooden leg ... '''

There is very little emotion in the second article and many statements appear objective. For example: 'It was disclosed that ... ' and 'It is believed that...', 'It has been alleged ... '

Though there is a slight political slant to the left, the second article does attempt to present both sides of the argument and not just one.

The tone of register of the first article is informal and colloquial, this is in contrast to the more formal tone of register of the second article.

The first article is lighthearted and entertaining as this is the way in which the popular press presents news articles. The final sentence 'On page 3, Jimmy poses with Samantha Fox' is hyperbolic to ridicule and parody popular press newspapers.

The second article presents the news in a more factual and informative way but tries to be interesting so that it is comprehensible and readable.'

The differences occur in the two articles because they have a different aim, a different political slant and a different audience.

Fiction

Some of you may want to try your hand at parody but prefer to deal in fiction rather than the reporting of fact. (You might, of course, argue that some popular newspapers are mainly fiction!) Fiction is a vast area, so select a precise field to operate within. Romantic and horror fiction are both a lot of fun to do; children's fiction is another possibility. Try starting like a very traditional example of the genre and then subvert it. Give the story a twist in the tail: don't punish the baddy or kill the evil alien or have the hero and heroine live happily ever after. Of course this will only be funny and effective if you have convinced the reader in the first instance. And if you are going to convince them, you really need to know what you are sending up very well.

Out of interest, try and write the first paragraph of each of a love, science fiction, war and children's story. Don't make life easy for yourself by too direct a reference to the subject matter. Now ask a friend or relative what sort of writing they come from. Also ask them how they could tell. What were the giveaway clichés of situation and language? Which of the four did they think you wrote most convincingly?

Now write the rest of that story and ensure that the style is consistent, but consistently extreme. In the last page or so destroy the reader's expectations.

If you think that is a bit too much like hard work, you can start with something more straightforward. Adverts and newspaper articles are among the most definable of styles.

Newspapers

Don't be utterly lazy, merely producing a 'Sun slag-off' as our NME correspondent termed it in an earlier chapter. Find a story in the popular press and re-write it as it might appear in a quality paper. Ensure that it is a story that they would cover: a political story perhaps, or a major disaster, i.e. not just a 'human interest' story. If you buy two papers, one quality, one popular, you ought to be able to find the same stories in both. Do your translation and then see if you have caught the tone.

To give you some immediate practice in style shifting, here are three versions of the same story. Please look only at the first article for the moment. These three stories come from a popular, a middle range and a quality paper respectively.

Look at the first article. Which sort of paper is it from? How can you tell? Take a careful look at isolated features of the text: graphics, headlines, quotes, adjectives and adverbs (emotive or factual?), sentence type and length. Don't simply go by general impression, be analytical.

Now attempt to come up with alternatives for these elements as you would expect them to appear in the other two sorts of paper. Having got thus far it ought to be relatively straightforward to produce an entire article.

Now compare yours with the originals. Which elements are you best and worst at? Which style of paper do you find it hardest to emulate?

Giant seas nightmare of hero Pat

TEENAGE hero Patrick Vaccaro yesterday relived his nightmare bid to save three fishermen pals after their boat capsized.

Sitting up in hospital, he revealed that he was near to exhaustion as he struggled to the beach after a seven-mile battle in mountainous waves.

He was able to direct rescuers to the stricken boat and lifeboatmen snatched 33-year-old Steve Woodbridge to safety in the Irish Sea.

But Pat, 18, of Meadow Road, Southport, was deeply saddened when he heard that the body of his best pal, Geoff Clements, 18, had been recovered at Blackpool yesterday.

The fourth man aboard the cabin cruiser Shady Lady – Colin Brookfield, 30 – is still missing.

Pat said: "I decided to try to make it ashore because it seemed the only chance for all of us.

"I left the others clinging to the boat and shouted 'Hold on, I'll be back.'

Exhaustion

"The waves were huge. At first I couldn't see a thing. I just kept going as they crashed over me.

"I was close to exhaustion when I saw lights on the pier. I just kept swimming and managed to crawl ashore.

"I came across a couple in a car and raised the alert."

After his battle with the sea, brave Pat wanted to go out with a helicopter crew to continue the search.

But he was persuaded to go to hospital instead.

Sea survivor vows 'never again'

A SURVIVOR of the fishing trip tragedy which killed two of his friends at the weekend, yesterday vowed: "I will never sail at sea again."

As 18-year-old Patrick Vacarro spoke from his hospital bed police were recovering the body of one of the victims, Geoffrey Clements, also 18, who was washed ashore at Blackpool.

Recovering from his ordeal, Patrick told how it took him eleven hours to swim from their 15-foot craft after it was capsized by a wave four miles offshore in the Irish Sea.

11-hour swim to raise alarm as fishing trip friends die

Express Staff Reporter

He added: "I expected it to take me two hours to get to shore, not 11. I have swum across Windermere a couple of times but never at sea like this."

At first I could see sandhills on shore, but when it started going dark I could not see anything. Then I saw street lights and was guided by them. It was a great relief when I reached the sea wall."

The other survivor was 33-year-old Steven Woodbridge, who spent 20 hours in the water before being winched to safety. Coastguards said they had expected people to survive just six hours in the cold water.

Mr. Vacarro, a gardener and tree-feller, of Meadow Avenue, Birkdale, Southport, was last night taken in a wheelchair to see Mr. Woodbridge, who was "improving" in the town's Infirmary intensive care unit.

The boat, the Sandy Lady, belonged to one of the two men who died – 30-year-old Colin Brookfield.

Patrick said when he got ashore at Southport early yesterday his legs buckled. "A couple took me into a caravan and put a blanket over me," he added.

The body of Mr. Clements, of Matlock Road, Birkdale, Southport, was found in the sea off Starr Gate, 20 miles from where the accident happened.

A search is still going on for the other victim.

Capsize survivor tells of 11-hour swim

By Sarah Boseley

A TEENAGER who swam for 11 hours in the Irish Sea to get help after a friend's boat capsized said yesterday that he would never sail at sea again.

Patrick Vaccaro, aged 18, volunteered to swim the four miles to the shore after heavy seas overturned the 15-foot glassfibre cabin cruiser Sandy Lady, in which he and three others had gone fishing.

One of his friends, Mr Steven Woodbridge, aged 33, was later winched to safety from the upturned hull and was said last night to be improving in the intensive care unit of Southport Infirmary. The body of Geoffrey Clements, 18, of Matlock Road, Birkdale, Southport, was found in the sea off Blackpool yesterday.

The boat's owner, Mr Colin Brookfield, 30, was still missing.

Mr Vaccaro, who said that his legs had buckled under him as he reached Southport beach, declared yesterday in hospital that in future he would restrict his sailing to the Lake District, where he swims and goes water skiing.

When the boat capsized he volunteered to swim to the coast to raise the alarm. He said: "I expected it to take me two hours to get to shore, not 11. I have swum across Windermere a couple of times, but never at sea like this.

"At first I could see sandhills on shore, but when it started going dark I could not see anything. Then I saw street lights and was guided by them. It was a great relief when I reached the sea wall."

Mr Vaccaro, a gardener and treefeller, of Meadow Avenue, Birkdale, said that he had swum breaststroke, with the currents against him the whole time. When he had reached the shore he had been helped by a couple who took him into their caravan and wrapped him in blankets.

He said the four men had set out on Friday to catch flatfish and mackerel. "The boat was capsized by a wave about four miles offshore. We managed to right her after about 10 minutes, but she was waterlogged. A few minutes later I set off to swim for the shore. I told the other three to stay on the boat."

When the coastguards found Mr Woodbridge the boat had turned over again. He had been in the water for 20 hours. Coastguards said that they did not usually expect people to survive for more than six in such cold water. A coastal search for the body of the fourth man was called off last night and will continue today.

Adverts

Keep an eye open for advertisements for new products or companies. Guess where else they might advertise and try to design an appropriate advertisement. If you've seen the poster, have a go at the Sunday supplement centre-spread. If you've seen the television commercial, design the poster. Again, chances are you'll get a chance to compare your effort with the professional job. Did you pick the right sort of layout and colours? Was your level of formality right – even if you didn't use the same words? Is your catchphrase better than theirs? If you produced one you're particularly pleased with you could ask a friend to see if they can tell the difference. If they can't, or think yours is better, perhaps you've discovered your future career!

Adverts do represent the most well-known example of persuasive writing. Try to make life a little more difficult for yourself. Instead of changing format only, think carefully about target audience. Look in magazines for different advertisements for the same product or service. There are many products which are used by a very wide-ranging group. However, within the group, different segments will be 'got at' by different adverts. Life insurance and charities are two good examples of this. Look at your examples and isolate the significant changes. Then find another product or service and try to write the yuppie advert, the family advert and the granny advert. If you are unclear what appeals to these groupings look at *Cosmopolitan* (career women/yuppies), the *Radio Times* (the ultimate family magazine) and *The People's Friend* (as read by my eighty-seven year-old grandmother).

More persuasive language

You might want to stretch yourself farther by tackling more difficult varieties of persuasive language. The convenient thing about being a language student is that you can always check your efforts against the real thing: language is all around us!

If you want some good examples of persuasive technique, a good way to start is by taping *Question Time*. Tape it rather than watching it, though: this will enable you to watch it by instalments and do some prediction exercises. This is how to go about it:

Listen to a question put to the panel.
Switch off and ask yourself, writing down your reply:
Which panel member will answer first?
Will they adopt a very formal or fairly informal style?
Will they allow their regional accent to come through or get as close to RP as they are able?
Will their tone be emotional or factual?
Will they use emotive or statistical lexis?
Will they sound impassioned and sincere, eminently reasonable, sarcastic?
Which speaker will disagree/oppose or support them?
How will their speech style be different?

This probably sounds impossibly difficult. In fact the tactics and techniques of speakers on such programmes are almost depressingly predictable. Nor is their individual identity that important: they are usually the token 'moderate left-winger', 'radical trade unionist' or 'right-wing Conservative'. They do tend to conform to type!

If you are not in the habit of watching these programmes you might need to watch a few to 'tune in'. This is probably educational, in any case.

If you really do find that task too difficult, you can do a more straightforward jotting down of distinctive features as you listen. Or you could follow an individual – such as the Prime Minister or Leader of the Opposition – through several contexts and see how they vary their persuasive technique. Prediction is more fun, though. You should eventually be able to write the script for them.

Poetry

Poetry and literary prose is a far harder nut to crack, but as we have said, they're only words – albeit fairly deviant and often sophisticated ones. It would increase your respect for the craft of poetry, if nothing else, to try and write something formally demanding, like a sonnet. Shakespeare makes it look easy. Believe us, it's not – and the surest way to discover this for yourself is to try. Making it rhyme, scan and say something sensible, never mind profound, is hard!

One quite entertaining and instructive way to produce a sonnet is to do a team effort. Six people each produce two lines of iambic pentameter. If that's pure jargon to you let us explain: all it means is that you want five iambs in each line, and an iamb is the name for two syllables – one unstressed, the other stressed (dee DUM). So an iambic pentameter has ten syllables which go dee DUM dee DUM dee DUM dee DUM dee DUM. A famous example is the opening to Gray's *Elegy*: 'The curfew tolls the knell of parting day'. Another is the opening of Shakespeare's *Twelfth Night*: 'If music be the food of love, play on'.

To return to what we want you to do. All six of you write two lines of iambic pentameter. The lines must have the same final rhyme (e.g. 'cat' and 'mat') but need not otherwise link. For instance: 'The sun sinks slowly 'neath the chimney pots' and 'One dress was stripey; t'other one had spots.'

Everyone is now given all of the lines, and working in pairs you try to make a poem of them. The poem must rhyme ababcdcdefef. Then the sonnet needs completing with a heroic couplet (that is, a rhyming couplet of iambic pentameter). It should aim to conclude the poem with a generalised statement which sums it up. This is the hardest bit. The surprising thing about this is that things which read remarkably like poems do arise, and six people given exactly the same lines come up with very different totalities – which tells you something about the several levels on which poems operate. Syntax is clearly very important.

If you find the idea preposterous take a look at these sonnets produced in half an hour by one of my A-level language groups:

> The lonely old man from Ridyard Estate,
> A broken down car parked up at his door
> No need to get up, no chance to be late,
> The wheels turn no more to do their tour.
>
> Birds at night fly high in the midnight sky
> As the trees rustled I heard a dog whine
> Something told me I was telling a lie
> Steps in the dark sent shivers up my spine
>
> Moonlight across the sea shone bright at night
> Footsteps in the white snow remind me of him
> Though the blood dripping from him was an ugly sight
> Killing him just didn't feel like a sin
>
> A lonely man, a lonely girl hopeless
> They got together but it was a mess.

> Moonlight across the sea shone bright at night
> The wheels turn no more to do their tours
> Though the dripping blood was an ugly sight
> Broken down cars parked at our doors.
>
> Footsteps in the white snow remind me of him
> The lonely old man fron Ridyard Estate
> Killing him just didn't seem like a sin
> No need to get up no chance to be late
>
> As the trees rustled I hear a dog whine
> Something told me I was telling a lie
> Steps in the dark sent shivers up my spine
> Birds at night fly high in the midnight sky
>
> They also count, who only sit and cry
> They mark the fact that all of us must die.

Another problem that some of us have with writing poetry is the very concentrated nature of its language. We are used to talking in longish units akin to sentences and we write in sentences, and suddenly to break grammatical rules and write 'stream of consciousness' or metaphorically seems tough. It also (and I think this is crucial) seems pretentious. Something called *The Metaphor Game* is a great help in overcoming inhibitions about writing poetry. (Our thanks to the poet Gillian Clarke who introduced this game to us.)

1 Someone is designated 'on' and thinks of a fairly famous person, alive or dead.
2 Everyone else asks questions such as what colour, type of food, tool, material, kind of transport, house does this person suggest to you? It is important that the person 'on' reacts quickly rather than pausing to consider. For example, if I were thinking of Marilyn Monroe I might come up with scarlet, hamburger (unglamorous but very American), hairdryer, black satin, red 'E' type and penthouse in answer to those questions.
3 The person 'on' gives the answers and also writes them down. Aim for about twelve.
4 Delete two which don't seem to go. (Of those I'd get rid of hamburger!)
5 Put the rest in alphabetical – and thus random – order. This stops you slipping into cliché.
6 Now, using the words given and exactly fifteen other words plus a title of up to eight words, write a poem.

Again, it is surprising what people come up with. It is also surprising how often people guess the mystery celebrity. This doesn't matter except that it does show how essentially they've been conveyed.

Once you've played this game a few times, you can actually manage it alone. You ask yourself the questions or simply write down a cluster of images. In this way you are trying to sum up 'Marilyn Monroeness' – not merely describe her. We hope you can see the distinction. Once again, even if what you create is not spectacularly good, it will have helped you to see how poetry can operate.

Here are two sets of answers or images:

antique suitcase	Beethoven
a tent	brown and sage green
black hat and blue duffle coat	fairly large house
boarded with a family	larger than average family
piano	public schools
South America	roast beef and Yorkshire pud
visiting friends and cinema	Rolls Royce
very very hairy	*Neighbours*
	walking dogs

Go through stages 4, 5 and 6 above and see what you come up with.

Now take a look overleaf at what our students wrote. They quite enjoyed it; we hope you did too!

Beethoven filled every corner of this brown, sage green room
She was alone in this fairly large house which was, at the moment, deserted by her
larger than average family

255

The lady, with her Margaret Thatcher hair style, sat at the piano,
on the polyester covered stool,
She recalls travelling to public schools in a Rolls Royce
and traditional dinners of Roast Beef and Yorkshire pud
Now, things have changed
She likes *Neighbours*, I've heard, and walking dogs.

He strolled, carrying his antique suitcase towards a
tent on a camping site,
He wore a black hat and blue duffle coat, his face
was brown
Previously, he boarded with a family
He loved his Aunty, and the sound of her playing the
piano
whilst he was playing in the nursery
He remembered the South American holiday, visiting
friends and cinema
He was now old and haggard, and very, very hairy.

Literary prose

Literary prose can seem even more impossible. It seems so normal, but how on earth do you produce it?

Perhaps the easiest way in is through autobiography and biography. Don't forget that there is nothing wrong with writing someone else's autobiography – you don't have to lay your soul bare to write in the first person: you simply adopt a persona. Of course you will need to understand that persona well enough to make them convincing, so it may well be that your own experience, knowledge or attitudes will be conveyed. If that was good enough for the Brontë sisters, it ought to be good enough for you!

Before you put pen to paper make a few decisions. Are you, in fact going to use the first person? Or is that a little too obvious a plea for sympathy? Do the advantages – namely being able to express thought and feeling directly – outweigh the disadvantage of limited point of view and knowledge? Might it be better (or more demanding) to try to write in the third person yet still make the reader sympathise with a specific character?

Are you going to use the present tense, thus involving the reader, or are you going to describe the past as over with and 'recollected in tranquility'?

If these questions have had you shaking your head in confusion and dismay perhaps looking at some examples may clarify what I mean. The following are the openings to two very famous autobiographical novels. Do you recognise them? It doesn't matter whether you do. The fact is that they represent two very different ways to present the central character.

There was no possibility of taking a walk that day. We had been wandering, indeed, in the lifeless shrubbery an hour in the morning; but since dinner (Mrs. Reed, when there was no company, dined early) the cold winter wind had brought with it clouds so sombre, and a rain so penetrating that further outdoor exercise was now out of the question.

I was glad of it; I never liked long walks, especially on chilly afternoons; dreadful to me was the coming home in the raw twilight, with nipped fingers and toes, and a heart saddened by the chidings of Bessie, the nurse, and humbled by the consciousness of my physical inferiority to Eliza, John, and Georgiana Reed.

The said Eliza, John, and Georgiana were now clustered round their mamma in the drawing-room: she lay reclined on a sofa by the fireside, and with her darlings about her (for the time neither quarrelling nor crying) looked perfectly happy. Me, she had dispensed from joining the group, saying, "She regretted to be under the necessity of keeping me at a distance; but that until she heard from Bessie, and could discover by her own observation that I was endeavouring in good earnest to acquire a more sociable and childlike disposition, a more attractive and sprightly manner – something lighter, franker, more natural, as it were – she really must exclude me from privileges intended only for contented, happy little children."

"What does Bessie say I have done?" I asked.

"Jane, I don't like cavillers or questioners; besides, there is something truly forbidding in a child taking up her elders in that manner. Be seated somewhere; and until you can speak pleasantly, remain silent."

A small breakfast-room adjoined the drawing-room; I slipped in there. It contained a bookcase; I soon possessed myself of a volume, taking care that it should be one stored with pictures. I mounted into the window-seat: gathering up my feet, I sat cross-legged, like a Turk; and, having drawn the red moreen curtain nearly close, I was shrined in double retirement.

Folds of scarlet drapery shut in my view to the right hand; to the left were the clear panes of glass, protecting, but not separating me from the drear November day. At intervals, while turning over the leaves in my book, I studied the aspect of that winter afternoon. Afar, it offered a pale blank of mist and cloud; near, a scene of wet lawn and storm-beat shrub, with ceaseless rain seeping away wildly before a long and lamentable blast.

I returned to my book – Bewick's *History of British Birds*: the letterpress thereof I cared little for, generally speaking; and yet there were certain picture pages that, child as I was, I could not pass quite as a blank.

Each picture told a story; mysterious often to my undeveloped understanding and imperfect feelings, yet ever profoundly interesting: as interesting as the tales Bessie sometimes narrated on winter evenings, when she chanced to be in good humour; and when, having brought her ironing-table to the nursery-hearth, she allowed us to sit about it, and while she got up Mrs. Reed's lace frills, and crimped her nightcap borders, fed our eager attention with passages of love and adventure taken from old fairy tales and older ballads; or (at a later period I discovered) from the pages of *Pamela*, and *Henry, Earl of Moreland*.

With Bewick on my knee, I was then happy: happy at least in my way. I feared nothing but interruption, and that came too soon. The breakfast-room door was opened.

"Boh! Madam Mope!" cried the voice of John Reed; then he paused: he found the room apparently empty.

"Where the dickens is she?" he continued. "Lizzy! Georgy! (calling to his sisters) Jane is not here: tell mamma she is run out into the rain – bad animal!"

"It is well I drew the curtain," thought I, and I wished fervently he might not discover my hiding-place: nor would John Reed have found it out himself; he was not quick either of vision or conception; but Eliza just put her head in at the door, and said at once: "she is in the window-seat, to be sure, Jack."

And I came out immediately, for I trembled at the idea of being dragged forth by the said Jack.

"What do you want?" I asked with awkward diffidence.

"Say, 'what do you want, Master Reed,'" was the answer. "I want you to come here;" and seating himself in an armchair, he intimated by a gesture that I was to approach and stand before him.

John Reed was a schoolboy of fourteen years old; four years older than I, for I was but ten. John had not much affection for his mother and sisters, and an antipathy to me. He bullied and punished me; not two or three times in the week, nor once or twice in a day, but continually: every nerve I had feared him, and every morsel of flesh on my bones shrank when he came near. There were moments when I was bewildered by the terror he inspired, because I had no appeal whatever against either his menaces or his inflictions; the servants did not like to offend their young master by taking my part against him, and Mrs. Reed was blind and deaf on the subject: she never saw him strike or heard him abuse me, though he did both now and then in her very presence; more frequently, however, behind her back.

Habitually obedient to John, I came up to his chair: he spent some three minutes in thrusting out his tongue at me as far as he could without damaging the roots: I knew he would soon strike, and while dreading the blow, I mused on the disgusting and ugly appearance of him who would presently deal it. I wonder if he read that notion in my face; for, all at once, without speaking, he struck suddenly and strongly. I tottered, and on regaining my equilibrium retired back a step or two from his chair.

"That is for your impudence in answering mamma a while since," said he. "Go and stand by the door, out of the way of the mirror and the windows.

I did so, not at first aware what was his intention; but when I saw him lift and poise the book and stand in act to hurl it, I instinctively started aside with a cry of alarm: not soon enough, however; the volume was flung, it hit me, and I fell, striking my head against the door and cutting it. The cut bled, the pain was sharp: my terror had passed its climax; other feelings succeeded.

"Wicked and cruel boy!" I said. "You are like a murderer – you are like a slave-driver – you are like the Roman emperors!"

Charlotte Brontë: Jane Eyre

Once upon a time and a very good time it was there was a moocow coming down along the road and this moocow that was coming down along the road met a nicens little boy named baby tuckoo ...

His father told him that story: his father looked at him through a glass: he had a hairy face.

He was baby tuckoo. The moocow came down the road where Betty Byrne lived: she sold lemon platt.

> O, the wild rose blossoms
> On the little green place.

He sang that song. That was his song.

> O, the green wothe botheth.

When you wet the bed it is warm then it gets cold. His mother put on the oilsheet. That had the queer smell.

His mother had a nicer smell than his father. She played on the piano the sailor's hornpipe for him to dance. He danced:

> Tralala lala,
> Tralala lala,
> Tralala tralaladdy
> Tralala lala.

Uncle Charles and Dante clapped. They were older than his father and mother but uncle Charles was older than Dante.

Dante had two brushes in her press. The brush with the maroon velvet back was for Michael Davitt and the brush with the green velvet back was for Parnell. Dante gave him a cachou every time he brought her a piece of tissue paper.

The Vances lived in number seven. They had a different father and mother. They were Eileen's father and mother. When they were grown up he was going to marry Eileen. He hid under the table. His mother said:

– O, Stephen will apologise.

Dante said:

– O, if not, the eagles will come and pull out his eyes. –

> Pull out his eyes,
> Apologise,
> Apologise,
> Pull out his eyes.
> Apologise,
> Pull out his eyes,
> Pull out his eyes,
> Apologise.

* * *

The wide playgrounds were swarming with boys. All were shouting and the prefects urged them on with strong cries. The evening air was pale and chilly and after every charge and thud of the footballers the greasy leather or flew like a heavy bird through the grey light.

He kept on the fringe of his line, out of sight of his prefect, out of the reach of the rude feet, feigning to run now and then. He felt his body small and weak amid the throng of players and his eyes were weak and watery. Rody Kickham was not like that: he would be captain of the third line all the fellows said.

Rody Kickham was a decent fellow but Nasty Roche was a stink. Rody Kickham had greaves in his number and a hamper in the refectory. Nasty Roche had big hands. He called the Friday pudding dog-in-the-blanket. And one day he had asked:

– What is your name?

Stephen had answered: Stephen Dedalus.

Then Nasty Roche had said:

– What kind of a name is that?

And when Stephen had not been able to answer Nasty Roche had asked:

– What is your father?

Stephen had answered:

– A gentleman.

Then Nasty Roche had asked:

– Is he a magistrate?

He crept about from point to point on the fringe of his line, making little runs now and then. But his hands were bluish with cold. He kept his hands in the side pockets of his belted grey suit. That was a belt round his pocket. And belt was also to give a fellow a belt.

James Joyce: A Portrait of the Artist as a Young Man

In the first passage, the reader is very much encouraged to pity the young girl. Adjectives and adverbials both direct us to see her as vulnerable and ill-used. Her cousin, John, is described in terms that make us react against him; the very place is made to seem depressing and oppressive and the conversation underlines Jane's powerlessness. (I could justify these assertions from the text – and would if my main job here were analysis. Could you?)

The second passage operates very differently. The narration is third person and our pity is not sought after so obviously. The boy is conveyed to us in his own childish words and we get his view of things even though he is not, overtly, the narrator. How is this achieved? Look carefully at the text.

Our first impression of Dante is not a positive one but she is certainly not given the John Reed treatment! The description of the boy on the football field does stress his vulnerability, his weakness, but again the effect is more subtly achieved. He doesn't plead his cause. We are shown, not told, the situation and get the impression (probably wrongly) that we can make our own minds up.

This distinction between showing and telling is a very important one. If you want to 'show', the less personal third person is probably better; if you want to 'tell them how it is', the emotional appeal is likely to be more effective from a first person narrator. Do remember, though, that it is perfectly possible to foreground a character and their feelings without making them the narrator. It may be vital to keep them in the dark about certain events or even about their own feelings. In the latter case I am thinking of Jane Austen's heroines. They are never the narrators: they are observed and judged, but they are nevertheless the focus of our interest and usually it is their viewpoint we adopt and sympathise with. The way Jane Austen engages our sympathy for her heroines is to report not only what they say but what they think. Taking your reader inside someone's head is a good way to ensure their sympathy and understanding. Again, an example may clarify:

His belief of her sister's insensibility she instantly resolved to be false; and his account of the real, the worst objections to the match, made her too angry to have any wish of doing him justice. He expressed no regret for what he had done which satisfied her; his style was not penitent, but haughty. It was all pride and insolence.

But when this subject was succeeded by his account of Mr. Wickham, – when she read with somewhat clearer attention a relation of events which, if true, must overthrow every cherished opinion of his worth, and which bore so alarming an affinity to his own history of himself, – her feelings were yet more acutely painful and more difficult of definition. Astonishment, apprehension, and even horror, oppressed her. She wished to discredit it entirely, repeatedly exclaiming, "This must be false! This cannot be! This must be the grossest falsehood!" – and when she had gone through the whole letter, though scarcely knowing anything of the last page or two, put it hastily away, protesting that she would not regard it, that she would never look in it again.

In this perturbed state of mind, with thoughts that could rest on nothing, she walked on; but it would not do; in half a minute the letter was unfolded again, and collecting herself as well as she could, she again began the mortifying perusal of all that related to Wickham, and commanded herself so far as to examine the meaning of every sentence. The account of his connection with the Pemberley family was exactly what he had related himself; and the kindness of the late Mr. Darcy, though she had not before known its extent, agreed equally well with his own words. So far each recital confirmed the other; but when she came to the will, the difference was great. What Wickham had said of the living was fresh in her memory, and as she recalled his very words, it was impossible not to feel that there was gross duplicity on one side or the other; and, for a few moments, she flattered herself that her wishes did not err. But when she read and re-read with the closest attention, the particulars immediately following of Wickhams resigning all pretensions to the living, of his receiving in lieu so considerable a sum as three thousand pounds, again was she forced to hesitate. She put down the letter, weighed every circumstance with what she meant to be impartiality – deliberated on the probability of each statement – but with little success. On both sides it was only assertion. Again she read on; but every line proved more clearly that the affair, which she had believed it impossible that any contrivance could so represent as to render Mr. Darcy's conduct in it less than infamous, was capable of a turn which must make him entirely blameless throughout the whole.

The extravagance and general profligacy which he scrupled not to lay to Mr. Wickham's charge, exceedingly shocked her; the more so, as she could bring no proof of its injustice. She had never heard of

him before his entrance into the –shire Militia, in which he had
engaged at the persuasion of the young man who, on meeting him
accidentally in town, had there renewed a slight acquaintance. Of
his former way of life nothing had been known in Hertfordshire but
what he told himself. As to his real character, had information been
in her power, she had never felt a wish of inquiring. His
countenance, voice, and manner had established him at once in the
possession of every virtue. She tried to recollect some instance of
goodness, some distinguished trait of integrity or benevolence, that
might rescue him from the attacks of Mr. Darcy; or at least, by the
predominance of virtue, atone for those casual errors under which
she would endeavor to class what Mr. Darcy had described as the
idleness and vice of many years' continuance. But no such
recollection befriended her. She could see him instantly before her,
in every charm of air and address; but she could remember no more
substantial good than the general approbation of the neighborhood,
and the regard which his social powers had gained him in the mess.
After pausing on this point a considerable while, she once more
continued to read. But, alas! the story which followed, of his designs
on Miss Darcy, received some confirmation from what had passed
between Colonel Fitzwilliam and herself only the morning before;
and at last she was referred for the truth of every particular to
Colonel Fitzwilliam himself – from whom she had previously
received the information of his near concern in all his cousin's
affairs, and whose character she had no reason to question. At one
time she had almost resolved on applying to him, but the idea was
checked by the awkwardness of the application, and at length wholly
banished by the conviction that Mr. Darcy would never have
hazarded such a proposal, if he had not been well assured of his
cousin's approbation.

She perfectly remembered everything that had passed in
conversation between Wickham and herself, in their first evening at
Mr. Philips's. Many of his expressions were still fresh in her
memory. She was *now* struck with the impropriety of such
communications to a stranger, and wondered it had escaped her
before. She saw the indelicacy of putting himself forward as he had
done, and the inconsistency of his professions with his conduct. She
remembered that he had boasted of having no fear of seeing Mr.
Darcy – that Mr. Darcy might leave the country, but that *he* should
stand his ground: yet he had avoided the Netherfield ball the very
next week. She remembered also that, till the Netherfield family had
quitted the country, he had told his story to no one but herself; but
that after their removal it had been everywhere discussed; that he
had then no reserves, no scruples in sinking Mr. Darcy's character,
though he had assured her that respect for the father would always
prevent his exposing the son.

How differently did everything now appear in which he was
concerned!

Jane Austen: Pride and Prejudice

Grasping who the narrator of a story is and whose viewpoint we are being asked to share are vital for analysis as well as for good writing: it's worth the time and trouble.

Try writing the opening of your own or your chosen character's autobiography in two stylistically different ways. You might do one in an emotional, first person, 'telling' way, the other in a more descriptive, third person 'showing' way. Which is better for your purposes? Which seems to come more easily to you?

Next you could experiment with tense. You probably wrote both your first versions in the past tense – it is almost second nature to use the past in storytelling. Have a go at using the present instead. Does it make it seem more immediate, dramatic and 'felt', or is your narrative now simply unclear? Might the best solution be to use the past most of the time, for the sake of clarity, but to insert passages of thought which are in the present? If you want to stick to the past but somehow convey just how the central protagonist felt then try using reported thought, for example, 'He looked at her. Was she really angry?'

If you want to be really daring, of course, you could try what is known as the 'stream of consciousness' technique. By this I mean that you write – unadulterated – what goes through the mind of your character. People don't think in sentences, or even complete utterances. They often leap from idea to idea as connections strike them. They miss out the ifs, buts and ands. It is not easy to write in this way convincingly but if you manage it it sounds authentic and saves a lot of unnecessary words of the 'He wondered whether ... ', 'She asked herself if ... ' sort. It also takes the reader more realistically inside the head of the character. We are not getting an edited, fit-for-publication version of their opinions and feelings: we are being allowed to spy on the real person. This technique is not a simple one, but it can be very effective. If this is the first time you've tried it, do persevere before abandoning it. Many of our students have written far more honestly and clearly (which is more surprising) using this technique as opposed to traditional narrative. Here is an example:

> Mummy was ill. She went to hospital. She went in with two legs, came out with one. She came to see him. She liked the new school, but a boy laughed at her, called her Long John Silver. He hated Neil Bye, he hit Neil Bye, made him cry. Mummy soon left, upset but holidays were soon, he would count down the days
>
> five
> four
> three
> two
> one
> yippeeee!
>
> He liked holidays, nothing to do. No more upset, no more work, no more anything. He saw family. He went to beaches. Blue water, hurt eyes.
>
> Soon he was back at school. Oh no! Next holidays seventy-two days.
>
> But mummy was ill again, very ill. Daddy came to school.
> Mummy dead.
> Cancer.

Before we leave stream of consciousness, you might also like to look at a professional example of it:

> At a certain moment, she supposed, the house would become so shabby that something must be done. If they could be taught to wipe their feet and not bring the beach in with them – that would be something. Crabs, she had to allow, if Andrew really wished to dissect them, or if Jasper believed that one could make soup from seaweed, one could not prevent it; or Rose's objects – shells, reeds, stones; for they were gifted, her children, but all in quite different ways. And the result of it was, she sighed, taking in the whole room from floor to ceiling, as she held the stocking against James's leg, that things got shabbier and got shabbier summer after summer. The mat was fading; the wall-paper was flapping. You couldn't tell any more that those were roses on it. Still, if every door in a house is left perpetually open, and no lockmaker in the whole of Scotland can mend a bolt, things must spoil. What was the use of flinging a green Cashmere shawl over the edge of a picture frame? In two weeks it would be the colour of pea soup. But it was the doors that annoyed her; every door was left open. She listened. The drawing-room door was open; the hall door was open; it sounded as if the bedroom doors were open; and certainly the window on the landing was open, for that she had opened herself. That windows should be open, and doors shut – simple as it was, could none of them remember it? She would go into the maids' bedrooms at night and find them sealed like ovens, except for Marie's, the Swiss girl, who would rather go without a bath than without fresh air, but then at home, she had said, 'the mountains are so beautiful.' She had said that last night looking out of the window with tears in her eyes. 'The mountains are so beautiful.' Her father was dying there, Mrs Ramsay knew. He was leaving them fatherless. Scolding and demonstrating (how to make a bed, how to open a window, with hands that shut and spread like a French-woman's) all had folded itself quietly about her, when the girl spoke, as, after a flight through the sunshine the wings of a bird fold themselves quietly and the blue of its plumage changes from bright steel to soft purple. She had stood there silent for there was nothing to be said. He had cancer of the throat. At the recollection – how she had stood there, how the girl had said 'At home the mountains are so beautiful', and there was no hope, no hope whatever, she had a spasm of irritation, and speaking sharply, said to James:
>
> 'Stand still. Don't be tiresome,' so that he knew instantly that her severity was real, and straightened his leg and she measured it.
>
> The stocking was too short by half an inch at least, making allowance for the fact that Sorley's little boy would be less well grown than James.

Virginia Woolf: To the Lighthouse

Try to rewrite that in the traditional, reported manner. You will find that it takes a lot more words and that it loses impact.

This is not to say that stream of consciousness is the only way to write or that the first person and past tense are worthless. What you need to decide is what suits you and your aims – just as you need to in your project work. You do not want to be the James Joyce or the Charlotte Brontë of the 1990s, but looking at different writers' techniques can and does help you to find your own voice and preferred style.

Informative and instructive writing

It may be, of course, that you do not want to find your voice as a literary, entertaining writer; that you would prefer to acquire expertise in more everyday, functional language use. We are thinking here of informative and instructive writing. It is all too easy to assume that these are bread and butter and straightforward. In fact, they are, in their own way, very demanding. You may not be trying to move or persuade people so you may not be choosing individual lexical items with as much care, but you are trying to be precise and clear. This has two main impacts upon your language. The first is that you do not want to waste the reader's time in unnecessary words: you need to be very strict with yourself about keeping to the point. The second is that you need to sequence your material carefully. In instructive writing – for example recipes – it is disastrous to get something out of order. Nor is it acceptable to add 'a fair bit' of sugar or 'a good dollop' of milk. Precision is all.

The same is true when writing informatively. It is of no use to anyone to say that the First World War happened 'this century', or that water boils 'when it gets really hot'. If people did not write things as fatuous as this there would be no trade in exam howlers. Informative writing necessitates intelligent selection and ordering of appropriate material and is most certainly an examination skill. What are essay answers if not examples of informative writing? What are analyses if not informative commentaries on others' writing and speaking?

Many people find informative/instructive writing the least interesting sort of work to produce. One way to kill two birds with one stone is to write something about your exam subject. Perhaps you could make your fortune writing *The Key To Success in A-Level English Language*.

Every time you decode a textbook and write your own notes you are producing informative writing with a specific audience. When you blend the material given to you by teachers with your own notes plus those from several different textbooks, you are doing the informative writer's job: that is, conveying a body of information as clearly, succinctly and appropriately as possible. You will probably need to think about layout: would subdivisions or numbered points help or simply distract? Have you prioritised material in order of importance, or chronologically or what? The main thing is that you do have a system and one which works for your material.

If you remain unclear about what the hallmarks of informative writing are, try using a body of material for different purposes, one informative, the other persuasive or entertaining. Here are a few simple, useful exercises:

Get some information on rape/child abuse/drug abuse (sorry if this sounds a gloomy collection!) Any doctor's surgery will furnish you with material, so will any Citizens' Advice Bureau. The NSPCC and Rape Crisis Line are also very willing to supply information.

Using the material you obtain, produce two pamphlets for home delivery. One should be unbiased, factual and purely informative, the other should aim to persuade householders to do something about this terrible problem.

As you write and design your two pamphlets, think carefully about layout:

What sort of graphics do you want?
Are you going to use any subheadings?
What tone are you attempting to convey?
How much detail do you want and how will you make it accessible to your readership?

Think next about the sort of words you want to employ: should they be emotive, hyperbolic and extreme or factual and unbiased? How colloquial or formal do you want to be?

This may, of course lead you to a consideration of audience. Generally, a younger audience will prefer a less formal style. A very young audience will need a simple lexical and structural level.

Another useful exercise is to switch audience. Take an AIDS pamphlet aimed at the general public. Redraft it for high school students or trainee nurses. How will the material differ? How much specialist lexis will you use? How will you avoid patronising or confusing a relatively young audience?

The high school audience is a very useful target group for informative writing. Try putting together an information pack on a social or health issue for fourth formers. Or a unit in a GCSE Biology or History course. This will probably involve you in some instructive as well as informative writing since you will presumably want them to do something once they have read or while they are reading your material. Which of these two options seems better to you? Why?

If you would rather write for someone older – perhaps A-Level students – then think of a topic you might reasonably expect them to be interested in. Avoid the obvious: 'How to play football' or 'Making job applications' have both been done to death. They are about as original as doing a persuasive piece on abortion or capital punishment. So what might be valid? A guide to higher education? A guide to holiday jobs abroad? Some facts about drug and alcohol abuse (again a little well worn, but worthy)? A young visitor's guide to your city? If you live in a tiny village or in the middle of nowhere it may well be that you have no tourists to write for. Many seventeen-year-olds start driving lessons. Would a more informal version of the Department of Transport's Driving Manual be a good idea? Only of course if you know what you are talking about!

This is a vital prerequisite for any piece of informative writing. You have no right to mislead people about which hi-fi or camera to buy, what the significant differences are between the major religions of the world or how to perform Latin American dancing faultlessly. If you write about something, you must know your stuff, which does not mean copying out great chunks of previously completed History, Geography or Science projects. That sort of cheating always shows.

As a writer you will need technical expertise, a system, industry, inspiration, the ideas of others – but do always find your voice – your own words.

Glossary of terms

The terms in this glossary are those whose first occurrences in the text are in capitals. They have been selected on two bases: either they seem to us to be words which may be unfamiliar to some readers, or they are well-known terms of which we would like you to have a working definition. They are listed in the glossary alphabetically.

In some cases we have felt the need to give two definitions – one which is as clear and simple as we can make it and one for those of you who want a rather more precise and linguistic definition.

Abstract nouns The names for ideas and emotions, things which exist notionally but not physically, e.g. 'love' and 'freedom'.

Accent The features of pronunciation which enable a listener to spot someone's regional and social derivation. Accent refers to sound only.

Active One of the two possible voices of verbs. In the active voice the subject of the sentence is the perpetrator of the verb. For example, in the sentence 'The dog bit the postman', 'The dog' is the subject of the verb part.
The other voice for verbs is the **Passive** (see separate entry).

Addressee The person spoken to.

Addresser The person speaking.

Adjective Function: to modify or tell us more about nouns and pronouns. Distribution: before nouns and after determiners, e.g. 'the happy girl'; as complements e.g. 'the girl is happy'; or after intensifiers e.g. 'the girl is very happy'.
Inflection: most adjectives can be made comparative by adding *er* e.g. more happy = 'happier', or superlative by adding *est* e.g. 'happiest'.

Adjunct The term used by some analysts for all the grammatically inessential elements in a sentence. The most common types of adjuncts are adjectives and adverbials.

Adverb Function: to modify or tell us more about a verb, adverb or adjective. Those modifying adverbs and adjectives, e.g. 'very', are often called intensifiers. Distribution: either before or after the word they modify – more usually after, more emphatically before.
Inflection: how-adverbials are often the adjective plus *ly*.

Adverbial The general name for a word or group of words working as an adverb i.e. modifying a verb, adverb or adjective.

Agent In passive structures, the person or thing which acted out the verb. If it is included, it follows the word 'by', e.g. 'The prisoner was interrogated by the Chief Inspector.' Here 'Chief Inspector' is the agent.

Anglo-Saxon More correctly, Old English.

Articles There are two articles: the definite 'the' used for particular nouns or ones already referred to and the indefinite 'a' used for less specific nouns.

Audience The people to whom a stretch of language is addressed.

Clause A main clause (or simple sentence) must have a main finite verb and a subject.

Cohesion (as a term used in discourse analysis) That which causes separate conversational elements to make joint sense. Much of this is achieved by word order – that is, the distribution of items.

Collocated The term used to describe words which habitually go together, e.g. 'mad as a' will usually be followed by 'hatter'; 'might and' by 'main' and 'unaccustomed as I am to' by 'public speaking'. Sometimes a writer deliberately surprises our expectations by using deviant collocations such as 'happy funeral'.

Colloquial A term for language which is informal. Colloquialisms are usually spoken rather than written and change more rapidly than more standard forms.

Complement The element of a sentence which follows a subject and a being or stative verb. It can be a noun or an adjective; in either case it completes the sense of the sentence.

Complex The term for sentences which have two or more clauses, at least one of which is subordinate.

Compound The term for sentences which have two or more main clauses, each with its own subject.
Subjects can also be referred to as compound when they involve two or more nouns e.g. 'Jack and Jill'.

Concrete nouns The names for things which are visible and tangible (e.g. 'tables', 'sun') as opposed to things which exist notionally but not physically.

Conditional Verb forms and clauses which convey possibility. Conditional clauses are often introduced by 'if' or 'unless'.

Conjunctions Function words which link items in a list, the elements of a compound subject or object, or two or more clauses.

Connotation (cf **Denotation**) The emotional associations or links which a lexical unit or word has, e.g. 'Christmas' links to Santa Claus, snow, parties and presents – for most people it has positive connotations. On the other hand 'murder' links to death, criminality and violence and thus has negative connotations. The connotations of 'girl' could be positive – youthful – or negative – patronised.

Continuous The marked form of the verb which indicates the progressive by the use of the ending *ing*, eg. 'talk' is simple and not progressive, 'talking' is continuous and progressive.

Co-ordinating conjunctions These can link the parts of a compound subject or items of a list, and/or more importantly, the two or more main clauses of a compound sentence. There are only a few co-ordinating conjunctions: 'and', 'but', 'or', 'nor', 'either' and 'neither'.

Declarative The linguistic label for the sentence function of stating facts or opinions. Declarative sentences can also be referred to as statements or assertions.

Decode To interpret the full meaning of a stretch of language. This includes both its text and subtexts – the denotations and the connotations of the words.

Denotation (cf. **Connotation**) The reference a word has to the thing, person or place it describes, i.e. its dictionary meaning; e.g. 'girl' = young female human being.

Determiners Function words which occur alongside and before nouns and specify quantity or significance. They include the two articles 'a' and 'the' and terms like 'some', 'this' and 'many'.

Dialect The elements of speech other than sound: words and grammar. When these are non-standard, i.e. not the same as Standard English, a speaker is regarded as having a localised dialect.

Discourse analysts Linguists who study stretches of spoken language (speech events) in order to generate rules about spoken language.

Dynamic The type or aspect of verbs which relate to action. Examples would be 'hit', 'wipe', 'frighten' or 'console'.

Elaborated code and variant (cf **Restricted code**) The sociologist Basil Bernstein suggested that this is used by more middle-class speakers. It is less context-bound than the restricted code and more generalised rather than anecdotal, but stresses personal opinion and role above group identity. It is advantageous in formal situations. Of course elaborated variant users also have access to restricted variant for more informal occasions.
(Bernstein's views are far from being uncriticised or proven. See Trudgill's book *Sociolinguistics* for a fuller discussion.)

Elucidation The sentence function in which a speaker clarifies what has been said. Elucidations can also support or oppose a previous remark.

Evaluation The sentence function in which a speaker gives a view of what has preceded.

Exclamatory The general name for sentences and utterances which convey surprise or other strong feeling.

False start The phenomenon of starting an utterance twice or re-phrasing.

Fillers Words added into discourse out of habit, or in order to gain thinking time. They are significant, but redundant in terms of meaning. Examples are 'well', 'sort of' and 'you know'.

Finite Verb forms which can occur alone in a main clause. They consist of all verb forms except the infinitive (e.g. 'to love', 'to take') and the participles ('loving', 'taken') which are referred to as **non-finite**.

Function words The small number of words whose main importance is grammatical rather than semantic. They have limited meaning alone but are significant in combination with other words. Function words include articles, determiners, pronouns, conjunctions and prepositions.

Habitual The term linguists use for actions which are regular. Habitual action is often signalled by verb form, e.g. 'I used to visit' rather than 'I visited'.

Idiolect The cluster of speech habits and sounds unique to an individual. It includes accent, pitch, word choice and style.

Imperative The more technical term for a command. As well as a sentence function it is a mood of verbs.

Indirect object In a sentence, the person or thing to or for whom the direct object is given/brought etc. In the sentence 'He bought her some flowers' the flowers are the direct object since they directly receive the action of the verb – the buying. He did not buy *her*, he bought *for* her, so she is the indirect object.
The indirect object can follow the verb but precedes the direct object.

Individuality The speech markers which allow you to recognise an individual. They include voice quality, volume/pitch and accent as well as pet words and phrases.

Initiating The first utterance in a conversation, important since it sets the tone for what follows and often indicates a dominant speaker.

Interaction The term for the social element of discourse. It involves group dynamics: who is dominant? Who initiates conversation? What role do speakers adopt?

Interrogative The term describing the questioning sentence function.

Intonation The rise and fall of pitch of a speaker's voice. It is very important in decoding meaning and is often linked to function, e.g. questions have a rising intonation, statements a flat one. The difference between a true question where the form and function are interrogative (e.g. 'Would you like a banana?') and a rhetorical question where the form is a question but the function is a statement (e.g. 'Do you want a punch on the nose?') is highlighted by different intonations.

Intransitive Verbs which cannot take an object e.g. 'go', 'be', 'seem'.

Latinate Words derived from Latin. They are often longer than the equivalent Old English word.

Lexical words The large group of words which have an ascribed, individual meaning. Syntax allows combinations of lexical and function words to create meaningful wholes.

Lexis The vocabulary of a language. Lexical items can be a group of words or a single word e.g. 'around the bend' or 'mad'. All the lexical items or lexemes of a language make up its **lexicon**.

Minor sentence A sentence which lacks one of the two necessary elements – a main verb or a subject.

Modified A word is modified in meaning when an adverbial or adjectival is placed with it. We are usually given more information or told how to feel about the word by the modifiers which go with it. These can be post- or pre-modifiers.

Morpheme The smallest possible grammatical unit. It is smaller than the word and includes inflections with fixed meaning such as plural *s* and past tense *ed*. Prefixes such as *un* meaning 'not' are also morphemes.

Move The name for each turn in a discourse which a speaker has.

Non-finite Verb forms which cannot function as the main verb of a clause. There are only three non-finite verb forms: the infinitive ('to bite') and the present and past participles ('biting' and 'bitten').

Non-fluency features A general term for the normal pauses, errors and slips which occur when people talk spontaneously.

Noun Function: to name a person, place or thing. Nouns are very often the subject or object of a sentence. Distribution: after articles ('a', 'the'), prepositions or verbs. Inflection: nouns can be inflected for number (*s/es* for plural) or case ('*s* for the genitive or possessive case).

Object The person, place or thing which receives the action of a verb in a sentence. In normal word order it follows the verb. Another name for it is the **direct object**.

Paralinguistic Features of conversation which are non-verbal but nevertheless convey meaning, for example shrugs or blown kisses. Non-verbal communication, involving gesture and facial expression, can be very important in decoding conversation.

Passive (cf **Active**) In the passive voice the subject of the sentence is the recipient of the action of the verb, e.g. in the sentence 'The postman was bitten by the dog', 'The postman' is the subject of the passive verb 'was bitten'.

Phatic communion The type of exchange which is redundant in terms of meaning but socially significant. It includes friendly noises like 'Morning', 'Nice sunny day' and 'How's things?'

Phrase A single element within a text which is longer than one word. It can be a verb such as 'look into', or a noun, adverbial or adjectival. It is differentiated from a clause because it lacks either the subject or predicate which a clause must have.

Idiomatic phrases have a fixed meaning which has little, if anything to do with the meaning of the words within the phrase – for example, 'a wild goose chase' has nothing to do with terrorising birds. Colloquial expressions are also of fixed meaning and tend to be spoken rather than written. Both idiomatic and colloquial expressions present non-native speakers with difficulty.

Pluperfect The tense which precedes the past and is signalled by 'had', e.g. 'When I had showered, I dressed.'

Post-modification This occurs after the noun or verb and often takes the form of a phrase or clause rather than a single word.

Pre-modification This occurs before the noun or verb and is more likely to consist of a single word or list of single words.

Predicate The term for all elements in a sentence except the subject. A predicate can be a verb only or a verb, indirect object and object, for example.

Prepositions Function words which relate one word to another, often in space: 'in', 'on' and 'under' are examples. Sometimes they are used after verbs to alter their meaning.

Pronouns Words which stand in place of nouns, though they cannot do so after an adjective. Personal pronouns can be first, second or third person; subject or object. There are also possessive pronouns denoting ownership, e.g. 'his', and reflexive pronouns indicating action perpetrated on oneself, e.g. 'himself'. Pronouns can also be used as interrogatives, e.g. 'which?' and to relate one clause to another, e.g. 'who'.

Proper nouns The capitalised nouns which name particular people (Jane), places (London) or things (The Bible). Unlike common nouns which are not individualised ('girl', 'city', 'book') most proper nouns cannot follow determiners such as 'a' and 'the'.

Received pronunciation The name for the most socially prestigious accent in Britain. It has no regional derivation, but is used by public school children, the Royal family and, traditionally, the BBC. It is more colloquially known as The Queen's English or BBC English.

Receiver The name for the recipient of a linguistic message, written or spoken. It includes both reader and listener.

Relative clause A post-modifying clause which is introduced by one of the relative pronouns. These are 'who', 'whom', 'whose', 'which' and 'that'.

Repetition The unnecessary repeating of a lexical unit.

Responses (as a term used in discourse analysis) The replies to **solicitations**. They are not exactly the same as answers to questions: there will be a link but it may be through the subtext rather than the text, e.g. 'Would you like to go to the park?' 'It's raining.'

Restricted code and variant A form of language use which the sociologist Basil Bernstein suggested was prevalent amongst some members of the working class. It is very context-dependent and clearly marks group membership. Some of its features include tag questions, heavy use of pronouns and anecdote. A speaker using only restricted variant, Bernstein argued, lacks stylistic range since this type of language use is only really meaningful to insiders and appropriate to relatively informal contexts. A speaker who only has access to this variant is thus disadvantaged in certain formal contexts like examinations, interviews and court cases.

Semantic field The grouping of words within areas of related meaning. Part of the meaning of each individual word is determined by the meanings of the other words in the same field, e.g. pink, crimson, red, magenta (colour); skirmish, battle, campaign (war); affection, passion, devotion, fondness (love).

Sender The name for the person communicating a linguistic message, whether written or spoken – it can therefore refer either to a writer or a speaker.

Sequencing The stylistic and linguistic ordering of words so that they make sense in terms of time. Tenses are particularly important in sequencing. In English we say 'If he comes, I will tell him'; in French the sequence is different, namely 'If he will come I will tell him.'

Simple The term for tenses which are unmarked, i.e. not progressive (ending in *ing*) and with no auxiliaries.
A sentence may be termed simple if it contains only one main clause and verb.

Solicitation The sentence function in which a speaker seeks information or clarification.

Standard English The form of English which is written and which most educated speakers use in formal contexts. It is more prestigious than non-standard English, though it must be stressed that this is for social and not linguistic reasons.

Stative A type of verb which expresses states of being and thought processes rather than actions. Examples are 'be', 'seem', 'know', 'realise' and 'mean'.

Stress What a speaker employs to foreground or highlight a word or morpheme. Greater volume and a rising intonation are both used.
In transcription, stress is marked by capitalisation or by a mark before the stressed sound.

Subtext The implications of a text which are understood though not stated.

Subject The person, place or thing governing the verb – and, in normal word order, preceding it. The verb may be either stative or dynamic.

Subordinating conjunctions Conjunctions which link clauses but introduce a clause which is dependent on or subordinate to the other, main clause. They establish complex relationships: of time ('while'), result ('because') or condition ('if').

Syntax The arrangement of words into sentences, in accordance with the accepted rules for that language.

Tense A category relating to verbs which marks when an action took place. The major tenses in English are the present, past and future, but further divisions can be made.

Text A stretch of language, written or spoken, which can be studied, analysed or described. It can be very short – 'One Way' on a traffic sign – or very long – *War and Peace* or the film *1900*.

Transitive The group of verbs which can be followed by a direct object e.g. 'bite', 'kiss', 'buy'.

Turn-taking In conversation, people usually wait their turn to speak. Some, out of eagerness or rudeness, interrupt, but the norm is for one speaker to yield the floor by prolonging a pause or glancing at the elected next speaker who then takes her turn.

Unvoiced pause A silent gap in speech, marked in transcription by (.)

Utterance The normal unit of division for spoken as opposed to written language. Its end is marked by a pause or by a new speaker taking over.

Verb Function: words of doing or being Distribution: between the subject and object or complement of the clause (the verb and object or complement are sometimes referred to as the predicate.) Inflection: important for tense: *ed* for the past in many verbs, *ing* to show the continuous. Also for person: *s* for the third person singular e.g. 'he likes'.

Voiced pause A gap in speech marked by a noise such as 'er' or 'erm'.

Word class The grammatical grouping of words according to their function. A more precise name for parts of speech. Words are often allocated to class according to their distribution (where they tend to occur) or their inflections (their word endings).

Acknowledgements

The authors and publishers would like to thank the following for permission to reprint copyright material:

A. P. Watt Ltd for extract from *Waterland* by Graham Swift
Michael Adams for article *Equal shares for [Palestine*
Aitken and Stone Limited for extract from *A House for Mr Biswas* by V. S. Naipaul, published by Andre Deutsch Limited
Andre Deutsch Ltd for *Not Waving but Drowning* from *Not Waving but Drowning* by Stevie Smith
Bogle L'Ouverture Publications Ltd for *Wha Fe Call I* from *Touch Mi Tell Mi* by Valerie Bloom
Sarah Boseley for article *Capsize survivor tells of 11-hour swim*
Bridgfords Estate Agents Ltd for property details
Butterworth Law Publishers Ltd for extracts from *The All England Law Reports*
Carcanet Press Limited for *Haymaking* from *Selected Poems* by Gillian Clarke
Chatto and Windus for extract from *Dinner at the Homesick Restaurant* by Anne Tyler
Chatto and Windus and the Estate of Wilfred Owen for *Anthem for Dead Youth* and *Anthem for Doomed Youth* from *The Collected Poems of Wilfred Owen* edited by Jon Stallworthy
Cover Stories for *Crow Resting* by Edward Pygge from New Statesman and Nation © New Statesman and Society
David Higham Associates for *Do Not Go Gentle Into That Good Night* from *The Poems* by Dylan Thomas, published by Dent
The Economist for extract from style guidelines
Elaine Greene Limited for extract from *Death of a Salesman* copyright © Arthur Miller 1949, published by Penguin Books Ltd
Express Newspapers plc for articles *Sea survivor vows 'never again'* and *Archbishop's moral mess* from the Daily Express
Faber and Faber Ltd for extract from *Lake Wobegon Days* by Garrison Keillor; *On Roofs of Terry Street* and *A Removal from Terry Street* from *Terry Street* by Douglas Dunn; *Hawk Roosting* from *Lupercal* by Ted Hughes
The Guardian for articles *Benefit rules tightened* by Simon Beavis, *Equal shares for Palestine* by Michael Adams and *Capsize survivor tells of 11-hour swim* by Sarah Boseley
The Health Education Authority for AIDS campaign advertisement
Hodder and Stoughton Limited for extracts from *Weekend* from *Watching Me, Watching You* by Fay Weldon; *Kennedy* by Theodore C. Sorensen
The Hogarth Press and the executors of the estate of Virginia Woolf for extract from *To the Lighthouse*
The Independent for article *Cross-channel ferry disaster* by David Usborne and Anne Spackman, first published 7.3.87.
Jonathan Cape Ltd for *Watchwords* from *Watchwords* by Roger McGough; extract from *Midnight's Children* by Salman Rushdie
Jonathan Cape Ltd and the executors of the estate of James Joyce for extract from *A Portrait of the Artist as a Young Man*

Just Seventeen for article on Tracie Spencer
Laurence Pollinger Limited and the estate of Frieda Lawrence Ravagli for extract from *Nottingham and the Mining Country* by D. H. Lawrence
Longman Group UK Limited for extracts from *Men, Women and Language* by Jennifer Coates
Martin Secker and Warburg Ltd for extracts from *The Life and Times of Michael K* by J. M. Coetzee; *Metamorphosis* by Franz Kafka; *Walter* by David Cook; *Wilt* by Tom Sharpe
Methuen and Co. Ltd for extract from *Linguistics and the Novel* by R. Fowler
Michael Joseph Ltd for extract from *The Diaries of Jane Somers* by Doris Lessing
National Union of Teachers for memorandum extract
New Internationalist for extract from *Dying for Doctors*
New Musical Express for extract from article by Danny Kelly and letter
Oxford University Press for extract from *The New Oxford Illustrated Dictionary* (1978)
Pedigree Petfoods for extract from advertisement
Peters Fraser and Dunlop Ltd for extract from *Separate Tracks* by Jane Rogers; *them and* [uz] by Tony Harrison; *Watch Your Step – I'm Drenched* from *The Apeman Cometh* by Adrian Mitchell, published by Jonathan Cape. Neither this nor any other of Adrian Mitchell's works is to be used in connection with any examination whatsoever.
Q for extract from article *I'm with the band*
Race Today Publications for *Sonny's Lettah* from *Inglan is a Bitch* by Linton Kwesi Johnson
Rex Features Ltd for two articles *Tame Tehran's Twerps* and *Head's Love for Girl, 15* from The Sun
Rosica Colin Limited for extracts from *Saturday Night and Sunday Morning* by Alan Sillitoe, © Alan Sillitoe 1958, 1986
Routledge for *Death of a Son* from *Selected Poems* by Jon Silkin
Saab Great Britain Ltd for extract from advertisement
The Salvation Army for leaflet extract
St Annes Music Ltd for *I'm Not in Love* by Gouldman and Stewart
Syndication International Ltd for article *Giant seas nightmare of hero Pat* from the Daily Mirror
Unwin Hyman, of HarperCollins Publishers Limited for *Song for Last Year's Wife* by Brian Patten
Warner Chappell Music Ltd for *It's Easy to Remember* by Rodgers and Hart © Warner Chappell Music Ltd and *All I Have to Do is Dream* by Boudleaux Bryan © Acuff Rose Opryland Music
Weidenfeld and Nicolson Ltd for extract from *The Radiant Way* by Margaret Drabble
William Heinemann Ltd for extracts from *The Blindfold Horse* by Shusha Guppy; *Waterland* by Graham Swift; *Staying On* by Paul Scott
George Wimpey plc for property details

Every effort has been made to trace the copyright holders of the extracts reprinted in this book. The publishers apologise for any inadvertent omissions, which they will be pleased to rectify in a subsequent reprint.